The Political

BLACKWELL READINGS IN CONTINENTAL PHILOSOPHY

Series Editor: Simon Critchley, University of Essex

Each volume in this superb new series provides a detailed introduction to and overview of a central philosophical topic in the Continental tradition. In contrast to the author-based model that has hitherto dominated the reception of the Continental philosophical tradition in the English-speaking world, this series presents the central issues of that tradition, topics that should be of interest to anyone concerned with philosophy. Cutting across the stagnant ideological boundaries that mark the analytic/Continental divide, the series will initiate discussions that reflect the growing dissatisfaction with the organization of the English-speaking philosophical world. Edited by a distinguished international forum of philosophers, each volume provides a critical overview of a distinct topic in Continental philosophy through a mix of both classic and newly commissioned essays from both philosophical traditions.

The Body: Classic and Contemporary Readings
Edited and introduced by Donn Welton

Race
Edited by Robert Bernasconi

The Religious
Edited by John D. Caputo

The Political
Edited by David Ingram

The Political

Edited by
David Ingram

First published 2002

2 4 6 8 10 9 7 5 3 1

Blackwell Publishers Inc.
350 Main Street
Malden, Massachusetts 02148
USA

Blackwell Publishers Ltd
108 Cowley Road
Oxford OX4 1JF
UK

Library of Congress Cataloging-in-Publication Data has been applied for.

ISBN 0–631–21547–6 (hardback); 0–631–21548–4 (paperback)

British Library Cataloguing in Publication Data
A CIP catalogue record for this book is available from the British Library.

Typeset in 10.5/12.5pt Bembo
by Kolam Information Services Pvt. Ltd, Pondicherry, India
Printed in Great Britain by
MPG Books Ltd, Bodmin, Cornwall

This book is printed on acid-free paper.

CONTENTS

LIST OF CONTRIBUTORS

Judith Butler is Maxine Elliot Professor in the Departments of Rhetoric and Comparative Literature at the University of California, Berkeley. She is the author of *Subjects of Desire: Hegelian Reflections in Twentieth-Century France* (1987), *Gender Trouble: Feminism and the Subversion of Identity* (1990), *Bodies That Matter: On the Discursive Limits of Sex* (1993), *The Psychic Life of Power: Theories of Subjection* (1997), and *Excitable Speech* (1997), as well as numerous articles and contributions on philosophy, feminist and queer theory. Her most recent work on Antigone and the politics of kinship is entitled *Antigone's Claim: Kinship Between Life and Death* (2000).

Simone Chambers is an Associate Professor of Political Science at the University of Colorado. Professor Chambers is writing a book, *Public Reason and Deliberation*, investigating the deliberative turn of contemporary liberalism. Her primary areas of scholarship include political philosophy, ethics, critical theory, and constitutional theory. She is the author of *Reasonable Democracy: Jürgen Habermas and the Politics of Discourse* (1996) and the co-editor of *Deliberation, Democracy, and the Media* (2000) and *Alternative Conceptions of Civil Society* (2001).

David Ingram is Professor of Philosophy at Loyola University, Chicago. His major publications include *Group Rights: Reconciling Equality and Difference* (2000), *Reason, History and Politics: The Communitarian Grounds of Legitimation in the Modern Age* (1995), *Critical Theory and Philosophy* (1990), and *Habermas and the Dialectic of Reason* (1987).

William McBride is Professor of Philosophy at Purdue University. His major publications include *Fundamental Change in Law and Society: Hart and Sartre on Revolution* (1970), *The Philosophy of Marx* (1977), *Social Theory at a Crossroads* (1980), *Sartre's Political Theory* (1991), *Social and Political Philosophy* (1994), *Philosophical Reflections on the Changes in Eastern Europe* (1999), and *From Yugoslav Praxis to Global Pathos: Anti-Hegemonic Post-Post-Marxist Essays* (2001). He is also editor of *Sartre and Existentialism*

(1997) and co-editor of *Phenomenology in a Pluralistic Context* (1983) and *The Task of Philosophy After Postmodernity* (2001).

Eduardo Mendieta is Assistant Professor of Philosophy at the State University of New York, Stony Brook. He is the editor and translator of Enrique Dussel's *The Underside of Modernity*, which also contains essays by Karl Otto Apel and Paul Ricoeur. He co-edited *Liberation Theologies, Postmodernity and the Americas* (1997). Currently he is writing a book entitled *The Geography of Utopia: Modernity's Spatiotemporal Regimes*.

Iris Marion Young is Professor of Political Science at the University of Chicago. She is the author of *Inclusion and Democracy* (2000), *Justice and the Politics of Difference* (1990), *Intersecting Voices: Dilemmas of Gender, Political Philosophy, and Policy* (1997), and *Throwing Like a Girl and Other Essays in Feminist Philosophy and Social Theory* (1990).

PREFACE

I have designed *The Political* in conformity with the structure of other volumes within the Blackwell series on Continental philosophy. These volumes contain representative selections of works written by some of the most important Continental philosophers of the twentieth century. In addition, they contain commentaries by well-known scholars. The commentaries both apply selections to contemporary issues and events and provide the reader with useful background information situating selections and authors within their respective contexts.

Although I must claim responsibility for the choice of philosophers represented in this volume, I have given my commentators considerable leeway in choosing and commenting on selections. Notwithstanding the daunting challenge of choosing the one important "soundbite" that succinctly encapsulates the essential thought of a thinker throughout his or her lifetime, I am satisfied that the selections chosen here reflect the distinctive ideas of their respective authors. Needless to say, distilling an adequate selection of excerpts, like those collected by Bill McBride from Sartre's *Critique of Dialectical Reason*, sometimes required painstaking effort.

The choice of philosophers represented in this volume was somewhat less complicated. That choice was determined partly by my decision to represent the most important schools of Continental philosophy and partly by my preference for thinkers whose contributions to political thought in the narrow sense of the term distinguished them from other social theorists within their school. However, choosing which schools to represent was somewhat problematic. Although phenomenology, existentialism, post-modernism, poststructuralism, and critical theory designate familiar methods, approaches, and schools within Continental philosophy, they are hardly distinctive. For example, besides being influenced by phenomenology, most existentialist political thought owes much to the Hegelian–Marxist tradition. The latter is also the dominant undercurrent coursing through the various currents of thought within critical theory, which in turn draws heavily from phenomenology and existentialism. Again, although many attempts have been made to distinguish postmodernism and poststructuralism, the truth of the matter is that philosophers falling within these schools have so much in common that it hardly matters whether one classifies them as postmodernist or poststructuralist.

Besides the ambiguity and vagueness of the organizing categories chosen for this volume, legitimate questions might be raised about my inclusion of postcolonialism and my exclusion of feminism. My decision to exclude feminism as one of the organizing categories of this volume does not reflect a negative judgment of feminism. Indeed, as I point out in the introduction of this volume, feminists working within the Anglo-American tradition of philosophy have made important contributions to political thought. But this has not been the case with their Continental counterparts. Simone de Beauvoir, Luce Irigaray, Julia Kristeva, and other feminists working within the Continental tradition have made important contributions to social thought and social ontology, but they have not devoted much energy to addressing political issues in the narrow sense intended here. Nevertheless, despite the relative scarcity of major Continental feminist political philosophers, I am happy to note that several of the selections and commentaries contained in this volume explicitly address feminist political concerns.

My decision to include postcolonialism as an organizing category might also be questioned on the grounds that it does not reflect a major method, approach, or school within Continental philosophy proper. Although technically correct, this objection falsely presumes that Continental philosophy is a self-contained tradition informing the thought of only French and German (or perhaps Continental European) philosophers. In fact, Continental philosophy is global and multicultural. Philosophers in Asia, Africa, North and South America, and Australia have elaborated this tradition in ways that respond to their own historical circumstances. Conversely, French and German philosophers have elaborated this tradition in ways that respond to events emanating from Europe's outer periphery, its former and present colonies, spheres of influence, and so forth. Such has been the encounter of Continental philosophy with colonialism and imperialism. My selection of postcolonialism, however, reflects a new phase in this encounter: here, instead of Europeans looking out from the center to the periphery, we find non-Europeans looking in from the periphery to the center. Stated differently, in postcolonial philosophy we have Africans, Asians, and non-European, non-white Americans using Continental philosophy to critically examine Continental philosophy's own Eurocentric myopia with respect to the inhabitants of its former colonies and the Third World at large.

As for the organization of this volume, I have arranged the categories of political thought in an order of logical progression. Phenomenology is arguably the first major movement of twentieth-century Continental philosophy, and it is the one to which all others refer. Later movements, such as poststructuralism and postmodernism, must be understood in part as reacting to it, as well as to the existentialism and Marxism that build upon it. In order to fully appreciate any of these movements, however, one must have at least some elementary grasp of Anglo-American political philosophy and its distinctive methods as well as some cursory knowledge of the history of nineteenth-century German political philosophy, all of which has been provided in the introduction.

A final word of gratitude to those who aided in the production of this volume: I would like to thank my assistant Darin McGinnis for editorial assistance in preparing earlier drafts of the introduction. I would also like to thank Beth Remmes and Jack Messenger at Blackwell Publishers for their helpful advice in the production of the volume. I owe a further debt of gratitude to Loyola for funding work on this project during the summer of 2000.

Finally, I would like to acknowledge the following institutions for granting permission to recopy the primary text sources used in this anthology: the University of Chicago Press for use of sections 24, 26, 28, 29, 31, 32, and 34 of Hannah Arendt's *The Human Condition*; Harcourt, Inc. for use of Hannah Arendt's "On Violence," originally published in *The Crisis of the Republic*, copyright © 1969, 1970, 1971, 1972 by Hannah Arendt, reprinted by permission of Harcourt, Inc.; Verso Publishers for use of selections from Jean-Paul Sartre's *Critique of Dialectical Reason*, vol. 1, translated by Alan Sheridan-Smith, London: Verso, 1991, vol. 2, translated by Quintin Hoare, London: Verso, 1991; MIT Press for use of Jürgen Habermas's "Three Normative Models of Democracy" and "On the Internal Relation between the Rule of Law and Democracy," published in *The Inclusion of the Other: Studies in Political Theory*, translation copyright 1998 Massachusetts Institute of Technology, originally published as *Die Einbeziehung Des Anderen: Studien Zur Politische Theorie*, copyright Suhrkamp Verlag, Frankfurt am Main, Germany; Automedia/Semiotext(e) for use of Michel Foucault's "What is Critique?" reprinted from *Politics of Truth*, ed. Lisa Hochroch and S. Lotringer; the University of Minnesota Press for use of Jean-François Lyotard's "Memorandum on Legitimation," originally published in *The Postmodern Explained: Correspondence 1982–85*, English translation copyright 1992 by Power Publications, Sydney, Australia, North American edition copyright 1993 by the Regents of the University of Minnesota, original, French language, edition copyright 1988 Editions Galilée, Paris; and the *Radical Philosophy Review* for use of Enrique Dussel's "Six Theses Towards a Critique of Political Reason: The Citizen as Political Agent," originally published in vol. 3, no. 2 of the *Review*.

INTRODUCTION

David Ingram

This volume contains selections and commentaries highlighting some of the major movements and figures of contemporary Continental political philosophy. Because the expression "contemporary Continental political philosophy" is a mouthful to digest for those who are strangers to the arcane world of academic philosophy, a few preliminary remarks about what I mean by it are clearly in order.

First, let us begin with "political." We often use this term as if it clearly designated a world of activity distinguishable from what are otherwise characterized as "social," "economic," and "legal" worlds – spheres of activity that no doubt impinge upon the political. For our purposes, we may think of the political as that sphere of life by which people collectively govern their lives by laying down general rules of conduct, or laws. By "philosophy" I have in mind deep reflection on the meanings of concepts and on the necessary conditions for the possibility of certain types of things. So constructed, "political philosophy" is roughly cognate with thinking hard about the presuppositions underlying political order. These presuppositions include: the nature and justification of political rights and duties; the meaning and role of power – as distinct from violence – in maintaining political order; the metaphysical reality of political groups and their political relationships; the constitution of political identity and community; and the relationship of the political to the non-political, i.e., economic, social, cultural, and purely personal, aspects of human existence.

Now that we have some understanding of what political philosophy purports to do, let's examine that part of it that is strictly "Continental." By "contemporary Continental philosophy" I mean varieties of twentieth-century philosophy that originated in Germany and France. So construed, contemporary Continental philosophy is often distinguished from what is commonly known in the profession as Anglo-American philosophy, which (not surprisingly) consists of varieties of philosophy that chiefly originated in England and North America.[1]

Continental and Anglo-American Philosophies:
A Contrast in Styles

Anglo-American political philosophy

In order to appreciate the unique contributions of contemporary Continental political philosophy one must contrast it with its Anglo-American counterpart. Contemporary Anglo-American political philosophy traces its origins to two sources. The first is the empiricist political tradition. It begins in the late sixteenth century with the experimental philosophy of Francis Bacon (1561–1626) and continues through contemporary pragmatism, whose major exponents are John Dewey (1859–1952) and Richard Rorty (b. 1931). This tradition is skeptical of metaphysical concepts, dogmatic traditions, and abstract ideas that lack any reference to particular observable events and things. The second source is rationalism, conceived *not* as a method for discovering knowledge – the view held by René Descartes (1596–1650) – but as a method of ordering it. Combining these sources, Anglo-American political philosophy has allied itself closely with science (chiefly economics) and logic. Striving for logical rigor, Anglo-American philosophers have sought to analyze the meaning of concepts in terms of their necessary and sufficient conditions for employment. Clarifying concepts aids in establishing necessary connections between concepts and propositions. In turn, deductive logic provides the formal procedure for justifying knowledge. Ultimately, Anglo-American political philosophers typically defend their theoretical generalizations by showing how they logically follow from hypothetical theorems of rational choice and probability; and they also do so by appealing to factual propositions about particular things and events that can be confirmed by direct observation.

The two major traditions of Anglo-American political theory, social contractarianism and utilitarianism, exemplify this approach in different ways. Spurning any appeal to metaphysical abstractions regarding divine providence and the highest good, the first great social contract theorist, Thomas Hobbes (1588–1679), argued that the problem of political order could be understood only by examining human behavior scientifically. Observing first-hand the harsh realities of religious and economic civil war in England, Hobbes concluded that the particular objects comprising political order were individuals who were compelled by a passion for self-preservation to war with one another over scarce provisions of material goods, power, and honor. Having deduced the necessity of conflict from laws of human behavior, which he modeled on Galileo's laws of physical motion (chiefly the law of inertia) and facts about scarcity, Hobbes concluded that conflict could only be avoided by everyone voluntarily agreeing to cooperate with one another peaceably. Although he insisted that rationally calculating egoists would realize that cooperation was in their best long-term interest, he also conceded that rational self-interest might tempt some of them to violate the "social compact" uniting them unless a sovereign ruler with unlimited power enforced it.[2]

Subsequent thinkers in the "social contract" tradition of political philosophy, like John Locke (1632–1704), disputed Hobbes's defense of absolute government by arguing that rational persons recognized moral limits on their behavior. Because these limits also implied the perfect freedom and equality of each with everyone, absolute government was both unnecessary and unjust. Thus, in Locke's opinion, the social compact itself was bound and limited by a distinctly moral type of reason, which informed any individual who consulted it that each and every person possessed certain natural or inalienable rights to self-preservation and property that could not be overridden by anyone, including the government.[3]

Thanks chiefly to John Rawls's and Robert Nozick's recent defense of rights,[4] morality-based social contract theory continues to enjoy greater support among Anglo-American political philosophers than its rational-choice, Hobbesian counterpart.[5] Retaining the empiricist focus on individuals as the basic units of political order, Rawls, who is arguably the greatest political philosopher of the twentieth century, conceives the social contract as a hypothetical thought experiment (what he calls the "original position") in which "we" imagine ourselves to be negotiating impartial terms of mutual cooperation. Impartiality is here guaranteed by the imposition of a "veil of ignorance," which prevents us from knowing anything about our individual circumstances. Unanimity, or universal agreement, is guaranteed by a theory of rational choice, which stipulates "primary goods" – including liberty, self-respect, economic resources, access to political power, and so on – that any rational being supposedly needs and desires, simply in order to exercise the basic moral powers associated with a fully just scheme of cooperation and pursue a fulfilling plan of life. Using the above devices of instrumental and moral reasoning. Rawls concludes that contractors in the original position would agree to order their society in accordance with two fundamental principles of justice: an unconditional principle commanding that each individual enjoy the greatest liberty compatible with a like liberty for all; and a more conditional principle commanding that social and economic inequalities (a) be attached to positions and offices open to all under conditions of fair equality of opportunity and (b) be to the greatest benefit of the least advantaged members of society (the "difference principle").

Leaving aside the complicated argument by which Rawls adduces them, how do such principles affect our understanding of a just society? According to Rawls, a just society should secure basic equal liberties (the first principle) before securing a fair distribution of income, wealth, and social bases of self-respect, such as jobs and the like (the second principle). In other words, it is most important that a society first guarantee freedom of conscience, of thought, of speech, of association, of movement, of occupation, of personal property, and of political participation (including the right to vote, run for office, etc.). This is because these liberties are especially necessary for fully exercising the two moral powers indispensable for stable, long-term cooperation: the capacity to understand and act from a public conception of justice; and the capacity to form, revise, and pursue a rational conception of the good.[6]

Although Rawls believes that a private property holding democracy is compatible with his principles, he denies Locke's and Nozick's claim that there exists a natural right to private property in the means of production (such as agriculture, industry, and finance). And, although he holds that a liberal, market-based socialist society is also compatible with these principles, he denies that there exists a natural right to worker-owned and worker-managed firms. Most important, Rawls doubts that the United States – or for that matter any welfare state that only protects against sickness, injury, poverty, and loss of employment without also fully realizing fair equality of opportunity (in education and training) – satisfactorily brings about the "fair value of political liberty" demanded by his first principle. In his opinion, only societies that "disperse the ownership of wealth and capital, and thus prevent a small part of society from controlling the economy and indirectly political life itself" do so. For, according to his theory, the aim of justice is not to redistribute income to those with less – which, after all, is compatible with very large and inherited inequalities of wealth that undermine the fair value of political liberty and large disparities of income that violate the difference principle – but to "put all citizens in a position to manage their own affairs and to take part in social cooperation on a footing of mutual respect under appropriately equal conditions."[7]

Rawls presented his social contract theory as a better alternative to the other major tradition of Anglo-American political philosophy: utilitarianism. However, utilitarianism itself initially came to prominence in the nineteenth century in response to weaknesses in social contract theory. Taking the skeptical implications of empiricism seriously, the founder of modern utilitarianism, Jeremy Bentham (1748–1832), argued that the social contract theorists' appeal to "natural" or "rationally intuitable" rights amounted to "nonsense on stilts." For Bentham, the very idea of an inalienable, or unconditional, right is a contradiction in terms. Unconditional liberty, he reasoned, is unconstrained liberty, or violence. Constrained liberty – the peaceful and cooperative order established by a system of rights – is liberty that has been limited by law for the sake of the public good. Because the requirements of public welfare define the limits of our rights, Bentham concluded that the true foundation for political order was not liberty, but utility, or the general welfare.[8] For Bentham and his followers (notably James Mill, his son John Stuart Mill, and Henry Sidgwick) the demand to maximize the greatest happiness for the greatest number could only be satisfied in a democracy wherein (in principle) each individual would be allowed to express his or her preferences through voting.

Subsequent social contract theorists like Rawls later criticized utilitarianism for subordinating the rights of individuals to the well-being of society and the tyranny of the majority. However, even Rawls conceded that the concrete application of his two principles of justice in adjudicating debates regarding the scope of constitutional rights could not dispense with a consideration of economic and social realities.

Anglo-American political philosophers continue to debate the merits of social contract theory and utilitarianism; and they continue to take liberal (constitutional) democracy as the exemplary model of political order. However, alternative styles of philosophizing have challenged the empiricism and abstract individualism of these approaches. For example, some feminists, like Susan Moller Okin, accept the basic framework of social contract theory (such as Rawls's) but question its narrow application to legal and economic institutions.[9] By excluding the family from its list of basic political structures, this theory neglects the single-most important system of patriarchal domination – a system whose injustices radiate outward to all other sectors of society, including the legal and political. Other feminists, such as Carole Pateman, are more radical in rejecting the theory in principle. For her, social contract theory posits a self-assertive possessive individualism that "always generates political right in the form of relations of domination and subordination."[10] Following Pateman's lead, Charles Mills and other critical race theorists have argued that the kind of *a priori* reasoning used by social contract theorists to defend ideal principles of justice necessarily abstracts from the real "racial contract" underlying "global white supremacist society."[11] Consequently, color-blind principles of equality adduced by Rawls and other contractarians are not useful in combatting forms of institutional racism that remain untouched by anti-discrimination law, and they may even work against color-sensitive affirmative action policies that are. Finally, self-styled communitarians like Charles Taylor, Alasdair MacIntyre, and Michael Sandel argue that privileging the individual over community falsifies the nature of political life and encourages an unhealthy deference to individual rights and self-assertion at the expense of social duties and communal solidarity.[12] Their appeal to historical traditions and richer notions of human being reflects their view that rationalist generalizations about rights and empiricist generalizations about preferences conceal the deeper unities, tensions, structures, and forces shaping our political identity. These social facts about identity formation suggest conceptions of freedom, equality, and social interaction that are more in keeping with notions of patriotic sacrifice and public-minded civic involvement characteristic of the older republican tradition than with the kind of self-interested power politics and self-absorbed preoccupation with career and family characteristic of our current liberal society. As we shall see, similar objections to liberal-democratic theory and practice are often voiced by Continental political philosophers, some of whom have directly influenced Anglo-American communitarian thought.

Continental political philosophy

Continental political philosophy traces its roots back to two major thinkers: Jean-Jacques Rousseau (1712–78) and Immanuel Kant (1724–1804). These philosophers also worked within the social contractarian tradition, but they differed from their English counterparts in conceiving the social contract as either constituting or conditioning a special kind of moral freedom. According to Rousseau, self-preservation requires that individuals exchange their natural independence for a state of mutual cooperation. The dependence of each on the other, however, need not entail a diminution of individual freedom so long as the dependence is entirely reciprocal. So long as the terms of social cooperation embody a General Will – aims that are shared by each and every citizen – no one is subject to any will but one's own.[13] More importantly, not only does obeying the General Will guarantee that one is not subject to the arbitrary will of another; it guarantees that one is willing something moral, namely the good of each and every person. In Rousseau's opinion, moral willing such as this actually embodies a higher form of rational freedom than merely satisfying one's preferences without external interference. Satisfying one's preferences can be a form of slavery if these preferences are simply taken for granted instead of being deliberately and rationally chosen. By contrast, rationally examining the universal compatibility of one's preferences with everyone else's breaks the causal determination of habit and instinct, thereby rendering one truly *self-determining*, or responsible for one's own behavior.

Rousseau's idea of moral freedom was later taken up by Kant, albeit in a somewhat different way. While Rousseau conceived of moral freedom in chiefly political terms, Kant conceived of it in metaphysical terms. On Rousseau's model, the General Will is the outcome of democratic deliberation. In order to assure that deliberation approximates unanimous consensus, Rousseau reasoned that citizens must be relatively few in number, share common lifestyles and interests, and not delegate their legislative powers to elected representatives; in order to assure that deliberation be moral and impartial, he reasoned that citizens must be virtuous (public spirited and patriotic) and relatively equal in economic status and political influence.

On Kant's model, by contrast, moral freedom is vested in a kind of metaphysical agency. On one hand, moral agency is conceived as subject to no other law than the moral law. Its rational willing has no other cause than itself; it is purely self-determining. On the other hand, the empirical, embodied agent remains subject to the mechanistic laws of nature. The contradiction between the two aspects of the self – morally free rational agency and causally determined embodied subjectivity – is resolved by Kant in one of the most famous sections of his masterpiece, *The Critique of Pure Reason* (1781). The necessity and universality attributed to causal laws can be explained, he reasoned, only if these laws are thought to be the product of reason itself, the mental faculty responsible for establishing necessary conceptual relations.

Previous philosophers working within the empiricist and rationalist traditions had also distinguished reason from sense experience by noting the former's capacity to discern or analyze necessary logical connections between concepts. But Kant was the first to propose that reason performed a more basic function: the *synthesis* of sensory experience into a predictable, causally ordered world of objects. This *transcendental* employment of reason provides the key to Kant's resolution of the freedom/determinism problem. The metaphysical idea of freedom that underwrites moral self-determination is not contradicted by the fact of causal determinism, since causal determinism is just a condition that our mind (or more precisely, the unifying activity of our reasoning) imposes on sensory experience. Reason, understood as a unitary faculty combining moral willing and transcendental synthesis, is entirely self-determining, since it ultimately legislates both moral and causal laws.

One can hardly underestimate the revolutionary impact that Kant's theory of moral and transcendental self-determination had on subsequent Continental philosophers. This impact was political, as well. Although Kant, unlike Rousseau, was not an advocate of unlimited democratic sovereignty but, like Locke and other liberals, an advocate of limited, constitutional government,[14] his metaphysical conception of self-determination implied an unlimited (or permanent) political revolution.[15] According to Kant, the strongest justification for constitutional government is not the establishment of legal rights. Legal rights, of course, are necessary for protecting our capacity to act independently of arbitrary violence. As distinct from violence, legal coercion simply forces would-be rights violators to respect the freedom of bodily movement that each needs to pursue a rational plan of life. So understood, respect for the law need not be motivated out of moral respect for others. Indeed, Kant says that even a "race of devils" would find it in their mutual self-interest to consent to a system protecting their negative freedom from external interference.

Yet Kant also observes that the establishment of lawful peaceful cooperation serves a higher purpose than securing freedom from external domination; it also makes possible the safe, *autonomous* exercise of inwardly directed moral virtue. In "An Answer to the Question: What is Enlightenment?" (1784), Kant argues that moral virtue is exercised fully only by enlightened autonomous agents, who reject any deference to dogmatic authority by obeying only the dictates of their own rational conscience. According to

Kant, this means that the duty to become morally self-determining requires that humanity embark on an indefinite process of political reform, gradually overthrowing all traditions and institutions that contradict the demands of moral reason. Ultimately, moral duty demands nothing less than the establishment of an ideally just polity wherein each citizen is free from external constraint and united by a General Will.

The moral perfectionism guiding Kant's political philosophy – above all, its rationalist injunction to radically question all taken-for-granted assumptions and authorities – has recently become a topic of renewed interest among philosophers and serves as the focal point of one of the selections contained in this volume. Such perfectionism was certainly taken seriously by Kant's epigones, who (predictably enough) proceeded to apply the injunction to think critically to Kant's own philosophy. The immediate successors to Kant's transcendental philosophy – Johann Gottfried Fichte (1762–1814), Friedrich Wilhelm Joseph von Schelling (1775–1854), and Georg Friedrich Wilhelm Hegel (1770–1831) – criticized what they perceived to be its dogmatic and inconsistent assumption of a dualism between reason (the faculty of concepts and universal ideas) and sense perception (the faculty of intuiting particular objects). In particular, they rejected Kant's view that reason was only a subjective, psychological faculty. By rigorously adhering to Kant's belief that transcendental reason designated an absolutely unconditioned, self-determining agency whose unifying activity extended to sense perception, they dissolved whatever dualism remained between subjective reason and its objective, limiting other. For them, *absolute idealism* implied *objective idealism*, or the notion that nature and society are informed by a unitary *spiritual* agency that seeks to progressively realize its essence as free, self-determining agency. The price they paid for thinking of reason in this all-encompassing (or totalizing) sense, however, was one that Kant himself had explicitly refused in *The Critique of Pure Reason*: Reason that absolutely and unconditionally embraces all reality – including its "other" – must incorporate an element of contradiction, or *dialectic*, within itself.

Among German idealists, it is Hegel who is often credited with having developed the most elaborate and influential system of dialectical thought. According to Hegel, reason (Spirit) evolves historically, and takes on concrete meaning and living force only insofar as it is embodied in particular objective social institutions, such as scientific practices, legal precepts, and religious, artistic, and philosophical movements.[16] The endpoint of spiritual progress is a world that has been fully understood and mastered by a humanity that has perfectly realized its own freedom in the form of a modern, rational, constitutional state. Although Hegel's model of a constitutional state allows room for individual freedom – and to that extent is not inherently opposed to the founding idea of liberalism – he emphatically insists that such freedom is but a conditional, subordinate moment in the total life of the community. For Hegel, neither the freedom nor the identity of the individual exists outside of communal attachments to family, civil association, and state. Just as one's preferences, values, and character are shaped by one's relationships to others, so too is one's freedom shaped by the customs and laws of one's society.[17]

Because one's freedom and identity are mutually dependent upon the freedom and identity of others, full self-determination presupposes that individual and community be harmonized in accordance with a General Will. Unlike Rousseau, Hegel believed that the General Will can be made compatible with a modern, highly differentiated and economically stratified social order, but only if individual differences are mediated by superordinate group (or corporate) memberships and identifications. At each ascending level of incorporation there exists a more extensive and universal membership. Thus, the interests of employees would be determined immediately by their particular membership in a company, with the interests of this company being determined by the more extensive and general interests of other companies like it; in turn, the interests of these companies would converge with the more general interests of other types of business, and these (commercial) interests would converge with one of several national interests.

Hegel rejected two other liberal ideas in conjunction with his theory of mediation: the separation of powers and the universal franchise. Hegel preferred the idea of integrating executive, legislative, and judicial functions under a supreme sovereign power so as to avoid constitutional crises regarding the delegation of authority. Furthermore, not only did he defend a representative form of government that excluded all but a few members of the propertied class from voting, but he dispensed with the notion of unmediated, unorganized voting. In his opinion, allowing individuals to vote in accordance with their individual conscience, unmediated by any corporate ties, only encourages them to place their particular interests ahead of the general interests of society. This adversarial notion of democracy, which he attributes to the English and American systems, is replaced in his theory by an older system incorporating the administrative harmonizing of group interests combined with their political representation by corporate bodies and estates. According to this model of political participation, members of particular sectors of civil society elect representatives from their own sector. For example, as a banker I would be incorporated into a financial sector and would thus be entitled to vote for a candidate representing the particular interests of that sector in a national parliament consisting of both a commercial and an agricultural chamber of deputies (the latter chamber consisting of inherited seats). Ultimately, whatever conflicts existed between these two chambers would be subsumed under the protective aegis of the national interest and resolved (mediated) by representatives of an impartial state bureaucracy. The final act of mediating particular and universal interest would be the unitary – largely symbolic – ratification of legislation by a hereditary monarch.

Interestingly, Hegel's greatest contribution to Continental political philosophy might not be his own political philosophy, which continued to inspire British and Italian philosophers well into the twentieth century,[18] but his *dialectical* method of articulating it. This method of philosophizing designates a mode of rational argumentation that is quite distinct from that found in Anglo-American political philosophy. As noted above, Anglo-American political philosophers conceive of rational argumentation as a process of deducing complex claims from foundational principles. Logical inferences like these in turn presuppose the analytical clarification of political concepts in terms of their necessary and sufficient conditions. Like Kant, Hegel thinks that the activity of drawing logical distinctions is only one aspect of reasoning, and a subordinate one at that. The other aspect of reasoning involves synthesizing what are otherwise analytically distinct and opposed terms. This kind of reasoning typically occurs when we try to give a complete explanation for the possibility of something actually existing. Rather than justify complex ideas by tracing them back to a few foundational principles in linear fashion – the method preferred by most Anglo-American political philosophers – we proceed in the reverse order: we show how simple, abstract ideas are meaningless, incoherent, or simply lacking concrete reality until progressively defined in terms of a totality of supporting ideas.

This process is circular in the same way that any process of deep reflection or textual interpretation is. When I reflect on myself, I split myself into opposing selves: the self (subject) that reflects and the self (object) that is reflected upon. This distinction is only relative, since both selves are implicated in the unitary self of reflection; and it is circular in a progressive way, since each act of reflection progressively deepens and alters my own sense of myself: my identity. Like understanding any text, my reflective understanding of my own autobiography involves interpreting particular events in light of a narrative totality consisting of past and (anticipated) future events. Part and whole define one another in a reciprocal or circular manner, but the circle is never closed; like a progressive spiral, each additional reading (or interpretation) of the text continually alters the text's identity and meaning. Deeper meanings are continually discovered so that the text is brought into ever greater coherence and meaningfulness. So construed, reflective reason – unlike analytic reason – is not simply a method of logically relating truths that are discovered independently, via empirical observation, but is itself a process of constituting truth, progressively changing what we take the identity of things (including ourselves) to be.

A simple example will suffice to illustrate this point. Recall for a moment Bentham's critique of the social contract tradition. That tradition assumes that freedom is something that adheres in the individual in a natural way, prior to any civil or legal association. If we analyze the bare, abstract concept of freedom, we arrive at the idea of choosing and acting in a way that is unconstrained by external impediments. To say that I am free in this *negative* sense is just to say that nothing and no one is forcing me to do something I don't want to do. Because civil laws limit what I want to do (e.g., taking Jill's property without asking her permission), it is reasonable to think of them as limiting my freedom. Analytically speaking, law *qua* external constraint opposes my freedom *qua* internal desire and volition. However, deeper reflection on the conditions for the possibility of freedom shows that this distinction is only conceptual and not real. Outside of a legal order, my desires and volitions would come into conflict with Jill's: either my freedom would limit hers or hers would limit mine. Legal coercion and constraint protects us both from the freedom-denying encroachments of the other. So understood, real freedom necessarily presupposes as one of its conditions of possibility its opposite: legal coercion. Conversely, legal coercion presupposes its opposite: freedom. Without individuals acting freely and entering into potentially conflict-laden relations with one another, law serves no purpose. Furthermore, law cannot effectively constrain unless it is freely obeyed, which can happen (according to Rousseau, Kant, and Hegel) only if it represents a General Will to which all can identify. In the final analysis, my negative freedom to be left alone to pursue my business unhindered by others depends upon the coercive enforcement of legal rights, whose own morally binding efficacy in turn depends upon my *positive* freedom to participate (however indirectly) in a collective act of self-legislation and self-determination.

The dialectical relationship between individual self-determination (and personal identity) and communal self-determination (and collective identity) is one of the enduring themes of Continental political philosophy that distinguishes it from its

Anglo-American counterpart. The reflective undermining (or deconstruction, to use a more contemporary phrase) of all fixed identities is another distinguishing feature. To reflect on something is to change its superficial (external or apparent) meaning and identity in relation to its deeper, essential conditions of possibility. Absolute idealists like Hegel reflectively altered (reversed) the meaning and identity of individuality by grounding it in sociality; they did the same with respect to individual freedom (by grounding it in communal coercion). Reflecting even deeper on the conditions of rationality, Post-Hegelian materialists like Karl Marx (1818–83) and Friedrich Nietzsche (1844–1900) later argued that rational reflection itself is but a surface reflection of deeper economic and psychological forces.

In his youth, Marx allied himself closely with a group of reform-minded philosophers known as Young Hegelians. These philosophers used Hegel's own ideas to undermine what they perceived to be the conservative implications of Hegel's thought. The most useful of these was the idea that religion reflected a distorted understanding of humanity. According to Hegel, religion projects the universal and infinitely creative powers of the human spirit outward, in the form of an all-powerful God who confronts humanity as an alien, freedom-restricting power. True emancipation of humanity comes when it overcomes religious alienation by recognizing its own universality and infinity in philosophical insight.

Young Hegelians like Ludwig Feuerbach (1804–72) thus sought the key to human emancipation in atheistic humanism. Indeed, Feuerbach believed that all forms of absolute idealism – including Hegel's philosophy of Spirit – involve religious mystification. For him, abstract ideas – including that of universal reason (Spirit) – were meaningless and empty apart from the particular, embodied lives of sensuous human beings. Marx agreed. However, he went beyond Feuerbach by attacking the state and its abstract legal apparatus as a more serious kind of religious alienation. According to Marx, in Hegel's political philosophy, the legal machinery of the state confronts the particular, conflicting wills of private persons as a monolithic General Will that is imposed upon them as an external force, from the top down. In order to overcome the alienation between concrete individuals of need (civil society) and abstract citizens embodying a General Will (state), Marx proposed that conflict-ridden civil society transform itself into a harmonious moral society through the exercise of direct, universal suffrage in the manner suggested by Rousseau. In essence, this would amount to the overcoming of both coercive state and coercive (conflict-ridden) civil society in the form of a perfect moral community.[19]

Marx soon realized that the source of conflict and alienation lay deeper than he thought. The modern bureaucratic state and its liberal-democratic order was indeed an expression of alienation. For Marx, the very concept of individual rights – though liberating in its own limited way – was premised on the economic alienation of private property holders, who viewed their competitors as limits on their freedom.[20] Liberal democracy was merely the arena in which conflicting wills canceled, dominated, or subsumed each other. The achievement of full human emancipation could therefore not stop at liberal democratic reform; the realization of true moral community required a communist solution: the abolition of private property.

Marx believed that communism was the key to satisfying all of humanity's metaphysical yearnings for communal solidarity, freedom, and wholeness. Religion, ethics, and philosophical speculation, he thought, were but substitute gratifications for and illusory reflections of humanity's infinite communal capacity for self-determination. Persons are forced to rely on such ideological opiates – which also function to legitimate the status quo – because they have externalized their free, communal creativity in the form of an alien economic system that now deforms and stifles that creativity.[21] The detailed division of labor required to maintain profitable forms of industrial efficiency under capitalism cripples the mental and physical development of workers, transforming them into one-dimensional automatons – slaves, all of them, to the machines they operate. While their individuality and freedom are effaced by the repetitive and mindless drudgery of their work, the freedom and individuality of their bosses is hardly less alienated.[22] For the freedom of consumers and producers, capitalists and workers alike is severely constrained by the laws of the market, which ceaselessly demand ever-greater conformity (mass consumption and mass production) and competition, all for the sake of accumulating profit rather than satisfying basic human needs.

In the final analysis, capitalism appears to invert the very individualism, freedom, communal productivity, and rationality it supposedly embodies. What it upholds in theory – the free, equitable, and dignified cooperation among individual contractors for the public good of all – it denies in practice, exploiting the labor of some for the profit of others, degrading humans (whom Kant famously regarded as "ends-in-themselves") to undignified means. Its irrational anarchy – exemplified in periodic business cycles of over-and under-production and the increasing division between rich and poor – is destructive of the very productive capacities it presupposes.[23] Only in a community whose members democratically planned and consciously controlled all decisions regarding the production and distribution of goods would the irrationality and immorality of capitalism, in Marx's judgment, be overcome.[24]

But how does humanity arrive at this promised land? Like Hegel before him, Marx viewed history as unfolding an irreversible logic of progressive stages of social evolution. However, as Hegel had earlier noted, social evolution is not linear, but dialectical; in order to achieve an unalienated community of fully realized, reconciled, and self-determining individuals, humanity must lose its primitive communal solidarity and equality and traverse successive stages of alienated class society. No Spirit – or logic of self-determination, reconciliation, or of any other idea – providentially guides this process. Rather, the process is blindly propelled by economic contradictions between *forces* and *relations* of production.[25] For example, the transition from feudalism to capitalism was in some sense necessitated by the inability of feudal property relations – the guild system in the cities and the manorial system in the countryside – to feed, clothe, and shelter the growing workforce. New relations of production, allowing for unfettered competition among free contractors who possessed complete ownership over mobile and fluid capital, enabled new productive technologies to be efficiently implemented in factories. The transition from capitalism to socialism is also necessitated by a similar dialectic. Capitalist productive forces generate too much wealth to be fully consumed and invested by capitalists, so they scale back production and employment, thereby worsening the crisis of over-production. Only by replacing private with social appropriation of (social) wealth will this contradiction be resolved.

Marx deepened Hegel's critique of analytic social contract theory and utilitarianism by showing how ideologies in general, and not just ideologies of atomistic individualism and freedom, are conditioned by material (or economic) contradictions. For Marx, the legal rights to contract and associate with one another, vote in elections, and speak openly are mere formal abstractions. Unless persons also have the material resources, opportunities, and capacities to exercise such rights equally, they are not real rights. But Marx's dialectical subsumption of political and legal theory under (analytically distinct) economic theory is more radical than it first appears. The economic realization of political and legal theory renders it superfluous. Legal and political rights merely reflect and adjudicate class conflicts born of inequality; eliminating the latter therefore deprives the former of its *raison d'être*.

The absence of any sustained political theory in Marx's thought thus reflects his cynical view that political philosophy in general is symptomatic of – and ideologically supportive of – an alienated and unjust social condition. Saying this, however, does not change the fact that Marx himself saw the realization of a stateless, communist society as in some sense the fulfilment of humanistic ideals.

These ideals – of freedom, equality, justice, solidarity, and individuality – are precisely those that came under attack by Friedrich Nietzsche, the last great progenitor of contemporary Continental political philosophy. While Marx offered an economic critique of bourgeois political ideology, Nietzsche offered a psychological one. In his opinion, humanistic ideals have their source in the resentment that weaker classes of persons feel towards stronger classes. Incapable of asserting their own Will to Power and taking responsibility for their own value judgments, the great "herd" of mediocre persons fears those who are more creative, assertive, and powerful and resent them for it. "Rights" (freedom), "equality," "justice," and "solidarity" are just rationalizations for denying the stronger their superior creativity. However, by denying creative and assertive instincts, morality denies what is most vital to human life. Hence, in contrast to the positive nihilism of the noble creator, who denies the existence of any limiting norm outside of his own will, the negative nihilism of the moral follower amounts to a total denial of life's instinctive impulse toward radical self-determination.[26]

In the final analysis, Nietzsche's psychological reflection on morality suggests that the very concepts of individuality, selfhood, and agency need to be radically questioned. Anticipating Freud's theory of the instincts, Nietzsche argues that the self, conceived as a continuous self-determining locus of identity, is itself the product of an act of social repression. Moral training requires that the primitive, assertive subject of vital instincts be restrained. Moral conditioning accomplishes this by training the subject to reflect upon itself as an object. Reflection objectifies the self, turns it into a moral subject whose identity can be normatively fixed and monitored from within as well as from without. Ultimately, the moral identity of the individual self is subsumed under the legal and political identity of society. Indeed, for Nietzsche, all fundamental legal and political categories reflect a more primary impulse to discipline and punish instinctual drives. The invention of "legal freedom" goes hand in hand with legal coercion, which, in turn, is justified in terms of the social contract, the notion of a General Will, or transcendent rational identity. Because persons are artificially defined as legally free by the moral code (and, to some extent, are conditioned to be that way), they can be held responsible for their acts, and punished accordingly.

If individuality, freedom, and other moral/rational ideas are just rationalizations designed to punish dangerous instincts and volitions – and, as such, are not necessitated by nature – then they can (and, in Nietzsche's view, should) be dispensed with, at least where it concerns exceptionally creative and assertive persons. In discarding God, morality, objective truth, and other metaphysical illusions as artificial limits on their Will to Power, such persons achieve the status of "overmen," that is, they continually overcome any temptation to deny their volatile (and at times contradictory) creativity and assertiveness. So in thrall are they to their dynamic natures that they cease being individuals who possess continuous, consistent, and integrated identities.

Contemporary Continental Schools of Political Thought

Contemporary Continental political thought is deeply imbued with the history of political thought running from Rousseau to Nietzsche. The distinctive feature of this tradition that sets it apart from Anglo-American political philosophy is its ceaseless questioning of the entire tradition of Western metaphysical thought that has shaped our basic categories of reasoning. For Continental philosophers, rational analysis and deduction of political ideas often conceals the deeper social, economic, and psychological contexts in which such ideas acquire their concrete meaning. The articulation of this context, in turn, shows that whatever meaning political ideas possess is far from clear, often implicating what appear to be extrinsic – if not opposed – social, economic, and psychological significations. It also shows that whatever validity such ideas possess is highly contingent and qualified, if not altogether ambivalent. Indeed, the very nature of dialectical reflection compels most Continental political philosophers to adopt a skeptical attitude toward their subject matter that would be unthinkable for Anglo-American philosophers intent on positively reconstructing workable theories of justice.

That said, there exists a significant diversity among schools of Continental thought that resists any summary judgment about that tradition's skeptical tendencies. My attempt in this anthology to provide the reader with a representative sampling of classical texts drawn from what are arguably the most significant schools of thought – phenomenology, existentialism, poststructuralism, postmodernism, and critical theory – is intended to highlight this diversity. Because practical limits have forced me to select just one philosopher from each school as best illustrating its strengths and weaknesses, students and teachers are encouraged to supplement these readings with those drawn from other sources. Another reason for doing so – which will soon become apparent – is the richness and diversity of each school. Philosophers working within any one school typically (and often strongly) disagree with one another on points of method and substance. To take just one example, the most important living representative of the Frankfurt School tradition of critical theory, Jürgen Habermas, develops a theory of law that shares a lot in common with the liberal-democratic theory of justice advanced by the most important living representative of Anglo-American social contract theory, John Rawls. This approach to justice stands in marked contrast to that adopted by Habermas's predecessors in the Frankfurt School tradition, who were chiefly influenced by a Marxist–Hegelian critique of liberal democracy.

Phenomenology

Among the several varieties of Continental philosophy represented in this volume, phenomenology appears to be the furthest removed from political concerns. Its founder, Edmund Husserl (1859–1938), shared the same desire for conceptual clarity that animated Anglo-American analytic philosophers at the turn of the century. However, while the latter focused chiefly on language and propositional logic, Husserl directed his attention to experience.

For Husserl, all meaning derives its determinate sense from the *intentions*, or meaning-giving acts, of a subject. Contrary to what empiricists taught, particular events and things are always immediately given (intended) in experience as meaningful in a general sense, i.e., as a type of thing (e.g., a telescope as distinct from a stick-like thing). Persons often differ in how they intend things (an aborigine sees a stick-like thing where a scientist perceives a telescope). But they also agree that whatever they experience is out there in the world. According to Husserl, agreement in the way we intend events and things is guaranteed by the fact that each shares in common with others an impersonal, transcendental structure of intentionality. Reflectively experiencing this subjectivity and its acts without distortion requires methodically bracketing, or suspending, all our "natural" everyday presuppositions about the external, three-dimensional nature of the experienced world. So construed, phenomenology "reduces" the experienced world to the world as experienced, thereby enabling the phenomenologist to reflect on how the phenomenon of external, three-dimensional objectivity is constituted from within the internal, experiential horizon of pure (transcendental) consciousness.[27]

Husserl touted phenomenology as a method for recovering our original way of experiencing reality, as a pure phenomenon of consciousness, or directly intuited psychic appearance. "To the things themselves!" became a rallying cry for achieving a kind of pristine experience of things unmediated and undistorted by cultural biases of any sort. Above all, Husserl promoted phenomenology as a more scientific (and more experientially rigorous) way of knowing reality than empirical science itself, whose experimental methods required abstracting from the lived experience of things. In his opinion, the history of science and philosophy since antiquity exhibited an experientially unjustified, metaphysical presumption about the nature of things, uncritically defining them as static substances possessing quantifiable (measurable) essences and changeable accidental qualities. By abstracting from the richer lifeworld that gives meaning and purpose to our experience, natural science cannot fathom its own deeper moral justification, which is freedom and responsibility through philosophical (specifically, phenomenological) enlightenment. By reducing all knowledge to abstract natural scientific understanding, scientism unwittingly promotes nihilism, or value skepticism.[28]

Husserl's most important disciple, Martin Heidegger (1889–1976), radicalized this phenomenological critique of scientism (or metaphysical objectivism) further. To begin with, Heidegger noted that Husserl's own appeal to transcendental subjectivity suffered from the same metaphysical dualism that plagued Kant's transcendental philosophy. The idea of an innate, universal stratum of conscious life that constitutes the meaningfulness of a world without belonging to it exhibits an experientially unjustified abstraction, or objectification, of subject and object (self and world). For Heidegger, phenomenology rather reveals the world as the context or experiential horizon of a concretely situated existential understanding. Existential understanding exemplifies immediate involvement in, not reflective consciousness of, practical life, which is just to say that beings do not originally or primarily manifest themselves as intentional "objects" (as Husserl would have it).[29]

Heidegger thus showed how our fundamental experience of the world is relative to our mode of being (with)in it. When I relate to the world in the practical mode of instrumental activity, I do not relate to it as an abstract field of objects "present-at-hand" possessing quantifiable properties. Rather, I relate to it as a tacit network of interrelated involvements "ready-to-hand": the hammer, my hammering, the aim of hammering, and the instrumental context that activates and situates this aim, appear together as one syndrome of concrete understanding (or know-how). Only when breakdowns occur in our routine practical understanding (as when the handle on the hammer breaks in two) does a shift to an objective, reflective mode of being occur in which the ready-to-hand being of the hammer is abstracted out of its context of practical involvements and manifests itself as a static, present-at-hand thing with discrete, quantifiable properties. The interruption of the hammering event calls forth a derivative (non-originary) experience of both the hammerer (as self-conscious subject who no longer feels at home in the world) and the hammer (as isolable object capable of being analyzed into discrete properties and talked about in thematic, scientific terms).

Significantly, Heidegger increasingly came to see modern science and technology (especially since Galileo, Bacon, and Descartes) as instituting a qualitatively distinct way of being-in-the-world which, he felt, dangerously concealed our more originary way of understanding it.[30] According to Heidegger, poetic and artistic modes of revealing reality authentically reveal the primal oneness and integrity obtaining between human existing and world. Modern science and technology, by contrast, project an instrumental relationship on to our understanding of the world, thereby reducing things (including persons) to abstract quantities for purposes of prediction and control.

The political implications of Heidegger's critique of modern science and technology were only developed in detail by his student, Hannah Arendt (1906–75). Nevertheless, Heidegger's critique of objectifying empiricism and rationalism that informed his deep distrust of analytic philosophy, scientific utilitarianism, and humanism of all varieties, resonated with his political views. To many observers, this critique reverberated in his contempt for social engineering and socialist planning, on one hand, and his distrust of liberal democracy as a reflection of abstract individualism, on the other. Coupled with his own lack of political understanding, this anti-modernist sentiment led him to embrace the nationalistic collectivism advocated by the Nazis.

Arendt's politics couldn't be further removed from Heidegger's. While she shared his phenomenologically based suspicion of empiricist and rationalist political philosophy, she concluded that at least one kind of democratic action was central to one dimension of world disclosure. In her opinion, common deliberation about shared rules of conduct opens up a "public space" in which words and deeds "disclose" the world in original and unpredictable ways.

In some respects her thinking about world disclosure parallels Heidegger's distrust of modern social engineering. This view is most forcefully expressed in *The Human*

Condition (1958), where she distinguished three modalities of being-in-the-world: labor (instrumental activity aimed at consumption); work (instrumental and expressive activity aimed at cultural fabrication); and action (expressive and communicative activity aimed at deliberation). In Arendt's opinion, modern administrative states (including liberal democracies) end up privileging labor above political action. Such states either eliminate political life altogether, replacing its argumentative multivocity with top-down scientific economic management – this is the example followed by bureaucratic socialist regimes, which make a mockery of Marx's own post-political communist ideal. Or, they dilute political life by reducing it to the passive act of voting for pre-selected slates of administrative elites – the example followed by liberal welfare democracies, which allow powerful economic interests to dictate political choices. In both cases, the public space necessary for sustaining free, equal political deliberation and elevated cultural life is subordinated to an all-encompassing economy of mass production and mass consumption. Subsequently, just as Heidegger had favorably compared the ancient Greeks to the moderns for having a more original and authentic experience of being, so Arendt compares them favorably for having a more original and authentic experience of the political, exemplified by general and direct citizen participation in the competitive (agonal) expression of diverse opinions.

Despite her sentimental preference for the Greek *polis* over the modern welfare state, Arendt was not entirely anti-modernist in her sympathies. More precisely, she viewed modern subjectivism and objectivism as opening up fundamentally ambivalent possibilities for being-in-the-world. On one hand, modernity initiates a "crisis of culture" whose secular destruction of traditional religious authority opens the way for the state's totalitarian administration of atomized individuals.[31] Their sole purpose in life is now reduced to production and consumption. On the other hand, it makes possible a more radical form of freedom, captured by Kant's notion of self-determination. For Arendt, however, the spontaneous willing of something absolutely new and original essentially consists in the revolutionary founding of laws and constitutions, which have their ultimate warrant in acts of deliberation and promise-making.

Showing no particular ideological preference, Arendt extolled both worker councils and town-hall meetings as retaining some of the former freedom associated with the revolutionary establishment of new political institutions. However, her favorable comparison of the American Revolution to its French counterpart did display an ideological preference: for freedom over social equality. The elimination of social inequality, she noted, could only be done in the name of a unitary (totalitarian) General Will, whose existence (as Rousseau himself had already implied) would be incompatible with the vital heterogeneity and dissent we associate with the political. In contrast to the unlimited power, or violence, exercised by a singularly sovereign will, the legitimate power generated by a plurality of free wills generates its own self-sustaining counter-balance. Not only does the constitutional separation of executive, judicial, and legislative powers ensure a more stable and secure exercise of political freedom through its protection of rights, but it makes possible a more efficient exercise of power. For, unlike violence, power that is collectively constituted, legitimately recognized, and freely obeyed encounters less resistance from those on whom it is exercised. Indeed, political power is nothing more than the power of speech and action, which arises from the discursive plurality of the public space.[32]

The essay of Arendt's included in this volume, "On Violence," is one of her best known and most important, not the least because it elaborates the distinction between illegitimate violence and legitimate power within the context of the student and Black Power movements of the 1960s. The accompanying commentary by Iris Marion Young defends Arendt's basic distinction against the mainstream view of political power, while taking issue with her criticism of the student and Black Power movements.

The mainstream view, famously propounded by Max Weber, holds that political power is synonymous with the state's territorial monopoly over violence. Although Arendt never provides a precise definition of violence, she clearly agrees with Weber that official acts of state can constitute as genuine a form of violence as revolutionary acts directed against the state. Violence is here characterized less by irrational acts of destruction than by calculated applications of instruments aimed at coercing and constraining political agents in a manner that disrupts their freely and publicly recognized consensual relationships. So construed, bureaucratically processed policies that circumvent channels of public accountability and debate are violent, in that they impose ends on political agents without their free, public consent.

Although Arendt agrees with Weber that official acts of state may be (and perhaps typically are) acts of violence, she denies that political actions that generate political power are. As Young points out, power and official violence may be exercised together – indeed, no use of official means to coerce behavior will be effective for long unless backed by the power of the people. However, the democratic plurality that generates political power is conceptually distinct from and very possibly incompatible with the top-down, centralized coercion exercised by the state. (As we shall see, this conception of power resonates with the views of many other contemporary Continental thinkers – most notably Foucault, Habermas, and Lyotard – for whom the idea of centralized, top-down domination is a premodern holdover from the days of absolute monarchy.)[33] So, despite the fact that Arendt does not deny that democratic polities enact coercive statutes, she insists that the force of these laws is dependent upon democratic consent. As Kant and earlier social contract theorists well understood, coercive law serves a legitimate political end: the protection of persons against violence, both official and non-official. Less well understood by them was the fact that the very legitimacy of law depends on its being the expression of a voluntary, public agreement between equals who have communicated their aims to one another. Young thus observes that, for Arendt, political power needs no justification – no moral support from God, Nature, tradition, or any other transcendent authority – beyond the prior and present action that generates and sustains it. Violence, by contrast, does require justification. Because it constitutes an external constraint on and interruption of political action (and very often an overturning of transcendent moral authority as well), it must base its justification on the avoidance of some great future evil.

Young concludes her commentary by returning to the opening themes of her essay: the legitimacy of counterforce exercised by student and Black Power movements of the 1960s; the illegitimacy of excessive police force; and the illegitimacy of NATO's bombing of Serbia and Kosovo in 1999. Arendt thought that the student movements represented dangerously violent efforts to circumvent the political process. In her opinion, any attempt to use politics to further social aims (racial and economic injustice) subordinates the impartial rule of law to a particular bureaucratic agenda. Young disagrees. Like Hannah Pitkin, she wonders what politics could be about if not the public administration of health, education, and welfare – all social aims. As for the student and Black Power movements of the 1960s, and the recent anti-globalization movements at the turn of the millennium, Young argues that the public demonstrations fueled by these movements, while certainly disruptive of authority, were typically expressions of democratic political power directed against official, bureaucratic violence. The violence frequently associated with these demonstrations was mainly an exercise of non-violent political power. The real violence was more often exercised by officials of the state, who sought, in vain, to control and contain a democratic action that further threatened its authority to dictate decisions unilaterally. Young thus finds excessive policing interventions (both domestic and international) to be acts of violence that are illegitimate for want of democratic political backing. However, despite her belief that, by definition, no act of violence can ever be legitimate, she does allow that some such acts may be morally justifiable. Measured acts of extra-legal violence required for defending oneself or others can be morally justified (though never legal or politically legitimate), as when oppressed minorities use arms to protect themselves against a majority that is out to destroy them. But police brutality and the recent NATO intervention in Serbia and Kosovo are not, in her opinion, examples of such measured acts.

Existentialism

Although it is no longer as dominant as it once was, phenomenology has exerted an impact on virtually every school of Continental thought. Twentieth-century existentialism is no exception to this rule, having traced some of its own ideas back to Heidegger.

Heidegger's existentialism mirrors two conflicting tendencies. The first emphasizes the historical contingency (throwness) of human existence. As historically contingent, I find myself (thrown) in(to) a situation that is not entirely of my own making, and this situation at least partly defines who I am (my being). The second aspect – which harks back to Søren Kierkegaard's notion of a "leap of faith" – emphasizes the capacity of radical self-choice. For Heidegger, one can resolve to embrace the prospective aspect of one's contingency (one's death) as a liberating acceptance of the utter nothingness supporting one's life. Accepting this nihilism positively, as Nietzsche taught, opens one to the possibility of radically redefining who one is *ex nihilo* or *ab initio*.

This conception of existential decision has a long pedigree (Arendt, whose own notion of political freedom also implies spontaneous self-constitution, traces it back to St Augustine's treatment of the will's natality). The conception forms the core of twentieth-century French existentialism, whose most famous exponents include Alexander Kojeve, Jean Hyppolyte, Simone de Beauvoir, Albert Camus, Maurice Merleau-Ponty, and Jean-Paul Sartre, who was arguably the most influential and most political of them all.[34] In Sartre's philosophy, it reemerges as a tragic moment in political life. Sartre's first *magnum opus*, *Being and Nothingness* (1943), develops the thesis of radical freedom within the context of a profoundly dualistic and Cartesian reinterpretation of Heidegger's existentialism. The "nothingness" that resides at the heart of existential consciousness resists any assimilation to factical "being." Indeed, consciousness is just the continual "annihilation" of being; in choosing itself, consciousness chooses its own possibilities for understanding its situation. Consequently, the world that appears to consciousness as resistant "being" is in reality only an ensemble of possibilities that may or may not be freely affirmed by consciousness. The world (my situation) is as I choose to define it.

The tragic moment of radical self-definition arises from the fact of social interaction. My definition of the world conflicts with that of others. Such conflict would appear to be resolvable if each consciousness were willing to subsume his or her freedom under a higher, shared consciousness, such as Rousseau's General Will or Hegel's Spirit. For Sartre, however, no resolution is possible, since my freedom is entirely a product of my own radical self-choice. Contrary to Hegel's optimistic view, I cannot allow the other to recognize me on his terms without at the same time allowing him to define me; but to allow him to reduce me to such an object would amount to an utter violation (annihilation) of my subjectivity. Consequently, for Sartre, radical freedom seems irreconcilably opposed to political reciprocity.

This dialectic continues to inform Sartre's later political writings, such as the monumental *Critique of Dialectical Reason* (1960), which, in stark contrast to Arendt's writing, attempts to synthesize existentialism with Marx's historical materialism. At first glance, the merger of Marxism and existentialism seems plausible enough. As I noted above, Marx himself sees alienation, or otherness, as something to be negated in revolutionary practice. Scarcity, or need, confronts consciousness as lack and limit; and capitalism confronts humanity as the system of need, scarcity, and alienation *par excellence*. However, as a social and political institution, capitalism can be practically negated only in collective political action. Collective action, in turn, is freedom enhancing; for as long as individuals do not collectively organize themselves, they are just so many inert atoms to be externally regimented (serially connected) by business and state. Only by spontaneously "fusing" themselves together in revolutionary solidarity with the projected aim of totally redefining their practical conditions can such individuals aspire to radical self-determination.

Tragically, material scarcity comes back to haunt the revolution. The spontaneous fusion of individuals into anarchic revolutionary groups requires the collective imposition of discipline and "fraternal terror" in preventing defections. The need for total unanimity that Arendt had earlier diagnosed as symptomatic of totalitarianism becomes crystalized in the form of bureaucratic institutions, whose management of scarcity in the name of social equality and freedom now requires – once again – the reduction of individuals to an inert, alienated mass of atoms.

The selections of Sartre's work chosen for this volume by the eminent Sartre scholar, William McBride, consist of extended excerpts from volume one of Sartre's monumental *Critique*. This work was written during a time of great revolutionary ferment throughout the Third World, in which Marxism was indeed, in Sartre's words, the "unsurpassable horizon of our time." As McBride proceeds to argue, there is not a little irony in this assertion; for Sartre's *Critique* is an attempt to deploy Marx's own dynamic, existential analysis of history in showing how institutionalized Marxist regimes inevitably betray their own emancipatory promise by congealing into repressive regimes. The irony is perhaps even greater for those of us writing today, since this betrayal has led to institutionalized Marxism being surpassed in all but a few countries. Still, as McBride rightly notes, the passing of institutionalized Marxism in today's world does not mean the surpassing of Marxism as an existential truth about our contemporary condition. Wherever scarcity and inequality exist – and whenever regimes of whatever political persuasion harden into bureaucratic orders maintaining class distinctions – conflict and anarchic freedom will continue to resurface. Today's triumphalist celebration of unrestrained global capitalism can become tomorrow's revolutionary situation.

McBride devotes considerable care in contrasting Sartre's political philosophy with the other philosophical perspectives represented in this volume. In stark contrast to the normative, quasi-contractualist theories advanced by Hannah Arendt and Jürgen Habermas, Sartre's approach is strictly phenomenological (descriptive of political experience rather than prescriptive or directive with respect to possible political conduct). The sober realism of Sartre's political descriptions do not inspire (and are not intended to inspire) much hope in political institutions, democratic or otherwise. In this respect, his views parallel those of Michel Foucault and Jean-François Lyotard, the leading exponents of poststructuralist and postmodernist political philosophy. However, McBride also observes that Sartre's tendency to view history from the standpoint of its overall trajectory (completion or direction) seems curiously antiquated and idealistic by their lights. Like Marx and Hegel before him, Sartre interpreted history as an epic struggle pitting humanity's irresistible quest for freedom against material exploitation, deprivation, and alienation.

For our purposes, it suffices to note that the enduring contribution of Sartre's *Critique* to political thought resides in its phenomenological description of the origination and stagnation of the political as reflected in its most elementary unit: the group. More precisely, like Arendt, Sartre uncovers the essence of the political in the spontaneous fusion of individuals in a revolutionary moment, such as when the otherwise passive working-class inhabitants of the Quartier Saint-Antoine attacked the *Bastille* (the fortress-prison overlooking their district) at the onset of what we today call the French Revolution. Like Arendt, Sartre appreciates the extent to which this political act was born of institutional violence (state-imposed oppression) and thus incorporated counter-violence. However, unlike Arendt, he also appreciates the extent to which revolutionary acts like this are not simply motivated for the sake of freedom taken in the abstract, but are motivated for the sake of concrete freedom, or freedom from material want.

Most contemporary political philosophers understand the intimate relationship between social inequality and political struggle; that is why they devote so much of their effort to discussing the relationship between political legitimacy and distributive justice. This focus, which forms the heart of Rawls's and Habermas's political philosophies, is not Sartre's, however. For as McBride points out, the violence that gives birth to the revolutionary group is later internalized within the regime it founds. In short, for Sartre, no existing state and no existing set of political and legal institutions is entirely free of violence, or of favoring the domination of one economic class by another. Hence, no existing state is legitimate or sovereign (equally representative of all the people).

Can we then not speak of political legitimacy and sovereignty? McBride never answers this question, but it would appear that for Sartre, at least, these terms could at best apply only to a revolutionary group-in-fusion at that moment when the will of each individual within the group spontaneously harmonizes in solidarity with the wills of all the other individuals in the group. This general will (to use a Rouseauian term) ceases to function as a vehicle of free self-determination as soon as the group interiorizes its own violent act in the form of internal discipline. The fraternity that sustains liberty and equality requires that each swear an oath to all the others not to waver from the cause. This oath, in turn, requires a kind of "fraternal terror," which, as McBride points out, makes possible the transformation of the group into a hierarchically structured political organization (party). With the institutionalization of the group in the form of legal or state-exercised power, we return to a situation where a few privileged persons (namely, those in authority and their monied clientele) actively dominate a mass of alienated, passive persons. The return to a potentially revolutionary situation also suggests that the liberatory imperative of practical reason, which aims at abolishing material want through revolutionary praxis, is dialectical in a wholly negative sense. For revolutionary transformation of self and social reality into a totally harmonious system of freedom inevitably fails by generating new forms of scarcity, new forms of alienation, and new revolutionary situations.

Critical Theory

One of the most important contemporary schools of Continental political thought seems to have fully appreciated the lessons of its phenomenological and existential counterparts. The critical theory associated with the early Frankfurt Institute (f. 1923) began as a sub-movement within neo-Marxist social thought and evolved into a neo-Kantian defense of liberal democracy.[35] While some of its early proponents openly embraced Sartre's existentialist Marxism – this was the case with Herbert Marcuse – later proponents, gravitating around the research of Jürgen Habermas, have sought to mute both Marxist and existential themes in favor of more expressly political themes drawn from Arendt's phenomenology.

Proponents of critical theory are often described as "neo-Marxist" because they revised or rejected many assumptions implicit in Marx's teaching and in the teaching of his more orthodox epigones.[36] First, they held that the emergence of state-regulated corporate capitalism would forestall any immanent socialist revolution. Second, they believed that any political reform of capitalism would require democratic political struggle in which individual rights were respected. Third, they returned to Hegel's insight that ideas and ideology – indeed, all the cultural achievements of art, religion, and philosophy – are more than just mere reflections of alienated class society, but are determining factors in human society generally. Finally, they held that the philosophical tensions in Marx's thought – between idealism and materialism, theory and practice, freedom and determinism, metaphysical universalism and historical relativism, moral criticism and scientific explanation – could be satisfactorily understood only by appealing to insights drawn from Freudian psychoanalysis and structural linguistics.

For our purposes, the most relevant connection between critical theory and Continental political philosophy concerns its synthesis of Heideggerian phenomenology and Hegelian dialectics. One of the earliest progenitors of critical theory, Georg Lukács (1885–1971), anticipated Heidegger's critique of science and technology by resurrecting Hegel's critical distinction between dialectical and analytical reasoning. According to Lukács, the kind of analytical, empirical knowledge of social reality promoted by science encourages the adoption of a methodological individualism that conceals the dialectical relationship between individuals (subject) and society (object). Behavioral social science and analytic political philosophy view society as an objectified ensemble of isolated individuals and events externally related to one another by means of deterministic economic laws and coercive contracts. Abstracting from the lived, practical experience of real social agents, such analytical reasoning both reflects and ideologically reinforces the fragmented, alienated, machine-like fatalism of capitalism. For Lukács, the apparent fatalism of capitalism can only be penetrated by workers, who in their everyday working lives experience the contradiction between their alienated existence as passive objects (capital) and their free social practice, which provides the essential dynamic unifying the total system. In this respect, his critique of analytical reason is not so different from Sartre's.

Extending Lukács's critique further, first-generation critical theorists like Theodor Adorno (1903–69), Max Horkheimer (1895–1971), and Herbert Marcuse (1898–1979) later came to share Heidegger's dystopian assessment of science and technology as at once concealing and oppressive. Like Heidegger, they equated this alienated, calculating mode of existence with modern rationality (inaugurated by the Enlightenment) but traced its origin back to the dawn of Western metaphysics. The "dialectic of enlightenment," as they called it, documents the moment at which rational "progress" betrayed its own promise of individual emancipation and happiness, degenerating into totalitarian domination.[37]

This pessimistic appraisal of modernity seems warranted by the horrific social catastrophes of the twentieth century. Yet, as Habermas rightly notes, it was irrationality and prejudice – not reason – that underlay them. Hence, unlike his predecessors, he has sought to vindicate the legacy of rational enlightenment and, along with it, the ideal of liberal democracy.

Habermas's earlier work built upon his predecessor's reconstruction of Marxist social theory. However, in doing so, he drew upon the expressly anti-Marxist political philosophy of Hannah Arendt. *Knowledge and Human Interests* (1968), for example, implicitly readapts Arendt's seminal distinction between labor, work, and action in showing how political activity is irreducibly distinct from economic activity. Contrary to Marx's own reduction of historical progress to economic necessity, Habermas argues that advances in moral–practical knowledge, institutionalized in law and democracy, typically precede rather than follow developments and applications of productive technologies. Because science and morality develop in accordance with their own irreducibly distinct rationales, economic (scientific and technological) progress is no guarantee of moral progress (in the establishment of a just society).

Habermas's distinction between moral and scientific forms of progress closely parallels Arendt's distinction between communicative and instrumental types of action. Most importantly, these distinctions enable him to defend the emancipatory legacy of the Enlightenment. Rationality is not exhausted by the calculated deployment of efficient means in dominating nature; nor is it exhausted by the kind of analytical and experimental methodology deployed by the empirical sciences. In the context of resolving practical disagreements, rationality rather entails reaching agreement through non-violent (open and free) dialogue.

Just as instrumental action is necessary for procuring economic self-preservation, so is communicative action necessary for procuring moral and political self-preservation. And just as analytical and empirical methods of reasoning guide the former, so dialectical (dialogical) and reflective forms of reasoning guide the latter. Logical inference and experimentation – exemplified in natural science – advance our interest in economic self-preservation by enabling the discovery of causal relations that can be used for prediction and control of objectifiable (quantifiable) processes. By contrast, dialogue and reflection – exemplified in interpretative science (history, literature, moral philosophy, psychoanalysis, etc.) – advance our interest in moral and political self-preservation by forging mutual understanding between subjects. Ultimately, our rational interest in freedom and knowledge is advanced only in open and undistorted dialogue, for it is by reflecting our opinions off of the opposing opinions of others that we gain transparent insight into prejudices and other unconscious compulsions.

Despite his concern about how scientific and technological modes of thinking indirectly encourage citizens to reduce problems of social justice to problems of maintaining stable economic growth – thereby also encouraging them to abdicate political action in deference to top-down planning by technical experts – Habermas is much less opposed to modern economic and administrative realities than is Arendt. In *The Theory of Communicative Action* (1981), Habermas concedes that the ever-growing complexity of modern democracy partially "unburdens" citizens of their responsibility for politically coordinating their lives. This, he notes, is a mixed blessing. Having become separated from the consensual communication of our everyday lifeworld, market economy and government administration efficiently coordinate interaction through instrumental/strategic media of money and power. Together with technical and scientific specialization, quasi-self-regulating "systems" such as these increase overall efficiency in the production and distribution of goods. At the same time, they threaten to "colonize" or supplant the communicative lifeworld from whence they spring. Hence, the crisis of culture and politics diagnosed earlier by Arendt remains a problem for Habermas as well.

Habermas's most recent attempt to ground liberal democracy in an ethics of discourse, *Between Facts and Norms* (1993), reframes this problem in terms of a tension between the ideal norms implicit in moral and political dialogue – which presume the possibility of achieving unanimous consensus under conditions of perfect equality and freedom – and the essential facts of modern, liberal society, which include social division, power and income stratification, and economic and administrative constraints. While denying that the tension between facts and norms renders liberal democracy a mere sham (the conclusion reached by Arendt), Habermas acknowledges that it does pose a political challenge. Having shown that egalitarian norms structure procedures and institutions at all level of governance and political life, Habermas can only hope that citizens will be sufficiently inspired by them to embark on a progressive course of legal, political, and social reform.

The two essays included in this volume, "Three Normative Models of Democracy" (1996) and "On the Internal Relation Between the Rule of Law and Democracy" (1996), show how Habermas's theory of communicative action provides a third alternative to the two dominant conceptions of legal equality and democracy currently circulating among political theorists. The *liberal* conception conceives of democracy as a process by which private citizens elect representatives and leaders who are delegated responsibility for enacting and implementing policies that fairly balance competing interests and maximize overall utility. Democracy here provides a voting mechanism for recalling officials who fail to protect the interests of the most powerful and numerous citizens. Although the state is delegated the task of coordinating conflicting aims, its interventions in the private sector are severely limited; for citizens are endowed with constitutional rights that permit them maximal (negative) freedom to pursue their private aims independent of external interference, governmental or otherwise.

The *republican* (or communitarian) conception of democracy, by contrast, conceives democracy in much more expansive terms. For civic republicans and communitarians, democracy involves more than passive voting; it entails active participation among all citizens in debating proposals, setting legislative agendas, and voting directly on policies. Following Rousseau, civic republicans decry the delegation of policy making to elected officials. According to them, these officials impose laws as if they were mere technical means for balancing competing interests and maximizing overall welfare rather than ethical codes for reinforcing civic-minded patriotism, virtue, and solidarity. Civic republicans reject this economics-based vision of political life, which views democracy as a market mechanism for satisfying the needs of the most powerful or numerous interest groups; and instead promote a communication-based vision aimed at generating mutual understanding and consensus. Since they regard the state as the primary vehicle for moral education and socialization, they privilege the positive freedom (right) to participate as equals in a communal process of democratic self-determination over the negative freedom to act without interference. In their opinion, the morally binding authority of the law has no transcendental warrant beyond what citizens have voluntarily imposed on themselves; hence for them, there is no higher law vested in reason, God, or nature (as liberals believe), and they even insist that the constitution is subject to radical alteration, should the people so ordain it.

Habermas thinks that liberal and republican models of democracy both have disadvantages. The republican model restricts democracy to ethical socialization; its presumption that the state is a direct extension of a unified, homogeneous people endowed with unlimited sovereignty verges on the totalitarian. Because there is no higher law than what the majority at any moment happens to deem is ethically proper, dissenting minorities are especially vulnerable to tyranny. The liberal model suffers from an opposite defect. Although it provides constitutional protection of individuals embracing widely opposed ethical viewpoints, it does so by uncoupling higher law from democratic politics altogether. Because basic rights are vested in a transcendent foundation (God, nature, reason) that is indifferent to changing social realities, such rights are invariably conceived in the most minimal of ways: as guarantees protecting (negative) freedom from interference. Here, positive political rights to participation and social rights to welfare are without standing. Consequently, the power of the state to intervene in mitigating the tyranny of market forces in generating extreme inequalities in power and wealth remains unjustified.

The "deliberative" or "procedural" conception of democracy advanced by Habermas overcomes these disadvantages. Like the liberal model, it accepts the reasonableness of ethical pluralism. It thus endorses the need for constitutional protections (including judicial review of democratic legislation) and concedes a legitimate role for strategic negotiations aimed at compromising opposed interests as well as administrative interventions aimed at aggregating and maximizing them efficiently. However, like the republican model it sees basic rights – indeed all laws – as outcomes of a fair procedure of collective interpretation. Not only is the concrete scope of individuals' "subjective" rights (negative freedom) defined by democratic legislation, but legislating in a way that does not discriminate against the reasonable needs of all citizens requires some active participation among citizens in generating public opinion and setting the legislative agenda. Contrary to the republican model, citizens need not define their lives in terms of politics; nor need they aspire to some ideal of ethical virtue. Rather, the very impulse toward civic-minded deliberation aimed at reaching consensus on the scope of rights will lead them to appreciate the costs that their lifestyles impose on the lives of others; and this in turn will encourage them to transform what were once opposed interests into mutually complementary ones.

Because subjective rights that guarantee the private autonomy of individuals pursuing their own personal aims are without concrete meaning and force apart from laws designed to interpret and enforce them, such rights are in some sense internally related to the political rights that guarantee the public autonomy of citizens engaged in legislative deliberation. Implicit in the modern concept of law (the rule of law) is the idea of equality before the law. Seen from the vantage point of discourse ethics, this idea specifies a conception of justice, or moral legitimacy, which imposes an obligation to obey the law only if "all those possibly affected by it could consent to it after participating in rational discourses." In short, if human rights possessed a prepolitical authority external and impervious to potential democratic consent ("as though they were preexisting moral facts"), this would "contradict" the essential autonomy of legal subjects. Stated somewhat differently, if citizens did not have democratic influence on the enactment and implementation of rights, then such rights could not function as reliable guarantees protecting their freedom against the state. Conversely, if there were no legal subjects whose subjective rights were at stake, law – and therefore democracy – would serve no purpose. Furthermore, at least some basic rights – such as freedom of speech and association – are necessary conditions for institutionalizing democracy. Consequently, far from being opposed – as the liberal and republican models each suggest – popular democratic sovereignty and basic human rights, subjective rights (private autonomy) and political rights (public autonomy) are "co-original," or mutually co-dependent.

If Habermas is right, the implications of this analysis for our understanding of equal rights is momentous. According to the liberal paradigm of law, rights are accorded equally to persons in virtue of what they possess in common: their basic, transcendent humanity. As such, rights apply to everyone in the *same* way. It would be a violation of formal consistency to say that P's right to X entitles P to Y and not hold that Q's right to X entitles Q to Y as well. This formal conception of equality, however, yields unjust results when applied to people whose actual circumstances are far from equal. Take the right to life, for example. It cannot mean the same thing for women and fetuses as it means for men. If it means anything at all when applied to fetuses (assuming for the sake of argument that it does apply to them), it means that they cannot be aborted except in extreme cases. If it means anything for women, it means that they have a right to abortion (at least under certain circumstances).

Unlike the liberal paradigm, the social welfare paradigm of law recognizes that equal rights will entail different entitlements to persons situated in different circumstances. However, like the liberal paradigm, it sees rights as entitlements that descend from some prior norm, for example, some generalization about the essential needs of women, fetuses, and men. Because it proceeds paternalistically, viewing rights as pregiven "goods" to be distributed to private individuals for the sake of pursuing their productive lives – and here Habermas's critique strongly resonates with Foucault's critique of normalizing "bio-power" (see below) – it tends to overgeneralize and artificially fix the "essential" needs of various classes of citizenry. Thus, social rights aimed at protecting pregnant women on the job often end up stereotyping them as "expectant mothers," regardless of whether some of the women in question do not view themselves this way. The procedural paradigm of law proposed by Habermas does not succumb to this defect. Instead of conceiving rights as pregiven goods aimed at satisfying pregiven needs, it conceives them as the product of a dialogic procedure involving all affected persons (in this case, especially women), in which needs are themselves clarified and modified.

Simone Chambers's commentary weighs the advantages and disadvantages of Habermas's proceduralism. The advantages of proceduralism revolve around its theoretical modesty. According to Habermas, political philosophy overshoots its proper mark of reconstructing universal normative foundations when it tries to offer concrete, substantive visions of justice. If the universal norms underwriting communicative action imply any standard of justice at all, it is only one that tells us how to go about fairly deciding for ourselves what is substantively just. However, because that procedural (or formal) standard is so general and empty of substantive prescriptive meaning and force, its power to regulate our deliberation is correspondingly weak.

Seen from one perspective, this weakness is a strength. It forces us, who are members of particular polities, to give these standards substantive meaning and force in a way that best suits our peculiar historical circumstances. As Chambers notes, given their country's peculiar historical experience with a particularly virulent form of fascism, Germans might rightly interpret their formal right to free speech, which is generally implied by universal democratic procedure, as strongly prohibiting types of hate speech that Americans, with a different history, would insist on legally tolerating. Yet seen from another perspective, the general vagueness of our democratic duty to protect free speech really is a weakness, in that it does not explicitly rule out prohibitions against any type of speech that a reasonable majority happens to believe is unacceptably hateful. Conceivably, a reasonable but uninformed majority might find any speech advocating strong views (such as atheism, or the class antagonism of capitalist society) to be so "hateful" and "divisive" as to be dangerous and unworthy of legal toleration.

In addition to this objection – that a procedural theory of deliberative democracy lacks sufficient content to legitimate (or delegitimate) actual decisions regarding issues of substantive justice – there is the related criticism, expressed by Lyotard among others (see below), that the theory is caught up in a vicious circle. The theory is supposed to ground prior norms that limit and guide actual democratic deliberation, but it is democratic deliberation that actually decides the meaning and force of these norms.

Chambers thinks these two objections miss their mark. First, Habermas supplements his procedural theory of democracy with an empirical account of the real social preconditions that have to obtain in order for procedures of democratic deliberation to yield just outcomes. Some of these preconditions – such as the cultivation of individual autonomy and mutual respect between persons – expressly rule out forms of racial discrimination, speech censorship, and other forms of substantive injustice even if the procedures, taken by themselves, do not. Second, the charge of circularity loses its force once we concede that not just any interpretation of the procedures of democratic association preferred by a reasonable majority can count as legitimate. For instance, given what we know about the actual effects of segregation, a majority could not legitimately interpret the general procedure of democratic equality in a way that permitted "separate but equal" facilities for blacks and whites. Nor could such a majority legitimately censor talk of atheism and class conflict without strong proof showing that it threatened democracy.

Despite her defense of Habermas's procedural theory of democracy, Chambers is concerned that Habermas has not sufficiently clarified the institutional and social preconditions that would have to obtain in order for democratic procedural justice to be fully (or even minimally) realized. Because of this neglect, there remains the impression that a procedural theory of democracy is devoid of substantive, critical content. Furthermore, even if, as Habermas insists, the precise nature of this content must, in the final analysis, be resolved upon by citizens and not by social theorists, it is unclear how citizens can do so rationally in light of the current distortions wrought upon the deliberative process by economic and social inequalities. Chambers's concern here recalls – in a manner that is at once paradoxical and searching – the dialectic of theory and practice that originally occupied Habermas's Marxist predecessors in the critical theory tradition: how can citizens embark on a radical politics of enlightened democratic reform, if the current social, economic, and political institutions circumscribing democratic deliberation do not permit rationally enlightened deliberation?

Poststructuralism

The schools of philosophy we have discussed so far share one thing in common: they take as their starting point the political agent's subjective (or intersubjective) point of view. This point of view, however, can be criticized for being too subjective (unscientific) or too question-begging as a normative foundation. For this reason poststructuralists seek a different starting point.

As its name implies, poststructuralism grew out of an earlier school of thought known as structuralism.[38] Structuralism was a predominantly French movement that established itself in linguistics and anthropology. Like Marx before them, structuralists sought to show that the subjective phenomena of conscious life are surface reflections of deeper structures. During the first decades of the twentieth century, the French linguist Ferdinand de Saussure had already argued that the meaning of any word (signifier) is partly determined by structural relationships with other words within a system of differences and resemblances rather than (as Husserl taught) by the intentions of a speaker relating to singular objects of consciousness. By the 1950s, French anthropologist Claude Lévi-Strauss was arguing that all thought is structured in accordance with certain binary distinctions (for instance, between nature and culture).

Poststructuralists accept the principle that consciousness is structured by impersonal rules but reject the idea that such rules are universal, or hard-wired into the brain. In their opinion, structures of thought, language, and behavior are relative to particular historical and cultural systems. These systems, in turn, are constituted by equally impersonal power relations, which are at once arbitrary and objective, conditioning the conscious choices of "subjects" in a largely unconscious way.

Hegel, Marx, and Heidegger had all earlier discussed the way in which the conscious life of the individual subject is preconsciously conditioned by particular, historically and culturally relative frames of understanding and behaving. Louis Althusser (1918–90) and his student Michel Foucault (1926–84) radicalized this insight further. Althusser argued that within each type of society there exists a "structure in dominance" that conditions – without totally determining – other structures. In feudal society that dominant structure is the political system; in *laissez-faire* capitalism it is the economic (or market) system; and in late, state-regulated capitalism it is the ideological (educational and communication) system. Althusser also noted the existence of a fourth structure alongside the political, the economic, and ideological systems of production: science. Following Gaston Bachelard (1884–1962), he observed that scientific structures do not progressively evolve in any continuous sense, but undergo "epistemological breaks" in which earlier structures are downgraded to the status of mere ideology.[39]

Foucault extended his mentor's epistemological relativism to incorporate all human sciences (including Marx's own historical materialist critique of capitalism, which Althusser had regarded as non-ideological). Refining Nietzsche's views about power, Foucault sought to undermine faith in the sovereign self-sufficiency and universal normativity of humanity, conceived as a transcendent form of subjective purposiveness. According to Foucault, the course of human history reveals no deep meaning and purpose and therefore displays no sense of progress. A sober look at Western thought since the Middle Ages rather suggests that it has traversed a sequence of global paradigms of knowledge that are radically discontinuous and historically contingent. Each paradigm (*episteme*) is governed by its own peculiar manner of conceiving meaning, life, human agency, and reality. Each paradigm has its own rules of language, speech, and behavior and its own rules about what counts as a true statement.[40]

Foucault's brilliant genealogy of penal reform and the exercise of sovereign political power in *Discipline and Punish* (1975) provides an excellent illustration of these paradigms. Until the mid-seventeenth century, knowledge and truth were conceived analogically; knowing something involved tracing its metaphorical relationships to other things. According to this model, the sovereign ruler was virtually identified with his kingdom, so that any law-breaking was regarded as a kind of treason, or violation of the sovereign's own personal power and bodily integrity. Punishment – which often took the form of public torture and disfigurement – therefore served as a ritual, symbolic reenactment of the monarch's absolute, personal power. Furthermore, since merely being suspected of criminal activity by the monarch was considered to be an affront to his person (which was presumed to be relatively infallible in its judgment), a suspect was presumed to be at least partly guilty. Hence, torturing the suspect served to expiate his guilt as well as reveal the full truth of its criminal extent. Failure to extract a confession did not invalidate the sovereign's original suspicion, but it did exonerate the suspect from any further suspicion of criminality.

The passing away of torture as a privileged form of punishment corresponds to the passing away of absolute sovereignty. It also corresponds to the emergence of two new paradigms of knowledge and truth. The classical paradigm that emerged in the mid-seventeenth century defined knowledge in terms of representing (often in minute detail) a plethora of particular things in accordance with their proper classifications. Applied to the political sphere, this meant that legitimate sovereignty had to correspond to the moral limits imposed by impartial reason. Not only would sovereign power have to be limited constitutionally and divided into separate powers, but it would have to represent (in some democratic form) the interests and powers of the population. Accordingly, punishment could no longer be justified as a personal act of vengeance on the part of a being who was above the moral law. Rather, punishment had to be rethought contractually, as the repayment of a debt that was owed to society at large. Respecting the dignity and autonomy of the criminal as one who was responsible for his crime required extracting this debt in a way that did not do violence to his rational, moral nature. Imprisonment, based upon a precise calculus of social harm and responsibility, thus replaced torture. If anything remained of the public spectacle, it was the labor-gangs who "represented" the moral fault of their criminal idleness in their hard work and passive confinement.

The theme of labor suggests the refiguration of sovereign power and punishment according to a newer, humanistic paradigm of knowledge and truth. The emergence of capitalism had already rendered the premodern dismemberment and destruction of the body costly. The laboring power of the criminal's body was something to be preserved, strengthened, and disciplined. The classical, retributive model of punishment – based upon the contractarian idea of repaying past debts – did not yet capture the utilitarian need to rehabilitate the criminal as a future, productive member of society. Beginning in the nineteenth century, we thus see punishment serving newer and different ends. No longer is one punished according to what one did (a discrete and quantifiable act) but according to what one will do, based upon a psychiatric examination of one's character. In short, punishment increasingly has as its aim the disciplining of the body as a source of productivity; and discipline, as a softer and less visible – albeit more global – form of punishment, has as its aim the training of a pliant, productive population.

The new humanism sees knowledge and truth as produced, rather than represented, by humanity. Since Kant, German idealists had insisted that humanity transcendentally produces the unified world in which it inhabits through its own knowing activity. The "truth" of human science (psychology, sociology, etc.) thus resides in its functionality for producing and maintaining this (social) world. More precisely, human science articulates general norms of (human) conduct which are then rigorously applied to a study of individual deviance. Such knowledge no doubt increases the power of governmental authorities. However, in Foucault's judgment, the new paradigm of knowledge actually contradicts both contractualist (populist) and functionalist (statist) views of political power.

Both contractualist and functionalist views of political power presuppose the metaphysical primacy of a subject (or plurality of subjects). The humanistic paradigm extends this presupposition further by making subjectivity the productive ground of objectivity. However, as Foucault notes, this dialectical relationship is incoherent: the subject is defined as both unconditioned (transcendental and other-worldly) and conditioned (finite and this-worldly) simultaneously. A more consistent, post-humanist standpoint would suggest that subjectivity is itself a more or less passive product of impersonal practices and power relationships.

On Foucault's model, power is neither inherent in individual subjects as a property they can freely (contractually) delegate to the state from the bottom up, nor is it inherent in the state as a kind of centralized, top-down control (or influence) superimposed unilaterally over passive individuals. Rather, power consists mainly of impersonal effects that function within relationships characterized by reciprocal resistance. For example, in games each player strategically influences the behavior of the other player; since each player is calling forth the behavior of the other (the initiative is had by both and neither of them) no one is in total control over what is happening. Power is inherently relational and active, existing only in the exercise of actual resistance.[41]

Power relations such as these structure most human relationships, right down to the most intimate relations involving kith and kin. Foucault, however, is chiefly interested in the way in which they structure public institutions such as hospitals, prisons, schools, business organizations, and governmental agencies. Power relations are always structured by institutional norms, but these are seldom obeyed in any conscious and voluntary way. On the contrary, such norms assume an almost invisible form, shaping bodily habits through such "micro-techniques" as confessional practices, clinical exams, statistical dossiers, case studies, exercises, spatial confinements, and methods of surveillance. These micro-techniques find their original employment in local institutional settings, such as military barracks, monasteries, hospitals, and prisons, but gradually cross-fertilize and reinforce one another. When concentrated in the hands of the state, they constitute a formidable type of "bio-power" that can mold discipline within schools, factories, and households. Yet, despite its "carceral" effects, "bio-power," like any power relationship, requires that those upon whom it is exercised have flexible leeway to act according to their own initiative – a possibility that invariably calls forth a corresponding strategy of resistance.

The selection of Foucault's writing chosen for this volume amends this account of power in a way that is more reminiscent of existential phenomenology than structuralism. By emphasizing the subject's own critical agency in constituting his or her subjectivity through acts of resistance, "What is Critique?" reflects a later turn toward more traditional philosophical themes in which ethics, freedom, and responsibility are invested with new meaning.

In Judith Butler's opinion, this 1978 lecture shows that Foucault is not the prophet of "moral despair" his critics (such as Habermas) make him out to be.[42] But he is not a moralist either, in the sense of providing certain foundations, orientations, regulations, and prescriptions for ethical and political conduct. Rather, Foucault's "contribution to normative theory" (as Butler puts it) consists in rearticulating modern ethical virtue in terms of one kind of critical comportment. More precisely, such comportment involves *not* advancing judgments about the goodness or badness, rightness or wrongness, of institutionalized norms, but exposing the limits of all normative undertakings, including that of judging.

Foucault's position here is heavily indebted to Kant's own understanding of enlightenment. For Kant, enlightenment consists in critically examining the limits of reason itself, understood as a distinctly modern nexus of scientific, moral (legal), and aesthetic discourses and practices. But whereas Kant was concerned to show that these limits correspond to necessary and universal conditions of possible knowledge, moral action, and aesthetic experience that in some sense bestow unconditional legitimacy on the respective norms governing these aspects of existence (an undertaking later renewed by Habermas), Foucault is concerned to show (like Nietzsche and Marx before him) that these limits are historically contingent and transgressible. Because showing this is tantamount to uncovering the arbitrary power relations that sustain these limits – which are also norms – genealogy, as Nietzsche and Foucault understand the term – is an exercise of delegitimation.

How is this related to ethics and political thought? Butler answers this question by reminding us that, for Foucault, the norms governing knowledge, morality (legality), and aesthetic experience (pleasure and desire) define and limit our very sense of who we are. They define what it means to be a person, a citizen, a gendered subject, and so on. Hence critically questioning these norms immediately opens up a space for resisting their authority. Enlightenment (critique) makes possible the transgressive "desubjuga-tion" and "re-stylization" of the subject. So construed, the ethical virtue that best accords with modern enlightenment is none other than the ongoing project of self-choice, or self-transformation, extolled by existentialists.

Of course, genealogical critique is in no position to command virtue. Even less can it transcendentally establish its condition of possibility – freedom to remake (originate) oneself. Indeed, even Butler concedes that Foucault's reference to our "originary freedom" is rather paradoxical, given the fact that, on his account, there is no subject of freedom apart from normative practices that constitute a person as such a subject. As she notes, Foucault's reference to an "originary freedom" must be understood as less philosophical assertion than performative speech-act, or offer of a possible restaging (or reperformance) of norms already in effect.

This seemingly paradoxical appeal to "originary freedom" in the ethical domain parallels a similar appeal in the political domain. Foucault says that political critique means "putting forth universal and indefeasible rights to which every government, whatever it may be, whether a monarch, a magistrate, and educator or a pater familias, will have to submit." According to Butler, Foucault's claim that political critique "puts forth" universal rights implies nothing about their philosophical status. Rather, putting forth such rights is simply another way of creatively invoking publicly recognized norms (such as the publicly recognized right to question morally), not in order to accede to the governability of the powers that be, but in order to resist them. Stated somewhat more paradoxically, critical appeals to universal rights are not metaphysical proclamations but acts of resisting governance that are first made possible by governance.

Postmodernism

Foucault's theory of power relations starkly contradicts the consensual, voluntaristic conception of political power articulated by social contract theorists and supporters of discursive democracy, like Arendt and Habermas. It also contradicts the functionalist, systems-theoretical conception of power developed by Marxists and critical theorists. In both of these latter instances, power is seen as emanating from a unified subject: either an intersubjective will generated by voluntary agreement or an impersonal will generated by the functional "needs" and "goals" of a system. Foucault's theory, by contrast, suggests a more radical decentralization of power whose main accompaniment is the decentering – or rather dissolution – of subjective agency.

Postmodernism renews this attack on rational unity and subjective agency by reflexively undermining – in a kind of negative dialectic – any stable sense of identity and meaning. Unlike poststructuralist critiques of humanism, which question the normative meaning of conscious life from an external perspective, postmodernist critiques of humanism question this meaning internally, by reflecting on its inherent contradictions. Postmodernists insist that any attempt to justify political norms rationally, by drawing sharp conceptual boundaries and identifying universal principles, is either question-begging or incoherent. Arguing in a more political vein, they insist that reason as such is negatively dialectical. In their opinion, conceptual analysis, logical inference, and totalizing synthesis imply a preference for hierarchy, unity, and order that is itself deeply implicated in forms of political domination.[43]

In sum, postmodernism emerged as a reaction to cultural modernism, or the idea (stressed by Kant) that different aspects of culture, value, and meaning could be conceptually distinguished and rationally grounded in universal principles. Cultural modernism, for instance, assumes that the moral values regulating moral and legal life can be grounded in universal principles of justice (human rights). These values and principles, in turn, are held to be rationally distinct from values of truth (probability) and efficiency – and principles of mathematics, physics, etc. – governing science and technology. Values regulating aesthetic experience ostensibly possess an equal degree of autonomy, referring to non-moral and non-cognitive principles of formal harmony. In all three instances, cultural modernism exhibits a dual preference for rational purity and distinctness, on one hand, and rational order and (universal) principle, on the other.

As postmodernists see it, the problem with cultural modernism is that its preference for rational purity and universal order ends up excluding certain values and differences by privileging others. For example, Jacques Derrida and Jean-François Lyotard observe that, in the West, possession of human rights has been closely linked to possession of reason, which has almost always been defined in such a way as to privilege some persons (e.g., white European men of independent economic means) while excluding others (women, children, non-Europeans, wage laborers, etc.).[44] Here, the rational policing of conceptual borders has served to deny some persons full admission to universal humanity on account of their differences from the dominant (or mainstream) nationality, gender, race, or class.

Just as cultural modernists deploy notions of rational purity and difference to exclude some from participation in universal rights, so they also deploy notions of rational order and unity to suppress differences requiring legal recognition and protection. For example, Lyotard has criticized Habermas's attempt to ground democracy in consensus-oriented communicative rationality on the grounds that it encourages people to suppress their differences for the sake of reaching universal agreement.[45] But, as he notes, under conditions of cultural modernity, individuals will reason about things differently in ways that will inevitably lead them to adopt incommensurable views about justice, public welfare, and ultimate ends. Democracy must therefore be conceived as a system of divided power-sharing in which minority groups are guaranteed some form of representation in political bargaining and compromise.

Lyotard's view that cultural modernity in fact privileges social fragmentation and conflict instead of rational unity and consensus stems from his postmodern critique of reason, or "grand narratives" that appeal to universal norms. This critique bears a strong resemblance to Hegel's own critique of abstract universals. Hegel noted that the meaningfulness of any idea is inversely proportional to its breadth of scope, or generality. The broader the scope, the emptier its meaning and (conversely) the narrower the scope, the fuller its meaning. Ultimately, ideas of reason acquire concrete meaning and prescriptive force by being embedded in particular, context-relative institutions, technologies, norms, and strategies. Hence, for Lyotard, there are only "small narratives," or situation-specific modes of reasoning.

The contextuality of reason is closely related to another postmodern theme: the undecidability of meaning. Semantic undecidability is most obvious in cases involving written texts. As Derrida has shown, every rereading of a text dialectically reveals new meanings that contradict earlier ones. Since neither the author nor his or her original context of authorship is present to fix meaning in any unambiguous, authoritative sense, it is up to the reader to fill in missing sense. But given the indefinite opportunities for reading a text, and given the uniquely different background (context) of expectations guiding each new reading, the opportunities for uncovering new meaning are indefinite. For this reason, Derrida concludes that reading both alters meaning (i.e., generates different and opposed meanings from the same text) and renders it indefinite and incomplete. Here, it is reason itself – the very act of seeking coherent unity and analytic clarity – that *deconstructs*, or undermines, such unity and clarity.[46]

The theme of semantic undecidability also figures in Lyotard's account of the two major conceptions of political rationality operant in modern theories of democracy.[47] According to one theory, democratic governance involves scientifically calculating public utilities. This calculation is "undecidable" because voting tabulations seldom if ever provide a coherent ranking of preferences. The absorption of greater amounts of complex and conflicting information thus outstrips the decisional capacities of the state. Indeed, rational undecidability penetrates to the very heart of scientific reasoning. As Lyotard notes, scientific measurement and prediction are relative to the decisions of scientific observers (the Heisenberg Principle of Uncertainty), and even consistency seems to contradict completeness in the realm of mathematical logic (Gödel's Theorem).

The other conception of political rationality, which appeals to democratic discussion as a way of rationally legitimizing decisions, also succumbs to undecidability. The dissolution of "Reason" into a plurality of incommensurable reason-giving practices, or "language games" (as Lyotard, following Wittgenstein, calls them) that are temporally and geographically localized *vis-à-vis* historically unique contexts of action suggests a very different view of political life from that given by social contract theorists and consensus theorists. Contrary to Habermas, whatever general social conventions regulate these practices are inherently indeterminate and open to continual reinterpretation and renegotiation by speakers on a moment by moment basis. Because she who grabs the initiative first has the privilege of defining the terms of discourse to her advantage, communication is more conflict-oriented than Habermas realizes.

To be sure, Lyotard no less than Habermas is concerned about the way in which the terms of discourse can be so slanted in favor of one of the parties that the other is simply reduced to silence. Today, there is much talk about accommodating differences under a neutral, constitutional framework. But the assumption, by Rawls and others, that what are otherwise incommensurable and conflicting "comprehensive doctrines" will converge (or "overlap") on constitutional matters for radically opposed reasons, needs to be seriously questioned.[48] Unless this constitutional consensus can be formulated – and more importantly, concretely applied – in ways that do not privilege any subgroup, such a consensus will involve committing what Lyotard calls a *differend*, or injustice whereby "a plaintiff is deprived of the means of arguing and by this fact becomes a victim."

A differend occurs whenever the settling of a conflict between two parties "is made in the idiom of one of them in which the wrong suffered by the other signifies nothing."[49] For example, because Native Americans are forced to defend their territorial claims in the alien languages of economic utility, private property, and contract, they are prevented from appealing to the deeper rationale underlying their claim, namely that their land designates a spiritual inheritance bequeathed to them by their ancestors that grounds their very communal identity. By effectively denying Native Americans an equal right to defend their claims in their own language, damage is done to their sense of identity and self-worth.

Of course, a postmodernist like Lyotard would hesitate to accord any supreme value to claims about "tribal identity," since all distinctions are essentially undermined by the complexity and fluidity of our relationships, languages, practices, and understandings. In his words, "the social subject itself seems to dissolve in this dissemination of language games . . . (for) the social bond is not woven with a single thread (but) by the intersection of at least two (and in reality an indeterminate number of) language games obeying different rules." In this fragmented political world, the old ideal of democratic legitimation through consensus or majority rule must give way to a new ideal based upon challenging the terms of discourse in a never ending struggle to allow new and dissident subaltern voices a right to be heard.

My commentary on Lyotard's "Memorandum on Legitimation" (1986) draws out some of the implications of this view of political fragmentation for current debates about identity politics and political legitimation. For Rawls, Habermas, and other liberals of Kantian bent, the rule of law designates a uniquely legitimate form of polity because it supposedly vests legislative authority in universal rational imperatives. According to this view, basic human rights have their justification in an impartial authority that transcends what any particular person or group of persons might want at any given time or place. Despotism (and totalitarianism), by contrast, reduces the meaning and prescriptive force of law to the will of a particular, dominant person, group, or people in excluding and suppressing other, subaltern wills.

Lyotard doubts whether Kantian conceptions of liberalism avoid despotism. Because universal human rights specify a wholly indeterminate idea, they do not logically entail (determine) any prescriptive, legally enforceable rights. Whatever meaning and prescriptive force attaches to these rights is determined by what a particular person or group of persons at a particular place and time decide(s). Unless each person is somehow made to think like everyone else in the polity, it is hard to see how any enforceable set of rights could not be despotic for at least some persons. But trying to make everyone alike, according to some idea of universal, rational equality, is itself despotic. For, as Lyotard notes, the standard for universal rational equality, if meaningful and prescriptive, will invariably end up privileging a particular group's understanding of this idea. Thus, white Europeans like Kant invariably understood "equality among rational persons" to mean equality among persons like *themselves*; which in practice meant denying full rights to non-Europeans, women, wage workers, and anyone else deemed subrational.[50]

Because of the despotism implicit in conflating particular rights and universal norms – a conflation we invite whenever we attempt to derive rights from norms – Lyotard urges us to accept the radical incommensurability between rational norm and context-specific command. Since democratic politics is ultimately about choosing specific rights and enforcing specific judgments and commands, he doubts whether any rights or commands can be absolutely impartial between persons and groups. At best, he suggests that the decision-making process itself can aspire to some legitimacy so long as it ensures that each group is fairly represented and heard.

Such respect for group differences can lead us to adopt two sorts of "identity politics." The first is reflected in tolerating differences (e.g., over the interpretation of basic rights), protecting aboriginals and other discriminated or endangered groups, and guaranteeing political representation for oppressed minorities. Racial redistricting in the US, language laws in Quebec, tribal sovereignty for aboriginals inhabiting North America, and international respect for illiberal but otherwise decent collectivist regimes are some of the examples I discuss that reflect this kind of identity politics. The second kind of identity politics, however, views any privileging of identity as potentially suppressive of differences. Concern about oppressing "double minorities" (minorities within minorities) and denying the complexity, interdependency, fluidity, and individuality of "identities" leads not only Habermas, but also Lyotard, to question the priority of preserving groups at the expense of restricting the subversive effects of free speech and association.

In the final analysis, there is no rational decision procedure for determining when it is appropriate to defend "identity politics" and when it is appropriate to subvert and deconstruct it by appeal to freedom of speech and association. Indeed, recent examples of alliance building between labor and environmental organizations in fighting against globalization suggest that we may not have to choose between these options. Free interaction between groups can transform their identities and bring about consensus where none existed – without having to suppress differences for the sake of reaching agreement.

Postcolonialism

My all-too brief overview of contemporary currents of Continental political thought would not be complete without including the eccentric perspective of postcolonial liberation philosophy. The reasons for doing so are compelling. To begin with, virtually all of the Continental political philosophers discussed in this volume have addressed colonialism or other global political phenomena. In this respect, they have been considerably less ethnocentric than their Anglo-American counterparts, whose vision up until very recently has seemed to be especially occluded by analytical methods of conceptual abstraction. Still, despite their attempt to think through the relationship between the particular and the universal dialectically, Continental political thinkers have been bogged down by a Hegelian–Marxist perspective that (arguably) reflects a Eurocentric bias – one that, in its own way, privileges the point of view of the privileged with regard to race. Thus, while Sartre, Lyotard, and Marcuse explicitly addressed colonialism in Africa (often citing the seminal work of such freedom fighters as West Indian/African social theorist Frantz Fanon),[51] they did so in a manner that privileged a Western Marxist (or post-Marxian socialist) perspective that viewed the world in terms of a class struggle between workers and capitalists. The same could be said of Foucault's interventions on behalf of China and Iran, or of Habermas's defense of a post-national world in the era of globalization. With the possible exception of Foucault,[52] none of them fully grasped the connection between revolution and religion (fundamentalist or liberationist). None of them really addressed the dynamics of national succession and group rights in any detail – not even Arendt and Habermas, who certainly devoted considerable effort to discussing the problem of nationalism, anti-semitism, and imperialism within a Eurocentric perspective.[53] Most important of all, none of them adequately stressed the degree to which European polities were impli-cated in a system of global racial (specifically "white") supremacy.[54]

The liberation philosophy of the Mexican–Argentinian philosopher Enrique Dussel attempts to "balance the accounts," as it were, by exposing this Eurocentric bias from the standpoint of those who occupy the "periphery" in today's global economic–political nexus: not only those who inhabit the Third World but all who find themselves marginalized, disenfranchised, exploited, and oppressed. The bias I have in mind takes many forms. One form of bias – which prevails among both Continental and Anglo-American philosophers – is the notion that there is a single model of the state that is universally appropriate for all countries. Up until the 1970s, Marxist philosophers favored the single-party (democratic centrist) model of socialism pioneered by the former Soviet Union and entrenched in virtually all communist countries. With the passing of communism, the favored model has been liberal, multiparty democracy. This model, not surprisingly, reflects the sorts of economic and political institutions that have taken hold in Europe, North America, and in most "advanced" industrialized nations of the world. The expectation is that so-called "undeveloped" societies in the Third World and former communist bloc will become just like these "advanced" societies, institutionalizing liberal market economies and formal democracies, replete with the same constitutional separation of powers, rights, and multipartisan competition for political power.

Another form of bias that is often connected with the first assumes that global capitalism will enable all the countries of the world and their inhabitants to enjoy the same affluent standard of living enjoyed by persons of average means inhabiting advanced industrial societies. By "equalizing" the standard of living throughout the globe and by encouraging international trade, global capitalism (so the argument goes) will "break down" cultural and other protectionist barriers, unleash a global demand for individual freedom and corresponding civil and political rights, and will eventually bring about world peace under the auspices of a united federation of mutually (and commercially) self-interested democracies.

As postcolonial philosophers like Dussel point out, there is scant evidence to show that global capitalism will fulfill these high expectations. The opening up of markets since the 1980s has, if anything, magnified the economic disparities between rich and poor countries – and between rich and poor within all countries. As these inequalities worsen and people become desperate, heightened political conflict takes its toll on democracy and the rule of law. Furthermore, the economic relationships between developed and undeveloped countries do not replace older forms of imperialism and colonialism so much as modify them. Former colonies have achieved legal independence from their colonizers but not economic or political independence. Global corporations still control much of the assets in these countries and they threaten to withdraw them unless governments meet their demands. Meanwhile, international financial institutions like the World Bank and World Trade Organization dictate severe austerity policies to countries desperately needing loans. These policies, in turn, weaken the power of governments to help their worst-off citizens, thereby placing additional stress on fragile democratic institutions.

There is another reason why the political question cannot be divorced from the social question, which takes us back to the first bias mentioned above: the privileging of a specific model of multipartisan democratic politics. The stability of democratic institutions in advanced industrial capitalist societies partly depends on the maintenance of a relatively secure, social welfare "safety net" for the worst off. It also depends, less positively, on the political marginalization of the poor and lower middle class, who are without education and financial resources to influence politicians. It is not without reason, therefore, that Western-styled democracies have gotten a "bad rap" among their own citizens for being corrupt bastions of political favoritism bought and sold by the wealthy. Indeed, the marginalization of the poor and powerless and the privileging of the wealthy and powerful reflect a deeper contradiction between capitalism and democracy that is insufficiently appreciated by political philosophers writing from the centers of European and North American capitalism. If the contradiction were appreciated by them, they would be less sanguine about espousing the universal justice of this oligarchic form of democracy for all societies, regardless of economic circumstances.

In conjunction with a masterful commentary by the eminent Dussel translator and scholar, Eduardo Mendieta, the selection included in this volume, "Six Theses Towards a Critique of Political Reason" (2000), does for liberal-democratic theory what Sartre's Critique did for Marxist theory: it exposes the dialectical contradictions of liberal-democratic regimes that seek to stay afloat in a sea of global capitalism. Liberal-democratic theorists from Kant to Habermas attempt to define political legitimacy in terms of formal procedures of justice. Formal procedures of justice are characterized by two features: they do not dictate any substantive outcomes in the distribution of goods (income, political influence, etc.) and they do not expressly privilege any group over another. Both of these features follow from the presumed universality of formal procedures, which ostensibly reflect the impartiality of pure political reason informing the rule of law. By contrast, material (substantive) conceptions of justice – like the dialectical conceptions of reason that ground them – are thought to be too historically and culturally specific, and too partial with respect to certain groups (for example, the poor), to count as rationally justifiable in a philosophical sense.

In Dussel's opinion, the exclusion of the material dimension of ethical life (including, as Mendieta notes, the neurobiological) from the formal is terribly shortsighted. Formal conceptions of justice that guarantee equal freedoms are all but useless unless those to whom these conceptions apply have their basic needs satisfied. This condition more or less obtains in the capitalist centers of Europe, North America, and Asia, but it does not obtain in the Third World periphery, most of whose inhabitants (which comprise 85 percent of the world's population) suffer from chronic starvation and disease. However, given the threat that global capitalism poses to the fragile ecological balance of the planet, even those who are lucky enough to inhabit the center find their lives at risk. The growth imperative driving global capitalism threatens the destruction of non-renewable resources, the pollution of the planet, the forced migration and displacement of desperate populations living in wastelands, and, in short, the development of underdevelopment. Hence, even advanced industrial societies need to supplement their formal procedures of justice with more material ones.

Dussel notes that, far from being alien to Western liberal thought, the "material" principle of collective self-preservation informs its deepest rationale for political order. Social contractarians like Locke quickly narrowed this rationale to the formal preservation of individual (and unequal) private property. However, because the principle of collective self-preservation insufficiently protects individual freedom, Dussel supplements it with two other principles: a formal principle of democratic justice that owes much to Habermas's discourse theory; and a (feasibility) principle of instrumental or strategic practicality, which enjoins interpreting material and formal principles in light of context-sensitive applications and particular, community-specific conceptions of the good.

Significantly, Dussel's interpretation of the formal principle of democratic justice deviates from Habermas's in one crucial respect. As Mendieta notes, Habermas's discourse ethic is dialectical, in that it enjoins the mutual transformation of differing perspectives into a single, common perspective (consensus). So construed, discourse ethics provides a formal (procedural) model of Hegel's "struggle for recognition," in that interlocutors relate to one another as equals, bound by the exact same (or recipro-cal) obligations. By contrast, Dussel's discourse ethic is anti-dialectical (or "analectical," from the Greek root *ano*, meaning "beyond"). Following the lead of Jewish phenom-enologist Emmanuel Levinas, Dussel holds that we have a greater obligation to the "Other" than the "Other" has to us. This follows from the fact that the "Other" places a moral command upon us that is in some sense unconditional and transcendent – not contingent on the mutual satisfaction of our needs and interests.

In order to dispel any confusion that might arise from this idea of unconditional response, we must note that Dussel ascribes a very distinctive meaning to it. For Dussel, the "Other" is precisely the other one: the excluded, marginalized, vulnerable, and oppressed – they who traditionally have been treated as subaltern, subhuman, or less than independent by Western thinkers. In short, in keeping with the "preference for the poor" implicit in the Catholic liberation theologies that have informed Dussel's own thinking over the years, our primary obligation is to aid the most dominated, oppressed, and vulnerable among us, even if this requires discriminating against those who are privileged (including ourselves). Moreover, such an obligation requires elevating our ethical duty to the level of revolutionary politics, the emancipatory aim of which is nothing less than the overcoming of racial and ethnic genocide that global capitalism disproportionately inflicts upon Third World populations.

Unrepentant humanist that he is, Dussel thinks of the three principles cited above as three inseparable aspects of universal political reason (Level A) that can be instantiated in diverse political constitutions and institutions (Level B) depending on cultural and economic circumstances. The latter, in turn, comprise the ideals that guide political critique (Level C): tracing the victimization of groups back to the political order, proposing alternatives to that order, and organizing groups that will implement these alternatives. In sum, Dussel has no reservations about defending a teleological conception of political rationality that has as its main goal the emancipatory redemption of the victims of the global order (thesis 4), through partisan political praxis (thesis 5) aimed at the eventual liberation of humanity at large (thesis 6). Normative political philosophy must become descriptive social theory and transformative praxis simultaneously. All-encompassing in its revolutionary scope and synthesis of distinct (if not opposed) discourses and practices, it remains – at least in this respect – the very epitome of dialectical reason.

Notes

1   This way of dividing philosophy reflects a Western (more precisely, Eurocentric) bias that has only recently been challenged by philosophers working within Asian, African, and Latin American philosophical perspectives. One such perspective – the liberation philosophy developed by the Argentine–Mexican philosopher Enrique Dussel – is represented in this volume.

2   T. Hobbes, *Leviathan* (1651), ed. C. B. Macpherson (Harmondsworth: Penguin Books, 1968).

3   J. Locke, *Two Treatises of Government* (1689), ed. P. Laslett (Cambridge: Cambridge University Press, 1967).

4   Cf. J. Rawls, *A Theory of Justice* (Cambridge, MA: Harvard University Press, 1971; revd. edn. 1999); and R. Nozick, *Anarchy, State, and Utopia* (New York: Basic Books, 1974).

5   Hobbesian social contract theory has become more popular in recent years, thanks in large part to the efforts of David Gauthier (*The Logic of the Leviathan* [Oxford: Clarendon Press, 1969]), Jean Hampton (*Hobbes and the Social Contract Tradition* [Cambridge: Cambridge University Press, 1986]), and Gregory Kavka (*Hobbesian Moral and Political Theory* [Princeton, NJ: Princeton University Press, 1986]).

6   J. Rawls, *Political Liberalism* (New York: Columbia University Press, 1993), Lecture VIII.

7   Rawls, *Theory of Justice* (revised edition), pp. xiv–xv.

8   J. Bentham, *An Introduction to the Principles of Morals and Legislation* (1789), ed. J. H. Burns and H. L. A. Hart (Oxford: Clarendon Press, 1996).

9   Susan Moller Okin, *Justice, Gender, and the Family* (New York: Basic Books, 1989).

10 Carole Pateman, *The Sexual Contract*, (Stanford, CA: Stanford University Press, 1988).

11 Charles Mills, *The Racial Contract* (Ithaca, NY: Cornell University Press, 1997).

12 Cf. C. Taylor, *Sources of the Self: The Making of Modern Identity* (Cambridge: Cambridge University Press, 1989); A. MacIntyre, *After Virtue* (Notre Dame, IN: Notre Dame University Press, 1981); and M. Sandel, *Liberalism and the Limits of Reason* (Cambridge: Cambridge University Press, 1982). For a discussion of Anglo-American debates between liberals and communitarians and their relationship to similar debates in Continental

philosophy, see David Ingram, *Reason, History, and Politics: The Communitarian Grounds of Reason in the Modern Age* (Albany: State University of New York Press, 1995), esp. chs. 1, 3, and 4.

13 J.-J. Rousseau, *On the Social Contract* (1762) in *Jean-Jacques Rousseau: The Basic Political Writings*, ed. Peter Gay (Indianapolis, IN: Hackett, 1987).

14 I. Kant, *The Metaphysics of Morals* (1797), trans. M. J. Gregor (Cambridge: Cambridge University Press, 1991).

15 Although Kant held that the revolutionary overthrow of any government was deeply immoral and criminal, he nonetheless believed that disinterested onlookers like himself could identify with the protagonists of the French Revolution, conceived as a symbol of eternal progress in moral freedom. Cf. H. Reiss, ed., *Kant's Political Writings* (Cambridge: Cambridge University Press, 1970).

16 G. F. W. Hegel, *Hegel's Phenomenology of Spirit* (1807), trans. A. V. Miller (Oxford: Oxford University Press, 1977).

17 G. F. W. Hegel, *Hegel's Philosophy of Right* (1821), trans. T. M. Knox (Oxford: Oxford University Press, 1977).

18 See, for example, the political writings of W. J. Bradley, Bernard Bosenquet, T. H. Green, and Benedetto Croce.

19 K. Marx, *Critique of Hegel's Philosophy of Right* (1843).

20 K. Marx, *On the Jewish Question* (1843).

21 K. Marx and F. Engels, *The German Ideology* (1845).

22 K. Marx, *The Paris Manuscripts of 1844*.

23 K. Marx, *Capital*, vol. 1. (1867).

24 K. Marx, *The Civil War in France* (1870).

25 K. Marx and F. Engels, *The Communist Manifesto* (1848).

26 F. Nietzsche, *The Genealogy of Morals* (1887).

27 E. Husserl, *Ideas Pertaining to a Pure Phenomenology and to a Phenomenological Philosophy* (Bk. I-1913), trans. F. Kersten (the Hague: Kluwer, 1982).

28 E. Husserl, *The Crisis of the European Sciences and Transcendental Phenomenology: An Introduction to Phenomenological Philosophy* (1938), trans. D. Carr (Evanston, IL: Northwestern University Press, 1970).

29 M. Heidegger, *Being and Time* (1927), trans. J. Stambaugh (Albany: State University of New York Press, 1996).

30 M. Heidegger, *The Question Concerning Technology and Other Essays*, ed. W. Lovett (New York: Harper & Row, 1977).

31 II. Arendt, *Between Past and Future: Six Exercises in Political Thought* (New York: Viking Press, 1961).

32 H Arendt, *On Revolution* (New York: Viking Press, 1962).

33 For a discussion of the similarities and differences between Arendt's political philosophy and those of Lyotard and Habermas, see Ingram, *Reason, History, and Politics*, chs. 7 and 8.

34 For a good discussion of French existential political theory and French politics, see Mark Poster, *Existential Marxism in Postwar France: From Sartre to Althusser* (Princeton, NJ: Princeton University Press, 1975).

35 For an introductory survey of the Frankfurt School tradition of critical theory, see David Ingram, *Critical Theory and Philosophy* (New York: Paragon House, 1990) and the companion volume of essays, *Critical Theory: The Essential Readings*, ed. D. Ingram and J. Simon (New York: Paragon House, 1991).

36 I provide a succinct description and analysis of the several varieties of neo-Marxism in "Continental Philosophy: Neo-Marxism," in *The Columbia History of Western Philosophy*, ed. R. H. Popkin (New York: Columbia University Press, 1999), 721–30.

37   See T. Adorno and M. Horkheimer, *Dialectic of Enlightenment* (1944), trans. J. Cumming (New York: Herder & Herder, 1972); and H. Marcuse, *One-Dimensional Man* (Boston: Beacon Press, 1964).

38   An excellent discussion of the various currents of poststructuralist political thought may be found in M. Ryan, *Marxism and Deconstruction: A Critical Articulation* (Baltimore, MD: Johns Hopkins University Press, 1982).

39   L. Althusser, *For Marx*, (New York: Vintage, 1969).

40   M. Foucault, *The Order of Things* (New York: Vintage, 1970).

41   M. Foucault, "The Subject and Power," in *Michel Foucault: Beyond Structuralism and Hermeneutics*, ed. H. Drefus and P. Rabinow (Chicago: University of Chicago Press, 1982).

42   See my discussion of the debate between Habermas and Foucault in "Foucault and Habermas on the Subject of Reason," in *The Foucault Companion*, ed. G. Gutting (Cambridge: Cambridge University Press, 1994).

43   Other important postmodernist political theorists include Jean Baudrillard and Jean-Luc Nancy. For a discussion of their work see D. Kellner, *Jean Baudrillard: From Marxism to Postmodernism and Beyond* (Palo Alto, CA: Stanford University Press, 1989) and Ingram, *Reason, History, and Politics*, ch. 4.

44   See Ingram's commentary on "Memorandum on Legitimation" below, p. 241.

45   For a comparison of Lyotard and Habermas, see D. Ingram, "The Subject of Justice in Postmodern Discourse: Aesthetic Judgement and Political Rationality," in *Habermas and the Unfinished Project of Modernity*, ed. M. P. D'Entreves and S. Benhabib (Cambridge: Polity Press, 1996), 268–30, and Ingram, *Reason, History, and Politics*, ch. 7.

46   J. Derrida, *Positions*, trans. A. Bass (Chicago: University of Chicago Press, 1972).

47   J.-F. Lyotard, *The Postmodern Condition: A Report on Knowledge*, trans. B. Massumi and G. Bennington (Minneapolis: University of Minnesota Press, 1984).

48   Rawls, *Political Liberalism*.

49   J.-F. Lyotard, *The Differend: Phrases in Dispute*, trans. Georges Van den Abbeele (Minneapolis: University of Minnesota Press, 1988).

50   In *Observations on the Feeling of the Beautiful and Sublime* (1764), trans. John. T. Goldthwait (Berkeley: University of California Press, 1960), 111–113, Kant notoriously stated that "so fundamental is the difference between [the black and white] races of man . . . it appears to be as great in regard to mental capacities as in color," so that "a clear proof that what [a Negro] said was stupid" was that "this fellow was quite black from head to foot." In a later essay, "On the Different Races of Man" (1775), in Emmanuel Chukwudi Eze (ed.), *Race and the Enlightenment: A Reader* (Oxford: Blackwell Publishers, 1997), 38–48, Kant develops a hierarchical scheme of races based upon inherited cognitive and moral potentials. Kant's better known views about women, servants, and dependents are stated in *The Metaphysics of Morals*, trans. Mary Gregor (New York: Cambridge University Press, 1991), 126, where he invokes his famous distinction between "passive" and "active" citizens. Elsewhere in the same treatise (pp. 86–7), however, Kant condemns the injustice of establishing colonies by fraud and force, even when its aim is to civilize 'savages' (American Indians, Hottentots, and the inhabitants of New Holland) who are not in "a rightful condition."

51   See Sartre's "Introduction" to Fanon's *The Wretched of the Earth*, trans. Constance Farrington (New York: Grove Weidenfeld, 1968), Marcuse's reference to Fanon in *One-Dimensional Man*, and Lyotard's essays on the Algerian War as a member of the movement *socialisme ou barbarie*.

52   See Foucault's sympathetic discussion of the 1979 Iranian Revolution, "A quoi rêvent les Iraniens?" in *Nouvel Observateur* 726 (Oct. 9–16, 1978): 48–9; "Réponse de Michel Foucault à une lectrice Iranienne," *Nouvel Observateur* 731 (Nov. 13, 1978): 26; and the series of brief articles he wrote for *Corriere della Sera* in 1978–9.

53 See H. Arendt, *The Origins of Totalitarianism* (New York: Harcourt Brace, 1951) and
     J. Habermas, *The Inclusion of the Other*, ed. C. Cronin and P. De Greiff (Cambridge, MA:
     MIT Press, 1998).

54 For a powerful defense of viewing Western political systems as instantiating white global
     supremacy, see Charles Mills, *Blackness Visible* (Ithaca, NY: Cornell University Press, 1998),
     ch. 5.

PART I

PHENOMENOLOGY

POLITICAL ACTION AND THE DIALECTIC OF POWER AND VIOLENCE

1

SELECTIONS FROM *THE HUMAN CONDITION*

Hannah Arendt

Action

All sorrows can be borne if you put them into a story or tell a story about them.

ISAK DINESEN

Nam in omni actione principaliter intenditur ab agente, sive necessitate naturae sive voluntarie agat, propriam similitudinem explicare; unde fit quod omne agens, in quantum huiusmodi, delectatur, quia, cum omne quod est appetatsuum esse, ac in agendo agentis esse modammodo amplietur, sequitur de necessitate delectatio. . . . Nihil igitur agit nisi tale existens quale patiens fieri debet.

(For in every action what is primarily intended by the doer, whether he acts from natural necessity or out of free will, is the disclosure of his own image. Hence it comes about that every doer, in so far as he does, takes delight in doing; since everything that is desires its own being, and since in action the being of the doer is somehow intensified, delight necessarily follows. . . . Thus, nothing acts unless [by acting] it makes patent its latent self.)

DANTE

24 The Disclosure of the Agent in Speech and Action

Human plurality, the basic condition of both action and speech, has the twofold character of equality and distinction. If men were not equal, they could neither understand each other and those who came before them nor plan for the future and foresee the needs of those who will come after them. If men were not distinct, each human being distinguished from any other who is, was, or will ever be, they would need neither speech nor action to make themselves understood. Signs and sounds to communicate immediate, identical needs and wants would be enough.

Human distinctness is not the same as otherness – the curious quality of *alteritas* possessed by everything that is and therefore, in medieval philosophy, one of the four basic, universal characteristics of Being, transcending every particular quality. Otherness, it is true, is an important aspect of plurality, the reason why all our definitions are distinctions, why we are unable to say what anything is without distinguishing it from something else. Otherness in its most abstract form is found only in the sheer multiplication of inorganic objects, whereas all organic life already shows variations and distinctions, even between specimens of the same species. But only man can express this distinction and distinguish himself, and only he can communicate himself and not merely something – thirst or hunger, affection or hostility or fear. In man, otherness, which he shares with everything that is, and distinctness, which he shares with everything alive, become uniqueness, and human plurality is the paradoxical plurality of unique beings.

Speech and action reveal this unique distinctness. Through them, men distinguish themselves instead of being merely distinct; they are the modes in which human beings appear to each other, not indeed as physical objects, but *qua* men. This appearance, as distinguished from mere bodily existence, rests on initiative, but it is an initiative from which no human being can refrain and still be human. This is true of no other activity in the *vita activa*. Men can very well live without laboring, they can force others to labor for them, and they can very well decide merely to use and enjoy the world of things without themselves adding a single useful object to it; the life of an exploiter or slaveholder and the life of a parasite may be unjust, but they certainly are human. A life without speech and without action, on the other hand – and this is the only way of life that in earnest has renounced all appearance and all vanity in the biblical sense of the word – is literally dead to the world; it has ceased to be a human life because it is no longer lived among men.

With word and deed we insert ourselves into the human world and this insertion is like a second birth, in which we confirm and take upon ourselves the naked fact of our original physical appearance. This insertion is not forced upon us by necessity, like labor, and it is not prompted by utility, like work. It may be stimulated by the presence of others whose company we may wish to join, but it is never conditioned by them; its impulse springs from the beginning which came into the world when we were born and to which we respond by beginning something new on our own initiative.[1] To act, in its most general sense, means to take an initiative, to begin (as the Greek word *archein*, "to begin," "to lead," and eventually "to rule," indicates), to set something into motion (which is the orginal meaning of the Latin *agere*). Because they are *initium*, newcomers and beginners by virtue of birth, men take initiative, are prompted into action. [*Initium*] *ergo ut esset, creatus est homo, ante quem nullus fuit* ("that there be a beginning, man was created before whom there was nobody"), said Augustine in his political philosophy.[2] This beginning is not the same as the beginning of the world;[3] it is not the beginning of something but of somebody, who is a beginner himself. With the creation of man, the principle of beginning came into the world itself, which, of course, is only another way of saying that the principle of freedom was created when man was created but not before.

It is in the nature of beginning that something new is started which cannot be expected from whatever may have happened before. This character of startling unexpectedness is inherent in all beginnings and in all origins. Thus, the origin of life from inorganic matter is an infinite improbability of inorganic processes, as is the coming into being of the earth viewed from the standpoint of processes in the universe, or the evolution of human out of animal life. The new always happens against the overwhelming odds of statistical laws and their probability, which for all practical, everyday purposes amounts to certainty; the new therefore always appears in the guise of a miracle. The fact that man is capable of action means that the unexpected can be expected from him, that he is able to perform what is infinitely improbable. And this again is possible only because each man is unique, so that with each birth something uniquely new comes into the world. With respect to this somebody who is unique it can be truly said that nobody was there before. If action as beginning corresponds to the fact of birth, if it is the actualization of the human condition of natality, then speech corresponds to the fact of distinctness and is the actualization of the human condition of plurality, that is, of living as a distinct and unique being among equals.

Action and speech are so closely related because the primordial and specifically human act must at the same time contain the answer to the question asked of every newcomer: "Who are you?" This disclosure of who somebody is, is implicit in both his words and his deeds; yet obviously the affinity between speech and revelation is much closer than that between action and revelation,[4] just as the affinity between action and beginning is closer than that between speech and beginning, although many, and even most acts, are performed in the manner of speech. Without the accompaniment of speech, at any rate, action would not only lose its revelatory character, but, and by the same token, it would lose its subject, as it were; not acting men but performing robots would achieve what, humanly speaking, would remain incomprehensible. Speechless action would no longer be action because there would no longer be an actor, and the actor, the doer of deeds, is possible only if he is at the same time the speaker of words. The action he begins is humanly disclosed by the word, and though his deed can be perceived in its brute physical appearance without verbal accompaniment, it becomes relevant only through the spoken word in which he identifies himself as the actor, announcing what he does, has done, and intends to do.

No other human performance requires speech to the same extent as action. In all other performances speech plays a subordinate role, as a means of communication or a mere accompaniment to something that could also be achieved in silence. It is true that speech is extremely useful as a means of communication and information, but as such it could be replaced by a sing language, which then might prove to be even more useful and expedient to convey certain meanings, as in mathematics and other scientific disciplines or in certain forms of teamwork. Thus, it is also true that man's capacity to act, and especially to act in concert, is extremely useful for purposes of self-defense or of pursuit of interests; but if nothing more were at stake here than to use action as a means to an end, it is obvious that the same end could be much more easily attained in mute violence, so that action seems a not very efficient substitute for violence, just as speech, from the viewpoint of sheer utility, seems an awkward substitute for sign language.

In acting and speaking, men show who they are, reveal actively their unique personal identities and thus make their appearance in the human world, while their physical identities appear without any activity of their own in the unique shape of the body and sound of the voice. This disclosure of "who" in contradistinction to "what" somebody is – his qualities, gifts, talents, and shortcomings, which he may display or hide – is implicit in everything somebody says and does. It can be hidden only in complete silence and perfect passivity, but its disclosure can almost never be achieved as a wilful purpose, as though one possessed and could dispose of this "who" in the same manner he has and can dispose of his qualities. On the contrary, it is more than likely that the "who," which appears so clearly and unmistakably to others, remains hidden from the person himself, like the *daimōn* in Greek religion which accompanies each man throughout his life, always looking over his shoulder from behind and thus visible only to those he encounters.

This revelatory quality of speech and action comes to the fore where people are *with* others and neither for nor against them – that is, in sheer human togetherness. Although nobody knows whom he reveals when he discloses himself in deed or word, he must be willing to risk the disclosure, and this neither the doer of good works, who must be without self and preserve complete anonymity, nor the criminal, who must hide himself from others, can take upon themselves. Both are lonely figures, the one being for, the other against, all men; they, therefore, remain outside the pale of human intercourse and are, politically, marginal figures who usually enter the historical scene in times of corruption, disintegration, and political bankruptcy. Because of its inherent tendency to disclose the agent together with the act, action needs for its full appearance the shining brightness we once called glory, and which is possible only in the public realm.

Without the disclosure of the agent in the act, action loses its specific character and becomes one form of achievement among others. It is then indeed no less a means to an end than making is a means to produce an object. This happens whenever human togetherness is lost, that is, when people are only for or against other people, as for instance in modern warfare, where men go into action and use means of violence in order to achieve certain objectives for their own side and against the enemy. In these instances, which of course have always existed, speech becomes indeed "mere talk," simply one more means toward the end, whether it serves to deceive the enemy or to dazzle everybody with propaganda; here words reveal nothing, disclosure comes only from the deed itself, and this achievement, like all other achievements, cannot disclose the "who," the unique and distinct identity of the agent.

In these instances action has lost the quality through which it transcends mere productive activity, which, from the humble making of use objects to the inspired creation of art works, has no more meaning than is revealed in the finished product and does not intend to show more than is plainly visible at the end of the production process. Action without a name, a "who" attached to it, is meaningless, whereas an art work retains its relevance whether or not we know the master's name. The monuments to the "Unknown Soldier" after World War I bear testimony to the then still existing need for glorification, for finding a "who," an identifiable somebody whom four years of mass slaughter should have revealed. The frustration of this wish and the unwillingness to resign oneself to the brutal fact that the agent of the war was actually nobody inspired the erection of the monuments to the "unknown," to all those whom the war had failed to make known and had robbed thereby, not of their achievement, but of their human dignity...

26   The Frailty of Human Affairs

Action, as distinguished from fabrication, is never possible in isolation; to be isolated is to be deprived of the capacity to act. Action and speech need the surrounding presence of nature for its material, and of a world in which to place the finished product.

Fabrication is surrounded by and in constant contact with the world: action and speech are surrounded by and in constant contact with the web of the acts and words of other men. The popular belief in a "strong man" who, isolated against others, owes his strength to his being alone is either sheer superstition, based on the delusion that we can "make" something in the realm of human affairs – "make" institutions or laws, for instance, as we make tables and chairs, or make men "better" or "worse"[5] – or it is conscious despair of all action, political and non-political, coupled with the utopian hope that it may be possible to treat men as one treats other "material."[6] The strength the individual needs for every process of production becomes altogether worthless when action is at stake, regardless of whether this strength is intellectual or a matter of purely material force. History is full of examples of the impotence of the strong and superior man who does not know how to enlist the help, the co-acting of his fellow men. His failure is frequently blamed upon the fatal inferiority of the many and the resentment every outstanding person inspires in those who are mediocre. Yet true as such observations are bound to be, they do not touch the heart of the matter.

In order to illustrate what is at stake here we may remember that Greek and Latin, unlike the modern languages, contain two altogether different and yet interrelated words with which to designate the verb "to act." To the two Greek verbs *archein* ("to begin," "to lead," finally "to rule") and *prattein* ("to pass through," "to achieve," "to finish") correspond the two Latin verbs *agere* ("to set into motion," "to lead") and *gerere* (whose original meaning is "to bear").[7] Here it seems as though each action were divided into two parts, the beginning made by a single person and the achievement in which many join by "bearing" and "finishing" the enterprise, by seeing it through. Not only are the words interrelated in a similar manner, the history of their usage is very similar too. In both cases the word that originally designated only the second part of action, its achievement – *prattein* and *gerere* – became the accepted word for action in general, whereas the words designating the beginning of action became specialized in meaning, at least in political language. *Archein* came to mean chiefly "to rule" and "to lead" when it was specifically used, and *agere* came to mean "to lead" rather than "to set into motion."

Thus the role of the beginner and leader, who was a *primus inter pares* (in the case of Homer, a king among kings), changed into that of a ruler; the original interdependence of action, the dependence of the beginner and leader upon others for help and the dependence of his followers upon him for an occasion to act themselves, split into two altogether different functions: the function of giving commands, which became the prerogative of the ruler, and the function of executing them, which became the duty of his subjects. This ruler is alone, isolated against others by his force, just as the beginner was isolated through his initiative at the start, before he had found others to join him. Yet the strength of the beginner and leader shows itself only in his initiative and the risk he takes, not in the actual achievement. In the case of the successful ruler, he may claim for himself what actually is the achievement of many – something that Agamemnon, who was a king but no ruler, would never have been permitted. Through this claim, the ruler monopolizes, so to speak, the strength of those without whose help he would never be able to achieve anything. Thus, the delusion of extraordinary strength arises and with it the fallacy of the strong man who is powerful because he is alone.

Because the actor always moves among and in relation to other acting beings, he is never merely a "doer" but always and at the same time a sufferer. To do and to suffer are like opposite sides of the same coin, and the story that an act starts is composed of its consequent deeds and sufferings. These consequences are boundless, because action, though it may proceed from nowhere, so to speak, acts into a medium where every reaction becomes a chain reaction and where every process is the cause of new processes. Since action acts upon beings who are capable of their own actions, reaction, apart from being a response, is always a new action that strikes out on its own and affects others. Thus action and reaction among men never move in a closed circle and can never be reliably confined to two partners. This boundlessness is characteristic not of political action alone, in the narrower sense of the word, as though the boundlessness of human interrelatedness were only the result of the boundless multitude of people involved, which could be escaped by resigning oneself to action within a limited, graspable framework of circumstances; the smallest act in the most limited circumstances bears the seed of the same boundlessness, because one deed, and sometimes one word, suffices to change every constellation.

Action, moreover, no matter what its specific content, always establishes relationships and therefore has an inherent tendency to force open all limitations and cut across all boundaries.[8] Limitations and boundaries exist within the realm of human affairs, but they never offer a framework that can reliably withstand the onslaught with which each new generation must insert itself. The frailty of human institutions and laws and, generally, of all matters pertaining to men's living together, arises from the human condition of natality and is quite independent of the frailty of human nature. The fences inclosing private property and insuring the limitations of each household, the territorial boundaries which protect and make possible the physical identity of a people, and the laws which protect and make possible its political existence, are of such great importance to the stability of human affairs precisely because no such limiting and protecting principles rise out of the activities going on in the realm of human affairs itself. The limitations of the law are never entirely reliable safeguards against action from within the body politic, just as the boundaries of the territory are never entirely reliable safeguards against action from without. The boundlessness of action is only the other side of its tremendous capacity for establishing relationships, that is, its specific productivity; this is why the old virtue of moderation, of keeping within bounds, is indeed one of the political virtues *par excellence*, just as the political temptation *par excellence* is indeed *hubris* (as the Greeks, fully experienced in the potentialities of action, knew so well) and not the will to power, as we are inclined to believe.

Yet while the various limitations and boundaries we find in every body politic may offer some protection against the inherent boundlessness of action, they are altogether helpless to offset its second outstanding character: its inherent unpredictability. This is not simply a question of inability to foretell all the logical consequences of a particular act, in which case an electronic computer would be able to foretell the future, but arises directly out of the story which, as the result of action, begins and establishes itself as soon as the fleeting moment of the deed is past. The trouble is that whatever the character and content of the subsequent story may be, whether it is played in private or public life, whether it involves many or few actors, its full meaning can reveal itself only when it has ended. In contradistinction to fabrication, where the light by which to judge the finished product is provided by the image or model perceived beforehand by the craftsman's eye, the light that illuminates processes of action, and therefore all historical processes, appears only at their end, frequently when all the participants are dead. Action reveals itself fully only to the storyteller, that is, to the backward glance of the historian, who indeed always knows better what it was all about than the participants. All accounts told by the actors themselves, though they may in rare cases give an entirely trustworthy statement of intentions, aims, and motives, become mere useful source material in the historian's hands and can never match his story in significance and truthfulness. What the storyteller narrates must necessarily be hidden from the actor himself, at least as long as he is in the act or caught in its consequences, because to him the meaningfulness of his act is not in the story that follows. Even though stories are the inevitable results of action, it is not the actor but the storyteller who perceives and "makes" the story. . . .

28   Power and the Space of Appearance

The space of appearance comes into being wherever men are together in the manner of speech and action, and therefore predates and precedes all formal constitution of the public realm and the various forms of government, that is, the various forms in which the public realm can be organized. Its peculiarity is that, unlike the spaces which are the work of our hands, it does not survive the actuality of the movement which brought it into being, but disappears not only with the dispersal of men – as in the case of great catastrophes when the body politic of a people is destroyed – but with the disappearance or arrest of the activities themselves. Wherever people gather together, it is potentially there, but only potentially, not necessarily and not forever. That civilizations can rise and fall, that mighty empires and great cultures can decline and pass away without external catastrophes – and more often than not such external "causes" are preceded by a less visible internal decay that invites disaster – is due to this peculiarity of the public realm, which, because it ultimately resides on action and speech, never altogether loses its potential character. What first undermines and then kills political communities is loss of power and final impotence; and power cannot be stored up and kept in reserve for emergencies, like the instruments of violence, but exists only in its actualization. Where power is not actualized, it passes away, and history is full of examples that the greatest material riches cannot compensate for this loss. Power is actualized only where word and deed have not parted company, where words are not empty and deeds not brutal, where words are not used to veil intentions but to disclose realities, and deeds are not used to violate and destroy but to establish relations and create new realities.

Power is what keeps the public realm, the potential space of appearance between acting and speaking men, in existence. The word itself, its Greek equivalent *dynamis*, like the Latin *potentia* with its various modern derivatives or the German *Macht* (which derives from *mögen* and *möglich*, not from *machen*), indicates its "potential" character. Power is always, as we would say, a power potential and not an unchangeable, measurable, and reliable entity like force or strength. While strength is the natural quality of an individual seen in isolation, power springs up between men when they act together and vanishes the moment they disperse. Because of this peculiarity, which power shares with all potentialities that can only be actualized but never fully materialized, power is to an astonishing degree independent of material factors, either of numbers or means. A comparatively small but well-organized group of men can rule almost indefinitely over large and populous empires, and it is not infrequent in history that small and poor countries get the better of great and rich nations. (The story of David and Goliath is only metaphorically true; the power of a few can be greater than the power of many, but in a contest between two men not power but strength decides, and cleverness, that is, brain power, contributes materially to the outcome on the same level as muscular force.) Popular revolt against materially strong rulers, on the other hand, may engender an almost irresistible power even if it foregoes the use of violence in the face of materially vastly superior forces. To call this "passive resistance" is certainly an ironic idea; it is one of the most active and efficient ways of action ever devised, because it cannot be countered by fighting, where there may be defeat or victory, but only by mass slaughter in which even the victor is defeated, cheated of his prize, since nobody can rule over dead men.

The only indispensable material factor in the generation of power is the living together of people. Only where men live so close together that the potentialities of action are always present can power remain with them, and the foundation of cities, which as city-states have remained paradigmatic for all Western political organization, is therefore indeed the most important material prerequisite for power. What keeps people together after the fleeting moment of action has passed (what we today call "organization") and what, at the same time, they keep alive through remaining together is power. And whoever, for whatever reasons, isolates himself and does not partake in such being together, forfeits power and becomes impotent, no matter how great his strength and how valid his reasons.

If power were more than this potentiality in being together, if it could be possessed like strength or applied like force instead of being dependent upon the unreliable and only temporary agreement of many wills and intentions, omnipotence would be a concrete human possibility. For power, like action, is boundless; it has no physical limitation in human nature, in the bodily existence of man, like strength. Its only limitation is the existence of other people, but this limitation is not accidental, because human power corresponds to the condition of plurality to begin with. For the same reason, power can be divided without decreasing it, and the interplay of powers with their checks and balances is even liable to generate more power, so long, at least, as the interplay is alive and has not resulted in a stalemate. Strength, on the contrary, is indivisible, and while it, too, is checked and balanced by the presence of others, the interplay of plurality in this case spells a definite limitation on the strength of the individual, which is kept in bounds and may be overpowered by the power potential of the many. An identification of the strength necessary for the production of things with the power necessary for action is conceivable only as the divine attribute of one god. Omnipotence therefore is never an attribute of gods in polytheism, no matter how superior the strength of the gods may be to the forces of men. Conversely, aspiration toward omnipotence always implies – apart from its utopian *hubris* – the destruction of plurality.

Under the conditions of human life, the only alternative to power is not strength – which is helpless against power – but force, which indeed one man alone can exert against his fellow men and of which one or a few can possess a monopoly by acquiring the means of violence. But while violence can destroy power, it can never become a substitute for it. From this results the by no means infrequent political combination of force and powerlessness, an array of impotent forces that spend themselves, often spectacularly and vehemently but in utter futility, leaving behind neither monuments nor stories, hardly enough memory to enter into history at all. In historical experience and traditional theory, this combination, even if it is not recognized as such, is known as tyranny, and the time-honored fear of this form of government is not exclusively inspired by its cruelty, which – as the long series of benevolent tyrants and enlightened despots attests – is not among its inevitable features, but by the impotence and futility to which it condemns the rulers as well as the ruled.

More important is a discovery made, as far as I know, only by Montesquieu, the last political thinker to concern himself seriously with the problem of forms of government. Montesquieu realized that the outstanding characteristic of tyranny was that it rested on isolation – on the isolation of the tyrant from his subjects and the isolation of the subjects from each other through mutual fear and suspicion – and hence that tyranny was not one form of government among others but contradicted the essential human condition of plurality, the acting and speaking together, which is the condition of all forms of political organization. Tyranny prevents the development of power, not only in a particular segment of the public realm but in its entirety; it generates, in other words, impotence as naturally as other bodies politic generate power. This, in Montesquieu's interpretation, makes it necessary to assign it a special position in the theory of political bodies: it alone is unable to develop enough power to remain at all in the space of appearance, the public realm; on the contrary, it develops the germs of its own destruction the moment it comes into existence.[9]

Violence, curiously enough, can destroy power more easily than it can destroy strength, and while a tyranny is always characterized by the impotence of its subjects, who have lost their human capacity to act and speak together, it is not necessarily characterized by weakness and sterility; on the contrary, the crafts and arts may flourish under these conditions if the ruler is "benevolent" enough to leave his subjects alone in their isolation. Strength, on the other hand, nature's gift to the individual which cannot be shared with others, can cope with violence more successfully than with power – either heroically, by consenting to fight and die, or stoically, by accepting suffering and challenging all affliction through self-sufficiency and withdrawal from the world; in either case, the integrity of the individual and his strength remain intact. Strength can actually be ruined only by power and is therefore always in danger from the combined force of the many. Power corrupts indeed when the weak band together in order to ruin the strong, but not before. The will to power, as the modern age from Hobbes to Nietzsche understood it in glorification or denunciation, far from being a characteristic of the strong, is, like envy and greed, among the vices of the weak, and possibly even their most dangerous one.

If tyranny can be described as the always abortive attempt to substitute violence for power, ochlocracy, or mob rule, which is its exact counterpart, can be characterized by the much more promising attempt to substitute power for strength. Power indeed can ruin all strength and we know that where the main public realm is society, there is always the danger that, through a perverted form of "acting together" – by pull and pressure and the tricks of cliques – those are brought to the fore who know nothing and can do nothing. The vehement yearning for violence, so characteristic of some of the best modern creative artists, thinkers, scholars, and craftsmen, is a natural reaction of those whom society has tried to cheat of their strength.[10]

Power preserves the public realm and the space of appearance, and as such it is also the lifeblood of the human artifice, which, unless it is the scene of action and speech, of the web of human affairs and relationships and the stories engendered by them, lacks its ultimate *raison d'être*. Without being talked about by men and without housing them, the world would not be a human artifice but a heap of unrelated things to which each isolated individual was at liberty to add one more object; without the human artifice to house them, human affairs would be as floating, as futile and vain, as the wanderings of nomad tribes. The melancholy wisdom of *Ecclesiastes* – "Vanity of vanities; all is vanity. . . . There is no new thing under the sun, . . . there is no remembrance of former things; neither shall there be any remembrance of things that are to come with those that shall come after" – does not necessarily arise from specifically religious experience; but it is certainly unavoidable wherever and whenever trust in the world as a place fit for human appearance, for action and speech, is gone. Without action to bring into the play of the world the new beginning of which each man is capable by virtue of being born, "there is no new thing under the sun"; without speech to materialize and memorialize, however, tentatively, the "new things" that appear and shine forth, "there is no remembrance"; without the enduring permanence of a human artifact, there cannot "be any remembrance of things that are to come with those that shall come after." And without power, the space of appearance brought forth through action and speech in public will fade away as rapidly as the living deed and the living word.

Perhaps nothing in our history has been so short-lived as trust in power, nothing more lasting than the Platonic and Christian distrust of the splendor attending its space of appearance, nothing – finally in the modern age – more common that the conviction that "power corrupts." The words of Pericles, as Thucydides reports them, are perhaps unique in their supreme confidence that men can enact *and* save their greatness at the same time and, as it were, by one and the same gesture, and that the performance as such will be enough to generate *dynamis* and not need the transforming reification of *homo faber* to keep it in reality.[11] Pericles' speech, though it certainly corresponded to and articulated the innermost convictions of the people of Athens, has always been read with the sad wisdom of hindsight by men who knew that his words were spoken at the beginning of the end. Yet short-lived as this faith in *dynamis* (and consequently in politics) may have been – and it had already come to an end when the first political philosophies were formulated – its bare existence has sufficed to elevate action to the highest rank in the hierarchy of the *vita activa* and to single out speech as the decisive distinction between human and animal life, both of which bestowed upon politics a dignity which even today has not altogether disappeared.

What is outstandingly clear in Pericles' formulations – and, incidentally, no less transparent in Homer's poems – is that the innermost meaning of the acted deed and the spoken word is independent of victory and defeat and must remain untouched by any eventual outcome, by their consequences for better or worse. Unlike human behavior – which the Greeks, like all civilized people, judged according to "moral standards," taking into account motives and intentions on the one hand and aims and consequences on the other – action can be judged only by the criterion of greatness because it is in its nature to break through the commonly accepted and reach into the extraordinary, where whatever is true in common and everyday life no longer applies because everything that exists is unique and *sui generis*.[12] Thucydides, or Pericles, knew full well that he had broken with the normal standards for everyday behavior when he found the glory of Athens in having left behind "everywhere everlasting remembrance [*mne meia aidia*] of their good and their evil deeds." The art of politics teaches men how to bring forth what is great and radiant – *tamegala kai lampra*, in the words of Democritus; as long as the *polis* is there to inspire men to dare the extraordinary, all things are safe; if it perishes, everything is lost.[13] Motives and aims, no matter how pure or how grandiose, are never unique; like psychological qualities, they are typical, characteristic of different types of persons. Greatness, therefore, or the specific meaning of each deed, can lie only in the performance itself and neither in its motivation nor its achievement.

It is this insistence on the living deed and the spoken word as the greatest achievements of which human beings are capable that was conceptualized in Aristotle's notion of *energeia* ("actuality"), with which he designated all activities that do not pursue an end (are *ateleis*) and leave no work behind (no *par' autas erga*), but exhaust their full meaning in the performance itself.[14] It is from the experience of this full actuality that the paradoxical "end in itself" derives its original meaning; for in these instances of action and speech[15] the end (*telos*) is not pursued but lies in the activity itself which therefore becomes an *entelecheia*, and the work is not what follows and extinguishes the process but is imbedded in it; the performance is the work, is *energeia*.[16] Aristotle, in his political philosophy, is still well aware of what is at stake in politics, namely, no less than the *ergon tou anthrōpou*[17] (the "work of man" *qua* man), and if he defined this "work" as "to live well" (*eu zēn*), he clearly meant that "work" here is no work product but exists only in sheer actuality. This specifically human achievement lies altogether outside the category of means and ends; the "work of man" is no end because the means to achieve it – the virtues, or *aretai* – are not qualities which may or may not be actualized, but are themselves "actualities." In other words, the means to achieve the end would already be the end; and this "end," conversely, cannot be considered a means in some other respect, because there is nothing higher to attain than this actuality itself.

It is like a feeble echo of the prephilosophical Greek experience of action and speech as sheer actuality to read time and again in political philosophy since Democritus and Plato that politics is a *technē*, belongs among the arts, and can be likened to such activities as healing or navigation, where, as in the performance of the dancer or play-actor, the "product" is identical with the performing act itself. But we may gauge what has happened to action and speech, which are only in actuality, and therefore the highest activities in the political realm, when we hear what modern society, with the peculiar and uncompromising consistency that characterized it in its early stages, had to say about them. For this all-important degradation of action and speech is implied when Adam Smith classifies all occupations which rest essentially on performance – such as the military profession, "churchmen, lawyers, physicians and opera-singers" – together with "menial services," the lowest and most unproductive "labour."[18] It was precisely these occupations – healing, flute-playing, play-acting – which furnished ancient thinking with examples for the highest and greatest activities of man.

29   *Homo Faber* **and the Space of Appearance**

The root of the ancient estimation of politics is the conviction that man *qua* man, each individual in his unique distinctness, appears and confirms himself in speech and action, and that these activities, despite their material futility, posses an enduring quality of their own because they create their own remembrance.[19] The public realm, the space within the world which men need in order to appear at all, is therefore more specifically "the work of man" than is the work of his hands or the labor of his body.

The conviction that the greatest that man can achieve is his own appearance and actualization is by no means a matter of course. Against it stands the conviction of *homo faber* that a man's products may be more – and not only more lasting – than he is himself, as well as the *animal laborans'* firm belief that life is the highest of all goods. Both, therefore, are, strictly speaking, unpolitical, and will incline to denounce action and speech as idleness, idle busybodyness and idle talk, and generally will judge public activities in terms of their usefulness to supposedly higher ends – to make the world more useful and more beautiful in the case of *homo faber*, to make life easier and longer in the case of the *animal laborans*. This, however, is not to say that they are free to dispense with a public realm altogether, for without a space of appearance and without trusting in action and speech as a mode of being together, neither the reality of one's self, of one's own identity, nor the reality of the surrounding world can be established beyond doubt. The human sense of reality demands that men actualize the sheer passive givenness of their being, not in order to change it but in order to make articulate and call into full existence what otherwise they would have to suffer passively anyhow.[20] This actualization resides and comes to pass in those activities that exist only in sheer actuality.

The only character of the world by which to gauge its reality is its being common to us all, and common sense occupies such a high rank in the hierarchy of political qualities because it is the one sense that fits into reality as a whole our five strictly individual senses and the strictly particular data they perceive. It is by virtue of common sense that the other sense perceptions are known to disclose reality and are not merely felt as irritations of our nerves or resistance sensations of our bodies. A noticeable decrease in common sense in any given community and a noticeable increase in superstition and gullibility are therefore almost infallible signs of alienation from the world.

This alienation – the atrophy of the space of appearance and the withering of common sense – is, of course, carried to a much greater extreme in the case of a laboring society than in the case of a society of producers. In his isolation, not only undisturbed by others but also not seen and heard and confirmed by them, *homo faber* is together not only with the product he makes but also with the world of things to which he will add his own products; in this, albeit indirect, way, he is still together with others who made the world and who also are fabricators of things. We have already mentioned the exchange market on which the craftsmen meet their peers and which represents to them a common public realm in so far as each of them has contributed something to it. Yet while the public realm as exchange market corresponds most adequately to the activity of fabrication, exchange itself already belongs in the field of action and is by no means a mere prolongation of production; it is even less a mere function of automatic processes, as the buying of food and other means of consumption is necessarily incidental to laboring. Marx's contention that economic laws are like natural laws, that they are not made by man to regulate the free acts of exchange but are functions of the productive conditions of society as a whole, is correct only in a laboring society, where all activities are leveled down to the human body's metabolism with nature and where no exchange exists but only consumption.

However, the people who meet on the exchange market are primarily not persons but producers of products, and what they show there is never themselves, not even their skills and qualities as in the "conspicuous production" of the Middle Ages, but their products. The impulse that drives the fabricator to the public market place is the desire for products, not for people, and the power that holds this market together and in existence is not the potentiality which springs up between people when they come together in action and speech, but a combined "power of exchange" (Adam Smith) which each of the participants acquired in isolation. It is this lack of relatedness to others and this primary concern with exchangeable commodities which Marx denounced as the dehumanization and self-alienation of commercial society, which indeed excludes men *qua* men and demands, in striking reversal of the ancient relationship between private and public, that men show themselves only in the privacy of their families or the intimacy of their friends.

The frustration of the human person inherent in a community of producers and even more in commercial society is perhaps best illustrated by the phenomenon of genius, in which, from the Renaissance to the end of the nineteenth century, the modern age saw its highest ideal. (Creative genius as the quintessential expression of human greatness was quite unknown to antiquity or the Middle Ages.) It is only with the beginning of our century that great artists in surprising unanimity have protested against being called "geniuses" and have insisted on craftmanship, competence, and the close relationships between art and handicraft. This protest, to be sure, is partly no more than a reaction against the vulgarization and commercialization of the notion of genius; but it is also due to the more recent rise of a laboring society, for which productivity or creativity is no ideal and which lacks all experiences from which the very notion of greatness can spring. What is important in our context is that the work of genius, as distinguished from the product of the craftsman, appears to have absorbed those elements of distinctness and uniqueness which find their immediate expression only in action and speech. The modern age's obsession with the unique signature of each artist, its unprecedented sensitivity to style, shows a preoccupation with those features by which the artist transcends his skill and workmanship in a way similar to the way each person's uniqueness transcends the sum total of his qualities. Because of this transcendence, which indeed distinguishes the great work of art from all other products of human hands, the phenomenon of the creative genius seemed like the highest legitimation for the conviction of *homo faber* that a man's products may be more and essentially greater than himself.

However, the great reverence the modern age so willingly paid to genius, so frequently bordering on idolatry, could hardly change the elementary fact that the essence of who somebody is cannot be reified by himself. When it appears "objectively" – in the style of an art work or in ordinary handwriting – it manifests the identity of a person and therefore serves to identify authorship, but it remains mute itself and escapes us if we try to interpret it as the mirror of a living person. In other words, the idolization of genius harbors the same degradation of the human person as the other tenets prevalent in commercial society.

It is an indispensable element of human pride to believe that who somebody is transcends in greatness and importance anything he can do and produce. "Let physicians and confectioners and the servants of the great houses be judged by what they have done, and even by what they have meant to do; the great people themselves are judged by what they are."[21] Only the vulgar will condescend to derive their pride from what they have done; they will, by this condescension, become the "slaves and prisoners" of their own faculties and will find out, should anything more be left in them than sheer stupid vanity, that to be one's own slave and prisoner is no less bitter and perhaps even more shameful than to be the servant of somebody else. It is not the glory but the predicament of the creative genius that in his case the superiority of man to his work seems indeed inverted, so that he, the living creator, finds himself in competition with his creations which he outlives, although they may survive him eventually. The saving grace of all really great gifts is that the persons who bear their burden remain superior to what they have done, at least as long as the source of creativity is alive; for this source springs indeed from *who* they are and remains outside the actual work process as well as independent of *what* they may achieve. That the predicament of genius is nevertheless a real one becomes quite apparent in the case of the *literati*, where the inverted order between man and his product is in fact consummated; what is so outrageous in their case, and incidentally incites popular hatred even more than spurious intellectual superiority, is that even their worst product is likely to be better than they are themselves. It is the hallmark of the "intellectual" that he remains quite undisturbed by "the terrible humiliation" under which the true artist or writer labors, which is "to feel that he becomes the son of his work," in which he is condemned to see himself "as in a mirror, limited, such and such." ...

31   The Traditional Substitution of Making for Acting

The modern age, in its early concern with tangible products and demonstrable profits or its later obsession with smooth functioning and sociability, was not the first to denounce the idle uselessness of action and speech in particular and of politics in general.[22] Exasperation with the threefold frustration of action – the unpredictability of its outcome, the irreversibility of the process, and the anonymity of its authors – is almost as old as recorded history. It has always been a great temptation, for men of action no less than for men of thought, to find a substitute for action in the hope that the realm of human affairs may escape the haphazardness and moral irresponsibility inherent in a plurality of agents. The remarkable monotony of the proposed solutions throughout our recorded history testifies to the elemental simplicity of the matter. Generally speaking, they always amount to seeking shelter from action's calamities in an activity where one man, isolated from all others, remains master of his doings from beginning to end. This attempt to replace acting with making is manifest in the whole body of argument against "democracy," which, the more consistently and better reasoned it is, will turn into an argument against the essentials of politics.

The calamities of action all arise from the human condition of plurality, which is the condition *sine qua non* for that space of appearance which is the public realm. Hence the attempt to do away with this plurality is always tantamount to the abolition of the public realm itself. The most obvious salvation from the dangers of plurality is mon-archy, or one-man-rule, in its many varieties, from outright tyranny of one against all to benevolent despotism and to those forms of democracy in which the many form a collective body so that the people "is many in one" and constitute themselves as a "monarch."[23] Plato's solution of the philosopher-king, whose "wisdom" solves the perplexities of action as though they were solvable problems of cognition, is only one – and by no means the least tyrannical – variety of one-man rule. The trouble with these forms of government is not that they are cruel, which often they are not, but rather that they work too well. Tyrants, if they know their business, may well be "kindly and mild in everything," like Peisistratus, whose rule even in antiquity was compared to "the Golden Age of Cronos";[24] their measures may sound very "untyrannical" and beneficial to modern ears, especially when we hear that the only – albeit unsuccessful – attempt to abolish slavery in antiquity was made by Periandros, tyrant of Corinth.[25] But they all have in common the banishment of the citizens from the public realm and the insistence that they mind their private business while only "the ruler should attend to public affairs."[26] This, to be sure, was tantamount to furthering private industry and indus-triousness, but the citizens could see in this policy nothing but the attempt to deprive them of the time necessary for participation in common matters. It is the obvious short-range advantages of tyranny, the advantages of stability, security, and productivity, that one should beware, if only because they pave the way to an inevitable loss of power, even though the actual disaster may occur in a relatively distant future.

Escape from the frailty of human affairs into the solidity of quiet and order has in fact so much to recommend it that the greater part of political philosophy since Plato could easily be interpreted as various attempts to find theoretical foundations and practical ways for an escape from politics altogether. The hallmark of all such escapes is the concept of rule, that is, the notion that men can lawfully and politically live together only when some are entitled to command and the others forced to obey. The com-monplace notion already to be found in Plato and Aristotle that every political commu-nity consists of those who rule and those who are ruled (on which assumption in turn are based the current definitions of forms of government – rule by one or monarchy, rule by few or oligarchy, rule by many or democracy) rests on a suspicion of action rather than on a contempt for men, and arose from the earnest desire to find a substitute for action rather than from any irresponsible or tyrannical will to power.

Theoretically, the most brief and most fundamental version of the escape from action into rule occurs in the *Statesman*, where Plato opens a gulf between the two modes of action, *archein* and *prattein* ("beginning" and "achieving"), which according to Greek understanding were interconnected. The problem, as Plato saw it, was to make sure that the beginner would remain the complete master of what he had begun, not needing the help of others to carry it through. In the realm of action, this isolated mastership can be achieved only if the others are no longer needed to join the enterprise of their own accord, with their own motives and aims, but are used to execute orders, and if, on the other hand, the beginner who took the initiative does not permit himself to get involved in the action itself. To begin (*archein*) and to act (*prattein*) thus can become two altogether different activities, and the beginner has become a ruler (an *archōn* in the twofold sense of the word) who "does not have to act at all (*prattein*), but rules (*archein*) over those who are capable of execution." Under these circumstances, the essence of politics is "to know how to begin and to rule in the gravest matters with regard to timeliness and untimeliness"; action as such is entirely eliminated and has become the mere "execution of orders."[27] Plato was the first to introduce the division between those who know and do not act and those who act and do not know, instead of the old articulation of action into beginning and achieving, so that knowing what to do and doing it became two altogether different performances.

Since Plato himself immediately identified the dividing line between thought and action with the gulf which separates the rulers from those over whom they rule, it is obvious that the experiences on which the Platonic division rests are those of the household, where nothing would ever be done if the master did not know what to do and did not give orders to the slaves who executed them without knowing. Here indeed, he who knows does not have to do and he who does needs no thought or knowledge. Plato was still quite aware that he proposed a revolutionary transformation of the *polis* when he applied to its administration the currently recognized maxims for a well-ordered household.[28] (It is a common error to interpret Plato as though he wanted to abolish the family and the household; he wanted, on the contrary, to extend this type of life until one family embraced every citizen. In other words, he wanted to eliminate from the household community its private character, and it is for this purpose that he recommended the abolition of private property and individual marital status.)[29] According to Greek understanding, the relationship between ruling and being ruled, between command and obedience, was by definition identical with the relationship between master and slaves and therefore precluded all possibility of action. Plato's contention, therefore, that the rules of behavior in public matters should be derived from the master–slave relationship in a well-ordered household actually meant that action should not play any part in human affairs.

It is obvious that Plato's scheme offers much greater chances for a permanent order in human affairs than the tyrant's efforts to eliminate everybody but himself from the public realm. Although each citizen would retain some part in the handling of public affairs, they would indeed "act" like one man without even the possibility of internal dissension, let alone factional strife: through rule, "the many become one in every respect" except bodily appearance.[30] Historically, the concept of rule, though originating in the household and family realm, has played its most decisive part in the organization of public matters and is for us invariably connected with politics. This should not make us overlook the fact that for Plato it was a much more general category. He saw in it the chief device for ordering and judging human affairs in every respect. This is not only evident from his insistence that the city-state must be considered to be "man writ large" and from his construction of a psychological order which actually follows the public order of his utopian city, but is even more manifest in the grandiose consistency with which he introduced the principle of domination into the intercourse of man with himself. The supreme criterion of fitness for ruling others is, in Plato and in the aristocratic tradition of the West, the capacity to rule one's self. Just as the philosopher-king commands the city, the soul commands the body and reason commands the passions. In Plato himself, the legitimacy of this tyranny in everything pertaining to man, his conduct toward himself no less than his conduct toward others, is still firmly rooted in the equivocal significance of the word *archein*, which means both beginning and ruling; it is decisive for Plato, as he says expressly at the end of the *Laws*, that only the beginning (*arche*) is entitled to rule (*archein*). In the tradition of Platonic thought, this original, linguistically predetermined identity of ruling and beginning had the consequence that all beginning was understood as the legitimation for rulership, until, finally, the element of beginning disappeared altogether from the concept of rulership. With it the most elementary and authentic understanding of human freedom disappeared from political philosophy.

The Platonic separation of knowing and doing has remained at the root of all theories of domination which are not mere justifications of an irreducible and irresponsible will to power. By sheer force of conceptualization and philosophical clarification, the Platonic identification of knowledge with command and rulership and of action with obedience and execution overruled all earlier experiences and articulations in the political realm and became authoritative for the whole tradition of political thought, even after the roots of experience from which Plato derived his concepts had long been forgotten. Apart from the unique Platonic mixture of depth and beauty, whose weight was bound to carry his thoughts through the centuries, the reason for the longevity of this particular part of his work is that he strengthened his substitution of rulership for action through an even more plausible interpretation in terms of making and fabrication. It is indeed true – and Plato, who had taken the key word of his philosophy, the term "idea," from experiences in the realm of fabrication, must have been the first to notice it – that the division between knowing and doing, so alien to the realm of action, whose validity and meaningfulness are destroyed the moment thought and action part company, is an everyday experience in fabrication, whose processes obviously fall into two parts: first, perceiving the image or shape (*eidos*) of the product-to-be, and then organizing the means and starting the execution.

The Platonic wish to substitute making for acting in order to bestow upon the realm of human affairs the solidity inherent in work and fabrication becomes most apparent where it touches the very center of his philosophy, the doctrine of ideas. When Plato was not concerned with political philosophy (as in the *Symposium* and elsewhere), he describes the ideas as what "shines forth most" (*ekphanestaton*) and therefore as variations of the beautiful. Only in the *Republic* were the ideas transformed into standards, measurements, and rules of behavior, all of which are variations or derivations of the idea of the "good" in the Greek sense of the word, that is, of the "good for" or of fitness.[31] This transformation was necessary to apply the doctrine of ideas to politics, and it is essentially for a political purpose, the purpose of eliminating the character of frailty from human affairs, that Plato found it necessary to declare the good, and not the beautiful, to be the highest idea. But this idea of the good is not the highest idea of the philosopher, who wishes to contemplate the true essence of Being and therefore leaves the dark cave of human affairs for the bright sky of ideas; even in the *Republic*, the philosopher is still defined as a lover of beauty, not of goodness. The good is the highest idea of the philosopher-*king*, who wishes to be the ruler of human affairs because he must spend his life among men and cannot dwell forever under the sky of ideas. It is only when he returns to the dark cave of human affairs to live once more with his fellow men that he needs the ideas for guidance as standards and rules by which to measure and under which to subsume the varied multitude of human deeds and words with the same absolute, "objective" certainty with which the craftsman can be guided in making and the layman in judging individual beds by using the unwavering ever-present model, the "idea" of bed in general.[32]

Technically, the greatest advantage of this transformation and application of the doctrine of ideas to the political realm lay in the elimination of the personal element in the Platonic notion of ideal rulership. Plato knew quite well that his favorite analogies taken from household life, such as the master–slave or the shepherd–flock relationship, would demand a quasi-divine quality in the ruler of men to distinguish him as sharply from his subjects as the slaves are distinguished from the master or the sheep from the shepherd.[33] The construction of the public space in the image of a fabricated object, on the contrary, carried with it only the implication of ordinary mastership, experience in the art of politics as in all other arts, where the compelling factor lies not in the person of the artist or craftsman but in the impersonal object of his art or craft. In the *Republic*, the philosopher-king applies the ideas as the craftsman applies his rules and standards; he "makes" his City as the sculptor makes a statue;[34] and in the final Platonic work these same ideas have even become laws which need only be executed.[35]

Within this frame of reference, the emergence of a utopian political system which could be construed in accordance with a model by somebody who has mastered the techniques of human affairs becomes almost a matter of course; Plato, who was the first to design a blueprint for the making of political bodies, has remained the inspiration of all later utopias. And although none of these utopias ever came to play any noticeable role in history – for in the few instances where utopian schemes were realized, they broke down quickly under the weight of reality, not so much the reality of exterior circumstances as of the real human relationships they could not control – they were among the most efficient vehicles to conserve and develop a tradition of political thinking in which, consciously or unconsciously, the concept of action was interpreted in terms of making and fabrication.

One thing, however, is noteworthy in the development of this tradition. It is true that violence, without which no fabrication could ever come to pass, has always played an important role in political schemes and thinking based upon an interpretation of action in terms of making; but up to the modern age, this element of violence remained strictly instrumental, a means that needed an end to justify and limit it, so that glorifications of violence as such are entirely absent from the tradition of political thought prior to the modern age. Generally speaking, they were impossible as long as contemplation and reason were supposed to be the highest capacities of man, because under this assumption all articulations of the *vita activa*, fabrication no less than action and let alone labor, remained themselves secondary and instrumental. Within the narrower sphere of political theory, the consequence was that the notion of rule and the concomitant questions of legitimacy and rightful authority played a much more decisive role than the understanding and interpretations of action itself. Only the modern age's conviction that man can know only what he makes, that his allegedly higher capacities depend upon making and that he therefore is primarily *homo faber* and not an *animal rationale*, brought forth the much older implications of violence inherent in all interpretations of the realm of human affairs as a sphere of making. This has been particularly striking in the series of revolutions, characteristic of the modern age, all of which – with the exception of the American Revolution – show the same combination of the old Roman enthusiasm for the foundation of a new body politic with the glorification of violence as the only means for "making" it. Marx's dictum that "violence is the midwife of every old society pregnant with a new one," that is, of all change in history and politics,[36] only sums up the conviction of the whole modern age and draws the consequences of its innermost belief that history is "made" by men as nature is "made" by God.

How persistent and successful the transformation of action into a mode of making has been is easily attested by the whole terminology of political theory and political thought, which indeed makes it almost impossible to discuss these matters without using the category of means and ends and thinking in terms of instrumentality. Perhaps even more convincing is the unanimity with which popular proverbs in all modern languages advise us that "he who wants an end must also want the means" and that "you can't make an omelette without breaking eggs." We are perhaps the first generation which has become fully aware of the murderous consequences inherent in a line of thought that forces one to admit that all means, provided that they are efficient, are permissible and justified to pursue something defined as an end. However, in order to escape these beaten paths of thought it is not enough to add some qualifications, such as that not all means are permissible or that under certain circumstances means may be more important than ends; these qualifications either take for granted a moral system which, as the very exhortations demonstrate, can hardly be taken for granted, or they are overpowered by the very language and analogies they use. For to make a statement about ends that do not justify all means is to speak in paradoxes, the definition of an end being precisely the justification of the means; and paradoxes always indicate perplexities, they do not solve them and hence are never convincing. As long as we believe that we deal with ends and means in the political realm, we shall not be able to prevent anybody's using all means to pursue recognized ends.

The substitution of making for acting and the concomitant degradation of politics into a means to obtain an allegedly "higher" end – in antiquity the protection of the good men from the rule of the bad in general, and the safety of the philosopher in particular,[37] in the Middle Ages the salvation of souls, in the modern age the productivity and progress of society – is as old as the tradition of political philosophy. It is true that only the modern age defined man primarily as *homo faber*, a toolmaker and producer of things, and therefore could overcome the deep-seated contempt and suspicion in which the tradition had held the whole sphere of fabrication. Yet, this same tradition, in so far as it also had turned against action – less openly, to be sure, but no less effectively – had been forced to interpret acting in terms of making, and thereby, its suspicion and contempt notwithstanding, had introduced into political philosophy certain trends and patterns of thought upon which the modern age could fall back. In this respect, the modern age did not reverse the tradition but rather liberated it from the "prejudices" which had prevented it from declaring openly that the work of the craftsman should rank higher than the "idle" opinions and doings which constitute the realm of human affairs. The point is that Plato and, to a lesser degree, Aristotle, who thought craftsmen not even worthy of full-fledged citizenship, were the first to propose handling political matters and ruling political bodies in the mode of fabrication. This seeming contradiction clearly indicates the depth of the authentic perplexities inherent in the human capacity for action and the strength of the temptation to eliminate its risks and dangers by introducing into the web of human relationships the much more reliable and solid categories inherent in activities with which we confront nature and build the world of the human artifice.

32   The Process Character of Action

The instrumentalization of action and the degradation of politics into a means for something else has of course never really succeeded in eliminating action, in preventing its being one of the decisive human experiences, or in destroying the realm of human affairs altogether. We saw before that in our world the seeming elimination of labor, as the painful effort to which all human life is bound, had first of all the consequence that work is now performed in the mode of laboring, and the products of work, objects for use, are consumed as though they were mere consumer goods. Similarly, the attempt to eliminate action because of its uncertainty and to save human affairs from their frailty by dealing with them as though they were or could become the planned products of human making has first of all resulted in channeling the human capacity for action, for beginning new and spontaneous processes which without men never would come into existence, into an attitude toward nature which up to the latest stage of the modern age had been one of exploring natural laws and fabricating objects out of natural material. To what an extent we have begun to act into nature, in the literal sense of the word, is perhaps best illustrated by a recent, casual remark of a scientist who quite seriously suggested that "basic research is when I am doing what I don't know what I am doing."[38]

This started harmlessly enough with the experiment in which men were no longer content to observe, to register, and contemplate whatever nature was willing to yield in her own appearance, but began to prescribe conditions and to provoke natural processes. What then developed into an ever-increasing skill in unchaining elemental processes, which, without the interference of men, would have lain dormant and perhaps never have come to pass, has finally ended in a veritable art of "making" nature, that is, of creating "natural" processes which without men would never exist and which earthly nature by herself seems incapable of accomplishing, although similar or identical processes may be commonplace phenomena in the universe surrounding the earth. Through the introduction of the experiment, in which we prescribed man-thought conditions to natural processes and forced them to fall into man-made patterns, we eventually learned how to "repeat the process that goes on in the sun," that is, how to win from natural processes on the earth those energies which without us develop only in the universe.

The very fact that natural sciences have become exclusively sciences of process and, in their last stage, sciences of potentially irreversible, irremediable "processes of no return" is a clear indication that, whatever the brain power necessary to start them, the actual underlying human capacity which alone could bring about this development is no "theoretical" capacity, neither contemplation nor reason, but the human ability to act – to start new unprecedented processes whose outcome remains uncertain and unpredictable whether they are let loose in the human or the natural realm.

In this aspect of action – all-important to the modern age, to its enormous enlargement of human capabilities as well as to its unprecedented concept and consciousness of history – processes are started whose outcome is unpredictable, so that uncertainty rather than frailty becomes the decisive character of human affairs. This property of action had escaped the attention of antiquity, by and large, and had, to say the least, hardly found adequate articulation in ancient philosophy, to which the very concept of history as we know it is altogether alien. The central concept of the two entirely new sciences of the modern age, natural science no less than historical, is the concept of process, and the actual human experience underlying it is action. Only because we are capable of acting, of starting processes of our own, can we conceive of both nature and history as systems of processes. It is true that this character of modern thinking first came to the fore in the science of history, which, since Vico, has been consciously presented as a "new science," while the natural sciences needed several centuries before they were forced by the very results of their triumphal achievements to exchange an obsolete conceptual framework for a vocabulary that is strikingly similar to the one used in the historical sciences.

However that may be, only under certain historical circumstances does frailty appear to be the chief characteristic of human affairs. The Greeks measured them against the ever-presence or eternal recurrence of all natural things, and the chief Greek concern was to measure up to and become worthy of an immortality which surrounds men but which mortals do not possess. To people who are not possessed by this concern with immortality, the realm of human affairs is bound to show an altogether different, even somehow contradictory aspect, namely, an extraordinary resiliency whose force of persistence and continuity in time is far superior to the stable durability of the solid world of things. Whereas men have always been capable of destroying whatever was the product of human hands and have become capable today even of the potential destruction of what man did not make – the earth and earthly nature – men never have been and never will be able to undo or even to control reliably any of the processes they start through action. Not even oblivion and confusion, which can cover up so efficiently the origin and the responsibility for every single deed, are able to undo a deed or prevent its consequences. And this incapacity to undo what has been done is matched by an almost equally complete incapacity to foretell the consequences of any deed or even to have reliable knowledge of its motives.[39]

While the strength of the production process is entirely absorbed in and exhausted by the end product, the strength of the action process is never exhausted in a single deed but, on the contrary, can grow while its consequences multiply; what endures in the realm of human affairs are these processes, and their endurance is as unlimited, as independent of the perishability of material and the mortality of men as the endurance of humanity itself. The reason why we are never able to foretell with certainty the outcome and end of any action is simply that action has no end. The process of a single deed can quite literally endure throughout time until mankind itself has come to an end.

That deeds possess such an enormous capacity for endurance, superior to every other man-made product, could be a matter of pride if men were able to bear its burden, the burden of irreversibility and unpredictability, from which the action process draws its very strength. That this is impossible, men have always known. They have known that he who acts never quite knows that he is doing, that he always becomes "guilty" of consequences he never intended or even foresaw, that no matter how disastrous and unexpected the consequences of his deed he can never undo it, that the process he starts is never consummated unequivocally in one single deed or event, and that its very meaning never discloses itself to the actor but only to the backward glance of the historian who himself does not act. All this is reason enough to turn away with despair from the realm of human affairs and to hold in contempt the human capacity for freedom, which, by producing the web of human relationships, seems to entangle its producer to such an extent that he appears much more the victim and the sufferer than the author and doer of what he has done. Nowhere, in other words, neither in labor, subject to the necessity of life, nor in fabrication, dependent upon given material, does man appear to be less free than in those capacities whose very essence is freedom and in that realm which owes its existence to nobody and nothing but man.

It is in accordance with the great tradition of Western thought to think along these lines: to accuse freedom of luring man into necessity, to condemn action, the spontaneous beginning of something new, because its results fall into a predetermined net of relationships, invariably dragging the agent with them, who seems to forfeit his freedom the very moment he makes use of it. The only salvation from this kind of freedom seems to lie in non-acting, in abstention from the whole realm of human affairs as the only means to safeguard one's sovereignty and integrity as a person. If we leave aside the disastrous consequences of these recommendations (which materialized into a consistent system of human behavior only in Stoicism), their basic error seems to lie in that identification of sovereignty with freedom which has always been taken for granted by political as well as philosophic thought. If it were true that sovereignty and freedom are the same, then indeed no man could be free, because sovereignty, the ideal of uncompromising self-sufficiency and mastership, is contradictory to the very condition of plurality. No man can be sovereign because not one man, but men, inhabit the earth – and not, as the tradition since Plato holds, because of man's limited strength, which makes him depend upon the help of others. All the recommendations the tradition has to offer to overcome the condition of non-sovereignty and win an untouchable integrity of the human person amount to a compensation for the intrinsic "weakness" of plurality. Yet, if these recommendations were followed and this attempt to overcome the consequences of plurality were successful, the result would be not so much sovereign domination of one's self as arbitrary domination of all others, or, as in Stoicism, the exchange of the real world for an imaginary one where these others would simply not exist.

In other words, the issue here is not strength or weakness in the sense of self-sufficiency. In polytheist systems, for instance, even a god, no matter how powerful, cannot be sovereign; only under the assumption of one god ("One is one and all alone and evermore shall be so") can sovereignty and freedom be the same. Under all other circumstances, sovereignty is possible only in imagination, paid for by the price of reality. Just as Epicureanism rests on the illusion of happiness when one is roasted alive in the Phaleric Bull, Stoicism rests on the illusion of freedom when one is enslaved. Both illusions testify to the psychological power of imagination, but this power can exert itself only as long as the reality of the world and the living, where one is and appears to be either happy or unhappy, either free or slave, are eliminated to such an extent that they are not even admitted as spectators to the spectacle of self-delusion.

If we look upon freedom with the eyes of the tradition, identifying freedom with sovereignty, the simultaneous presence of freedom and non-sovereignty, of being able to begin something new and of not being able to control or even foretell its consequences, seems almost to force us to the conclusion that human existence is absurd.[40] In view of human reality and its phenomenal evidence, it is indeed as spurious to deny human freedom to act because the actor never remains the master of his acts as it is to maintain that human sovereignty is possible because of the incontestable fact of human freedom.[41] The question which then arises is whether our notion that freedom and non-sovereignty are mutually exclusive is not defeated by reality, or to put it another way, whether the capacity for action does not harbor within itself certain potentialities which enable it to survive the disabilities of non-sovereignty. . . .

34 Unpredictability and the Power of Promise

In contrast to forgiving, which – perhaps because of its religious context, perhaps because of the connection with love attending its discovery – has always been deemed unrealistic and inadmissible in the public realm, the power of stabilization inherent in the faculty of making promises has been known throughout our tradition. We may trace it back to the Roman legal system, the inviolability of agreements and treaties (*pacta sunt servanda*); or we may see its discoverer in Abraham, the man from Ur, whose whole story, as the Bible tells it, shows such a passionate drive toward making convenants that it is as though he departed from his country for no other reason than to try out the power of mutual promise in the wilderness of the world, until eventually God himself agreed to make a Covenant with him. At any rate, the great variety of contract theories since the Romans attests to the fact that the power of making promises has occupied the center of political thought over the centuries.

The unpredictability which the act of making promises at least partially dispels is of a twofold nature: it arises simultaneously out of the "darkness of the human heart," that is, the basic unreliability of men who never can guarantee today who they will be tomorrow, and out of the impossibility of foretelling the consequences of an act within a community of equals where everybody has the same capacity to act. Man's inability to rely upon himself or to have complete faith in himself (which is the same thing) is the price human beings pay for freedom; and the impossibility of remaining unique masters of what they do, of knowing its consequences and relying upon the future, is the price they pay for plurality and reality, for the joy of inhabiting together with others a world whose reality is guaranteed for each by the presence of all.

The function of the faculty of promising is to master this twofold darkness of human affairs and is, as such, the only alternative to a mastery which relies on domination of one's self and rule over others; it corresponds exactly to the existence of a freedom which was given under the condition of non-sovereignty. The danger and the advantage inherent in all bodies politic that rely on contracts and treaties is that they, unlike those that rely on rule and sovereignty, leave the unpredictability of human affairs and the unreliability of men as they are, using them merely as the medium, as it were, into which certain islands of predictability are thrown and in which certain guideposts of reliability are erected. The moment promises lose their character as isolated islands of certainty in an ocean of uncertainty, that is, when this faculty is misused to cover the whole ground of the future and to map out a path secured in all directions, they lose their binding power and the whole enterprise becomes self-defeating.

We mentioned before the power generated when people gather together and "act in concert," which disappears the moment they depart. The force that keeps them together, as distinguished from the space of appearances in which they gather and the power which keeps this public space in existence, is the force of mutual promise or contract. Sovereignty, which is always spurious if claimed by an isolated single entity, be it the individual entity of the person or the collective entity of a nation, assumes, in the case of many men mutually bound by promises, a certain limited reality. The sovereignty resides in the resulting, limited independence from the incalculability of the future, and its limits are the same as those inherent in the faculty itself of making and keeping promises. The sovereignty of a body of people bound and kept together, not by an identical will which somehow magically inspires them all, but by an agreed purpose for which alone the promises are valid and binding, shows itself quite clearly in its unquestioned superiority over those who are completely free, unbound by any promises and unkept by any purpose. This superiority derives from the capacity to dispose of the future as though it were the present, that is, the enormous and truly miraculous enlargement of the very dimension in which power can be effective. Nietzsche, in his extraordinary sensibility to moral phenomena, and despite his modern prejudice to see the source of all power in the will power of the isolated individual, saw in the faculty of promises (the "memory of the will," as he called it) the very distinction which marks off human from animal life.[42] If sovereignty is in the realm of action and human affairs what mastership is in the realm of making and the world of things, then their chief distinction is that the one can only be achieved by the many bound together, whereas the other is conceivable only in isolation.

In so far as morality is more than the sum total of *mores*, of customs and standards of behavior solidified through tradition and valid on the ground of agreements, both of which change with time, it has, at least politically, no more to support itself than the good will to counter the enormous risks of action by readiness to forgive and to be forgiven, to make promises and to keep them. These moral precepts are the only ones that are not applied to action from the outside, from some supposedly higher faculty or from experiences outside action's own reach. They arise, on the contrary, directly out of the will to live together with others in the mode of acting and speaking, and thus they are like control mechanisms built into the very faculty to start new and unending processes. If without action and speech, without the articulation of natality, we would be doomed to swing forever in the ever-recurring cycle of becoming, then without the faculty to undo what we have done and to control at least partially the processes we have let loose, we would be the victims of an automatic necessity bearing all the marks of the inexorable laws which, according to the natural sciences before our time, were supposed to constitute the outstanding characteristic of natural processes. We have seen before that to mortal beings this natural fatality, though it swings in itself and may be eternal, can only spell doom. If it were true that fatality is the inalienable mark of historical processes, then it would indeed be equally true that everything done in history is doomed.

And to a certain extent this is true. If left to themselves, human affairs can only follow the law of mortality, which is the most certain and the only reliable law of a life spent between birth and death. It is the faculty of action that interferes with this law because it interrupts the inexorable automatic course of daily life, which in its turn, as we saw, interrupted and interfered with the cycle of the biological life process. The life-span of man running toward death would inevitably carry everything human to ruin and destruction if it were not for the faculty of interrupting it and beginning something new, a faculty which is inherent in action like an ever-present reminder that men, though they must die, are not born in order to die but in order to begin. Yet just as, from the standpoint of nature, the rectilinear movement of man's life-span between birth and death looks like a peculiar deviation from the common natural rule of cyclical movement, thus action, seen from the viewpoint of the automatic processes which seem to determine the course of the world, looks like a miracle. In the language of natural science, it is the "infinite improbability which occurs regularly." Action is, in fact, the one miracle-working faculty of man, as Jesus of Nazareth, whose insights into this faculty can be compared in their originality and unprecedentedness with Socrates' insights into the possibilities of thought, must have known very well when he likened the power to forgive to the more general power of performing miracles, putting both on the same level and within the reach of man.[43]

The miracle that saves the world, the realm of human affairs, from its normal, "natural" ruin is ultimately the fact of natality, in which the faculty of action is ontologically rooted. It is, in other words, the birth of new men and the new beginning, the action they are capable of by virtue of being born. Only the full experience of this capacity can bestow upon human affairs faith and hope, those two essential characteristics of human existence which Greek antiquity ignored altogether, discounting the keeping of faith as a very uncommon and not too important virtue and counting hope among the evils of illusion in Pandora's box. It is this faith in and hope for the world that found perhaps its most glorious and most succinct expression in the few words with which the Gospels announced their "glad tidings": "A child has been born unto us."

Notes

1   This description is supported by recent findings in psychology and biology which also stress the inner affinity between speech and action, their spontaneity and practical purposelessness. See especially Arnold Gehlen, *Der Mensch: Seine Natur und seine Stellung in der Welt* (1955), which gives an excellent summary of the results and interpretations of current scientific research and contains a wealth of valuable insights. That Gehlen, like the scientists upon whose results he bases his own theories, believes that these specifically human capabilities are also a "biological necessity," that is, necessary for a biologically weak and ill-fitted organism such as man, is another matter and need not concern us here.

2   *De civitate Dei* xii. 20.

3   According to Augustine, the two were so different that he used a different word to indicate the beginning which is man (*initium*), designating the beginning of the world by *principium*, which is the standard translation for the first Bible verse. As can be seen from *De civitate Dei* xi. 32, the word *principium* carried for Augustine a much less radical meaning; the beginning of the world "does not mean that nothing was made before (for the angels were)," whereas he adds explicitly in the phrase quoted above with reference to man that nobody was before him.

4   This is the reason why Plato says that *lexis* ("speech") adheres more closely to truth than *praxis*.

5   Plato already reproached Pericles because he did not "make the citizen better" and because the Athenians were even worse at the end of his career than before (*Gorgias* 515).

6   Recent political history is full of examples indicating that the term "human material" is no harmless metaphor, and the same is true for a whole host of modern scientific experiments in social engineering, biochemistry, brain surgery, etc., all of which tend to treat and change human material like other matter. This mechanistic approach is typical of the modern age; antiquity, when it pursued similar aims, was inclined to think of men in terms of savage animals who need be tamed and domesticated. The only possible achievement in either case is to kill man, not indeed necessarily as a living organism, but *qua* man.

7   For *archein* and *prattein* see especially their use in Homer (cf. C. Capelle, *Wörterbuch des Homeros und der Homeriden* [1889]).

8   It is interesting to note that Montesquieu, whose concern was not with laws but with the actions their spirit would inspire, defines laws as *rapports* subsisting between different beings (*Esprit des lois*, Book I, ch. 1; cf. Book XXVI, ch. 1). This definition is surprising because laws had always been defined in terms of boundaries and limitations. The reason for it is that Montesquieu was less interested in what he called the "nature of government" – whether it was a republic or a monarchy, for instance – than in its "principle . . . by which it is made to act, . . . the human passions which set it in motion" (Book III, ch. 1).

9   In the words of Montesquieu, who ignores the difference between tyranny and despotism: "Le principle du gouvernement despotique se corrompt sans cesse, parcequ'il est corrompu par sa nature. Les autres gouvernements périssent, parceque des accidents particuliers en violent le principe: celui-ci périt par son vice intérieur, lorsque quelques causes accidentelles n'empêchent point son principle de se corrompre" (*op. cit.*, Book VIII, ch. 10).

10 The extent to which Nietzsche's glorification of the will to power was inspired by such experiences of the modern intellectual may be surmised from the following side remark: "Denn die Ohnmacht gegen Menschen, nicht die Ohnmacht gegen die Natur, erzeugt die desperateste Verbitterung gegen das Dasein" (*Wille zur Macht*, No. 55).

11 In the above-mentioned paragraph in the Funeral Oration Pericles deliberately contrasts the *dynamis* of the *polis* with the craftsmanship of the poets.

12 The reason why Aristotle in his *Poetics* finds that greatness (*megethos*) is a prerequisite of the dramatic plot is that the drama imitates acting and acting is judged by greatness, by its distinction from the commonplace (1450b25). The same, incidentally, is true for the beautiful, which resides in greatness and *taxis*, the joining together of the parts (1450b34 ff.).

13 See fragment B157 of Democritus in Diels, *op. cit.*

14 For the concept of *energeia* see *Nicomachean Ethics* 1094a1–5; *Physics* 201b31; *On the Soul* 417a16, 431a6. The examples most frequently used are seeing and flute-playing.

15 It is of no importance in our context that Aristotle saw the highest possibility of "actuality" not in action and speech, but in contemplation and thought, in *theōria* and *nous*.

16 The two Aristotelian concepts, *energeia* and *entelecheia*, are closely interrelated (*energeia . . . synteinei pros tēn entelecheian*): full actuality (*energeia*) effects and produces nothing besides itself, and full reality (*entelecheia*) has no other end besides itself (see *Metaphysics* 1050a22–35).

17 *Nicomachean Ethics* 1097b22.

18 *Wealth of Nations* (Everyman's edn.), II, 295.

19 This is a decisive feature of the Greek, though perhaps not of the Roman, concept of "virtue": where *aretē* is, oblivion cannot occur (cf. Aristotle *Nicomachean Ethics* 1100b12–17).

20 This is the meaning of the last sentence of the Dante quotation at the head of this chapter; the sentence, though quite clear and simple in the Latin original, defies translation (*De monarchia* i. 13).

21 I use here Isak Dinesen's wonderful story "The Dreamers," in *Seven Gothic Tales* (Modern
    Library edn.), especially pp. 340ff.

22 The classic author on this matter is still Adam Smith, to whom the only legitimate function
    of government is "the defence of the rich against the poor, or of those who have
    some property against those who have none at all" (*op. cit.*, II, 198ff.; for the quotation
    see II, 203).

23 This is the Aristotelian interpretation of tyranny in the form of a democracy (*Politics*
    1292a16 ff.). Kingship, however, does not belong among the tyrannical forms of govern-
    ment, nor can it be defined as one-man rule or monarchy. While the terms "tyranny" and
    "monarchy" could be used interchangeably, the words "tyrant" and *basileus* ("king") are
    used as opposites (see, for instance, Aristotle *Nicomachean Ethics* 1160b3; Plato *Republic*
    576D). Generally speaking, one-man rule is praised in antiquity only for household matters
    or for warfare, and it is usually in some military or "economic" context that the famous line
    from the *Iliad, ouk agathon polykoiraniē; heis koiranos estō, heis basileus* – "the rule by many is
    not good; one should be master, one be king" (ii. 204) – is quoted. (Aristotle, who applies
    Homer's saying in his *Metaphysics* [1076a3 ff.] to political community life [*politeuesthai*] in a
    metaphorical sense, is an exception. In *Politics* 1292a13, where he quotes the Homeric line
    again, he takes a stand against the many having the power "not as individuals, but
    collectively," and states that this is only a disguised form of one-man rule, or tyranny.)
    Conversely, the rule of the many, later called *polyarkhia*, is used disparagingly to mean
    confusion of command in warfare (see, for instance, Thucydides vi. 72; cf. Xenophon
    Anabasis vi. 1. 18).

24 Aristotle *Athenian Constitution* xvi. 2, 7.

25 See Fritz Heichelheim, *Wirtschaftsgeschichte des Altertums* (1938), I, 258.

26 Aristotle (*Athenian Constitution* xv. 5) reports this of Peisistratus.

27 *Statesman* 305.

28 It is the decisive contention of the *Statesman* that no difference existed between the consti-
    tution of a large household and that of the *polis* (see 259), so that the same science would
    cover political and "economic" or household matters.

29 This is particularly manifest in those passages of the fifth book of the *Republic* in which Plato
    describes how the fear lest one attack his own son, brother, or father would further general
    peace in his utopian republic. Because of the community of women, nobody would know
    who his blood relatives were (see esp. 463C and 465B).

30 *Republic* 443E.

31 The word *ekphanestaton* occurs in the *Phaedrus* (250) as the chief quality of the beautiful. In
    the *Republic* (518) a similar quality is claimed for the idea of the good, which is called
    phanotaton. Both words derive from *phainesthai* ("to appear" and "shine forth"), and in both
    cases the superlative is used. Obviously, the quality of shining brightness applies to the
    beautiful much more than to the good.

32 Werner Jaeger's statement (*Paideia* [1945], II, 416 n.), "The idea that there is a supreme art
    of measurement and that the philosopher's knowledge of value (*phronēsis*) is the ability to
    measure, runs through all Plato's work right down to the end," is true only for Plato's
    political philosophy, where the idea of the good replaces the idea of the beautiful. The
    parable of the Cave, as told in the *Republic*, is the very center of Plato's political philosophy,
    but the doctrine of ideas as presented there must be understood as its application to politics,
    not as the original, purely philosophical development, which we cannot discuss here.
    Jaeger's characterization of the "philosopher's knowledge of values" as *phronēsis* indicates,
    in fact, the political and non-philosophical nature of this knowledge; for the very word
    phronesis characterizes in Plato and Aristotle the insight of the statesman rather than the
    vision of the philosopher.

33 In the *Statesman*, where Plato chiefly pursues this line of thought, he concludes ironically: Looking for someone who would be as fit to rule over man as the shepherd is to rule over his flock, we found "a god instead of a mortal man" (275).

34 *Republic* 420.

35 It may be interesting to note the following development in Plato's political theory: In the *Republic*, his division between rulers and ruled is guided by the relationship between expert and layman; in the *Statesman*, he takes his bearings from the relation between knowing and doing; and in the *Laws*, the execution of unchangeable laws is all that is left to the statesman or necessary for the functioning of the public realm. What is most striking in this development is the progressive shrinkage of faculties needed for the mastering of politics.

36 The quote is from *Capital* (Modern Library edn.), p. 824. Other passages in Marx show that he does not restrict his remark to the manifestation of social or economic forces. For example: "In actual history it is notorious that conquest, enslavement, robbery, murder, briefly violence, play the great part" (ibid., 785).

37 Compare Plato's statement that the wish of the philosopher to become a ruler of men can spring only from the fear of being ruled by those who are worse (*Republic* 347) with Augustine's statement that the function of government is to enable "the good" to live more quietly among "the bad" (*Epistolne* 153. 6).

38 Quoted from an interview with Wernher von Braun, as reported in the *New York Times*, December 16, 1957.

39 "Man weiss die Herkunft nicht, man weiss die Folgen nicht . . . [der Wert der Handlung ist] unbekannt," as Nietzsche once put it (*Wille zur Macht*, No. 291), hardly aware that he only echoed the age-old suspicion of the philosopher against action.

40 This "existentialist" conclusion is much less due to an authentic revision of traditional concepts and standards than it appears to be; actually, it still operates within the tradition and with traditional concepts, though in a certain spirit of rebellion. The most consistent result of this rebellion is therefore a return to "religious values" which, however, have no root any longer in authentic religious experiences or faith, but are like all modern spiritual "values," exchange values, obtained in this case for the discarded "values" of despair.

41 Where human pride is still intact, it is tragedy rather than absurdity which is taken to be the hallmark of human existence. Its greatest representative is Kant, to whom the spontaneity of acting, and the concomitant faculties of practical reason, including force of judgment, remain the outstanding qualities of man, even though his action falls into the determinism of natural laws and his judgment cannot penetrate the secret of absolute reality (the *Ding an sich*). Kant had the courage to acquit man from the consequences of his deed, insisting solely on the purity of his motives, and this saved him from losing faith in man and his potential greatness.

42 Nietzsche saw with unequaled clarity the connection between human sovereignty and the faculty of making promises, which led him to a unique insight into the relatedness of human pride and human conscience. Unfortunately, both insights remained unrelated with and without effect upon his chief concept, the "will to power," and therefore are frequently overlooked even by Nietzsche scholars. They are to be found in the first two aphorisms of the second treatise in *Zur Genealogie der Moral*.

43 Jesus himself saw the human root of this power to perform miracles in faith – which we leave out of our considerations. In our context, the only point that matters is that the power to perform miracles is not considered to be divine – faith will move mountains and faith will forgive; the one is no less a miracle than the other, and the reply of the apostles when Jesus demanded of them to forgive seven times in a day was: "Lord, increase our faith."

ON VIOLENCE

I

These reflections were provoked by the events and debates of the last few years as seen against the background of the twentieth century, which has become indeed, as Lenin predicted, a century of wars and revolutions, hence a century of that violence which is currently believed to be their common denominator....

Since violence – as distinct from power, force, or strength – always needs *implements* (as Engels pointed out long ago),[1] the revolution of technology, a revolution in tool-making, was especially marked in warfare. The very substance of violent action is ruled by the means–end category, whose chief characteristic, if applied to human affairs, has always been that the end is in danger of being overwhelmed by the means which it justifies and which are needed to reach it. Since the end of human action, as distinct from the end products of fabrication, can never be reliably predicted, the means used to achieve political goals are more often than not of greater relevance to the future world than the intended goals....

The chief reason warfare is still with us is neither a secret death wish of the human species, nor an irrepressible instinct of aggression, nor, finally and more plausibly, the serious economic and social dangers inherent in disarmament, but the simple fact that no substitute for this final arbiter in international affairs has yet appeared on the political scene. Was not Hobbes right when he said: "Covenants, without the sword, are but words"?

Nor is a substitute likely to appear so long as national independence, namely, freedom from foreign rule, and the sovereignty of the state, namely, the claim to unchecked and unlimited power in foreign affairs, are identified. (The United States of America is among the few countries where a proper separation of freedom and sovereignty is at least theoretically possible insofar as the very foundations of the American republic would not be threatened by it. Foreign treaties, according to the Constitution, are part and parcel of the law of the land, and – as Justice James Wilson remarked in 1793 – "to the Constitution of the United States the term sovereignty is totally unknown." But the times of such clearheaded and proud separation from the traditional language and conceptual political frame of the European nation-state are long past; the heritage of the American Revolution is forgotten, and the American government, for better and for worse, has entered into the heritage of Europe as though it were its patrimony – unaware, alas, of the fact that Europe's declining power was preceded and accompanied by political bankruptcy, the bankruptcy of the nation-state and its concept of sovereignty.)...

The more dubious and uncertain an instrument violence has become in international relations, the more it has gained in reputation and appeal in domestic affairs, specifically in the matter of revolution. The strong Marxist rhetoric of the New Left coincides with the steady growth of the entirely non-Marxian conviction, proclaimed by Mao Tse-tung, that "Power grows out of the barrel of a gun." To be sure, Marx was aware of the role of violence in history, but this role was to him secondary; not violence but the contradictions inherent in the old society brought about its end. The emergence of a new society was preceded, but not caused, by violent outbreaks, which he likened to the labor pangs that precede, but of course do not cause, the event of organic birth. In the same vein he regarded the state as an instrument of violence in the command of the ruling class; but the actual power of the ruling class did not consist of or rely on violence. It was defined by the role the ruling class played in society, or, more exactly, by its role in the process of production. It has often been noticed, and sometimes deplored, that the revolutionary Left under the influence of Marx's teachings ruled out the use of violent means; the "dictatorship of the proletariat" – openly repressive in Marx's writings – came after the revolution and was meant, like the Roman dictatorship, to last a strictly limited period. . . .

On the level of theory there were a few exceptions. Georges Sorel, who at the beginning of the century tried to combine Marxism with Bergson's philosophy of life – the result, though on a much lower level of sophistication, is oddly similar to Sartre's current amalgamation of existentialism and Marxism – thought of class struggle in military terms; yet he ended by proposing nothing more violent than the famous myth of the general strike, a form of action which we today would think of as belonging rather to the arsenal of nonviolent politics. Fifty years ago even this modest proposal earned him the reputation of being a fascist, notwithstanding his enthusiastic approval of Lenin and the Russian Revolution. Sartre, who in his preface to Fanon's *The Wretched of the Earth* goes much farther in his glorification of violence than Sorel in his famous *Reflections on Violence* – farther than Fanon himself, whose argument he wishes to bring to its conclusion – still mentions "Sorel's fascist utterances." This shows to what extent Sartre is unaware of his basic disagreement with Marx on the question of violence, especially when he states that "irrepressible violence . . . is man recreating himself," that it is through "mad fury" that "the wretched of the earth" can "become men." These notions are all the more remarkable because the idea of man creating himself is strictly in the tradition of Hegelian and Marxian thinking; it is the very basis of all leftist humanism. But according to Hegel man "produces" himself through thought, whereas for Marx, who turned Hegel's "idealism" upside down, it was labor, the human form of metabolism with nature, that fulfilled this function. . . .

I quoted Sartre in order to show that this new shift toward violence in the thinking of revolutionaries can remain unnoticed even by one of their most representative and articulate spokesmen,[2] and it is all the more noteworthy for evidently not being an abstract notion in the history of ideas. . . .

The student rebellion is a global phenomenon, but its manifestations vary, of course, greatly from country to country, often from university to university. This is especially true of the practice of violence. Violence has remained mostly a matter of theory and rhetoric where the clash between generations did not coincide with a clash of tangible group interests. This was notably so in Germany, where the tenured faculty had a vested interest in overcrowded lectures and seminars. In America, the student movement has been seriously radicalized wherever police and police brutality intervened in essentially nonviolent demonstrations: occupations of administration buildings, sit-ins, et cetera. Serious violence entered the scene only with the appearance of the Black Power movement on the campuses. Negro students, the majority of them admitted without academic qualification, regarded and organized themselves as an interest group, the representatives of the black community. Their interest was to lower academic standards. They were more cautious than the white rebels, but it was clear from the beginning (even before the incidents at Cornell University and City College in New York) that violence with them was not a matter of theory and rhetoric. . . .

The new undeniable glorification of violence by the student movement has a curious peculiarity. While the rhetoric of the new militants is clearly inspired by Fanon, their theoretical arguments contain usually nothing but a hodgepodge of all kinds of Marxist leftovers. . . .Sartre with his great felicity with words has given expression to the new faith. "Violence," he now believes, on the strength of Fanon's book, "like Achilles' lance, can heal the wounds it has inflicted." If this were true, revenge would be the cure-all for most of our ills. . . . The rarity of slave rebellions and of uprisings among the disinherited and downtrodden is notorious; on the few occasions when they occurred it was precisely "mad fury" that turned dreams into nightmares for everybody. In no case, as far as I know, was the force of these "volcanic" outbursts, in Sartre's words, "equal to that of the pressure put on them." To identify the national liberation movements with such outbursts is to prophesy their doom – quite apart from the fact that the unlikely victory would not result in changing the world (or the system), but only its personnel. To think, finally, that there is such a thing as a "Unity of the Third World," to which one could address the new slogan in the era of decolonization "Natives of all under-developed countries unite!" (Sartre) is to repeat Marx's worst illusions on a greatly enlarged scale and with considerably less justification. The Third World is not a reality but an ideology[3] . . .

The one positive political slogan the new movement has put forth, the claim for "participatory democracy" that has echoed around the globe and constitutes the most significant common denominator of the rebellions in the East and the West, derives from the best in the revolutionary tradition – the council system, the always defeated but only authentic outgrowth of every revolution since the eighteenth century. But no reference to this goal either in word or substance can be found in the teachings of Marx and Lenin, both of whom aimed on the contrary at a society in which the need for public action and participation in public affairs would have "withered away,"[4] together with the state. Because of a curious timidity in theoretical matters, contrasting oddly with its bold courage in practice, the slogan of the New Left has remained in a declamatory stage, to be invoked rather inarticulately against Western representative democracy (which is about to lose even its merely representative function to the huge party machines that "represent" not the party membership but its functionaries) and against the Eastern one-party bureaucracies, which rule out participation on principle . . . .

II

If we turn to discussions of the phenomenon of power, we soon find that there exists a consensus among political theorists from Left to Right to the effect that violence is nothing more than the most flagrant manifestation of power. "All politics is a struggle for power; the ultimate kind of power is violence," said C. Wright Mills, echoing, as it were, Max Weber's definition of the state as "the rule of men over men based on the means of legitimate, that is allegedly legitimate, violence."[5] The consensus is very strange; for to equate political power with "the organization of violence" makes sense only if one follows Marx's estimate of the state as an instrument of oppression in the hands of the ruling class . . . .

In terms of our traditions of political thought, these definitions have much to recommend them. Not only do they derive from the old notion of absolute power that accompanied the rise of the sovereign European nation-state, whose earliest and still greatest spokesmen were Jean Bodin, in sixteenth-century France, and Thomas Hobbes, in seventeenth-century England; they also coincide with the terms used since Greek antiquity to define the forms of government as the rule of man over man – of one or the few in monarchy and oligarchy, of the best or the many in aristocracy and democracy. Today we ought to add the latest and perhaps most formidable form of such dominion: bureaucracy or the rule of an intricate system of bureaus in which no men, neither one nor the best, neither the few nor the many, can be held responsible, and which could be properly called rule by Nobody. (If, in accord with traditional political thought, we identify tyranny as government that is not held to give account of itself, rule by Nobody is clearly the most tyrannical of all, since there is no one left who could even be asked to answer for what is being done. It is this state of affairs, making it impossible to localize responsibility and to identify the enemy, that is among the most potent causes of the current world-wide rebellious unrest, its chaotic nature, and its dangerous tendency to get out of control and to run amuck.) . . .

However, there exists another tradition and another vocabulary no less old and time-honored. When the Athenian city-state called its constitution an isonomy, or the Romans spoke of the *civitas* as their form of government, they had in mind a concept of power and law whose essence did not rely on the command–obedience relationship and which did not identify power and rule or law and command. It was to these examples that the men of the eighteenth-century revolutions turned when they ransacked the archives of antiquity and constituted a form of government, a republic, where the rule of law, resting on the power of the people, would put an end to the rule of man over man, which they thought was a "government fit for slaves." They too, unhappily, still talked about obedience – obedience to laws instead of men; but what they actually meant was support of the laws to which the citizenry had given its consent. Such support is never unquestioning, and as far as reliability is concerned it cannot match the indeed "unquestioning obedience" that an act of violence can exact – the obedience every criminal can count on when he snatches my pocketbook with the help of a knife or robs a bank with the help of a gun. It is the people's support that lends power to the institutions of a country, and this support is but the continuation of the consent that brought the laws into existence to begin with. Under conditions of representative government the people are supposed to rule those who govern them. All political institutions are manifestations and materializations of power; they petrify and decay as soon as the living power of the people ceases to uphold them. This is what Madison meant when he said "all governments rest on opinion," a word no less true for the various forms of monarchy than for democracies. ("To suppose that majority rule functions only in democracy is a fantastic illusion," as Jouvenel points out: "The king, who is but one solitary individual, stands far more in need of the general support of Society than any other form of government."[6] Even the tyrant, the One who rules against all, needs helpers in the business of violence, though their number may be rather restricted.) However, the strength of opinion, that is, the power of the government, depends on numbers; it is "in proportion to the number with which it is associated,"[7] and tyranny, as Montesquieu discovered, is therefore the most violent and least powerful of forms of government. Indeed one of the most obvious distinctions between power and violence is that power always stands in need of numbers, whereas violence up to a point can manage without them because it relies on implements. A legally unrestricted majority rule, that is, a democracy without a constitution, can be very formidable in the suppression of the rights of minorities and very effective in the suffocation of dissent without any use of violence. But that does not mean that violence and power are the same. . . .

It is, I think, a rather sad reflection on the present state of political science that our terminology does not distinguish among such key words as "power," "strength," "force," "authority," and, finally, "violence" – all of which refer to distinct, different phenomena and would hardly exist unless they did. (In the words of d'Entrèves, "might, power, authority: these are all words to whose exact implications no great weight is attached in current speech; even the greatest thinkers sometimes use them at random. Yet it is fair to presume that they refer to different properties, and their meaning should therefore be carefully assessed and examined. . . . The correct use of these words is a question not only of logical grammar, but of historical perspective.")[8] To use them as synonyms not only indicates a certain deafness to linguistic meanings, which would be serious enough, but it has also resulted in a kind of blindness to the realities they correspond to. In such a situation it is always tempting to introduce new definitions, but – though I shall briefly yield to temptation – what is involved is not simply a matter of careless speech. Behind the apparent confusion is a firm conviction in whose light all distinctions would be, at best, of minor importance: the conviction that the most crucial political issue is, and always has been, the question of Who rules Whom? Power, strength, force, authority, violence – these are but words to indicate the means by which man rules over man; they are held to be synonyms because they have the same function. It is only after one ceases to reduce public affairs to the business of dominion that the original data in the realm of human affairs will appear, or, rather, reappear, in their authentic diversity.

These data, in our context, may be enumerated as follows:

Power corresponds to the human ability not just to act but to act in concert. Power is never the property of an individual; it belongs to a group and remains in existence only so long as the group keeps together. When we say of somebody that he is "in power" we actually refer to his being empowered by a certain number of people to act in their name. The moment the group, from which the power originated to begin with (*potestas in populo*, without a people or group there is no power), disappears, "his power" also vanishes. In current usage, when we speak of a "powerful man" or a "powerful personality," we already use the word "power" metaphorically; what we refer to without metaphor is "strength."

Strength unequivocally designates something in the singular, an individual entity; it is the property inherent in an object or person and belongs to its character, which may prove itself in relation to other things or persons, but is essentially independent of them. The strength of even the strongest individual can always be overpowered by the many, who often will combine for no other purpose than to ruin strength precisely because of its peculiar independence. The almost instinctive hostility of the many toward the one has always, from Plato to Nietzsche, been ascribed to resentment, to the envy of the weak for the strong, but this psychological interpretation misses the point. It is in the nature of a group and its power to turn against independence, the property of individual strength.

Force, which we often use in daily speech as a synonym for violence, especially if violence serves as a means of coercion, should be reserved, in terminological language, for the "forces of nature" or the "force of circumstances" (*la force des choses*), that is, to indicate the energy released by physical or social movements.

Authority, relating to the most elusive of these phenomena and therefore, as a term, most frequently abused,[9] can be vested in persons – there is such a thing as personal authority, as, for instance, in the relation between parent and child, between teacher and pupil – or it can be vested in offices, as, for instance, in the Roman senate (*auctoritas in senatu*) or in the hierarchical offices of the Church (a priest can grant valid absolution even though he is drunk). Its hallmark is unquestioning recognition by those who are asked to obey; neither coercion nor persuasion is needed. (A father can lose his authority either by beating his child or by starting to argue with him, that is, either by behaving to him like a tyrant or by treating him as an equal.) To remain in authority requires respect for the person or the office. The greatest enemy of authority, therefore, is contempt, and the surest way to undermine it is laughter.[10]

Violence, finally, as I have said, is distinguished by its instrumental character. Phenomenologically, it is close to strength, since the implements of violence, like all other tools, are designed and used for the purpose of multiplying natural strength until, in the last stage of their development, they can substitute for it.

It is perhaps not superfluous to add that these distinctions, though by no means arbitrary, hardly ever correspond to watertight compartments in the real world, from which nevertheless they are drawn. Thus institutionalized power in organized communities often appears in the guise of authority, demanding instant, unquestioning recognition; no society could function without it. . . .

Moreover, nothing, as we shall see, is more common than the combination of violence and power, nothing less frequent than to find them in their pure and therefore extreme form. From this, it does not follow that authority, power, and violence are all the same.

Still it must be admitted that it is particularly tempting to think of power in terms of command and obedience, and hence to equate power with violence, in a discussion of what actually is only one of power's special cases – namely, the power of government. Since in foreign relations as well as domestic affairs violence appears as a last resort to keep the power structure intact against individual challengers – the foreign enemy, the native criminal – it looks indeed as though violence were the prerequisite of power and power nothing but a facade, the velvet glove which either conceals the iron hand or will turn out to belong to a paper tiger. On closer inspection, though, this notion loses much of its plausibility. For our purpose, the gap between theory and reality is perhaps best illustrated by the phenomenon of revolution. . . .

Where commands are no longer obeyed, the means of violence are of no use; and the question of this obedience is not decided by the command–obedience relation but by opinion, and, of course, by the number of those who share it. Everything depends on the power behind the violence. The sudden dramatic breakdown of power that ushers in revolutions reveals in a flash how civil obedience – to laws, to rulers, to institutions – is but the outward manifestation of support and consent. . . .

No government exclusively based on the means of violence has ever existed. Even the totalitarian ruler, whose chief instrument of rule is torture, needs a power basis – the secret police and its net of informers. Only the development of robot soldiers, which, as previously mentioned, would eliminate the human factor completely and, conceivably, permit one man with a push button to destroy whomever he pleased, could change this fundamental ascendancy of power over violence. Even the most despotic domination we know of, the rule of master over slaves, who always outnumbered him, did not rest on superior means of coercion as such, but on a superior organization of power – that is, on the organized solidarity of the masters.[11] . . .

To switch for a moment to conceptual language: Power is indeed of the essence of all government, but violence is not. Violence is by nature instrumental; like all means, it always stands in need of guidance and justification through the end it pursues. And what needs justification by something else cannot be the essence of anything. The end of war – end taken in its twofold meaning – is peace or victory; but to the question And what is the end of peace? there is no answer. Peace is an absolute, even though in recorded history periods of warfare have nearly always outlasted periods of peace. Power is in the same category; it is, as they say, "an end in itself." (This, of course, is not to deny that governments pursue policies and employ their power to achieve prescribed goals. But the power structure itself precedes and outlasts all aims, so that power, far from being the means to an end, is actually the very condition enabling a group of people to think and act in terms of the means–end category.) And since government is essentially organized and institutionalized power, the current question What is the end of government? does not make much sense either. The answer will be either question-begging – to enable men to live together – or dangerously utopian – to promote happiness or to realize a classless society or some other nonpolitical ideal, which if tried out in earnest cannot but end in some kind of tyranny.

Power needs no justification, being inherent in the very existence of political communities; what it does need is legitimacy. The common treatment of these two words as synonyms is no less misleading and confusing than the current equation of obedience and support. Power springs up whenever people get together and act in concert, but it derives its legitimacy from the initial getting together rather than from any action that then may follow. Legitimacy, when challenged, bases itself on an appeal to the past, while justification relates to an end that lies in the future. Violence can be justifiable, but it never will be legitimate. Its justification loses in plausibility the farther its intended end recedes into the future. No one questions the use of violence in self-defense, because the danger is not only clear but also present, and the end justifying the means is immediate.

Power and violence, though they are distinct phenomena, usually appear together. Wherever they are combined, power, we have found, is the primary and predominant factor. The situation, however, is entirely different when we deal with them in their pure states – as, for instance, with foreign invasion and occupation. We saw that the current equation of violence with power rests on government's being understood as domination of man over man by means of violence. If a foreign conqueror is confronted by an impotent government and by a nation unused to the exercise of political power, it is easy for him to achieve such domination. In all other cases the difficulties are great indeed, and the occupying invader will try immediately to establish Quisling governments, that is, to find a native power base to support his dominion....

To substitute violence for power can bring victory, but the price is very high; for it is not only paid by the vanquished, it is also paid by the victor in terms of his own power. This is especially true when the victor happens to enjoy domestically the blessings of constitutional government. Henry Steele Commager is entirely right: "If we subvert world order and destroy world peace we must inevitably subvert and destroy our own political institutions first."[12] The much-feared boomerang effect of the "government of subject races" (Lord Cromer) on the home government during the imperialist era meant that rule by violence in faraway lands would end by affecting the government of England, that the last "subject race" would be the English themselves. The recent gas attack on the campus at Berkeley, where not just tear gas but also another gas, "outlawed by the Geneva Convention and used by the Army to flush out guerrillas in Vietnam," was laid down while gas-masked Guardsmen stopped anybody and everybody "from fleeing the gassed area," is an excellent example of this "back-lash" phenomenon. It has often been said that impotence breeds violence, and psychologically this is quite true, at least of persons possessing natural strength, moral or physical. Politically speaking, the point is that loss of power becomes a temptation to substitute violence for power – in 1968 during the Democratic convention in Chicago we could watch this process on television[13] – and that violence itself results in impotence. Where violence is no longer backed and restrained by power, the well-known reversal in reckoning with means and ends has taken place. The means, the means of destruction, now determine the end – with the consequence that the end will be the destruction of all power.

Nowhere is the self-defeating factor in the victory of violence over power more evident than in the use of terror to maintain domination, about whose weird successes and eventual failures we know perhaps more than any generation before us. Terror is not the same as violence; it is, rather, the form of government that comes into being when violence, having destroyed all power, does not abdicate but, on the contrary, remains in full control. It has often been noticed that the effectiveness of terror depends almost entirely on the degree of social atomization. Every kind of organized opposition must disappear before the full force of terror can be let loose....

To sum up: politically speaking, it is insufficient to say that power and violence are not the same. Power and violence are opposites; where the one rules absolutely, the other is absent. Violence appears where power is in jeopardy, but left to its own course it ends in power's disappearance. This implies that it is not correct to think of the opposite of violence as nonviolence; to speak of nonviolent power is actually redundant. Violence can destroy power; it is utterly incapable of creating it. Hegel's and Marx's great trust in the dialectical "power of negation," by virtue of which opposites do not destroy but smoothly develop into each other because contradictions promote and do not paralyze development, rests on a much older philosophical prejudice: that evil is no more than a privative *modus* of the good, that good can come out of evil; that, in short, evil is but a temporary manifestation of a still-hidden good. Such time-honored opinions have become dangerous. They are shared by many who have never heard of Hegel or Marx, for the simple reason that they inspire hope and dispel fear − a treacherous hope used to dispel legitimate fear. By this, I do not mean to equate violence with evil; I only want to stress that violence cannot be derived from its opposite, which is power, and that in order to understand it for what it is, we shall have to examine its roots and nature.

III

. . . To act with *deliberate* speed goes against the grain of rage and violence, but this does not make them irrational. On the contrary, in private as well as public life there are situations in which the very swiftness of a violent act may be the only appropriate remedy. The point is not that this permits us to let off steam − which indeed can be equally well done by pounding the table or slamming the door. The point is that under certain circumstances violence − acting without argument or speech and without counting the consequences − is the only way to set the scales of justice right again. (Billy Budd, striking dead the man who bore false witness against him, is the classical example.) In this sense, rage and the violence that sometimes − not always − goes with it belong among the "natural" *human* emotions, and to cure man of them would mean nothing less than to dehumanize or emasculate him. That such acts, in which men take the law into their own hands for justice's sake, are in conflict with the constitutions of civilized communities is undeniable; but their antipolitical character, so manifest in Melville's great story, does not mean that they are inhuman or "merely" emotional. . . .

Not many authors of rank glorified violence for violence's sake; but these few − Sorel, Pareto, Fanon − were motivated by a much deeper hatred of bourgeois society and were led to a much more radical break with its moral standards than the conventional Left, which was chiefly inspired by compassion and a burning desire for justice. To tear the mask of hypocrisy from the face of the enemy, to unmask him and the devious machinations and manipulations that permit him to rule without using violent means, that is, to provoke action even at the risk of annihilation so that the truth may come out − these are still among the strongest motives in today's violence on the campuses and in the streets.[14] And this violence again is not irrational. Since men live in a world of appearances and, in their dealing with it, depend on manifestation, hypocrisy's conceits − as distinguished from expedient ruses, followed by disclosure in due time − cannot be met by so-called reasonable behavior. Words can be relied on only if one is sure that their function is to reveal and not to conceal. It is the semblance of rationality, much more than the interests behind it, that provokes rage. To use reason when reason is used as a trap is not "rational"; just as to use a gun in self-defense is not "irrational." This violent reaction against hypocrisy, however justifiable in its own terms, loses its *raison d'être* when it tries to develop a strategy of its own with specific goals; it becomes "irrational" the moment it is "rationalized," that is, the moment the re-action in the course of a contest turns into an action, and the hunt for suspects, accompanied by the psychological hunt for ulterior motives, begins.

Although the effectiveness of violence, as I remarked before, does not depend on numbers – one machine gunner can hold hundreds of well-organized people at bay – nonetheless in collective violence its most dangerously attractive features come to the fore, and this by no means because there is safety in numbers. It is perfectly true that in military as well as revolutionary action "individualism is the first [value] to disappear";[15] in its stead, we find a kind of group coherence which is more intensely felt and proves to be a much stronger, though less lasting, bond than all the varieties of friendship, civil or private.[16] To be sure, in all illegal enterprises, criminal or political, the group, for the sake of its own safety, will require "that each individual perform an irrevocable action" in order to burn his bridges to respectable society before he is admitted into the community of violence. But once a man is admitted, he will fall under the intoxicating spell of "the practice of violence [which] binds men together as a whole, since each individual forms a violent link in the great chain, a part of the great organism of violence which has surged upward."[17] . . .

Violence in interracial struggle is always murderous, but it is not "irrational"; it is the logical and rational consequence of racism, by which I do not mean some rather vague prejudices on either side, but an explicit ideological system. Under the pressure of power, prejudices, as distinguished from both interests and ideologies, may yield – as we saw happen with the highly successful civil-rights movement, which was entirely nonviolent. ("By 1964 . . . most Americans were convinced that subordination and, to a lesser degree, segregation were wrong.")[18] But while boycotts, sit-ins, and demonstrations were successful in eliminating discriminatory laws and ordinances in the South, they proved utter failures and became counterproductive when they encountered the social conditions in the large urban centers – the stark needs of the black ghettos on one side, the overriding interests of white lower-income groups in respect to housing and education on the other. All this mode of action could do, and indeed did, was to bring these conditions into the open, into the street, where the basic irreconcilability of interests was dangerously exposed. . . .

Finally – to come back to Sorel's and Pareto's earlier denunciation of the system as such – the greater the bureaucratization of public life, the greater will be the attraction of violence. In a fully developed bureaucracy there is nobody left with whom one can argue, to whom one can present grievances, on whom the pressures of power can be exerted. Bureaucracy is the form of government in which everybody is deprived of political freedom, of the power to for the rule by Nobody is not no-rule, and where all are equally powerless we have a tyranny without a tyrant. . . .

What makes man a political being is his faculty of action; it enables him to get together with his peers, to act in concert, and to reach out for goals and enterprises that would never enter his mind, let alone the desires of his heart, had he not been given this gift – to embark on something new. Philosophically speaking, to act is the human answer to the condition of natality. Since we all come into the world by virtue of birth, as newcomers and beginnings, we are able to start something new; without the fact of birth we would not even know what novelty is, all "action" would be either mere behavior or preservation. No other faculty except language, neither reason nor consciousness, distinguishes us so radically from all animal species. To act and to begin are not the same, but they are closely interconnected.

None of the properties of creativity is adequately expressed in metaphors drawn from the life process. To beget and to give birth are no more creative than to die is annihilating; they are but different phases of the same, ever-recurring cycle in which all living things are held as though they were spellbound. Neither violence nor power is a natural phenomenon, that is, a manifestation of the life process; they belong to the political realm of human affairs whose essentially human quality is guaranteed by man's faculty of action, the ability to begin something new. And I think it can be shown that no other human ability has suffered to such an extent from the progress of the modern age, for progress, as we have come to understand it, means growth, the relentless process of more and more, of bigger and bigger. The bigger a country becomes in terms of population, of objects, and of possessions, the greater will be the need for administration and with it the anonymous power of the administrators. . . .

Moreover, there is the recent rise of a curious new brand of nationalism, usually understood as a swing to the Right, but more probably an indication of a growing, world-wide resentment against "bigness" as such. While national feelings formerly tended to unite various ethnic groups by focusing their political sentiments on the nation as a whole, we now watch how an ethnic "nationalism" begins to threaten with dissolution the oldest and best-established nation-states. . . .

Whatever the administrative advantages and disadvantages of centralization may be, its political result is always the same: monopolization of power causes the drying up or oozing away of all authentic power sources in the country. In the United States, based on a great plurality of powers and their mutual checks and balances, we are confronted not merely with the disintegration of power structures, but with power, seemingly still intact and free to manifest itself, losing its grip and becoming ineffective. . . .

Because of the enormous effectiveness of teamwork in the sciences, which is perhaps the outstanding American contribution to modern science, we can control the most complicated processes with a precision that makes trips to the moon less dangerous than ordinary weekend excursions; but the allegedly "greatest power on earth" is helpless to end a war, clearly disastrous for all concerned, in one of the earth's smallest countries. It is as though we have fallen under a fairyland spell which permits us to do the "impossible" on the condition that we lose the capacity of doing the possible, to achieve fantastically extraordinary feats on the condition of no longer being able to attend properly to our everyday needs. If power has anything to do with the we-*will*-and-we-can, as distinguished from the mere we-can, then we have to admit that our power has become impotent. The progresses made by science have nothing to do with the I-will; they follow their own inexorable laws, compelling us to do whatever we can, regardless of consequences. Have the I-will and the I-can parted company? Was Valéry right when he said fifty years ago: "*On peut dire que tout ce que nous savons, c'est-à-dire tout ce que nous pouvons, a fini par s'opposer à ce que nous sommes*"? ("One can say that all we know, that is, all we have the power to do, has finally turned against what we are.")

Again, we do not know where these developments will lead us, but we know, or should know, that every decrease in power is an open invitation to violence – if only because those who hold power and feel it slipping from their hands, be they the government or be they the governed, have always found it difficult to resist the temptation to substitute violence for it.

Appendices

II, page 74, note 2

The New Left's unconscious drifting away from Marxism has been duly noticed. See especially recent comments on the student movement by Leonard Schapiro in the *New York Review of Books* (December 5, 1968) and by Raymond Aron in *La Révolution introuvable*, Paris, 1968. Both consider the new emphasis on violence to be a kind of backsliding either to pre-Marxian utopian socialism (Aron) or to the Russian anarchism of Nechaev and Bakunin (Schapiro), who "had much to say about the importance of violence as a factor of unity, as the binding force in a society or group, a century before the same ideas emerged in the works of Jean-Paul Sartre and Frantz Fanon." Aron writes in the same vein: "*Les chantres de la révolution de mai croient dépasser le marxisme . . . ils oublient un siècle d'histoire*" (p. 14). To a non-Marxist such a reversion would of course hardly be an argument; but for Sartre, who, for instance, writes "*Un prétendu 'dépassement' du marxisme ne sera au pis qu'un retour au prémarxisme, au mieux que la redécouverte d'une pensée déjà contenue dans la philosophie qu'on a cru dépasser*" ("Question de Méthode" in *Critique de la raison dialectique*, Paris, 1960, p. 17), it must constitute a formidable objection. (That Sartre and Aron, though political opponents, are in full agreement on this point is noteworthy. It shows to what an extent Hegel's concept of history dominates the thought of Marxists and non-Marxists alike.)

Sartre himself, in his *Critique of Dialectical Reason*, gives a kind of Hegelian explanation for his espousal of violence. His point of departure is that "need and scarcity determined the Manicheistic basis of action and morals" in present history, "whose truth is based on scarcity [and] must manifest itself in an antagonistic reciprocity between classes." Aggression is the consequence of need in a world where "there is not enough for all." Under such circumstances, violence is no longer a marginal phenomenon. "Violence and counter-violence are perhaps contingencies, but they are contingent necessities, and the imperative consequence of any attempt to destroy this inhumanity is that in destroying in the adversary the inhumanity of the contraman, I can only destroy in him the humanity of man, and realize in me his inhumanity. Whether kill, torture, enslave . . . my aim is to suppress his freedom – it is an alien force, *de trop*." His model for a condition in which "each one is one too many . . . Each is *redundant* for the other" is a bus queue, the members of which obviously "take no notice of each other except as a number in a quantitative series." He concludes, "They reciprocally deny any link between each of their inner worlds." From this, it follows that praxis "is the negation of alterity, which is itself a negation" – a highly welcome conclusion, since the negation of a negation is an affirmation.

The flaw in the argument seems to me obvious. There is all the difference in the world between "not taking notice" and "denying," between "denying any link" with somebody and "negating" his otherness; and for a sane person there is still a considerable distance to travel from this theoretical "negation" to killing, torturing, and enslaving.

Most of the above quotations are drawn from R. D. Laing and D. G. Cooper, *Reason and Violence. A Decade of Sartre's Philosophy, 1950–1960*, London, 1964. Part Three. This seems legitimate because Sartre in his foreword says: "*J'ai lu attentivement l'ouvrage que vous avez bien voulu me confier et j'ai eu le grand plaisir d'y trouver un exposé très clair et très fidèle de ma pensée.*"

XIII, page 80, note, 13

It would be interesting to know if, and to what an extent, the alarming rate of unsolved crimes is matched not only by the well-known spectacular rise in criminal offenses but also by a definite increase in police brutality. The recently published *Uniform Crime Report for the United States*, by J. Edgar Hoover (Federal Bureau of Investigation, United States Department of Justice, 1967), gives no indication how many crimes are actually solved – as distinguished from "cleared by arrest" – but does mention in the Summary that police solutions of serious crimes declined in 1967 by 8 percent. Only 21.7 percent (or 21.9 percent of all crimes are "cleared by arrest," and of these only 75 percent could be turned over to the courts, where only about 60 percent of the indicted were found guilty! Hence, the odds in favor of the criminal are so high that the constant rise in criminal offenses seems only natural. Whatever the causes for the spectacular decline of police efficiency, the decline of police power is evident, and with it the likelihood of brutality increases. Students and other demonstrators are like sitting ducks for police who have become used to hardly ever catching a criminal.

A comparison of the situation with that of other countries is difficult because of the different statistical methods employed. Still, it appears that, though the rise of undetected crime seems to be a fairly general problem, it has nowhere reached such alarming proportions as in America. In Paris, for instance, the rate of solved crimes declined from 62 percent in 1967 to 56 percent in 1968, in Germany from 73.4 percent in 1954 to 52.2 percent in 1967, and in Sweden 41 percent of crimes were solved in 1967. (See "Deutsche Polizei," in *Der Spiegel*, April 7, 1967.)

Notes

1 *Herrn Eugen Dührings Umwälzung der Wissenschaft* (1878), Part II, ch. 3.

2 See appendix II, p. 84.

3 The students caught between the two superpowers and equally disillusioned by East and West, "inevitably pursue some third ideology, from Mao's China or Castro's Cuba." (Spender, *op. cit.*, p. 92.) Their calls for Mao, Castro, Che Guevara, and Ho Chi Minh are like pseudo-religious incantations for saviors from another world; they would also call for Tito if only Yugoslavia were farther away and less approachable. The case is different with the Black Power movement; its ideological commitment to the nonexistent "Unity of the Third World" is not sheer romantic nonsense. They have an obvious interest in a black–white dichotomy; this too is of course mere escapism – an escape into a dream world in which Negroes would constitute an overwhelming majority of the world's population.

4 It seems as though a similar inconsistency could be charged to Marx and Lenin. Did not Marx glorify the Paris Commune of 1871, and did not Lenin want to give "all power to the *soviets*"? But for Marx the Commune was no more than a transitory organ of revolutionary action, "a lever for uprooting the economical foundations of . . . class rule," which Engels rightly identified with the likewise transitory "dictatorship of the Proletariat." (See *The Civil War in France*, in Karl Marx and F. Engels, *Selected Works*, London, 1950, Vol. I, pp. 474 and 440, respectively.) The case of Lenin is more complicated. Still, it was Lenin who emasculated the *soviets* and gave all power to the party.

5 *The Power Elite*, New York, 1956, p. 171; Max Weber in the first paragraphs of *Politics as a Vocation* (1921). Weber seems to have been aware of his agreement with the Left. He quotes in the context Trotsky's remark in Brest-Litovsk, "Every state is based on violence," and adds, "This is indeed true."

6 Bertrand de Jouvenel, *Power: The Natural History of Its Growth* (1945), London, 1952, p. 98.

7 *The Federalist*. No. 49.

8 Passerin d'Entrèves, *The Notion of the State: An Introduction to Political Theory*, Oxford, 1967, p. 7. Cf. also p. 171, where, discussing the exact meaning of the words "nation" and "nationality," he rightly insists that "the only competent guides in the jungle of so many different meanings are the linguists and the historians. It is to them that we must turn for help." And in distinguishing authority and power, he turns to Cicero's *potestas in populo, auctoritas in senatu*.

9   There is such a thing as authoritarian government, but it certainly has nothing in common with tyranny, dictatorship, or totalitarian rule. For a discussion of the historical background and political significance of the term, see my "What is Authority?" in *Between Past and Future: Exercises in Political Thought*, New York, 1968, and Part I of Karl-Heinz Lübke's valuable study, *Auctoritas bei Augustin*, Stuttgart, 1968, with extensive bibliography.

10 Sheldon Wolin and John Schaar, in "Berkeley: The Battle of People's Park," *New York Review of Books*, June 9, 1969, are entirely right: "The rules are being broken because University authorities, administrators and faculty alike, have lost the respect of many of the students." They then conclude, "When authority leaves, power enters." This too is true, but, I am afraid, not quite in the sense they meant it. What entered first at Berkeley was student power, obviously the strongest power on every campus simply because of the students' superior numbers. It was in order to break this power that authorities resorted to violence, and it is precisely because the university is essentially an institution based on authority, and therefore in need of respect, that it finds it so difficult to deal with power in nonviolent terms. The university today calls upon the police for protection exactly as the Catholic church used to do before the separation of state and church forced it to rely on authority alone. It is perhaps more than an oddity that the severest crisis of the church as an institution should coincide with the severest crisis in the history of the university, the only secular institution still based on authority. Both may indeed be ascribed to "the progressing explosion of the atom 'obedience' whose stability was allegedly eternal," as Heinrich Böll remarked of the crisis in the churches. See "Es wird immer später," in *Antwort an Sacharow*, Zürich, 1969.

11 In ancient Greece, such an organization of power was the polis, whose chief merit, according to Xenophon, was that it permitted the "citizens to act as bodyguards to one another against slaves and criminals so that none of the citizens may die a violent death." (*Hiero*, IV, 3.)

12 "Can We Limit Presidential Power?" in *The New Republic*, April 6, 1968.

13 See appendix XIII, p. 84.

14 "If one reads the SDS publications one sees that they have frequently recommended provocations of the police as a strategy for 'unmasking' the violence of the authorities." Spender (*op. cit.*, p. 92) comments that this kind of violence "leads to doubletalk in which the provocateur is playing at one and the same time the role of assailant and victim." The war on hypocrisy harbors a number of great dangers, some of which I examined briefly in *On Revolution*, New York, 1963, pp. 91–101.

15 Frantz Fanon, *The Wretched of the Earth*, Grove Press, 1968, p. 47.

16 J. Glenn Gray, *The Warriors* (New York, 1959; now available in paperback), is most perceptive and instructive on this point. It should be read by everyone interested in the practice of violence.

17 Fanon, *op. cit.*, pp. 85 and 93, respectively.

18 Robert M. Fogelson, "Violence as Protest," in *Urban Riots: Violence and Social Change*, Proceedings of the Academy of Political Science, Columbia University, 1968.

2

POWER, VIOLENCE, AND LEGITIMACY: A READING OF HANNAH ARENDT IN AN AGE OF POLICE BRUTALITY AND HUMANITARIAN INTERVENTION

.

Iris Marion Young

In the spring of 1999 I was completing a book on democracy. Its arguments assume a basic commitment to democratic values – the rule of law, liberty, equal respect, and a desire to work out disagreement through discussion. Suddenly I was paralyzed in my work. With NATO bombs raining on Yugoslavia, reflection on the essentially non-violent values of democracy felt irrelevant at best and arrogantly privileged at worst.

While living in Vienna in 1998 I had followed with horror the escalating attacks by Serbian soldiers on both armed and unarmed Albanian Kosovars, which seemed more immediate there than they had in the United States. Thus in the early months of 1999 I had hoped that the negotiations including the United States, Western European countries, Russia, and Yugoslavia would succeed in stopping this violence. When European negotiators delivered their final offer and it was rejected by Yugoslavia, for a few days I swallowed the self-righteous rhetoric of United States and European leaders, and I approved of the NATO war.

When it became clear that the war made the Serbian army more able and willing than before to force the flight of hundreds of thousands of Albanian Kosovars, and that NATO had foreseen these consequences without planning a response to them, I was dumbstruck. When it further appeared that NATO's strategy was to target civilians and cripple the economy of an entire country, I was overcome with shame and rage. Obsessed with this war and the fact that it was being waged by nineteen of the world's democracies, none of which had consulted with their citizens, I felt impelled to think about violence. But where could I turn to help me think? In this moment of rupture I reopened one of the only works of recent political theory that reflects specifically on the theme of violence, Hannah Arendt's essay, "On Violence."

Arendt there notes that political theorists have rarely reflected on violence as such. While there is a long tradition of theoretical writing on warfare, most of this theorizes strategy, balance of power, or the meaning of sovereignty violation, rather than reflecting specifically on the meaning and use of violence *per se*. Forty years later, her observation remains goods. Although the last decades of the twentieth century saw acts of violent horror that mock mid-century pledges of "never again," most contemporary political theorists have neglected systematic reflection on violence in public affairs.[2] Perhaps just as remarkable, in the vast recent literature interpreting and extending Arendt's ideas, there is little focused discussion about her conceptualization of violence and the logic of its relation to other key political concepts.[3]

In this essay I focus on Arendt's small text on violence, which distills and expands some of the insights and positions she developed in other texts, such as *The Origins of Totalitarianism, On Revolution,* and *The Human Condition.*[4] "On Violence" is a dense and suggestive essay. I find its positions confusing and that Arendt does not follow through on an elaboration of some of its important distinctions. Her central and self-consciously counter-intuitive claim is that power and violence are opposites. I aim to make sense of this contentious claim, and to explain how it challenges commonly accepted understandings of the relationship of state power and violence. I shall elaborate Arendt's claim that violence may sometimes be justified, but it cannot be legitimate. Through this reading of Arendt I will reflect on and evaluate manifestations of official violence which I believe enjoys too much acceptance in contemporary societies: the use of violent means by police and military intervention that claims to protect human rights.

Prelude: Clearing Away the Mess

Written at the height of the Vietnam War and in the wake of campus protest all over the world, "On Violence" reveals Arendt as the arrogant conservative many of us wish she were not. Despite her theoretical praise for council democracy, when something like it erupts on campus lawns in her neighborhood, Arendt reacts more like an annoyed professor than a republican citizen. She shares with the student protesters a revulsion of the war in Vietnam; indeed, this is one of her motives for writing the essay. She thinks that the logic of the student movements undermines the spirit of the university, however, especially when students demand to study subjects they deem more "relevant" than the standard curriculum.

Anti-war activists and curriculum reformers, however, apparently are not the people most to be feared. It is the "appearance of the Black Power movement on the campuses" (p. 75, this volume) that most disturbs her. Arendt heaps contempt on these students who demand courses in "non-existent subjects" like women's studies or Black studies, and asserts that this movement has succeeded in forcing universities to admit unqualified students. Arendt thought that universities were going to hell, that student radicals, especially Black student radicals, were responsible for this sorry situation, and that this tragedy was symptomatic of a general loss of public reason.

The interest of Black radicals, she says, is to lower academic standards, and to bring the cries of brute social need to ivied halls, where their din drowns out all deliberation. Influenced by Sartre, Fanon, Mao, Che, and other confused and dangerous revolutionaries, the Black student movement celebrates violence, and in so doing it abandons the nobility of the Civil Rights movement. "To expect people, who have not the slightest notion of what the *res publica*, the public thing, is, to behave non-violently and argue rationally in matters of interest is neither realistic nor reasonable" (p. 78). Arendt's attitude toward student radicals and especially toward Black radicals, as expressed in this text, is embarrassing and offensive. As some important recent commentary on Arendt's writing as a public intellectual points out, Arendt had a poor understanding of racism in America and of the movements around her resisting it.[5]

The text has other political flaws. Arendt surely overdraws the distinction between Marx, who for all his commitment to an idea of progress never gave up an understanding of praxis, and twentieth-century Marxism, in the persons of Sartre and Fanon, which she regards as naive, dangerous, corrupted, and mechanistic. In this text as in others, moreover, Arendt insists that the entrance of need onto the public stage of modernity leads to nothing but mischief. Many have argued that she is simply wrong about this, and I agree with them.[6] Arendt's ideas have many such problems and prejudices, but I do not need to repeat the criticisms that others have well made. The core conceptualization of violence and power that I wish to elaborate from Arendt's suggestive reflections, however, can be disentangled from these other concerns and set out on its own. Contemporary politics can learn much from doing so.

Violence as Rational and Instrumental

I find no definition of violence in Arendt's essay. I shall assume that by "violence" we mean acts by human beings that aim physically to cause pain to, wound, or kill other human beings, and/or damage or destroy animals and things that hold a significant place in the lives of people. Active threats to wound or kill also fall under a concept of violence.[7] In this essay Arendt reflects not on any and all forms and occasions of violence, but on violence in public affairs, those actions and events where individuals and groups express aggression, hate, disagreement, and conflict concerning issues of government and rules, coexistence and exclusion, etc., in violent ways. In this essay Arendt aims to overturn several misconceptions about such political violence. Before dwelling on the most important of those, namely Arendt's claim that violence is confused conceptually with power, I shall briefly review another mistake political theorists make about violence, according to Arendt.

One reason that few philosophers choose to theorize about violence, Arendt suggests, may be that they believe that violence is irrational and unpredictable. On this understanding, violence is pervasive but senseless. It ruptures routine, breaks and destroys people and things, but because of its unpredictability and irrationality there is little that theory can say about it. This statement is partly true and partly false. Violence is unpredictable in the same way that action is unpredictable, but it is not usually irrational.

A key characteristic of violence, says Arendt, is its reliance on instruments, the instruments of destruction. Violence is more or less fierce in proportion to the ability of its instruments to inflict damage and destruction on people and things. Not only does violence usually involve the use of instruments, the technical development and number of which magnify destructive effects, but the wounds and killing wrought in acts of violence are usually themselves instrumental. Wanton acts of violence are less common than calculated, deliberate, planned, and carefully executed violent stratagems aimed at specific objectives. In that sense most acts of violence are rational. They are, however, also unpredictable for the same reason that action itself is unpredictable.

In *The Human Condition* Arendt develops her particular concept of action, and distinguishes it from labor and work. Human activity counts as action insofar as it consists in initiative, in bringing something uniquely new into the world. An action is not predetermined from antecedent conditions. Consequently action is subject to interpretation. The agent has purposes of his or her own construction, which have their place in a narrative of his or her character and plans. Unlike labor or production, for Arendt, action is essentially social because it takes place in relation to others' plans and meanings. For this reason not only is an action unpredictable, a rupture of routine, but so is the reaction of others to an action. Action is an expression of natality, beginning, not only because it ruptures routine, but also because the response of others makes its consequences unpredictable. To the extent that people engage in violence as means to enact their purposes, violence is also unpredictable, a rupture in the course of events.

Violence appears as the most salient unpredictable phenomenon in human affairs only because modern theory tries to conceptualize politics within a science which can render its events predictable. Efforts to turn the study of politics into a science, according to Arendt, are as old as Plato. In their modern form, these efforts construct public affairs and the course of history as subject to regularities. Arendt mentions two models of history and politics as in principle predictable: an organic model and a production model. The organic model treats history and social change as like biological processes. The seeds of the present are in the past; societies and regimes grow, reach maturity, and eventually decay and die. Under the pens of thinkers such as Nietzsche and Sorel, Arendt suggests, violence becomes as inevitable in history as death is in nature. Violence can even become a positive aspect of politics in this framework, because it prunes away the dead wood and generates new growth.

The production model, on the other hand, imagines political events as under the control of a planner guiding them to their intended end. Many revolutionaries of both right and left act as though politics can realize a social plan. Those who try to reduce politics to bureaucratic administration display a similar image of public affairs as ideally under the control of rational plans and well-honed instruments which properly trained people can use to bring about predictable consequences. This productive model can also give a neutral or positive place to violence in history; to produce something out of raw material it is necessary to do violence to its initial form.

Perhaps noticing the instrumental character of violence accounts for its being inserted into a production model of politics. Both the production model and the organic model of politics and history, however, deny the specificity of human affairs as *action*. They endeavor to dissolve the novelty of human actions into instances of general trends and tendencies. Violence is closer to action than production, insofar as it constitutes a rupture in predictable routines, insofar as it relates subjects to one another, and insofar as the performer cannot predict its consequences because he or she cannot predict how others will react. While violence is connected to the realm of action in these ways, Arendt's main claim in this essay is that violence should be distinguished from power, understood as the capacity for collective action.

Confusion of Violence with Power

Perhaps another reason that political theorists reflect so little on violence as such, Arendt suggests, is that they assume that violence is already subsumed under their subject matter when they theorize political power. Theorists and political actors typically confuse violence with power. They either take power to be based on the capacity for violence, or they conceptualize violence as an extension of power. Arendt's main task in this essay is to distinguish these two concepts. I shall elaborate the meaning of her distinction, and argue that it has important normative implications.

Political philosophy should be careful to distinguish several apparently close concepts: power, force, strength, authority, and violence. Force is a strictly physical concept, the energy that moves and resists inertia, what imposes constraints or breaks through them. Strength counts as the ability both to exert and to resist force. A body is strong insofar as it can overcome the resistance of another, or insofar as it resists the force that aims to act upon, move, or transform it. A person is strong just insofar as he or she moves against the resistance of things and persons. Strength is indivisible and resides only in one body. Use of strength to exert force, though, can be magnified through instruments. By acquiring instrumental means of exerting force for the sake of destruction and the threat of destruction, individuals or groups often can induce the compliance of others with their commands or wishes. Violence relies on force and strength, and magnifies them with instruments.

Arendt insists, however, that power is conceptually and practically entirely different from violence. Power consists in collective action. Power is the ability of persons jointly to constitute their manner of living together, the way they organize their rules and institutions through reciprocal self-understanding of what the rules are and how they foster cooperation. Thus power relies not on bodies and instruments that exert force, but primarily on speech – the interpretation of meaning, the articulation of new ideas, the dynamics of persuasion, the linking of understanding and action. Power establishes and maintains institutions, that is, regulated and settled means of cooperating to bring about collective ends. It has its basis and continuance in the consent and support of those who abide by, live according to, and interpret rules and institutions to bring about new collective ends. Those who engage in collective action must communicate and cooperate, discuss their problems and jointly make plans. Insofar as successful institutions mobilize the cooperation of a large number of people in their operations, who understand the meaning and goals of the institutions, know the rules, and in general endorse their operations, they embody power.

Power is distinct from strength in that it exists *between* people rather than in them. Power is a feature of action and interaction insofar as people understand one another's words and deeds and coordinate with one another to achieve mutually understood ends. Thus power involves some kind of agreement, whether in word or action. Those who participate in the collective action that founds and maintains institutions and the enactment of their ends must know what they are doing and engage with one another to coordinate their actions.[8]

With these distinctions, Arendt stands opposed to a major tendency in modern political theory. She holds that the confusion of violence with power stems from a common understanding of state power as the exercise of sovereign domination. Political power, on this view, is nothing other than the rule of some over others, the exercise of command and successful obedience. While Max Weber is hardly alone in this view, his theory of the state may have exerted the most influence over contemporary thinking. For Weber, the state is the monopoly over the legitimate use of violence. In this paradigm, state and law are founded on the capacity for violence: the state and its legal system is simply the vehicle that a hegemonic group creates for itself to further its purposes, maintain itself in power, and rule over the rest.[9]

Arendt agrees that if in fact political power, government, means simply that state officials of whatever sort – kings, lords, presidents, cabinet ministers, generals – exercise dominion over the territory and actions of power, then power and violence are sensibly associated. There is no doubt that many rulers have relied on killing or torture and their threats to induce compliance with their wills and goals from subjects, and that they often succeed. "If the essence of power is the effectiveness of command, then there is no greater power than that which grows out of the barrel of a gun" (p. 37).

Arendt argues, however that the success and stability of even despotic regimes over a long term depends on eliciting the voluntary cooperation of at least a large mass of subjects with rulers and institutions that enact their living together and their common projects, that is on power understood as collective action. Even government understood as sovereign dominion depends for its success on a regularity of mutually understood, cooperative activities, and in this respect on the consent of those ruled.

Historically, such consent and support were often tied to beliefs in the *authority* of the rulers. Government as sovereignty has rested on the use of violence far less than on belief systems which have anointed certain individuals or groups with the *right* to the service and obedience of others. Ideologies of authority construct the ground of right in values and personages that transcend politics and mundane narrative time. Authoritarian hierarchical systems of government derive their power to a great extent from the commitment of subjects to these beliefs in the transcendent ground of the right to rule.[10] Thus Arendt suggests in "On Violence" that we should also distinguish the concept of authority from power. Authority is the quality of receiving unquestioned recognition and obedience as appeal to a transcendent origin from which the ruler's right derives. Power, on the other hand, in the sense of collective action, depends on persuading one another in the here and now to cooperate.

Modernity erodes authority, according to Arendt; the disenchantment of the world means it becomes more difficult for rulers to succeed in eliciting obedience by appealing to unquestioned transcendent foundations. The egalitarian and democratic impulses of modernity reject belief in the divine right of kings or the superior wisdom of philosopher princes that gives them the right of command. Moderns attempt to install science as a new kind of authority, and efforts to base a political hierarchy on expertism continue to be partially successful. The order of experts is not stable, however, because it rests on no timeless and otherworldly cosmology. Under these circumstances rulers who aim to exercise dominion over subjects must depend even more than before on the collective action of those ruled and their commitment to prevailing institutions and practices.

This fact becomes most apparent if and when people withdraw their consent, when people begin to act collectively toward different ends than those the rulers intend or desire. Rulers are helpless before such a shift in power. If they have the means of violence at their disposal – which usually means depending on the power of organized armies – they can attempt to impose their will on a disobedient public through force. The ruler can bomb neighborhoods, eliminate opponents, and keep a threatening watch over people to limit their ability to communicate and cooperate. Violence and the threat of violence can in this way destroy power, but never create or sustain it. Since power depends on collective action, it rests on the freedom of a plurality of distinct individuals aiming to foster their institutions. The tyrant who rules through violence is relatively impotent. While he may prevent action and resistance, and may be able to enforce service of his needs and desires, he can accomplish nothing worldly.

Of course history is cluttered with regimes structured by relations of ruler and subject, and these often rely on the threat of violence to compel obedience to the ruler's will when actions threaten to undermine or resist that will. But such regimes of domination are weak just insofar as they must depend on compulsion in this way. They are powerful only if the people they govern cooperate through consent and collective will sustaining the institutions in which they live together, express their meanings, and enact their collective goals.

Thus Arendt contrasts power and violence.

> Power and violence are opposites; where one rules absolutely, the other is absent. Violence appears where power is in jeopardy, but left to its own course it ends in power's disappearance. This implies that it is not correct to think of the opposite of violence as nonviolence; to speak of nonviolent power is already redundant. Violence can destroy power; it is ultimately incapable of creating it. (p. 80, this volume)[11]

Though violence and power are opposites in this conceptual and phenomenological sense, Arendt says that they often occur together. Although governments often rely on the use and threat of violence, systems of government that rest on command and obedience must also rely on the collective action of subjects – power – for their effectiveness. While movements to resist or overturn such regimes must mobilize mass power of collective organization to succeed, they often also use means of violence to aid their objectives. That epitome of violence, war, is also an example of power. A disciplined army depends on the solidarity of its soldiers, their willingness to work together and protect each other under stress.

Power and violence are opposites, but they often occur together. This sounds contradictory.[12] By interpreting Arendt's distinction between violence and power not only as conceptual, but also as *normative*, we can make sense of this statement. While violence and power *in fact* often occur together, they need not, and they *ought not*, at least not often and not very much. The interpretation of governance that identifies it with sovereign dominion is problematic because it conceives political power as necessarily oppressive, and living under government as necessarily a denial of freedom. There is another interpretation of government that does not assume the inevitability of a relation of command and obedience, and the necessary connection with violence these seem to entail. Arendt uses a Greek word for this alternative: *isonomy*. Jeffrey Isaac describes isonomy as "a concept of power and law whose essence did not rely on the command–obedience relation and which did not identify power and rule or law and command."[13] *Isonomy* names a process of governance as self-government, where the citizens have equal status and must rely on one another equally for developing collective goals and carrying them out. Just insofar as government in this form depends on speech and persuasion, it precludes violence and violence is its opposite. Government ought to be the exercise of power as the expression and result of people coming together, assessing their problems and collective goals, discussing together how to deal with them, and persuading one another to adopt rules and policies, then each self-consciously acting to effect them.

Arendt finds occasional historical bursts of sheer collective action and publicity, when a plurality of people through their mutual understanding and collective promising enact a public as the space of the appearance of singular and plural deeds and as the expressions of their freedom. People govern themselves by means of rules they formulate, understand, and trust one another to follow, as a condition of their own cooperative action. They enact collective projects that originate from their public deliberations upon their institutions, problems, and desires. In this fragile space of power there are no rulers to be obeyed, though there are often leaders and great persuaders.

> What makes a man a political being is his faculty of action; it enables him to get together with his peers, to act in concert, and to reach out for goals and enterprises that would never enter his mind, let alone the desires of his heart, had he not been given this gift – to embark on something new. (p. 82, this volume)

Such a statement about the meaning of political action – power in Arendt's sense – seems so abstract as to be vacuous. When people act in concert with their peers, what are they *doing*? What are these goals and enterprises that would otherwise never enter their minds, that are original ruptures in the passage of events, that exhibit this mysterious quality of natality? The question becomes even more acute when one takes account of Arendt's insistence that action is wholly distinct from labor and work, distinct from activities of producing what will meet needs and consuming those products, on the one hand, and from the fashioning of those works that not only build social surroundings, and serve as instruments of living and doing, but also stand as lasting monuments to a people and culture, on the other hand. If collective action neither serves the goals of building cathedrals nor producing food, then what are its goals and enterprises?

Some commentators have complained that Arendt's strong distinction between the social and the political is both unacceptably conservative and renders the concept of political power empty. Arendt decries what she perceives as a modern propensity for the public sphere and law increasingly to be dominated by discussion of how to alleviate *social* problems – poverty, unequal distribution of wealth, discrimination, urban blight and development, water and transportation planning, the organization of health care, and so on.[14] This deep distrust of an interest in bringing social issues into the light of public discussion partly explains her antipathy to the Black Power movement.

In the essay we are considering, Arendt's vitriolic remarks about bureaucracy are tied to this insistence that the political should not be tainted by the social. Attention to the social elevates the meeting of needs to the primary purpose of government, purges government of politics, and thereby levels it to the lowest common denominator.

Bureaucracy attempts to harness people's energies into a kind of machine in which the administration of things will meet needs. The goal of bureaucracy is to implement rules and procedures that determine routines that workers and clients can follow, rendering themselves fungible, to achieve production, distribution, and service delivery objectives as efficiently as possible. The purpose of bureaucracy, that is to say, is to reduce as much as possible any need for *action* in Arendt's sense.

> In a fully developed bureaucracy there is nobody left with whom one can argue, to whom one can present grievances, on whom the pressures of power can be exerted. Bureaucracy is the form of government in which everybody is deprived of political freedom, of the power to act; for the rule by Nobody is not no-rule, and where all are equally powerless we have a tyranny without a tyrant. (p. 82, this volume)

The bureaucratic principle is the opposite of power and collective action. Whereas people acting collectively are *mindful* of their goals and deliberate about the best means to achieve them, in the logic of bureaucracy the means are related to the ends not through opinion and deliberation, but through regulated routine, where distinct activities are efficiently organized. The whole point of bureaucratic logic is that participants should not have to think about how to achieve coordinated ends. Bureaucracies create hierarchies of command and obedience that are supposed to make the operation of routines more efficient. Just to the extent that people become disempowered, however, the bureaucracy becomes less able to fulfill its role of the administration of things and the meeting of needs. Its parts fail to coordinate; the system becomes irrational, or it becomes corrupt – its command mechanisms come to serve private gain rather than the achievement of collectively agreed upon ends. Thus even the effective pursuit of public administration depends on power in Arendt's sense – that people act collectively in a self-conscious way that involves deliberation, persuasion, and following through the collective will with implementation.

As I understand Arendt's concepts, the successful achievement of any socially organized ends depends on power. Collective action is awesome and monumental, but difficult to achieve and sustain. Military campaigns, imperial rule of extensive territory, the establishment of an effective health care service, and organization of a mass resistance movement that brings down a dictatorial regime, the conduct of constitutional dialogue over a period of years, these all require and manifest power in Arendt's sense. There seems to me to be no reason to exclude matters having to do with meeting needs, production and service provision, from the scope of activities to which such power can and should be brought to bear. It is not only bureaucratically organized meeting of needs that carries dangers of the dissipation or corruption of power; they all do. Power only exists as long as it is actively sustained by the plural participants in the endeavor who self-consciously coordinate with one another. If they withdraw their commitment or ease their communication, or if acts of violence break up their relationships, only a shell will be left.

Power, and the political, then, I interpret as an *aspect* of any social institution or collective activity, including some of those that enact sovereign dominion or repressive domination. Institutions cannot be effective for long unless they have occasions when participants set their collective goals, discuss what institutions, rules, and practices would best coordinate their actions to achieve those goals, and make commitments to one another to carry out their responsibilities in the system of cooperation.

Power is thus necessary for government, but it is also fragile. People easily and often lose this sense of public promise, and disperse into the impotent privacy of a concern for their own survival or pleasure. To the extent that governing institutions remain, they freeze into routinized bureaucracies, become cronyist semi-private operations, or elicit conformity through terror. The use of violence in public affairs is normatively question-able not only because killing and causing suffering are prima facie wrong. Violence is also morally problematic because its use, especially if routine, widespread, or massive, endangers power. "Violence appears where power is in jeopardy, but left to its own course it ends in power's disappearance" (p. 80, this volume). When rulers or those who most benefit from a given order of things find that they or their goals lose popular support, they often try to restore their power through the use of violence. Such actions may well reduce resistance but they do not restore power. Violence not only harms individuals, but it makes their lives difficult to carry on as before. When either rulers or resisters adopt the use of violence as a regular means of trying to elicit the cooperation of others, they tend to produce the opposite effect: flight, retreat into privacy, preemptive strikes, distrust of all by all. The use of violence in politics is problematic, moreover, because its consequences so easily and often escalate beyond the specific intentions its uses have. Violent acts tend to produce violent responses that radiate beyond the original acts.

Arendt's concept of power is abstract and incomplete. Although she discusses people's movements and revolutions as well as the activities of governments, her theory tends to ignore structural social relations, and their manner of channeling power to the systematic advantage of some and the disadvantage of others. Her conceptual distinction between power and violence, however, which I have interpreted as having normative significance as well, opens important possibilities for rethinking the relations of power and freedom.

Legitimacy and Justification

Thus far in their essay I have reviewed Arendt's discussion of several confusions about violence and politics to which Arendt believes many theorists have been prone: that violence is irrational or inevitable, and most importantly, that violence is the basis of power. In the following passage she signals another common confusion which she traces to this confusion of violence and power:

> Power needs no justification, being inherent in the very existence of political commu-nities; what it does need is legitimacy. . . . Power springs up whenever people get together to act in concert, but it derives its legitimacy from the initial getting together rather than from any action that then may follow. Legitimacy, when challenged, bases itself on appeal to the past, while justification relates to an end that lies in the future. Violence can be justifiable, but it never will be legitimate. Its justification loses in plausibility the farther its intended end recedes into the future. (p. 79, this volume)

Like so much else in this text, Arendt's claims here are provocative and suggestive, but she does not elaborate them further. In this section I will try to follow through on this distinction between legitimacy and justification. Making sense of these claims is key for the arguments about official violence that I will make in the next section. Power does not need justification, but does require legitimacy; violence calls for justification, but it can never be legitimate. What does this mean?

Both legitimacy and justification are concepts of moral reasoning. Both concern ways of giving reasons for an action or structure. In the passage quoted, Arendt offers only one hint about the difference in these forms of giving an account: legitimation appeals to the past, while justification appeals to the future in relation to the act.

To find more texts that will help unlock this mystery one can turn to *On Revolution*. There Arendt draws a connection between power, in the sense of original collective action, and the activity of founding new institutions which can preserve that power and give it embodiment in law.

> Power comes into being only if and when men join themselves together for the purpose of action, and it will disappear when, for whatever reason, they disperse and desert one another. Hence, binding and promising, combining and covenanting are the means by which power is kept in existence.... Just as promises and agreements deal with the future and provide stability in the ocean of future uncertainty where the unpredictable may break in from all sides, so the constituting, founding, and world-building capacities of men concern always not so much ourselves and our own time on earth as our "successor" and "posteriorities."[15]

Power consists in collective action, people coming together and supporting one another to do deeds and accomplish goals the like of which "would never enter his mind, let alone the desires of his heart, had he not been given this gift" ("On Violence," p. 82, this volume). Power is often fleeting, however; it springs out of relations between people who accomplish something, and then dissipates. For power to be a force in politics, it needs to be institutionalized, and this is what foundings accomplish. In founding a constitution the empowered collective gives itself relative permanence, a permanence guaranteed through covenants. In the moment of founding, participants in a public mutually promise to abide by principles that guide institutions, to organize and give their energy to the implementation of the institutions, and to be loyal to the institutions and to one another through them. The mutuality of promise making is important for Arendt. She cites the spirit of American revolutionaries who, she says, found legitimate power only in the reciprocity and mutuality of promises made between equals, as distinct from the spurious power of kings and aristocrats, which was not founded on mutual promising.

Arguments that government actions, policies, laws, or representatives are legitimate, then, are backward looking because they refer to founding promises. To say that these leaders or policies are legitimate is to make the argument that they are in conformity with, a present embodiment of, the principles and promises that institutionalize the public's power. Making such an argument, I suggest, requires more than the recital of a history or the citation of founding documents. An argument for the legitimacy of present officials, actions, or laws, I suggest, involves a *renewal* of the power that came into play in the original process, which itself reaffirms the promises, a new commitment of the collective's participants to one another on terms of mutuality and reciprocity. To argue that a government or policy or action is legitimate in these ways does not itself imply that they are just, right, or good. To the extent that institutionalizing power involves *mutual* promising, however, there is an implicit commitment to the justice or rightness of principles to guide future action, at least as concerning relations with one another.

With this notion of legitimation we can notice another important difference between Weber and Arendt. Despite his identification of the state with sovereign dominion that rests on monopoly over the means of violence, Weber agrees with Arendt that the naked imposition of domination by continual force and violence is an unsteady basis for ruling. State power is most stable, according to Weber, when it carries legitimacy. Weber's concept of legitimacy, however, is positivistic. Rulers have legitimacy for him just insofar as their subjects accept some rationalization of their ruling position. This could be a religious story about their divine right, or it could be a story about their aristocratic natures, or about how their greater intelligence or skill make them suited for leadership. Or it could be a story about how people have agreed to establish a constitution. As I understand Weber, the content of the story does not matter as much as that it functions to elicit consent from subjects.[16]

In the passage I quoted from *On Revolution*, Arendt distinguishes mutual promise and covenant that gives power legitimacy from simple consent. I take it that consent is only the absence of opposition and resistance, a willingness on the part of subjects to go along with the rules and decrees, and such consent usually has some basis in belief. Each subject consents alone, however, in relation to the state. Covenants to which accounts of the legitimacy of political officials and actions appeal, on the other hand, are public, indeed they are the effects and institutionalizations of publics that emerge from collective action.

As I understand Arendt's distinction, justification is a less complex affair than legitimation. First, only an action whose moral value is *in question* requires justification. This is why Arendt says that power needs no justification. The default position for power is that it is valuable; acting in concert enables a unique and wonderful kind of freedom that human beings experience in no other way. The default position for violence, on the other hand, is that it is a disvalue. Violence destroys, and it is not very violent unless it destroys valuable things – human lives or things meaningful to human lives and action.

Thus any act of violence calls for justification, account of why it is morally acceptable. When Arendt claims that such an account is always forward looking, she refers to the instrumental character of violence. A justification of violence can only appeal to the good it brings about, its consequences. Justification of violence cannot be retrospective in the ways that arguments about legitimacy are, because violence is always a rupture that breaks through the continuity of the present with the past. Arendt claims that the plausibility of a justification for violence declines the further its intended good consequence recedes into the future.

Arendt does not offer criteria for what justifies violence in politics. A thorough account would require more space than I have in this essay. The argument I will make next about official violence, however, presupposes some understanding of the limits of the justification of violence. I will assume that most acts of violence cannot be morally justified; they are in the service of wrongful efforts on the part of some people to dominate and coerce others into doing what they want, or to remove the resistance of others. A narrow range of violent actions may be justified, however, according to such considerations as the following: whether they are likely to prevent serious harm, under circumstances where other preventive measures are not available; and whether they are constrained in their consequences, that is, do not have harmful consequences that reach beyond their immediate effect, whether intended or unintended. Few real-world acts of violence satisfy these conditions, I suggest, especially in the context of politics and public affairs.

There is a final aspect to the distinction between the legitimation of power and the justification of violence that I interpret from Arendt's hints. Whereas arguments about the legitimacy of one act or policy can often appeal to previous arguments about legitimacy, arguments justifying violence cannot appeal as such to precedent. As I said above, there is a kind of default character to legitimacy that justifications of violence do not share. If it can be shown that a government is legitimate, then the presumption follows that its acts and policies are legitimate. The legitimacy of one law or policy helps reinforce the legitimacy of others. This is appropriate if legitimacy corresponds to a web of institutionalized power expressing the mutual commitments of a public. Because any act of violence is a rupture that endangers that potential or actual commitment and mutuality, however, each act of violence must be justified on its own, on a case by case basis, not by appeal to similar acts from the past, but by argument about its particular unique circumstances and consequences. While there may be very general moral principles and criteria that can be used in such arguments, no institution or authority can produce a set of rules that morally legitimate acts of violence in advance.

Official Violence

I will now apply this interpretation of the opposition of power and violence to a particular class of violent acts: those perpetrated by agents of the state as a means to achieve their mission of law enforcement. The two differing interpretations of state power that I have reviewed – the Weberian and the Arendtian – yield two radically different understandings of official violence. A Weberian interpretation finds the threat and use of violence to be an essential and normal component of the actions of legitimate state officials in carrying out their duties. The critical view of violence that I find in Arendt, on the other hand, along with her theory of power as collective action, imply that official violence is always questionable, and thus requires justification. Official violence often fails this justificatory test.

I examine official violence in two forms: police violence in domestic law enforcement and the use of military force by one or more states against another state or states with the aim of responding to violations of human rights or the threat of such violations. A Weberian interpretation of state power or sovereignty, I argue, has difficulty making sense of a concept of police brutality; Arendt's theory offers the conceptual means to do so. International "police actions" that claim to enforce international human rights law, or so-called humanitarian intervention, can be theorized on analogy with domestic law enforcement criteria. If one accepts Arendt's distinction between violence and power, I shall argue, then acts of so-called humanitarian intervention become questionable.

Police brutality

Arendt herself thematizes police brutality in her essay. She embeds her impassioned criticism of this mode of official violence in an arrogant interpretation of the student radicalism and Black community activism. Recall that she heaps contempt on students who demand courses in "non-existent subjects" like women's studies or Black studies, and asserts that these movements have succeeded in forcing universities to admit unqualified students by threatening violence.

Given these deep prejudices against student radicalism, it is especially interesting that she reserves the worst condemnation for official violence – for the impotent bigness of the United States and the Soviet Union amassing their weapons of mass destruction, and for the police who respond to protesters with gas, batons, and guns. Police brutality against essentially nonviolent demonstrations is responsible for radicalizing the student movement. Violent and massive police attacks on protesters at the Democratic Party convention in Chicago in 1968 were a sign of the utter impotence of both the Chicago city administration, its police force, and the members of the ruling Establishment of the country. When officials have lost power – that is, when they no longer have the support and cooperation of masses of people – they rarely resist the temptation to substitute violence for power. Almost inevitably, however, the resort to violence further undermines power, and violence becomes a senseless and irrational end in itself.

In one of her appendices Arendt hypothesizes that police brutality is linked to police inefficiency. To the extent that the police force is unable to prevent crimes or solve those committed, they resort to acts of naked violence against people in the streets. Whether or not her claimed correlations are correct, she expresses a judgment few juries in the US today share: it is not the prerogative of police officers to brutalize citizens when attempting to perform their duties. Arendt worries about a Black racism that responds with violent rage to "ill-designed integration policies whose consequences their authors can easily escape" (p. 77). She seems to fear a ragged horde rising up from the privacy of its poverty to obliterate what little is left of a civilized public sphere. She judges more horrible, however, the prospect of a white racist backlash in which "the climate of opinion in the country might deteriorate to the point where a majority of its citizens would be willing to pay the price of the invisible terror of a police state for law and order in the streets" (p. 77). Such words make an eerie echo in this age where prison-building is a growth industry, sweeping homeless people from the streets with fire hoses has become common, and the number of executions has quadrupled in ten years.

Today, it seems to me, perhaps even more than at the time Arendt wrote these words, we have "a kind of police backlash, quite brutal and highly visible." This is something that political philosophers do not generally discuss. In the late 1990s the United Stated Justice Department, not exactly a promoter of nonviolence and quiet reason in law enforcement, nevertheless found that some of the routine behavior of police departments in cities like Pittsburgh, PA was so egregious in its violation of the rights of citizens that it ordered and supervised changes. In Chicago front-page headlines reported at least a dozen questionable police shootings of citizens in 2000. Other citizen complaints are too numerous to report; local protests against policy brutality are nearly as regular as church services, but I sense little outrage among most of my neighbors. In November 1999 in Seattle we saw a police riot reminiscent of the Chicago of 1968 that Arendt condemns.

On those rare occasions when police are put on trial for their acts of violence against citizens, juries usually absolve them of guilt. Even in cases where unarmed people have been shot dead by several police officers, they and their advocates have been able to convince juries that their actions fall within their proper line of duty and that their role gives them discretion to use violence when they interpret a situation as requiring it to do their job. Arendt is probably right to suggest that one explanation for why such police violence is so little questioned is that many people believe that it will be used primarily to contain a minority that does not include them. I suggest that an additional explanation for a relatively widespread willingness to condone or excuse official violence results from the ideology of state power that understands it as founded in violence.

The idea that the state is nothing but monopoly of the legitimate use of violence slides easily for many people into the idea that the use of violence by legitimate agents of a legitimate state is itself legitimate. On this account, since the power of the state is ultimately grounded in control over the means of violence, the use of violence by agents of the state is simply an extension and expression of their power. It matters for this account that the state is legitimate, that it brings about and enforces a rule of law, that its agents obtain their offices through proper procedures and so on. Given a legitimate state whose officials are trying to enforce the law, however, many people think that the maintenance of such "law and order" requires the "show of force." Some might go further: law enforcement officials and other state agents ought to display their willingness to employ the means of violence in order to ensure obedience to the law, and they are most convincing in this display if they actually use violence on a regular basis.

Such an understanding of state power does have a concept of the abuse of power by police. When police use their power in ways that promote their personal gain, when they are corrupt or themselves criminal, they grossly abuse their power. A conception of state power which sees it as grounded in or inherently connected to violence, however, has great difficulty forming a concept of police brutality under circumstances when police believe they are properly doing their job. As long as the official is acting "in the line of duty" and claims that the violent acts are normal or necessary, it seems that many people find them morally acceptable.

As I have discussed above, on the alternative conceptualization suggested by Arendt, the power of states consists in the ways they institutionalize the ability for collective action. State institutions can organize decision making and executive bodies that mobilize to solve collective problems and then the energy to solve them. They actualize this potential only to the extent that people work in them with one another to bring about those results through consciously coordinated action. When state institutions fail to create and implement solutions to collective problems or enact collective visions, which is often, they lack power, and no amount of violence will compensate for that lack. Indeed, the use of violence against those who fail to join the effort is more likely to weaken the ability of the collective to act than to enhance it.

This does not mean that powerful state institutions cannot and should not sometimes force people to abide by its laws and regulations and contribute to its collective goals.

Coercion is an inevitable and proper aspect of legal regulation. The sovereigntist view of state power, however, too quickly equates coercion with the threat of violence. I do not have the space to develop a full argument for the claim here, but I suggest that successful coercion is usually more a result of power than of violence. Where there are settled laws and regulations whose objectives are clear and widely accepted, and which were legislated by means of legitimate procedures, then those who attempt to violate or circumvent the laws suffer various forms of sanction, shaming, and punishment often without any violence at all being brought to bear. Some people who would otherwise not do what these laws require are motivated to obey them because they fear these consequences, but this is not the same as saying that they are motivated by the threat of violence.

Arendt's account of power and violence suggests that the use of official violence is always deeply problematic and always calls for specific justification. It can never be regarded as normal and legitimate, because it cannot appeal to founding first principles that authorize it, and because each act of violence endangers the trust and security on which collective power rests. Some acts of official violence may be justified, but these can only be decided case by case according to restrictive criteria like those I outlined above: their scope is limited, their effects immediate and contained, and the harm they prevent worse than the one they inflict. Insofar as coercive regulation may rely on the use of physical restraint and force to subdue resisters, it may sometimes be justified. There ought to be the strongest presumption against the infliction of injury, however, let alone killing. My observation of contemporary police practices in the United States today, as well as many other places, leads me to conclude that both many police officers and citizens consider such acts a normal and acceptable extension of state power. Every specific act of official violence, however, needs as much justification as acts of violence committed by others, and nothing can legitimate them in advance.

Martha Minow points to a few cities in the United States that have embraced community policing as an alternative model by which to structure the entire practice of policing, where "the use of state power does not model the violence it is intended to prevent."[17] Community policing is a decades-old concept in the United States, of course; its concepts and practices in most cities, however, are confined only to a few neighborhoods or programs, alongside and in the context of more general models of policing that rely on threat and use of violence as normal. This balance should at least be reversed, with threats of violence infrequent and contained within a context of organized citizen cooperation and watchfulness.

So-called humanitarian intervention

The last two decades have seen swift support for the conviction that human rights principles should override the claim by states that sovereignty gives them absolute right to regulate what goes on in their territories in whatever way they choose. There is increasing support in the world for the principle that especially when there are serious and extensive violations of human rights by a state, or when a state is unable to protect its citizens from massive violence, that outside agents not only have a right but a duty to intervene to try to protect lives and well being. I endorse this general direction of international law that limits state sovereignty for the sake of promoting human rights. Nevertheless I find disturbing that some international actors appear to assume that such commitments to human rights themselves legitimate some states making war on others. Arendt's distinctions between power and violence, and particularly her argument that violence may sometimes be justified but never legitimate, are useful, I suggest, for reflecting on moral issues of so-called humanitarian intervention. I shall argue that these issues about the morally appropriate use of violence parallel those concerning domestic police action.

The judgment has become widespread that the sovereignty of states which seriously violate human rights can be overridden by outsiders who seek to prevent or sanction such violation. International law concerning human rights requires transparency and enforcement, and only state institutions have the powers these requirements imply. In the absence of global state institutions today, single states or coalitions of states recently have taken it upon themselves to act as global police, invading other states or bombing them from above, they claim for the purposes of enforcing human rights. The assumption seems to be strong that it is morally permissible and may be morally required for states to engage in military action against states that violate human rights.

A relatively new development in this evolving human rights regime consists in efforts to legitimate such interventions. Especially in the last decade, some of the world's strongest military powers and alliances have engaged in non-defensive military actions for which they have first sought and claimed to have received legal or quasi-legal authorization. Western powers sought and received the approval of the United Nations Security Council before they launched their war against Iraq. While the NATO war against Yugoslavia did not have the authorization of the United Nations, NATO claimed that it was legitimate because of the process of discussion and decision making that took place among the leaders of its nineteen members, as well as among a few states outside the alliance. In such processes, world military forces attempt to legitimate their actions when they appeal to international principles they claim have or ought to have the force of law, and when they can point to procedures of international discussion and decision making that they claim authorize their actions. The opinion seems to be taking hold of powerful international leaders and many of the general public, moreover, that the use of violence against rogue states is acceptable and normal, and needs little or no justification beyond a consensus that the state is a law breaker.

If Arendt's account of violence and power is right, however, such immediate and massive resort to violence as a tool of international law enforcement may be a sign of impotence more than power. I believe that this evolving situation where some states and perhaps also the United Nations speak and act as though they are legitimate agents empowered to do what they judge necessary to enforce the law may be at least as dangerous to peace and international stability as is international anarchy. There appears to be little international imagination for alternative methods of motivating or compelling compliance with human rights norms, and almost no international will to install competent institutions that could enact more settled discussion and cooperation among peoples of the world. When war, indeed devastating war, is almost the first resort of international police powers, and when states engage in what they believe is righteous violence, it opens gulfs of distrust.

On Arendt's account, the use of violence in international relations can be no more legitimate than in domestic life. While international violence, like domestic violence, may sometimes be justified, there too justification must be in terms of its consequences and not by appeal to any supposedly authorizing covenants or principles. Especially when air war and the use of indiscriminate weapons such as land mines are the preferred military means, the claim that such violence is justified is usually difficult to sustain in Arendt's terms: the destruction is too massive, the consequences too long term and unpredictable, too many lives are risked and lost, especially those of civilians. In this era when weapons of mass destruction continue to proliferate, their use against a state on one occasion stimulates their defensive accumulation by others. At the beginning of her essay Arendt declares that these frightful instruments of war have rendered such action irrational. "The technical development of implements of violence has now reached the point where no political goal could conceivably correspond to their destructive potential or justify their actual use in armed conflict. Hence, warfare – from time immemorial the final merciless arbiter in international disputes – has lost much of its effectiveness and nearly all its glamour" (p. 3).

So I will return to my beginning, the NATO war against Yugoslavia. There are significant similarities between this war and incidents of police brutality. NATO claimed that its actions were aimed at stopping the perpetration of crimes by a rogue state. That state had committed crimes against humanity, and NATO claimed to be acting as a legal agent for humanity itself, rather than acting to further its own specific treaty interests or the specific interests of its member nations. NATO officials spoke and acted as if this police-for-the-world role authorized it to use any and all military force in whatever way and for as long as necessary to achieve its objective, the military defeat of Yugoslavia and the capitulation of its president to the terms NATO set for the return of the Kosovar Albanians and the establishment of a government in which they would exercise self-government.

Both the conduct and outcome of the NATO war were disastrous, as far as I can tell, and morally wrong. The removal of the Organization for Security and Cooperation in Europe forces that had been in Kosovo to help keep the peace allowed Serbian forces to increase the level of terror it directed at the Kosovar Albanian people and force them to flee the province. As I mentioned above, NATO nations prepared neither themselves nor those most affected for a huge flood of refugees, and as a result many suffered greatly and unnecessarily. NATO chose to limit its action to an air war, which had the advantage of wreaking death and suffering on Serbians while risking hardly any Western European or North American lives. They bombed factories, urban and suburban residential neighborhoods, bridges, television stations, an embassy, and churches. The war was waged not against a state or regime, but against an entire people and society. The many civilians who were maimed or died as a result did not suffer from "collateral damage." They were victims of international police brutality.

Surely NATO cannot claim that more lives were saved by the war than were lost in it. Nor can NATO say that the Kosovar Albanians are better off today than they were in 1998: too many of their friends and family have died or been injured, too many of their homes, animals, businesses, and cultural institutions have been destroyed. The underground civilian shadow government they had built has all but disappeared, and they face a likely future of hostility with their neighbors. On the account of violence that I have derived from Arendt, war cannot be legitimated, as NATO tried to do, but it may perhaps be justified. Justification comes only by appeal to consequences, however, and by that account this war also cannot be justified.

Notes

1 Hannah Arendt, *On Violence* (New York: Harcourt Brace, 1969).

2 There are a few exceptions. See Ted Honderich, *Violence for Equality*, and Sergio Cotta, *Why Violence* (University of Florida Press, 1985).

3 John McGowan does focus specifically on the concept of violence in Arendt. See McGowan, "Must Politics be Violent? Arendt's Utopian Vision," in Craig Calhoun and John McGowan, eds., *Hannah Arendt and the Meaning of Politics* (Minneapolis: University of Minnesota Press, 1997), 263–96.

4 I am grateful to the following people for comments on an earlier version of this essay that saved me from much wrong-headedness: David Alexander, Bat-Ami Bar On, Leah Bradshaw, Michael Geyer, Bonnie Honig, Jeffrey Isaac, Patchen Markell, Martin Matustik, Nancy Rosenblum, Bill Scheverman, and Dana Villa.

5 See Robert Bernasconi, "The Double Face of the Political and the Social: Hannah Arendt and America's Racial Divisions," *Research in Phenomenology*, Vol. 26, 1996: 3–24; Anne Norton, "Heart of Darkness: Africa and African Americans in the Writings of Hannah Arendt," in Bonnie Honig, ed., *Feminist Interpretations of Hannah Arendt* (University Park: Pennsylvania State University Press, 1995), 247–62.

6 The best critique of Arendt's idea of the social and its separation from the political is Hanna Pitkin's. See *The Attack of the Blob* (Berkeley: University of California Press, 1999).

7 For the purposes of this essay, I am limiting discussion to physical forms of violence; their incidence is frequent and horrible enough to call urgently for inquiry. I recognize that there may well be phenomena of psychological violence, various ways that people are able to destroy the spirit of other persons without doing them bodily damage. Indeed, some of Arendt's other writings have rich veins to mine for such a concept of psychological violence. Because non-physical forms of violence present more serious conceptual problems, and because the phenomenon Arendt seems most concerned with in this essay is violence that involves bring physical pain to, wounds, or kills human beings, I limit my discussion here to that form.

8 *The Human Condition*, especially ch. 28.

9 Max Weber, "Politics as a Vocation," in H. H. Gerth and C. Wright Mills, eds., *From Max Weber* (New York: Oxford University Press, 1946), 77–8; Jürgen Habermas contrasts Weber's instrumental and positivistic view of state power with Arendt's view, which he interprets as more normative and based in communication. See Habermas, "Hannah Arendt on the Concept of Power," in *Philosophical–Political Profiles* (Cambridge, MA: MIT Press, 1983), 171–88.

10 See Arendt, "What is Authority?" in *Between Past and Future* (New York: Viking Press, 1961).

11 Compare Leah Bradshaw, "Political Authority and Violence," a paper presented at the Canadian Political Science Association meetings, Quebec City, August 2000.

12 Nancy C. M. Hartsock suggests that in fact Arendt does undermine her concept of power by saying that power and violence often occur together. See Hartsock, *Money, Sex and Power* (New York: Longman, 1983), 220–1.

13 Jeffrey Isaac, *Arendt, Camus and Modern Rebellion* (New Haven, CT: Yale University Press, 1992), 149.

14 See Pitkin, *The Attack of the Blob*.

15 Arendt, *On Revolution* (New York: Viking Press, 1965), 175.

16 Weber, "Politics as a Vocation," 79–81; "The Social Psychology of World Religions," in Gerth and Mills, *From Max Weber*, 294.

17 Martha Minow, "Between Nations and Between Intimates," unpublished ms., p. 27.

PART II

EXISTENTIALISM

REVOLUTIONARY PRAXIS AND THE DIALECTIC OF GROUPS AND INSTITUTIONS

3

SELECTIONS FROM *CRITIQUE OF DIALECTICAL REASON*

Jean-Paul Sartre

Everything we established in *The Problem of Method* follows from our fundamental agreement with historical materialism. But as long as we present this agreement merely as one option among others we shall have achieved nothing, and our conclusions will remain conjectural. I have proposed certain methodological rules; but they cannot be valid, in fact they cannot even be discussed, unless the materialist dialectic can be assumed to be true. It must be proved that a negation of a negation can be an affirmation, that conflicts – within a person or a group – are the motive force of History, that each moment of a series is *comprehensible* on the basis of the initial moment, though *irreducible* to it, that History continually effects totalizations of totalizations, and so on, before the details of an analytico-synthetic and regressive–progressive method can be grasped.

But these principles cannot be taken for granted; indeed most anthropologists (*anthropologistes*) would reject them....

There is a crisis in Marxist culture; there are many signs today that this crisis is temporary, but its very existence prohibits us from justifying the principles by their results.

The supreme paradox of historical materialism is that it is, at one and the same time, the only truth of History and a total *indetermination* of the Truth. The totalizing thought of historical materialism has established everything except its own existence. Or, to put it another way, contaminated by the historical relativism which it has always opposed, it has not exhibited the truth of History as it defines itself, or shown how this determines its nature and validity in the historical process, in the dialectical development of *praxis* and of human experience. In other words, we do not know what it means for a Marxist historian to *speak the truth*. Not that his statements are false – far from it; but he does not have the concept of *Truth* at his disposal....

So we must take up the whole problem once again, and explore the limits, the validity and the extent of dialectical Reason. We cannot deny that a *Critique* (in the Kantian sense of the term) of dialectical Reason can be made only by dialectical Reason itself; and indeed it must be allowed to ground itself and to develop itself as a free critique of itself, at the same time as being the movement of History and of knowledge.

This is precisely what has not been done until now: dialectical Reason has been walled up in dogmatism. . . .

If dialectical Reason is to be possible as the career of all and the freedom of each, as experience and as necessity, if we are to display *both* its total translucidity (it is no more than ourself) and its untranscendable severity (it is the unity of everything that conditions us), if we are to ground it as the rationality of *praxis*, of totalization, and of society's future, if we are then to *criticize* it as analytical Reason has been criticized, that is to say, if we are to determine its significance, then we must realize the situated experience of its apodicticity *through ourselves*. But let it not be imagined that this experience is comparable to the "intuitions" of the empiricists, or even to the kind of scientific experiments whose planning is long and laborious, but whose result can be observed instantaneously. The experience of the dialectic is itself dialectical: this means that it develops and organizes itself on all levels. At the same time, it is the very experience of living, since to live is to act and be acted on, and since the dialectic is the rationality of *praxis*. It must be *regressive* because it will set out from lived experience (*le vécu*) in order gradually to discover all the structures of *praxis*. . . .

When we have arrived at the most general conditionings, that is to say, at materiality, it will then be time to reconstruct, on the basis of the investigation, the schema of intelligibility proper to the totalization. This second part, which will be published later, will be what one might call a synthetic and progressive definition of "the rationality of action". In this connection, we shall see how dialectical Reason extends beyond analytical Reason and includes *within itself* its own critique and its own transcendence. However, the limited character of the project cannot be emphasized sufficiently. I have said — and I repeat — that the only valid interpretation of human History is historical materialism. So I shall not be restating here what others have already done a thousand times; besides, it is not my subject. . . .

Our real aim is theoretical. It can be formulated in the following terms: on what conditions is the knowledge *of a History* possible? To what extent can the connections brought to light be *necessary*? What is dialectical rationality, and what are its limits and foundation? Our extremely slight dissociation of ourselves from the letter of Marxist doctrine (which I indicated in *The Problem of Method*) enables us to see the meaning of this question as the disquiet of the genuine experience which refuses to collapse into non-truth. It is to this disquiet that we are attempting to respond. But I am far from believing that the isolated effort of an individual can provide a satisfactory answer — even a partial one — to so vast a question, a question which engages with the totality of History. If these initial investigations have done no more than enable me to define the problem, by means of provisional remarks which are there to be challenged and modified, and if they give rise to a discussion and if, as would be best, this discussion is carried on collectively in working groups, then I shall be satisfied. . . .

Before taking the discussion any further, we must make a clear distinction between the notions of totality and totalization. A totality is defined as a being which, while radically distinct from the sum of its parts, is present in its entirety, in one form or another, in each of these parts, and which relates to itself either through its relation to one or more of its parts or through its relation to the relations between all or some of them. If this reality is *created* (a painting or a symphony are examples, if one takes integration to an extreme), it can exist only in the imaginary (*l'imaginaire*), that is to say, as the correlative of an act of imagination. The ontological status to which it lays claim by its very definition is that of the in–itself, the inert. . . .

The *totality*, despite what one might think, is only a regulative principle of the totalization. . . .

On this basis, it is easy to establish the intelligibility of dialectical Reason; it is the very movement of totalization. . . .

Thus the dialectic is a totalizing activity. Its only laws are the rules produced by the developing totalization, and these are obviously concerned with the relation between unification and the unified, that is to say, the modes of *effective* presence of the totalizing process in the totalized parts. And knowledge, itself totalizing, is the totalization itself in so far as it is present in particular partial structures of a definite kind. . . . These remarks enable us to define the first feature of the *critical investigation*: it takes place *inside* the totalization and can be neither a contemplative recognition of the totalizing movement, nor a particular, autonomous totalization of the known totalization. Rather, it is a real moment of the developing totalization in so far as this is embodied in all its parts and is realized as synthetic knowledge of itself through the mediation of certain of these parts. In practice, this means that the critical investigation can and must be anyone's reflexive experience. . . .

To make myself clearer, let me say that – if, as we assume, the region of totalization is, for us, human history – the critique of dialectical Reason could not appear *before* historical totalization had produced that individualized universal which we call the dialectic, that is to say, before it was posited for itself in the philosophies of Hegel and Marx. Nor could it occur *before* the *abuses* which have obscured the very notion of dialectical rationality and produced a new divorce between *praxis* and the knowledge which elucidates it. Indeed, *Critique* derives its etymological meaning and its origin from the real need to separate the true from the false, to define the limits of totalizing activities so as to restore to them their validity. In other words, critical investigation could not occur *in our history*, before Stalinist idealism had sclerosed both epistemological methods and practices. It could take place only as the intellectual expression of that reordering which characterizes, in this "one World" of ours, the post-Stalinist period. Thus, when we claim that *anyone* can carry out the critical investigation, this does not mean it could happen at any period. It means anyone *today*. . . .

If there is any such thing as dialectical Reason, it must be defined as the absolute intelligibility of the irreducibly new, in so far as it is irreducibly new. It is the opposite of the positivist analytical enterprise of explaining new facts by reducing them to old ones. And, in a sense, the positivist tradition is so firmly anchored in us, even today, that the requirement of intelligibility may seem paradoxical. The new, *in so far as it is new*, seems to elude the intellect: the new *quality* is regarded as a brute fact or, at best, its irreducibility is taken to be temporary, and analysis is expected to reveal old elements in it. But in fact it is man who brings novelty into the world: it is his *praxis* (at the level of perception: colours, odours) which, through the partial or total reorganization of the practical field, produces a new instrument in the new unity of its appearance and function; it is the *praxis* of users which, coordinated with that of producers, will maintain the tool in the human world and, through use, link together its so-called "elements" in such a way as to preserve its irreducibility, in relation to men. . . .

As we shall see later, the practical individual enters into ensembles of very different kinds, for example, into what are called *groups* and what I shall call *series*. It is no part of our project to determine whether series precede groups or vice versa, either originally or in a particular moment of History. On the contrary: as we shall see, groups are born of series and often end up by realizing themselves in their turn. So the *only* thing which matters to us is to display the transition from series to groups and from groups to series as constant incarnations of our practical multiplicity, and to test the dialectical intelligibility of these reversible processes. In the same way, when we study class and class-being (*l'être de classe*) we shall find ourselves drawing examples from the history of the working class. But the purpose will not be to define the particular class which is known as the proletariat: our sole aim will be to seek the constitution of a class in these examples, its totalizing (and detotalizing) function and its dialectical intelligibility (bonds of interiority and of exteriority, interior structures, relations to other classes, etc.). In short, we are dealing with neither human history, nor sociology, nor ethnography. To parody a title of Kant's, we would claim, rather, to be laying the foundations for "Prolegomena to any future anthropology"....

Volume I of the *Critique of Dialectical Reason* stops as soon as we reach the "locus of history"; it is solely concerned with finding the intelligible foundations for a structural anthropology – to the extent, of course, that these synthetic structures are the condition of a directed, developing totalization. Volume II, which will follow shortly, will retrace the stages of the critical progression: it will attempt to establish that there is *one* human history, with *one* truth and *one* intelligibility – not by considering the material content of this history, but by demonstrating that a practical multiplicity, whatever it may be, must unceasingly totalize itself through interiorizing its multiplicity at all levels.

Book I: From Individual Praxis to the Practico-Inert

On the most superficial and familiar level, the investigation *first* reveals, in the unity of dialectical connections, unification as the movement of individual *praxis*, plurality, the organization of plurality, and the plurality of organizations. One need only open one's eyes to see this. Our problem concerns these connections. If there are individuals, *who*, or *what*, totalizes?

A simple but inadequate answer is that there would not even be the beginnings of partial totalization if the individual were not totalizing *through himself*. *The entire historical dialectic rests on individual* praxis *in so far as it is already dialectical*, that is to say, to the extent that action is itself the negating transcendence of contradiction, the determination of a present totalization in the name of a future totality, and the real effective working of matter. This much is clear, and is an old lesson of both subjective and objective investigation. Our problem is this: what becomes of *the* dialectic if there are only particular men each of whom is dialectical? As I have said, the investigation provides its own intelligibility. We must therefore see what is the real rationality of action, at the level of individual *praxis* (ignoring for the moment the collective constraints which give rise to it, limit it or make it ineffective).

Everything is to be explained through *need* (*le besoin*); need is the first totalizing relation between the material being, man, and the material ensemble of which he is part. This relation is *univocal*, and *of interiority*. Indeed, it is through need that the first negation of the negation and the first totalization appear in matter. Need is a negation of the negation in so far as it expresses itself as a *lack* within the organism; and need is a positivity in so far as the organic totality tends to preserve itself *as such* through it. . . .

Man, who produces his life in the unity of the material field, is led by *praxis* itself to define zones, systems and privileged objects within this inert totality. He cannot construct his tools – and this applies to the agricultural tools of primitive peoples as much as to the practical use of atomic energy – without introducing partial determinations into the unified environment, whether this environment is the whole world or a narrow strip of land between the sea and the virgin forest. Thus he sets himself in opposition to himself through the mediation of the inert; and, conversely, the constructive power of the labourer opposes the part to the whole in the inert within the "natural" unity. . . . *Labour* of any kind always exists only as a totalization and a transcended contradiction. . . .

From my window, I can see a road-mender on the road and a gardener working in a garden. Between them there is a wall with bits of broken glass on top protecting the bourgeois property where the gardener is working. Thus they have no knowledge at all of each other's presence; absorbed as they are in their work, neither of them even bothers to wonder whether there is anybody on the other side. Meanwhile, I can see them without being seen, and my position and this passive view of them at work situates me in relation to them: I am "taking a holiday", in a hotel; and in my inertia as witness I realize myself as a petty bourgeois intellectual; my perception is only a moment of an undertaking (such as trying to get some rest after a bout of "over-working", or some "solitude" in order to write a book, etc.), and this undertaking refers to possibilities and needs appropriate to my profession and milieu. From this point of view, my presence at the window is a passive activity (I want "a breath of fresh air" or I find the landscape "restful", etc.) and my present perception functions as a means in a complex process which expresses the whole of my life. Hence my initial relation to the two workers is negative: I do not belong to their class, I do not know their trades, I would not know how to do what they are doing, and I do not share their worries.

But these negations have a double character. In the first place, they can be perceived only against an undifferentiated background consisting of the synthetic relations which support me together with them in an *actual* immanence: I could not contrast their ends with mine without recognizing them as ends. The basis of comprehension is complicity in principle with any undertaking, even if one then goes on to combat or condemn it. Any new end, once determined, is set against the organic unity of all human ends. . . . It would be a mistake to suppose that my perception reveals me to myself as *a man* confronted by two other *men*: the concept of man is an abstraction which never occurs in concrete intuition. It is in fact as a "holiday-maker", confronting a gardener and road-mender, that I come to conceive myself; and in making myself what I am I discover them as they make themselves, that is, as their work produces them; but to the extent that I cannot see them as ants (as the aesthete does) or as robots (as the neurotic does), and to the extent that I have to project myself through them before their ends, in order to differentiate their ends from mine, I realize myself as a member of a particular society which determines everyone's opportunities and aims; and beyond their present activity, I rediscover their life itself, the relation between needs and wages, and, further still, social divisions and class struggles. . . .

If I try to locate myself in the social world, I discover around me various ternary or binary formations, the first of which are constantly disintegrating and the second of which arise from a turning totalization and may at any moment integrate themselves into a trinity. . . . If the idealist dialectic misused the triad, this is primarily because the *real* relation between men is necessarily ternary. But this trinity is not a designation or ideal mark of the human relation: it is inscribed *in being*, that is to say, in the materiality of individuals. In this sense, reciprocity is not the thesis, nor trinity the synthesis (or conversely): it is lived relations whose content is determined in a given society, and which are conditioned by materiality and capable of being modified only by action. . . .

At the same time, it is worth pointing out that this univocal relation of surrounding materiality to individuals is expressed *in our History* in a particular and contingent form since the whole of human development, at least up to now, has been a bitter struggle against *scarcity* . . .

The fact is that after thousands of years of History, three quarters of the world's population are undernourished. Thus, in spite of its contingency, scarcity is a very basic human relation, both to Nature and to men. In this sense, scarcity must be seen as that which makes us into *these* particular individuals producing *this* particular History and defining *ourselves* as men. It is perfectly possible to conceive of a dialectical *praxis*, or even of labour, without scarcity. In fact, there is no reason why the products required by the organism should not be practically inexhaustible, while a practical operation was still necessary in order to extract them from the earth. In that case, the inversion of the unity of human multiplicities through the counter-finalities of matter would still necessarily subsist. For this unity is linked to labour as to the original dialectic. But what would disappear is our quality as *men*, and since this quality is historical, the actual specificity of our History would disappear too. So today everyone must recognize this basic contingency as the necessity which, working both through thousands of years and also, quite directly, through the present, forces him to be exactly what he is. . . .

In pure reciprocity, that which is Other than me *is also the same*. But in reciprocity as *modified by scarcity*, the same appears to us as anti-human in so far as *this same man* appears as radically Other – that is to say, as threatening us with death. Or, to put it another way, we have a rough understanding of his ends (for they are the same as ours), and his means (we have the same ones) as well as of the dialectical structures of his acts; but we understand them as if they belonged to *another species*, our demonic double. Nothing – not even wild beasts or microbes – could be more terrifying for man than a species which is intelligent, carnivorous and cruel, and which can understand and outwit human intelligence, and whose aim is precisely the destruction of man. This, however, is obviously our own species as perceived in others by each of its members in the context of scarcity.

This, at any rate, is the basic abstract matrix of every reification of human relations in any society. At the same time, it is the first stage of *ethics*, in so far as this is *praxis* explaining itself in terms of given circumstances. The first movement of ethics, in this case, is the constitution of radical evil and of Manichaeism; it values and evaluates the breaking of the reciprocity of immanence by interiorized scarcity (though we cannot go into the production of values here), but only by conceiving it as a product of the *praxis* of the Other. . . .

It must be clearly understood here that the rediscovery of scarcity in this investigation makes absolutely no claim either to oppose Marxist theory, or to complete it. It is of a different order. The essential discovery of Marxism is that labour, as a historical reality and as the utilization of particular tools in an already determined social and material situation, is the real foundation of the organization of social relations. This discovery *can no longer* be questioned. What we are arguing, however, is this: the possibility of these social relations becoming contradictory is itself due to an inert and material negation re-interiorized by man. We are also arguing that *violence* as a negative relation between one *praxis* and another characterizes the immediate relation of all men, not as a real action but as an inorganic structure re-interiorized by organisms and that the possibility of reification is present in all human relations, even in the pre-capitalist period, and even in family relations or relations between friends. . . .

From the point of view of intelligibility, the important thing is to comprehend how a positive fact, such as the large-scale use of coal, could become the source of deeper and more violent divisions between people within a *working society*, a society which was also seeking to increase its social wealth by all available means; and to understand, too, how the constraints of the material complex which men inherit can negatively define the new expropriated, exploited and undernourished groups. Of course, this new mode of production could not have abolished scarcity, so it was not even conceivable that the means of production should be socialized. But this negative explanation is no more valuable than the attempt to explain the emigration of ancient Greeks by reference to their ignorance of the sciences of Nature. It would be both more reasonable and more intelligible to exhibit industrialization as a process which developed out of *previous* scarcity, which is a real factor in History (in so far as it is crystallized in institutions and practices), and therefore on the basis of the negation of men by matter through other men. . . .

Inert *praxis* which imbibes matter transforms natural, meaningless forces into quasi-human practices, that is to say, into passivized actions. Chinese peasants, as Grousset rightly says, are colonialists. For four thousand years, they have been appropriating arable land on the frontiers of their territory, from Nature and from the nomads. One aspect of their activity is the deforestation which has been going on for centuries. This *praxis* is living and real, and retains a traditional aspect: even recently the peasant was still tearing up scrub to clear a place for millet. But, at the same time, it inscribes itself on nature, both positively and negatively. Its positive aspect is that of the soil and the division of cultivation. Its negative aspect is a signification of which the peasants themselves are not aware, precisely because it is an absence – *the absence of trees*. . . . Traditionalist Chinese in previous centuries could not perceive it since their goal was conquest of the soil. They saw only the plenty represented by their harvests and had no eyes for *the lack*, which was for them, at most, a simple process of liberation, the elimination of an obstacle. . . . Above all deforestation as the elimination of obstacles becomes negatively a lack of protection: since the loess of the mountains and peneplains is no longer retained by trees, it congests the rivers, raising them higher than the plains and bottling them up in their lower reaches, and forcing them to overflow their banks.

Thus, the whole history of the terrible Chinese floods appears as an intentionally constructed mechanism.

If some enemy of mankind had wanted to persecute the peasants of China as a whole, he would have ordered mercenary troops to deforest the mountains systematically. The positive system of agriculture was transformed into an infernal machine. But the enemy who introduced the loess, the river, the gravity, the whole of hydrodynamics, into this destructive apparatus was the peasant himself. . . .

On this basis, deforestation as the action of Others becomes everyone's action as Other *in matter*; objectification is alienation, and at first this primitive alienation does not express exploitation, though it is inseparable from it, but rather the materialization of recurrence. There is no joint undertaking, but still the infinite flight of particular undertakings inscribes itself in being as a joint result. By the same token, Others are fused, as Others, in the passive synthesis of a false unity; and, conversely, the Oneness stamped on matter reveals itself as Other than Oneness. The peasant becomes his own material fatality; he produces the floods which destroy him. . . .

If materiality is everywhere and if it is indissolubly linked to the meanings engraved in it by *praxis*, if a group of men can act as a quasi-mechanical system and a thing can produce its own idea, what becomes of *matter*, that is to say, Being totally without meaning? The answer is simple: it does not appear *anywhere* in human experience. At any moment of History things are human precisely to the extent that men are things. A volcanic eruption destroys Herculaneum; in a way, this is man destroying himself by the volcano. It is the social and material unity of the town and its inhabitants which, within the human world, confers the unity of an event on something which without men would perhaps dissolve into an indefinite process without meaning. . . .

Matter eludes us precisely to the extent that it is given *to us* and *in us*. The universe of science is a strict chain of *significations*. These are produced by practice and return to it in order to illuminate it. But each of them appears as *temporary*; even if it is still in the system tomorrow, the permanent possibility of the overthrow of the ensemble will modify it. The monism which *starts from the human world* and *situates* man in Nature is the monism of materiality. This is the only monism which is realist, and which removes the *purely theological* temptation to contemplate Nature "without alien addition". It is the only monism which makes man neither a molecular dispersal nor a being apart, the only one which *starts* by defining him by his *praxis* in the general milieu of animal life, and which can transcend the following two true but contradictory propositions: all existence in the universe is material; everything in the world of man is human. . . .

Man lives in a universe where the future is a thing, where the idea is an object and where the violence of matter is the "midwife of History". But it is man who invests things with his own *praxis*, his own future and his own knowledge. . . .

A new characteristic of the symbiosis we are uncovering is what economists and some psychologists have called *interest*. . . . Interest is a certain relation between man and thing in a social field. It may be that it reveals itself fully, in human history, only with what is called real property. But it exists in a more or less developed form wherever men live in the midst of a material set of tools which impose their techniques on them. . . . There is a choice: either "everyone follows his interest", which implies that divisions between men are *natural* – or it is divisions between men, resulting from the mode of production, which make interest (particular or general, individual or class) appear as a real moment of the relations between men. In the first case, interest as a fact of nature is an entirely unintelligible *datum*; indeed, the induction which posits it as an *a priori* reality of human nature could never be justified. The whole of History; in so far as its motive force is provided by conflicts of interest, sinks entirely into the absurd; in particular, Marxism becomes no more than an irrational hypothesis: if conflicts of interest are *a priori* then relations of production are determined by them rather than by the mode of production; in other words, the mode of production is not *praxis* objectifying itself and finding the basis of its contradictions in its objectification, that is to say, in its becoming-matter; instead, it is a mere mediation through which individual interests determine the type and intensity of their conflicts. In effect, the immediate consequence of the law of interest (or the Darwinian "struggle for life") is that human relations are *a priori* antagonistic. . . .

In this sense, it is not diversity of interests which gives rise to conflicts, but conflicts which produce interests, to the extent that worked matter imposes itself on struggling groups as an independent reality through the temporary impotence which emerges from their balance of forces. And, in this sense, interest is always a negation not only of the Other but also of the practico-inert being both of matter and of men in so far as this being is constituted by everyone as the destiny of the Other. But, in the same moment, it is precisely this interchangeability of man and his product in the medium of the practico-inert. . . .

Thus *for this being* who reveals himself in the perpetual appropriation of his *praxis* by the technical and social environment, destiny threatens as a mechanical fatality; and his struggle against destiny as such cannot itself be conceived as free human affirmation: it must appear as a means of safeguarding, or at least serving, *his interest*. Interest therefore appears as the inorganic materiality of the individual or group seen as an absolute and irreducible being which subordinates itself to *praxis* as a way of preserving itself in its practico-inert exteriority. In other words, it is the passive, inverted image of freedom, and the only way in which freedom can produce itself (and become conscious of itself) in the shifting hell of the field of practical passivity. . . .

The man who looks at his work, who recognizes himself in it completely, and who also does not recognize himself in it at all; the man who can say both: "This is not what I wanted" and "I understand that this is what I have done and that I could not do anything else", and whose free *praxis* refers him to his prefabricated being and who recognizes himself equally in both – this man grasps, in an immediate dialectical movement, necessity as the *destiny in exteriority of freedom*.

Should we describe this as alienation? Obviously we should, in that *he returns to himself as Other*. However, a distinction must be made: alienation in the Marxist sense begins with exploitation. Should we go back to Hegel who sees alienation as a constant characteristic of all kinds of objectification? Yes and no. We must recognize that the original relation between *praxis* as totalization and materiality as passivity obliges man to objectify himself in a milieu which is not his own, and to treat an inorganic totality as his own objective reality. It is this relation between interiority and exteriority which originally constituted *praxis* as a relation of the organism to its material environment; and there can be no doubt that as soon as man begins to designate himself not as the mere reproduction of his life, but as the ensemble of products which reproduce his life, he discovers himself as *Other* in the world of objectivity; totalized matter, as inert objectification perpetuated by inertia, is in effect *non-human* or even *anti-human*. . . .

It is the necessity for the practical agent to discover himself in the organized inorganic as a material being, and this necessary objectification as grasping himself in the world and outside himself in the world, which makes man into what Heidegger calls a "being of distances". But it is very important to notice that he first discovers himself as the real object of his *praxis* in a milieu which is not that of his practical life, so that his knowledge of himself is knowledge of himself as inertia stamped with a seal. . . .

For those who have read *Being and Nothingness*, I can describe the foundation of necessity as practice: it is the For-Itself, as agent, revealing itself initially as inert or, at best, as practico-inert, in the milieu of the In-Itself. This, one might say, is because the very structure of action as the organization of the unorganized primarily relates the For-Itself to its alienated being as Being in itself. This inert materiality of man as the foundation of all knowledge of himself by himself is, therefore, an alienation of knowledge as well as a knowledge of alienation. . . .

Fundamental alienation does not derive, as *Being and Nothingness* might mislead one into supposing, from some prenatal choice: it derives from the univocal relation of interiority which unites man as a practical organism with his environment. . . .

We shall examine the most obvious, immediate and superficial gatherings of the practical field, as they appear in everyday experience. And, since many of them arise as simple internal determinations of a substance with which they are homogeneous, they can be treated formally not in their particularity, but in so far as through themselves they are social beings in the practico-inert field: through themselves they will manifest to us what might be called their ontological intelligibility, and in a later moment we will be able, through them, to understand and fix this more fundamental reality, class. In *The Problem of Method* I called these inorganic social beings *collectives*. . . .

In order to understand the collective one must understand that this material object realizes the unity of interpenetration of individuals as beings-in-the-world-outside-themselves to the extent that it structures their relations as practical organisms in accordance with the new rule of *series*. . . .

Let us illustrate these notions by a superficial everyday example. Take a grouping of people in the Place Saint-Germain. They are waiting for a bus at a bus stop in front of the church. I use the word "grouping" here in a neutral sense: we do not yet know whether this gathering is, as such, the inert effect of separate activities, or whether it is a common reality, regulating everyone's actions, or whether it is a conventional or contractual organization. These people – who may differ greatly in age, sex, class, and social milieu – realize, within the ordinariness of everyday life, the relation of isolation, of reciprocity and of unification (and massification) from outside which is characteristic of, for example, the residents of a big city in so far as they are united though not integrated through work, through struggle or through any other activity in an organized group common to them all. To begin with, it should be noted that we are concerned here with a plurality of isolations: these people do not care about or speak to each other and, in general, they do not look at one another; they exist side by side alongside a bus stop. . . .

In other words, the intensity of isolation, as a relation of exteriority between the members of a temporary and contingent gathering, expresses *the degree of massification* of the social ensemble, in so far as it is produced on the basis of given conditions. . . .

It is at precisely this level that material objects will be found to determine the serial order as the social reason for the separation of individuals. The practico-inert exigency, here, derives from scarcity: *there are not enough places for everyone.* . . .

The travellers waiting for the bus take tickets indicating the order of their arrival. This means that they accept *the impossibility of deciding which individuals are dispensable in terms of the intrinsic qualities of the individual*; in other words, that they remain on the terrain of common interest, and of the identity of separation as meaningless negation; positively, this means that they try to differentiate every Other from Others without adding anything to his characteristic *as Other* as the sole social determination of his existence. *Serial unity*, as common interest, therefore imposes itself as exigency and destroys all opposition. . . .

In order to understand the rationality of alterity as a rule of the social practico-inert field, we must, in effect, understand that this alterity is more complex and concrete than in the superficial and limited example in which we have observed it. Following up our investigation, we may find that some new characteristics emerge as seriality comes to be constituted in a larger field, and as the structure of more complex collectives. . . .

When I listen to a broadcast, the relation between the broadcaster and myself is not a human one: in effect, I am passive in relation to what is being said, to the political commentary on the news, etc. This passivity, in an activity which develops on every level and over many years, can *to some extent* be resisted: I can write, protest, approve, congratulate, threaten, etc. But it must be noted at once that these activities will carry weight only if a majority (or a considerable minority) of listeners who do not know me do likewise. So that, in this case, reciprocity is a gathering with one voice. Moreover, radio stations represent the point of view of the government or the special interests of a group of capitalists; so the listeners' activities (about programmes or about the opinions that are expressed) are unlikely to have any effect. . . .

The main point is that my inability to act on the series of *Others* (who may allow themselves to be convinced) reverts to me and makes *these Others* my destiny. Of course, this is not because of the broadcast on its own, but because it occurs in a wider context of mystificatory propaganda which lulls them into unawareness. . . .

In developing this example our investigation (*expérience*) of seriality has grown richer. . . .

As collectives are both a result of particular undertakings and a radical inversion of finality, they have peculiar powers which may have made it possible to believe in their subjective existence, but which need to be studied in objectivity. Because the economic system of a society is *a collective*, it can be conceived as a system which functions of itself, tending to persevere in its being. In particular, what Marx calls the process of capital must necessarily be understood through the materialist dialectic and in accordance with his rigorous interpretation of it. But if it is true that this process is partially responsible for "the atomisation of crowds" and also for recurrence, it is also true that it can exist as "a relation determined by production" only in and through this milieu of recurrence which it helps to maintain . . .

Thus it is not so much, as Marx says somewhat unfortunately in the *Manifesto*, "the united action of many members", but above all their separation and atomization which endows their real relations of production with the inhuman character of a thing. . . .

The real problem – which we cannot go into here – relates not so much to the past, where recurrence and alienation have always existed, as to the future: to what extent will a socialist society do away with atomism *in all its forms?* To what extent will collective objects, the signs of our alienation, be dissolved into a true inter-subjective community in which the only real relations will be those between men, and to what extent will the necessity of every human society remaining a detotalized totality maintain recurrence, flights and therefore unity-objects as limits to true unification? Must the disappearance of capitalist forms of alienation mean the elimination of *all* forms of alienation? . . .

Yet this "uniting of action" does occur; the proof is that bourgeois economists speak quite readily of the solidarity of the interests of workers and employers. Thus, the finished product is presented as if it were the result of a concerted undertaking, that is to say, of an action and work group comprising management, technicians, office staff and workers. But the bourgeois economist does not wish to see that this solidarity is expressed *in inert matter* as an inversion of the real relations; this false unity, as the inert seal which supposedly signifies *men*, can, in fact, refer only to relations of antagonism and seriality. . . .

If, as Marx has often said, everything is *other* in capitalist society, this is primarily because atomization, which is both the origin and the result of the process, makes social man an Other than himself, conditioned by Others in so far as they are Other than themselves. . . .

The worker will be saved from his destiny only if the human multiplicity as a whole is permanently changed into a group *praxis.* . . .

We have seen that the practico-inert field, considered in general and *a priori*, cannot, by any of its contradictions, occasion the form of practical sociality which we are about to study, namely the group. Groups always constitute themselves on the basis of certain particular contradictions which define a particular sector of the field of passive-activity, while one cannot have any *a priori* assurance that the same applies everywhere. . . .

The group constitutes itself as the radical impossibility of living, which threatens serial multiplicity. But this new dialectic, in which freedom and necessity are now one, is not a new incarnation of the transcendental dialectic: it is a human construction whose sole agents are individual men as free activities. For this reason, in order to distinguish it from constituent dialectics, we shall refer to it as the constituted dialectic. . . .

After 12 July 1789 the people of Paris were in a state of revolt. Their anger had deep causes, but as yet these had affected the people only in their common impotence. (Cold, hunger, etc., were all suffered either in resignation – serial behaviour falsely presenting itself as individual virtue – or in unorganized outbursts, riots, etc.). On the basis of what exterior circumstances were groups to be constituted? In the first place (in temporal order) the existence of an institutional, practical group, the electors of Paris, in so far as they had constituted themselves in accordance with royal decrees and *in so far as* they were in permanent session, in spite of, or contrary to these decrees, designated the inert gathering of Parisians as possessing, *in the dimension of collective praxis*, a practical reality. The electoral assembly was the active unity, as the being-outside-itself-in-freedom, of the inert gathering.

But this totalization was not enough: indeed *representation* consists in defining, by some procedure, an active group as a projection of the inert gathering in the inaccessible milieu of *praxis*. For example, in bourgeois democracies, elections are passive, serial processes. Each elector, of course, decides how to vote as Other and through Others; but instead of deciding in common and as a united *praxis* with the Others, he allows it to be defined inertly and in seriality by opinion. Thus an elected assembly represents the gathering *as long as* it has not met, as long as its members are the inert product of an inert alterity and as long as crude multiplicity, as a numerical relation between the parts, expresses the relations of impotence amongst collectives and power relations in so far as these forces are forces of inertia. *But as soon as* an assembly gets organized, as soon as it constitutes its hierarchy, and defines itself (by party alliances) as a definite group (characterized by the permanence of a majority, by a complex play around a shifting majority, by the complicity of all the parties against a single individual etc.), this real *praxis* . . . presents itself both as the faithful representation of the gathering – which being organized, it cannot in any way be – and as *its dialectical efficacity*. But the very fact of penetrating the gathering with a false totalised unity ("Frenchmen, *your* government . . . etc.") relegates the gathering to its statute of impotence. . .

And this totality as an object of *praxis* (the city to be besieged, disturbances to be prevented) was by itself a determination of the practico-inert field; the city was both the place, in its totalized and totalizing configuration (the threat of siege determining it as a container) and the population designated in the form of materiality sealed by the military action which produced it as a confined crowd. The *rumours*, the *posters*, the *news* (especially that of Necker's departure) communicated their common designation to everyone: *each was a particle of sealed materiality*. At this level, the totality of encirclement can be described as being lived *in seriality*. It was what is known as enthusiasm: people were running in the streets, shouting, forming gatherings, and burning down the gates of the toll houses. The bond between individuals was, in its various real forms, that of alterity as the immediate discovery of oneself in the Other. . .

Freedom – as a simple positive determination of *praxis* organized on the basis of its real objectives (defence against the troops of the Prince de Lambesc) – was manifested as the necessity of dissolving necessity. On this basis, a dialectic established itself at the Hôtel de Ville between the constituted authorities, which did not wish to hand out weapons, and which equivocated and found pretexts, and the crowd, which was increasingly threatening, and which, through the behaviour of the electors, of the provost of merchants, etc., revealed itself as a *unity-exis*. When rags were found in the boxes of arms promised by Flesselles, the crowd felt that it had been *tricked* – in other words, it interiorized Flesselles' actions and saw them, *not in seriality*, but in opposition to seriality as a sort of passive synthesis. . . . Everyone reacted in a new way: not as an individual, nor as an Other, but as an individual incarnation of the common person. There was nothing magical in this new reaction: it merely expressed the re-interiorization of a reciprocity.

From this moment on, there is something which is neither group nor series, but what Malraux, in *Days of Hope*, called the Apocalypse – that is to say, the dissolution of the series into a fused group. And this group, though still unstructured, that is to say, entirely *amorphous*, is characterized by being the direct opposite of alterity. . . .

As the possibility of repression in the Quartier Saint-Antoine appeared increasingly probable, residents of this district, *seen as third parties*, were directly threatened. However, this threat did not apply to them as "accidental individuals": they were not being sought for their individual activities (like a criminal in hiding).... Rather, they are threatened as *a moment* of a punitive campaign which will develop dialectically, as a free organized action, whose successive moments are foreseen by the enemy.... At this level, everyone, as a *third party*, became incapable of distinguishing his own safety from that of the Others....

The Other, by totalizing the practical community through his regulatory action, *effects for me* the integration which I myself should have realized but was unable to. Through him, in fact, my being-in-the-group becomes immanence; I am *amongst* third parties and I have no privileged statute. But this operation does not transform me into an object, because totalization by the third party only reveals a free *praxis* as a common unity which is already there and which already qualifies him.

In practice, this means that I am integrated into the common action when the common *praxis* of the third party posits itself as regulatory. I run with all the others; I shout: "Stop!"; everybody stops. Someone else shouts, "Let's go!" or, "To the left! To the right! To the Bastille!" And everyone moves off, following the regulatory third party, surrounding him and sweeping past him; then the group reabsorbs him as soon as another third party, by giving some order or by some action visible to all, constitutes himself as regulatory for a moment. But the order is not *obeyed*. Who would obey? And whom? It is simply the common *praxis* becoming, in some third party, regulatory of itself in me and in all the other third parties, in the movement of a totalization which totalizes me and everyone else....

The reality of the *praxis* of a (fused) group depends on the liquidation (either simultaneous or subject to temporal dislocations which can be ignored) of the serial, both in everyone and by everyone in everyone, and its replacement by community. This reality (which sometimes produces itself and sometimes does not) must therefore be comprehended in its intelligibility. But this intelligibility is defined *precisely* by the practical relation of the hostile *praxis* (through the material object) to the free action by which the third party unveils this *praxis* by opposing it....

The people have taken the Bastille. This public fact cannot be interpreted in the same way as the significations which it has just overthrown. This is why alienation – if it occurs – generally reveals itself *much later* and through confrontations. Thus the moment of victory presents itself to the victorious group – except in exceptional circumstances – as the pure objectification of freedom as *praxis*; and its character of irreducible novelty reflects for the group the novelty of its unity....

The intelligibility of the fused group depends, therefore, on the complex ensemble of a negative designation of its community, reactualized in the negation of this negation, that is, in the free constitution of individual *praxis* into common *praxis*. At this level, there is group behaviour and there are group thoughts in that the common *praxis* is self-elucidating; and the essential structure of these practical thoughts is the unveiling of the world as a new reality through a negation of the old reality of impotence, that is to say, through the negation of the impossibility of humanity. The fact that the origin of the grouping was Terror is not actually very significant; every *praxis* constitutes itself as an opening made in the future, and sovereignly affirms its own possibility – simply through the emergence of the undertaking itself – that is to say, it makes success into a structure of practical freedom. As the freedom of revolt reconstitutes itself as common violence against practico-inert necessity, its future objectification becomes, for it, the free violence of men against misery and impossibility of living. . . .

But, at the same time, this violence, always ready to attack any re-emergence of inertia within the group, dissolves itself in pure, unanimous sovereignty, in so far as, through the active member of the group, sovereign freedom is always *here* and *now*. However, as violence is always going on, whether against an external enemy or against insidious alterity within, the behaviour of a revolutionary, on 14 July as on 10 August, appears contradictory: he not only fights for freedom (that is to say, for the practical realization of a concrete objective), but also realizes sovereign freedom in himself as unity and ubiquity; at the same time, however, he commits violence on the enemy (in fact this is simply counter-violence) and he uses perpetual violence *in order to reorganize himself*, even going so far as to kill some of his fellow members. But there is not really any contradiction here: this common freedom gets its violence not only from the violent negation which occasioned it, but also from the reign of necessity, which it transcended but preserved in itself, and which constantly threatens to be reborn as a disguised petrification, that is to say, as a collapse into the inertia of the gathering. . . .

Whatever the origin of the group may be, the permanence of the dangers may require it to persist between the moments of real activity, as a permanent means of resisting the enemy. . . . The new exigency comes to the group to the extent that the third party reveals it, or in other words, in so far as individual *praxis* interiorizes the objective permanence of the common danger in the form of a common exigency. But this new state of the group (which manifests itself historically in every revolutionary situation) is defined by new characteristics, conditioned by new circumstances. . . .

Thus the ontological statute of the surviving group appears at first as the practical contrivance of a free, inert permanence of common unity in everyone. When freedom becomes common *praxis* and grounds the permanence of the group by producing its own inertia through itself and in mediated reciprocity, this new statute is called *the pledge (le serment)*. It goes without saying that pledges can take very different forms, from the explicit act of swearing an oath (for example, the Tennis Court oath; an oath as the synthetic link between members of a medieval commune) to the implicit assumption of a pledge as the already existing reality of the group (for example, by those who are born into the group and who grow up among its members). In other words, *the historical act of* making a pledge in common, though it is universal and *always* corresponds to a surviving group's resistance to the divisive tendency of (spatio-temporal) distance and differentiation, is not the only possible form of the common pledge, in so far as the pledge is a guarantee against the future, inertia produced in immanence and by freedom, and the foundation of all differentiation. . . .

A pledge is mediated reciprocity. All its derivative forms – for example a witness's oath in law, an individual swearing on the Bible, etc. – derive their meaning from this basic form of pledge. But we must be careful not to confuse this with a *social contract*. We are not trying to describe the basis of particular societies – which, as we shall see, would be absurd; we are trying to explain the necessary transition from an immediate form of group which is in danger of dissolution to another form, which is reflexive but permanent. . . .

The fundamental re-creation, within the pledge, is the project of substituting a real fear, produced by the group itself, for the retreating external fear, whose very distance is deceptive. And we have already encountered this fear as a free product of the group, and as a collective action of freedom against serial dissolution; we have seen it appear momentarily during the action itself; and it is called Terror. . . .

This is precisely what a pledge is: namely the common production, through mediated reciprocity, of a statute of violence; once the pledge has been made, in fact, the group has to guarantee everyone's freedom against necessity, even at the cost of his life and in the name of freely sworn faith. Everyone's freedom demands the violence of all against it and against that of any third party as its defence against itself (as a free power of secession and alienation). . . . The pledged group produces its objectification as a particular material product *in it* (the written pact, and the very hall in which it was signed, which was formerly a container, become, after dispersal, an interiorized product, a material mediation between the members). But this interior objectivity (which produces itself for everyone as an impossibility of going back beyond a certain past date, as an irreversibility of temporalization) is not the objectification of the group as *being*; it is the eternal, frozen preservation of its rising (of the reflexive, statutory rising through the pledge). It is the origin of humanity. . . .

Indeed, everyone lives *group-being* as a nature: he is "proud" *to belong to it*, he becomes *the* material referent (*signifié*) of the uniforms of the group (if there are any) – *but* as *the nature of freedom* (it is its frightening form of inertia, in so far as it comes to me as exigency). Thus the relations of common individuals within the group are ambivalent links of reciprocity (unless they are governed by the resumption of the struggle and the total objective): he and I *are brothers*. And this fraternity is not based, as is sometimes stupidly supposed, on physical resemblance expressing some deep identity of natures. . . .

We are brothers in so far as, following the creative act of the pledge, we *are our own sons*, our common creation. And, as in real families, fraternity is expressed in the group by a set of reciprocal and individual obligations, defined by the whole group on the basis of circumstances and objectives (obligations to help one another in general or in the particular and fully determinate case of an action or a concrete task). . . .

The violence and coercive force of *fraternity-terror* as a true relation of interiority between the members of the group are based on the myth of *rebirth*; they define and produce the traitor as absolute evil to precisely the extent that they define him as the man who destroyed *the previous unity*. In other words, both terror and the pledge relate to the deep fear of a dissolution of unity. They therefore posit it as the essential security and as the justification of any repressive violence. But the basic contradiction of the group – which is not resolved by the pledge – is that its real unity lies in common *praxis* or, to be precise, in the common objectification of this *praxis*. When the community affirms itself as the reign of common freedom, it cannot in fact – whatever it does – either realize the free interpenetration of individual freedoms or find an inert *being-one* which is common to all freedoms. . . .

This untranscendable conflict between the individual and the common, which oppose and define each other and each of which returns into the other as its profound truth, is naturally manifested in new contradictions within the organized group; and these contradictions are expressed by a new transformation of the group; the organization is transformed into a hierarchy, and pledges give rise to institutions. This is of course not a historical sequence; and indeed we shall see that – on account of dialectical circularity – any form can emerge either before or after any other and that only the materiality of the historical process can determine the sequence. . . .

The *being of the institution*, as the geometrical locus of intersections of the collective and the common, is the *non-being* of the group, produced as a bond between its members. . . . As an institutionalized *praxis*, it remains either *a power over everyone* (in the name of pledged faith) or, if everyone represents and maintains it, *his own free power over the Others*. . . .

Thus the new statute of power emerges everywhere, even in the army, the archetypal institutional group. In the context of the organized group, we defined it as the right to do one's duty; but here it must be defined as the duty to do one's best in order to get one's right to do one's duty recognized. Institutional man has to get this *recognition* by means of two opposed and simultaneous practices: on the one hand, when his institutional power is not directly threatened, his general tactic will be to liquidate the Other in himself so as to liquidate it in the Others (the officer who lives with his men and models his whole life on theirs); on the other hand, in the moment of exercising his power, institutional man will immediately constitute himself as the absolute Other, by adopting certain behaviour and dress; and he will base the firmness of the power exercised and of the decisions made, on his *institution-being (être-institution)*, that is to say, on inertia and the total opacity of the alterity which has become the particular institution's presence in him, and, hence, the group's presence as common *praxis*. At this level, in fact, mystification is very probable: with the institution remaining a practice and the group not being dissolved, the institution, in its negative being (which is really only the ubiquity of non-being) appears, in appropriate circumstances, as the ontological statute of the community. . . .

In this moment, freedom is completely hidden or else appears as the inessential and ephemeral slave of necessity. Necessity, on the other hand, is absolute in the sense that its free, practical form (necessity produced by freedom) merges with its form as serial alienation. The imperative and impotence, terror and inertia are based on each other. The institutional moment, in the group, corresponds to what might be called the systematic self-domestication of man by man. The aim is, in effect, to create men who (as common individuals) will define themselves, in their own eyes and amongst themselves, by their fundamental relation (mediated reciprocity) with institutions. More than half of this task is carried out by circular seriality: everyone systematically acting on himself and on everyone else through all, resulting in the creation of the strict correlate of the man-institution, that is to say, the institutionalized man. In so far as the ossification of the ossified *praxis* which is the institution is due to our own impotence, it constitutes for each and for all a precise index of *reification* . . . .

The institutional system as an exteriority of inertia necessarily refers to *authority* as its reinteriorization; and *authority*, as a power over all powers and over all third parties through these powers, is itself established by the system as an institutional guarantee of institutions.

The foundation of authority is in fact sovereignty, in so far as, after the stage of the fused group, it is the quasi-sovereignty of the regulatory third party. Thus the *leader* emerges at the same time as the group itself and produces the group which produces him, except that at this elementary moment of the investigation, the leader might be *anyone*. In other words, everyone's quasi-sovereignty is one of the constitutive bonds of the group . . . .

Thus *authority* fulfils a definite function: as the synthetic power of a single individual (possibly, though not necessarily, as an expression of a united sub-group), it gathers up the multiplicity of institutional relations and gives them the synthetic unity of a real *praxis*. Institutions claim to be the inorganic being-one of the serialized community; the leader claims to be the dissolution and synthetic reunification of this external passivity in the organic unity of the regulatory *praxis*, that is to say, of the *praxis* of the group in so far as it is reflected to him as the common *praxis* of a person.

But this is the essential contradiction of authority, of the individual reincarnation of the fused group and of Freedom–Terror; as such the leader himself enters the institutional multiplicity, since he is a real product of an institution. Thus the leader preserves institutions to precisely the extent that he apparently produces them as an internal exteriorization of his interiority, and he dissolves their inert-being in his historical *praxis*. But this historical *praxis* – as the reciprocity of the sovereign and of common individuals – is itself produced by the inert eternity of institutional relations . . . .

Now, the first point to notice is that, contrary to what is so often maintained, sovereignty in itself does not constitute any problem or require any foundation. The illusion that it does is due to the fact that the state of massification is normally regarded as logically and historically basic, and that the reified relationships which occur in societies based on exploitation are treated as the prototype of human relations. From the moment in which *absence of relationship* becomes the fundamental relation, one can ask how the type of synthetic relation known as Power can set itself up as the bond between the separate molecules. And all means of interpretation except two have been foresworn *a priori*. These two are, that Power emanates from God, and that Power emanates from certain intermittent metamorphoses which transform society into a totalized-totality, and that it expresses the constraints of collective representation, etc. Unfortunately, neither God nor the totalized group actually exist. If it were really necessary to find a foundation for sovereignty, we would be searching for a long time: for there is no such thing.

There is none *because* there is no need for one: sovereignty is simply the univocal relation of interiority between the individual as *praxis* and the objective field which he organizes and transcends towards his own end . . . .

Sovereignty within the group, therefore, does not have to explain its positive power, but rather the negative and limiting determinations to which it is subjected. In fact, we have seen how it became *quasi-sovereignty* in the tension of "transcendence-immanence". And from our point of view, this limitation is still the foundation of Power: the sovereignty of the leader can only be a *quasi-sovereignty*, since otherwise he would not be a regulatory third party and the bond of interiority would break . . . .

These remarks have nothing to do with the historical origins of sovereignty, but only with entirely abstract logical and dialectical relations, which must, however, be present as the intelligibility of any historical interpretation. Within groups, sovereignty is in fact at least relatively simple. But the ensembles in which sovereignty, in some form or other, manifests itself in its full development and power are *societies*. And we have already established that a society is not a group, nor a grouping of groups, nor even struggling groupings of groups. *Collectives* are both the matrix of groups and their grave; they remain as the indefinite sociality of the practico-inert, nourishing groups, maintaining them and transcending them everywhere by their indefinite multiplicity. Where there are several groups, the collective is either a mediation or battlefield.

Society, which our dialectical investigation has, up to this moment of its development, approached only very abstractly, thus yields up its highly formal and indeterminate structure: in the material context of needs, dangers, instruments and techniques, there can be no such thing as society unless there are, in some way or other, human multiplicities united *by a container or by a soil*, unless these multiplicities are divided, by Historical development, into groups and series, and unless the basic internal relation of the society – whether production (division of labour), consumption (type of distribution) or defence against the enemy (division of tasks) – is ultimately *that of groups to series*. And among the many differentiations of this internal bond, one of the easiest to grasp is the institutional ensemble, cloaked and reunited by the sovereign institution, by the State, in so far as a small group of organisers, administrators and propagandists take on the task of imposing *modified* institutions within collectives, as serial bonds which unite serialities. In short, what is known as the State can never be regarded as the product or expression of the totality of social individuals or even of the majority of them, since this majority is serial *anyway*, and could not express its needs and demands without liquidating itself as a series, so as to become a large group (which either immediately opposes authority or else renders it *completely* inoperative). It is at this level of the large group that dissolving alterity permits concrete needs and objectives to constitute themselves as *common* realities. And the idea of a diffuse popular sovereignty becoming embodied in a sovereign is a mystification. There is no such thing as diffuse sovereignty: the organic individual is sovereign in the abstract isolation of his work; and in fact, he immediately becomes alienated in the practico-inert, where he learns of *the necessity of impotence* (or of impotence as a necessity at the basis of his practical freedom).... Sovereignty does not rise from the collective to the sovereign; on the contrary, sovereignty (as command, as a phantom of unity, or as the legitimacy of freedom), descends through the sovereign to modify collectives, without changing their structure of passivity....

Thus, within a given society, the State cannot be said to be either legitimate or illegitimate; it is legitimate within a group, because it is produced in a milieu of pledged faith. But it does not really have *this legitimacy* when it acts on collectives, since *the Others* have not sworn anything either to groups or to one another....

Something like acceptance may therefore occur; but in itself this is ineffectual since it exists in every other only as an awareness of impotent recurrence. I obey because *I cannot* do otherwise; and in itself this confers serial pseudo-legitimacy on the sovereign: his power to command proves that he has a different nature from mine, or, in other words, that he is freedom....

Thus Marx was right when he wrote "Only *political superstition* still imagines today that civil life must be held together by the state, whereas in reality, on the contrary, the state is held together by civil life".

Marx was right, *subject to the* qualification that there is a circular process at work here and that the State, being produced and sustained by the dominant, rising class, constitutes itself as the organ of the contraction and integration of the class. And of course this integration takes place through circumstances, and as a historical totalization; but still, it takes place *through the State*, at least in part. Thus it would be wrong to see the State *either* as the concrete reality of society (as Hegel apparently wished to believe), *or* as a pure, epiphenomenal abstraction which merely gives passive expression to changes effected by the concrete development of its real society.

This is particularly important in so far as the State cannot take on its functions without positing itself as a mediator between the exploiting and the exploited classes. The State is a determination of the dominant class, and this determination is conditioned by class struggle. But it affirms itself as a deep negation of the class struggle. . . .

Every group, in fact, in so far as its own totalizing movement contains the abstract possibility of establishing its own sovereignty, constitutes itself *either* outside the State (even if it is more or less directly connected with it, through subventions, official encouragement, etc.), by positing the autonomy of its *praxis*, *or*, primarily in opposition to the State, as a denunciation and rejection of its transcendent sovereignty, through a practice of abstention, passive resistance, disobedience or revolt. . . .

Our investigation has now arrived at a shifting flight of elucidations: the practical unity of the group which organizes itself lies in its object, in groups external to it; it passes momentarily through every participant in an undertaking as an "excluded third party" (*tiers exclu*); and it resurfaces theoretically and practically in the activity of the sovereign. But it is never really given *inside* the group itself, in the way that the unity of the moments of an individual action lies in the unity of an active development. . . .

Thus the true efficacity of the group, as a *praxis* bogged down in matter, lies in its materiality – that is, in its becoming-process. But, in so far as *praxis* is process, goals lose their teleological character. Without ceasing to be genuine goals, they become destinies. . . .

This enables us to reach the concrete at last, that is to say, to complete our dialectical investigation. . . . Our study of the different structures, in an order of increasing complexity, has shown inertia reappearing inside groups, at first as the free violence of freedoms against freedoms and then becoming *a common being* in a reciprocally created inertia. This is what we have called freedom as necessity. On this basis, and through the force of inertia itself, this necessity, freely accepted under the pressure of increasingly urgent circumstances and in the milieu of scarcity, becomes pledged faith, and an agent of the re-exteriorization of interiority (organized and institutionalized relations) until the most extreme mode of exteriority (the institution) produces in its own institutional statute the conditions and means of re-interiorization.

Is there not a perpetual double movement of regroupment and petrification? We can ignore such questions: our purpose was to explain the intelligibility of these possibilities; and this we have done. . . .

At this level, it should be observed that the complex forms assumed, in and through circularity, by what are conventionally called *social realities*, need not be confined to any one specific level of intelligibility, and that it may be impossible to confine them to any particular practico-ontological statute. This is not just because groups have a serial destiny even in the moment of their practical totalization, or because a particular seriality may, in some circumstances, be transformed into a community. The most important reason is that the group is always marked by the series, that it becomes its reality in the milieu of freedom, and that a series is determined, even in its totally inorganic practico-inert layers, by the sovereign self-production of the group. It is therefore necessary to conceive of a specific statute for certain realities whose real unity is manifested as a bond of interiority between *common* and *serial multiplicities*. This applies, for example, to social classes (when defined within a system of exploitation)....

It should in fact be noted that the practice of the wage-contract "freely agreed" by both parties and characteristic of the industrial era posits the freedom of the worker as an absolute principle. Contractual reciprocity goes further because – at least formally – each freedom is guaranteed by that of the Other, and this presupposes that the employer would find in the worker a freedom equal to his own, or in other words, recognize him as a member of the human race. At first sight, this seems very different from racism in that colonial super-exploitation is based upon the "sub-humanity" of the natives. In the case of racism, the contradiction derives from the fact that the colonialist finds himself forced to use the "sub-human" whom he oppresses as such for properly human activities. The contradiction of early capitalism, however, is that the employer, under cover of a proclaimed reciprocity, treats the worker as an enemy: the free contract, at this period, concealed what was really forced labour. Labour was recruited by constraint, iron discipline was imposed on it, and employers protected themselves by perpetual blackmail and, frequently, by repression.

The contradiction therefore is both to recognize that the worker is free and to introduce him by compulsion into a system in which it is *also* recognized that he will be reduced to a sub-human level. At the same time, the viciousness of preventive or repressive measures shows that the worker is condemned *in advance* for any *possible* tendency to revolt, while at the same time his protestations are apparently seen as legitimate.

The process of alienation requires that the worker should be regarded as free at the moment of the contract, in order to be reduced to a commodity later.

Thus man freely becomes a commodity: he sells himself....

This is the dual practical character of the individual action of capitalists: the production of free workers in the form of human commodities in rigid, reciprocal conditioning, with a systematic preference for the machine over human labour, wherever the latter can be replaced by the former. Now, this dual character of the operation *as living praxis* is *precisely* what defines *oppression*: the power given to worked matter of (double) compulsion over free individuals in so far as they have been recognized (the free contract) in their freedom remains fundamentally unchanged, whether this worked matter is a machine (or the money to buy one) or a gun. And this oppression can be realized only in the form of permanent violence, that is to say, in so far as it is practised against an anti-human species whose freedom is essentially the freedom to do evil....

To refuse to define oneself as evil is to reject bourgeois Manichaeism; but this Manichaeism is simply another name for the humanism of the dominant class, and it has to be rejected as humanism. Now, an abstract rejection would still be an acceptance: in rejecting humanism as such, a worker *would be admitting* that he was non-human.

The new exigency, born of the transcendence of this contradiction, is that the rejection should be inscribed in the production of a true and positive humanism; and this presupposes that the worker takes away from the bourgeoisie the privilege of stating the truth of man for all, that is to say, truth itself. However, the bourgeois claims to be human by virtue of intelligence, culture, scientific knowledge, technical abilities, etc.: and while these powers must belong to everyone, the workers partly lack them. Furthermore, the idealist intellectualism of the bourgeoisie depends on analytical Reason: analytical Reason determines what is true. Thus the worker must either allow his class to be dissolved by a positivistic atomization and allow himself to be defined as isolated in ignorance and malevolence *or* he must recreate Reason, dissolve analytical rationality in a larger complex and, without losing the hope of escaping ignorance some day, find non–intellectual criteria and foundations for truth. Of course, as Marx said, the problems are not formulated until the means of resolving them are present; but *everything is already present: praxis* as the measure of man and the foundation of truth, and dialectic as the permanent dissolution of analytical Reason. . . .

We can conclude by saying that the dialectic, as the practical consciousness of an oppressed class struggling against its oppressor, is a reaction which is produced in the oppressed by the divisive tendency of oppression – but not at any arbitrary time or place: later we shall discover the material conditions which make this consciousness possible. But at any rate it is a transcendence of contemplative truth by effective practical truth, and of atomization (accompanied by serial agreement) towards the synthetic unity of the combat-group. . . .

Our aim is to define the formal conditions of History; we need not dwell on the relations of material reciprocity between classes in their real historical development. What has been established by our dialectical investigation is that for there to be any such thing as classes, they must be determined in reciprocity, whatever the mediating process may be. Besides, we know that the only intelligibility of their relationship is dialectical. From this point of view, analytical Reason can be seen to be an oppressive *praxis* for dissolving them, and its inevitable effect is to make the dialectic into the rationality of the oppressed class (on the basis of circumstances which have yet to be determined). The emergence of dialectical Reason in the working class as a dissolution of analytical Reason and as a determination of the bourgeois class in terms of its function and practice (exploitation-oppression) is induced; it is an aspect of the class struggle. . . .

Struggle, in the field of scarcity, as negative reciprocity, engenders the Other as Other than man, or as anti–human; but at the same time I comprehend him, in the very springs of my *praxis*, as a negation of which I am a concrete practical negation, and as mortal danger.

For each of the adversaries, this struggle is intelligible; or rather, at this level, it is intelligibility itself. Otherwise, reciprocal *praxis* would in itself have no meaning or goal. But what concerns us is the general problem of intelligibility, particularly at the concrete level. . . .

These questions bring us at last to the real problem of History. If History really is to be the totalization of all practical multiplicities and of all their struggles, the complex products of the conflicts and collaborations of these very diverse multiplicities must themselves be intelligible in their synthetic reality, that is to say, they must be compre-hensible as the synthetic products of a totalitarian *praxis*. This means that History is intelligible if the different practices which can be found and located at a given moment of the historical temporalization finally appear as partially totalizing and as connected and merged in their very oppositions and diversities by an intelligible totalization from which there is no appeal. It is by seeking the conditions for the intelligibility of historical vestiges and results that we shall, for the first time, reach the problem of totalization without a totalizer and of the very foundations of this totalization, that is to say, of its motive-forces and of its non-circular direction. Thus, the regressive movement of the critical investigation has demonstrated the intelligibility of practical structures and the dialectical relation which interconnects the various forms of active multiplicities. But, on the one hand, we are still at the level of synchronic totalization and we have not yet considered the diachronic depth of practical temporalization; and on the other hand, the regressive movement has ended with a question: that is to say, it has to be completed by a synthetic progression whose aim will be to rise up to the double synchronic and diachronic movement by which History constantly totalizes itself. So far, we have been trying to get back to the elementary formal structures, and, at the same time, we have located the dialectical foundations of a structural anthropology. These structures must now be left to live freely, to oppose and to co-operate with one another: and the reflexive investigation of this still formal project will be the object of the next volume. If the truth is *one* in its increasing internal diversification, then, by answering the last question posed by the regressive investigation, we shall discover the basic signification of History and of dialectical rationality.

4

SARTRE'S *CRITIQUE*

William L. McBride

Sartre's Move to Political Theory

Of the Continental European philosophers considered in this volume, Sartre is no doubt among the most famous in terms of public name recognition, but among the least known for his systematic political theory as such. The core piece of that theory, volume 1 of the *Critique of Dialectical Reason*, was published in 1960, the year that in retrospect, if a single year must be chosen, effectively marked the end of the dominance of existentialism as the most significant intellectual current in Europe. The death, in an automobile accident, of Albert Camus, from whom Sartre had been personally estranged for some time, and who had come under harsh criticism for his ambivalence about the war that the French government was still waging in a costly and losing effort to preserve colonialism in Algeria, occurred in January of that year. Maurice Merleau-Ponty, Sartre's closest former collaborator other than Simone de Beauvoir, was to die the following year, a year which also saw the widely heralded publication of Michel Foucault's *Madness and Civilization* (*Histoire de la folie*). Times were changing very rapidly, and the *Critique* itself, as I hope to show here, was a significant index and testimonial to these changes. But this work, at least in part by virtue of its author's strong identification with the earlier, immediate postwar (i.e., World War II) times and ways of thinking, never received the same degree of attention – adulation *or* condemnation – as had his earlier *Being and Nothingness*.

Part of the reason for this is the way in which the *Critique* was written: badly, by most standards. The original French version (there are two, with different pagination) consists of over 750 pages of small print, with paragraphs that not uncommonly run to three or four pages, and a table of contents of four lines. Even within the text itself there are few subdivisions, especially in the latter half, so that most of the subtitles to be found in Alan Sheridan-Smith's English translation were introduced by him. Sartre could write quite differently, as evidenced by his autobiography of his early years, *Les Mots* (1964), in which he deliberately cultivated a distinctive style, with short, pithy sentences interspersed throughout the text, that many find attractive. He always did, it is true, take the view that writing philosophy requires the use of a denser, more technical language than do other forms of literature; but *Being and Nothingness*, by contrast to the *Critique*, was at least clearly structured. The circumstances under which the *Critique* was written – Sartre's despair over the twin follies of the Algerian War and the Cold War, partially assuaged by drugs and alcohol consumed in large quantities, together with his Gargantuan appetite for writing *words* and more words – are reflected in the outcome: intellectually lucid, with some brilliant descriptive passages (some of which are to be found in the text that we have excerpted here), but as a whole turgid and daunting. Moreover, what was published in 1960 was only volume 1; the second volume, never completed, was first published, posthumously, in 1985.

For a fuller overview of the evolution of Sartre's political theory – from an early paper in the philosophy of law, through his numerous politically oriented essays that first appeared in the influential journal that he edited for many years, *Les Temps Modernes*, and on to the controversial, much-debated interview with his secretary, Benny Lévy, that was transcribed in the newspaper, *Le Nouvel Observateur*, just before his death – it will be useful to consult my own book by that title, *Sartre's Political Theory*,[1] and/or other secondary works on the topic. Here, I shall be concentrating on volume 1 of the *Critique* proper, considered in its historical setting, with sidelong glances at some of the other authors being considered in this collection and at a few of their (and Sartre's) contemporaries.

The Background: *Search for a Method*

First of all, however, it will be necessary to discuss a crucial independent Sartrean essay, *Search for a Method* (*Question de méthode*), which is to be found as the preliminary 100-odd pages of the two French editions of the work, but is not part of the English edition. (On the first page of the latter, with which our own excerpts here begin, it is referred to by the title that it was given in the UK, *The Problem of Method*; it is the same essay by another name.) Hazel Barnes's translation of it was published and available to Anglophone readers some thirteen years before the *Critique* itself. But what is even odder is that the original essay had been published in Polish translation three years before it first appeared in French!

Some background information is in order. With relatively slight variations from country to country, a rigid discipline had been in effect for many years in the Soviet Union, and since World War II in the so-called "Soviet Bloc" in Eastern Europe, with respect to what philosophers and writers in general were permitted by the authorities to publish. There, a dichotomy was presumed to obtain between, on the one hand, Marxist theory, which (with due allowances being made, at some times more than at others, for *some* differences of interpretation within the general framework) reflected the truth about the world, including history and politics and even epistemology and the philosophy of science, and, on the other hand, bourgeois theory, which expressed the false ideological premises of a ruling class trying desperately to cling to power. If and when professional philosophers in those countries published anything concerning contemporary "bourgeois" philosophy, they were expected to treat it in a hostile, polemical fashion. (Writing about the past *history* of philosophy was a somewhat different, more complicated matter.) Intellectuals who were members of the then-powerful French Communist Party were expected to observe the same discipline if they wished to continue to be members. Sartre, who was sympathetic with many of the communists' long-term goals and wished to conduct dialogue with them, but who at the same time, as the philosopher of freedom *par excellence*, could not accept either Party discipline or the rigidly deterministic view of the world that lay at the core of the "official," Marxist-Leninist interpretation of Marx's philosophy known as dialectical materialism, was repeatedly rebuffed and denounced by them as another bourgeois philosopher – a particularly dangerous one because of the great popularity of his existentialism, even though at times they accepted his *political* collaboration. Then, in 1956, came "the Thaw."

The trigger event for this was the death of the Soviet Union's long-time, tyrannical dictator, Joseph Stalin. His successor, Nikita Khrushchev, gave a secret speech that was soon leaked to Western sources, in which he acknowledged some of Stalin's crimes and proposed a few timid steps towards intellectual as well as political experimentation or liberalization. One of the small results of this new policy as it filtered down through Communist Party hierarchies was to allow the editors of a Polish intellectual journal, *Twórczość*, to plan a special edition on contemporary thought in France – long a cultural beacon to many Polish intellectuals – and to invite Sartre to contribute a piece on Marxism and existentialism. He accepted, and *Search for a Method*, first entitled "Marksism i Egzystencjalizm," was the outcome.

Sartre begins *Search for a Method* with a notoriously oversimplified story about the history of Western philosophy, according to which one or two great philosophical worldviews, associated with the names of the "great men" who first formulated them, have dominated every epoch. He relegates other contemporary thought-systems, which he characterizes (in a special usage of the term that differs from Marx's and virtually everyone else's) as "ideologies," to the function of being supplements, so to speak, to the dominant philosophies (or, alternatively, of being reactionary efforts to return to earlier worldviews). That is the way in which he now regards existentialism, he says: as a subordinate though important ideology in the shadow of Marxism, the dominant philosophy of the present epoch. "Mainstream" Marxism, as he points out rather uncontroversially, has become dogmatic and frozen, and so existentialism's task is to reinject considerations of the role of personal free choice into a body of thinking that has come to suppose that all human behavior is predetermined. Eventually, he concludes, Marxism itself will be replaced by a "philosophy of freedom," the nature of which we at present lack the intellectual tools to be able to anticipate.

In the couse of this discussion Sartre makes some quite disparaging remarks about those whom he frequently calls, simply, "the Marxists" – i.e., those who have arrogated that label to themselves – such as his witticism that these people write as if they had had no childhoods, but had come into existence on the day of their first job. He advocates the introduction of ideas derived from Freud, among others, into the better, more adequate social history that he envisages for the future. His "question of method" is, precisely, how to work to develop such a complex, comprehensive method, beyond the reductivist tendencies of both American social science behaviorism and "orthodox" Marxism; he proposes a method that he calls "progressive-regressive", a term borrowed from a French Marxist contemporary of his, Henri Lefebvre. The initial, "regressive" part would consist in trying to go beneath the surface appearances of existing societies in order to uncover underlying social and psychosocial structures – something that Sartre regards mainstream Marxism as having utterly failed to do, relying instead on *a priori* categories, and that he finds somewhat lacking even in the work of Marx himself. In an important sense, this *is* Sartre's quick, preliminary description of what volume 1 of the *Critique* is supposed to undertake. Volume 2, then, as Sartre indicates in the last sentence of volume 1 (and of our excerpts from the *Critique*), was to have exemplified the "progressive" part of the method, reconstructing segments of actual history on the basis of the discoveries made in volume 1. As a matter of fact, the bulk of what Sartre actually wrote toward volume 2, which, as I have indicated, has been published posthumously, is devoted to doing just that with respect to a period of Soviet history during the 1930s, when Stalin held sway.

Situating and Beginning to Read the Text

In starting to read our excerpts from the text, those who are at all familiar with *Being and Nothingness* will no doubt sense a "disconnect," because most of the language and many of the philosophical concerns are so different between the two works. This sense can be somewhat mitigated by a careful reading of a few lines that we have included from a footnote, in which Sartre addresses "those who have read *Being and Nothingness*" and proceeds to draw some parallels between the "for-itself" of the latter and the notion of *praxis* in the *Critique*, on the one hand, and between the "in-itself" and what he now calls the inert, or inert matter, on the other. Just so, there is a striking "disconnect" between the language of the *Critique*, engaged as much of it is in the investigation of underlying structures at a level of what one might call a "deep sociology" which borders on ontology, and what is, at least by comparison, the almost chatty style of *Search for a Method*, devoted to situating Sartre's newer philosophical interests within a global historical context. But Sartre does indicate the connection between the two, as he sees it, in the opening sentences of the *Critique*, in which he asserts it as his goal to justify the truth of "the materialist dialectic" which is the core of the Marxist worldview.

The words of the title, "critique of dialectical reason," are obviously intended to evoke memories of Kant, whose three critiques – of pure reason, of pure practical reason, and of judgment – define, for Sartre and indeed for many others, a complex worldview of their own that is still very much alive. Similarly, in his introductory remarks in the *Critique* proper Sartre uses a parody of another Kantian title to affirm his intention to present "prolegomena to any future anthropology" (with the word "anthropology" being understood in a very broad sense, roughly equivalent to "social theory," that is much more common in Europe than in the United States and that was familiar to Kant himself). But for Kant, as is well known, "dialectical" thinking within the domain of pure reason culminated in irresoluble antinomies. It was his great successor and critic, Hegel, who both made dialectic the core of his own thinking and saw it as the key to explaining all of reality. Marx, following Hegel, agreed in principle with this but saw Hegel's "core" insight as having been wrapped in a "mystical shell," that is, a belief that ultimate reality is spiritual, which Marx sought to shuck in favor of a materialist, but still dialectical, conception of the world. Sartre, in both the language and the insights of the *Critique*, situates himself squarely within this tradition. So, in fact, do most if not all of the other philosophers considered in the present volume, even though they all, to a greater or lesser extent, distance themselves from Hegel's optimism, which Marx shared in certain ways though not in others, about the possibility of acquiring absolute, comprehensive knowledge and of fully realizing human freedom.

In one passage that we have excerpted from the first half of the *Critique*, Sartre cautiously indicates a closer affinity to Hegel than to Marx on the issue, crucial for assessing just how "optimistic" his own theory ultimately is, of whether it might ever be possible to overcome all forms of alienation. It is a question that he will raise again, as an open and unanswered one, in a few very brief, isolated passages later in the work. But his earlier remarks strike me as ultimately indicative of his fundamental outlook: "alien-ation" in the limited sense of the capitalist forms of exploitation described by Marx could conceivably be eliminated, although it is by no means certain that it *will* be, but alienation in the broader, more all-pervasive sense in which Hegel often uses it is in principle ineliminable. Hegel, as an idealist for whom world history is ultimately to be conceived as a theodicy – a justification of the workings of Spirit – had a gloss on the ubiquitous workings of alienation that was, in the last analysis, Panglossian: this is the best of possible worlds, after all. Sartre, as a self-professed materialist, has no such resort. As a result, the *Critique* as a whole comes across to most readers as a far from upbeat work.

But, I would like to suggest by way of compensation, it just may have the merit of being *true*, in fulfillment of the hope expressed by Sartre in his opening paragraph. That is, a dialectical approach to society and history – viewing negations of negations as leading to affirmations, taking conflict to be the motor force of history, and other, related fundamental insights which Sartre enumerates in this text and countless others throughout the volume and which are foreign to a straightforward "analytic" approach to the sociopolitical world – may in fact yield a deeper and fuller understanding of that world, even if there is no guarantee that it will make us happier. In the ensuing excerpts he takes the line that this truth, if such it is, is not self-evident *a priori* but must rather be demonstrated in the course of working through the investigation itself.

The other obvious, complementary way of vindicating the truth or validity (perhaps a better word here, since what is in question is not a series of propositions, but rather an entire method and world-outlook) of dialectical reason as Sartre construes it is to see if it helps furnish insights into actual institutions and events. Sartre himself asserts, early in the text, that these insights of his have become accessible to "anyone" as a result of several developments – the previously mentioned theoretical contributions of Hegel and Marx, of course, but also two twentieth-century phenomena: the enormous "*abuses* . . . of dialectical rationality" that were carried out, in Marx's name, under Stalinism, and the increasingly "one-World" nature of the post-Stalinist global config-uration. (Although it is not made clear in the text of the translation, Sartre writes the words "one World" in English, a rarity for him.) Wilfrid Desan, in one of the first book-length studies of the *Critique*,[2] made a good case for applying Sartre's dialectical explanatory techniques to the United States civil rights movement, which reached its apogee in the years immediately following the *Critique*'s publication. Then came 1968, the year of student uprisings in Paris and throughout much of the world, as well as of the crushing of the so-called "Prague Spring" by the Soviet Army. The relatively formless, anti-political politics of the initial student movements, as they unfolded, showed some striking affinities with Sartre's account, very unconventional within the traditions of modern Marxist and non-Marxist political theory alike, of the formation and behavior of what he calls "groups." At the same time, the Soviet actions in Czechoslovakia deprived Sartre and many other Western intellectuals of any lingering hopes they might have had for a reversion of that post-but still quasi-Stalinist system to its self-professed original Marxian socialist ideals; in fact, I think that they can be seen in retrospect to have rendered nearly inevitable, to a greater extent than any other single event, that system's eventual demise, even though a little more than two decades were still to pass before this happened. In short, there is much about the apparent applicability of Sartre's approach, even when considered in this very preliminary and superficial way, that makes plausible his claims concerning its explanatory value.

The correctness, at least as I see it (and hope that readers of these excerpts may see it), of this observation did not, however, lead to very widespread recognition of Sartre's political philosophy as magisterial, much less prophetic, over those same ensuing years. During the Paris events in 1968 he participated in some student sit-ins as an observer, and was permitted to speak, but told to keep it very brief; rather than Sartre, the manifest intellectual hero to many of the student radicals was Louis Althusser, a Marxist theoretical "hard-linear" who was routinely given the label (even though he himself did not much like it) of "structuralist," the name of the dominant intellectual fad of that post-and anti-existentialist epoch. (Althusser, then still a member of the French Communist Party, ended up supporting that party's more politically establishmentarian position by refusing to endorse the students' demands; this initiated a series of events, beginning with a recurrence of his chronic mental illness, that marked the beginning of a precipitous decline in his tragic career. But that is another story.) Other major new French thinkers – all having in common with Sartre, as I have already noted, the Hegelian–Marxist heritage, but leading in different directions that are now often unfairly lumped together as "postmodern" – were already emerging or in the wings: Michel Foucault, mentioned at the outset of this essay; Jacques Derrida, Althusser's colleague in philosophy at Sartre's elite *alma mater*, the Ecole Normale Supérieure, whose bibliography begins in 1962 and who by 1968 had achieved international recognition; Jean-François Lyotard, whose *La Phénoménologie* was published the following year; and so on. Sartre – above all the existentialist Sartre of *Being and Nothingness*, but secondarily Sartre the dissident public intellectual and editor of *Les Temps Modernes* – had been a significant part of their intellectual formations, as Derrida in particular has generously acknowledged on numerous recent occasions; but at that point they regarded his past hegemony as a burden of which they were striving, rather successfully as it turned out, to be relieved. Sartre's radical new political philosophy was not something to which they wished to devote their attention.

If there is a single word that epitomizes the poststructuralists' wish to reject the philosophies of the past, especially the influential Hegelian and Marxist philosophies in their original, literal versions, it is "totality." Lyotard, in *The Postmodern Condition*, is especially emphatic about this, but he speaks for a whole movement or set of movements: revulsion at the claims of any philosophers to be able comprehensively to grasp any wholes, much less, as in Hegel's case, the whole of reality. The concept of totality is indeed a central element in *Althusser's* reconstruction of Marx, but for Sartre in the *Critique* it names only one possible perspective on any given society or segment of history – a fixed, external one which necessarily falsifies the actual evolutions of societies and hence cannot serve as the basis of accurate explanation. The contrasting, more valid perspective, in Sartre's terminology, is that of "totalization," which implies movement and open-endedness. He explains this contrast at some length in passages that we have excerpted from the early pages of the *Critique*. Sartre's ultimate project is to be able to view all of history as one vast, ongoing, complex, and not predetermined movement of totalization, but he more frequently applies this term, which he employs extensively, to *segments* of sociohistorical interactions. In a sense, then, Sartre's orientation in the *Critique* falls midway between an extreme postmodern position, which would entirely ban attempts to furnish what Lyotard and others have called "grand narratives" – generalizations about *any* significant aspect of reality – and the unabashedly totalistic, "God's-eye" view of society and history that is the central object of postmodernists' scorn. Sartre, no believer, refers to history as a "totalization without a Totalizer" and to societies as "detotalized totalities."

Nevertheless, despite the large amount of indeterminacy that has always been central to Sartre's philosophy from its earliest formulations, he unquestionably does propose, in the *Critique*, to develop intellectual tools to enable us to *explain* the sociopolitical world; in this thoroughly obvious sense, his principal purpose is far from that of Derridean "deconstruction," with its primarily Heideggerean and other Continental philosophical origins. But the kind of explanation that Sartre is seeking to provide is also quite unorthodox by what pass for the "mainstream" standards of Anglo-American philosophy. The analytic approach to the world, which his friend and severe critic, Claude Lévi-Strauss, proudly identifies with his own scientific structural anthropology in an early study of the *Critique* in his book, *La Pensés sauvage* (*The Savage Mind*),[3] but which could easily be extended to include most of the modern Western tradition of liberal political theory outside the orbit of Hegel and Marx and their successors, is inadequate to explain what it sets out to explain, according to Sartre. In particular, he argues, because it views its objects as fixed and essentially atemporal, it is incapable of dealing with *novelty*, the new. (One might think here, although Sartre does not mention this, of the large number of writers on democratic theory who take for granted what are assumed to be the fundamental rules of the democratic game, or to put it another way assume that everyone knows what democracy *is*; they then have great difficulty in understanding and attempting to pigeonhole new but untraditional forms of apparently democratic activity, such as the recent wave of protests concerning the World Trade Organization.)

The comparatively brief portion of the *Critique* which Sartre labels "Introduction" concludes with a short subsection outlining the overall plan of the remainder of the volume. Having begun to situate both conceptually and historically, and both in Sartre's own terms and in terms of some rival approaches, the nature and purpose of the *Critique* as we find them expressed especially in that Introduction, we may now begin to consider just how, in the bulk of the work, he goes about trying actually to justify dialectical reason's claims to explanatory superiority.

The Domain of the Practico-Inert

Beyond the Introduction, the book is divided into two halves, "From Individual Praxis to the Practico-Inert," and "From Groups to History." Sartre takes as his starting point the human individual, considered as an entity with *needs* in a world characterized by *scarcity*. Although themselves material, human beings are *organisms* who are condemned, so to speak, constantly to make free choices to act rather than, like inorganic matter, simply to be acted upon – in short, they are at core beings of what Sartre calls *praxis*. His selection of this Greek term has a number of implications. Among other things, it stands in contrast to *hexis*, passive habit; it evokes the early, more ethical and philosophical, writings of Marx, who defined *praxis* as "sensuous human activity," in contrast to the more deterministic later Marx preferred by communist orthodoxy; and it signals a shift of orientation in Sartre's account of human reality from the focus on the *consciousness* of the "for-itself" in *Being and Nothingness* to a new emphasis on *labor* or work. Human beings, as free *praxis*, are necessitated to work on inert matter in order to satisfy their needs. Thus a dialectical contrast can be seen to be built into the human condition at the most elementary level: the interaction between *praxis* and matter immediately creates a vast realm of reality which Sartre denominates "the practico-inert."

This initial Sartrean account drew early criticism, particularly from some Marxists, for taking the individual as its starting point; it was, they said, just more of the same, since the existentialist standpoint of *Being and Nothingness* had been highly individualistic – either basically solipsistic, totally centered on the individual self, or at best capable of dealing with dyadic relations between single selves and single Others, these relations being conceived as essentially conflictual. (It is the latter type of relationship that is captured in Sartre's famous metaphor of "the Look" in his earlier work.) But in fact a careful reading of some of the texts which we have excerpted from Book I of the *Critique* shows that Sartre did indeed modify his perspective a good deal. While still maintaining that *praxis* is basically individual – it is simply a fact that we are individuals, each with his or her separate body – and continuing to contend throughout his account that any *common* human activity, including the group *praxis* on which he concentrates in Book II, will always be constituted by individual *praxeis*, rather than ever being self-sufficient in the way in which Hegel and the Classical Greek political philosophers claimed that communities could be, he now takes considerable pains to acknowledge the fundamental importance of *reciprocity* and *triadicity*. His portrait of the vacationing bourgeois intellectual looking out the window of his country inn at a gardener working inside the wall of the property and a man simultaneously repairing the road outside the wall, each oblivious of the other but both seen by the unifying "third party" who happens in this case to be the intellectual – the first of several memorable phenomenological descriptions which we have excerpted – well illustrates this change of emphasis stemming from a new sense of greater social complexity on his part.

But this new insistence on reciprocity hardly signals the appearance of a Sartre who looks at the world through rose-colored glasses; far from it! While he regards scarcity – an extremely broad concept which never, to my mind, receives adequate definition either in the *Critique* proper or in *Search for a Method* where it was first introduced – as being a contingent fact about our world that might not obtain in other possible worlds, he depicts its pervasive presence among us, from the level of global hunger to the most mundane everyday interactions, as the source of oppression and violence. It is as a result of the fact that, given the existence of scarcity, there are too many of us, he contends, that Manichaean views of the other individual or tribe as a radically evil threat to ourselves originate; indeed, he suggests in one especially provocative passage, this perception constitutes "the first movement of ethics." Sartre's characterization of humanity, in this section, as an "intelligent, carnivorous, and cruel" species has frequently been compared to Thomas Hobbes's picture of the state of nature, *homo homini lupus* (man a wolf to man). But Hobbes's account *is* thoroughly individualistic, so extremely so that critics have justifiably questioned how any communication could ever take place in such a state (and incidentally underestimates the pack-orientation even of wolves!), whereas Sartre's insistence on dialectical reciprocity makes for a more realistic, though no more sanguine, account.

Indeed, this infernal domain of the practico-inert as initially experienced, according to Sartre, is one in which men are not only potential "wolves" to other men, but also to themselves. That is, the work that is cooperatively carried out under conditions of scarcity often results in the reduction of free human beings to a condition resembling the matter on which they are forced to work, as slaves of necessity. He illustrates his point with a couple of examples, one relatively recent, the other centuries-old: the negative effect, on the nascent working class which it created, of the positive discovery of coal's usefulness for the Industrial Revolution, and the ecologically devastating outcome of Chinese peasants' traditional deforestation practices. These examples help to bring out the sense in which Sartre considers himself a materialist, attempting to develop an adequate, monistic theory "which can transcend two true but contradictory propositions: all existence in the universe is material; everything in the world of man is human."

For most political philosophers within the broad liberal individualist tradition, the Archimedean point for explaining the motivation of human social interaction is some version of "self-interest" or simply "interest"; this concept undergirds, for instance, David Hume's account of the origins of the "artificial virtue" of justice, John Rawls's understanding of what it is that drives actors in actual society although not, as he insists rather disingenuously, the parties who decide on the rules of the game in his imaginary "original position," and indeed the entire tradition of bourgeois economic thought that claims Hume's acquaintance Adam Smith as its progenitor. Sartre proceeds to take on this conceptual dragon particularly in the form in which it has influenced even Marxist theorists, who should know better. In what I consider to be one of the most valuable pieces of sheer philosophical analysis in the book, he "deconstructs" the concept of interest, showing its nullity as a primitive explanatory concept. When workers themselves or their Marxist advocates appeal to "the interest of the working class," he shows, it is a useful way of asserting their freedom against the implicit claim that they are eternally condemned to be oppressed workers and that this is their *destiny*; but to regard "interest" as such as a *given* natural fact about every human being is in the last analysis to render social interaction unintelligible.

The final portion of Book I, "From Individual Praxis to the Practico-Inert," ranges over collective entities in general, with greatest emphasis being placed on the type of passive collection of human beings gathered around a common enterprise which in one way or another controls them that Sartre calls "the series." Two detailed illustrations, excerpted by us here, that he furnishes of this phenomenon are the queue of commuters waiting to board an urban bus in Paris and the government-sponsored radio broadcast that is being diffused to impotent listeners nationwide. He indicates that the capitalist system itself is a larger-scale instance of the same phenomenon of seriality, which atomizes individuals and makes both individuals and sets of individuals Other to one another. Is there, then, no hope, no chance of escaping the cycle of self-oppression that we all ultimately concur in reaffirming, in large and small ways, throughout most of our lives? For the Sartre of the *Critique*, there *is* hope: it lies in the novel type of freely formed social structure, at its outset radically different from the series, which he calls "the group."

The Taking of the Bastille and its Aftermath

The *Critique* reaches its dramatic climax, in the middle of the volume, with Sartre's analysis of this great event in French history, the beginning of what later came to be called the French Revolution. While very interesting in its own right (and in certain respects controversial, particularly with respect to the part played, or perhaps not played, by "outside agitators"), it is intended simply as an illustration of the formation of Sartrean groups. It is an extreme, or limiting case, illustration, at least if Sartre had his historical facts right: under conditions of great pressure in the form of a perceived external threat from the king's army to massacre the inhabitants of an entire, proto-working class neighborhood called the Quartier Saint-Antoine, a sea change, Apocalyptic in its intensity, occurred in the attitudes of these previously docile people, who first gathered in the streets and then eventually "took things into their own hands" by attacking and capturing the fortress-prison which occupied a commanding position overlooking the district. To the type of "hot," volatile, virtually formless social formation exemplified by the early stages of such a mob, which "decides" spontaneously on its goal – in this case the taking of the Bastille – when one of its members, anyone at all, gives the word ("*À la Bastille!*", or whatever), which everyone then immediately accepts and acts upon, Sartre gives the suggestive name, *le groupe en fusion*, the group in fusion or the fusing group. Unfortunately, the usually competent English translator chose for some reason to translate this expression as "the fused group," unwittingly suggesting a certain sense of fixedness and of its having been put together from the outside that is just the opposite of Sartre's intention. Nevertheless, the originality of Sartre's dialectical account of revolution comes through. It serves as a sort of regulative ideal for a political theory which accepts, and under certain circumstances may advocate, radical as opposed to merely incremental, institutional change.

At the risk of sounding flippant, I would like to suggest that the entire remainder of the *Critique* can be viewed as a downhill journey, and that Sartre himself presents it this way. It is also, not surprisingly, in this "downhill" portion of the work that Sartre deals, in his own unique fashion, with some of the central concepts of modern political philosophy, notably sovereignty, power and authority, acceptance, legitimacy, and the State. For if truth be told (and he admitted as much on occasion in interviews), his own emotional predilections in this area tended towards anarchism or, to use a slightly less extreme term, left libertarianism, and many of the detailed analyses that we have excerpted from this portion of the *Critique*, while purporting to remain at the level of explanation rather than moral exhortation, can in fact also be interpreted as furnishing systematic justifications of this position.

Once a group in fusion has achieved its initial objective, assuming that it does succeed, then, as Sartre demonstrates, there soon arises a felt need to create some more permanent structure in order to try to guard against a reversal. In the case of the group that captured the Bastille, for instance, there was a danger that the authorities might return with troops, and so an around-the-clock vigil was required, and so on. The first stage in ensuring greater permanence, then, takes the form of what Sartre calls "the surviving group," (*groupe de survivance*), although the expression for the next stage, "The Statutory Group," canonized by Sheridan-Smith as the heading of this portion of his translation, has come to be used more frequently in English. (The French noun *statut*, which Sartre employs and no doubt overuses in the *Critique*, can sometimes mean "statute," or rule, and sometimes bears a meaning much closer to "status"; the English translation almost invariably renders it as "statute," which makes for some unnecessarily peculiar-sounding passages.) In any event, the means adopted to ensure the group's survival is called by Sartre "the oath", *le serment*, which among other things recalls, as he himself indicates, the "Tennis Court Oath" that was taken by members of the nascent Constituent Assembly as the French Revolution escalated following the events at the Bastille. Here again – and this is my final such warning – there is some problem with the choice of word, since Sheridan-Smith's preferred English translation of *le serment* is actually "the pledge," although he also renders it as "the oath" in some passages. In this case, however, I am more sympathetic with what I take to have been the translator's reasoning, since Sartre intends his analysis to apply not only to such highly dramatic, world-historical events as the fateful decision by the Assembly members to solidify and make visible and permanent their resistance to the absolute monarchy, but also to much more banal group formations; and for the latter, "pledge" (e.g., a college fraternity or sorority pledge) is a more apt expression.

Sartre insists that this pledge or oath is not to be construed as his version of a social contract, since he is using his concept to explain the necessary dialectical logic of *any* group whose members wish to guarantee its permanence, whereas every contract is particular, with its own specific terms limited to its signatories, and hence incapable of serving as the moral/legal basis of a whole society. Of course, the notion of the social contract has typically been employed in just this way by many political philosophers, from Hobbes to Rawls and beyond, as a highly general, sometimes rather vague, term to impute legitimacy to governments by suggesting that they have a popular, and hence at least in some sense ultimately democratic, basis. Sartre is deeply suspicious of any such imputation. Talk of a social contract in general seems to him a mystification that falsely idealizes the real world with a view to inducing citizens' acquiescence to governments.

At times Sartre himself tends somewhat to idealize his "pledge," going so far as to call it "the origin of humanity" in one passage. His basic point is that, in taking the pledge to remain faithful to the group's goals and to one another, the members, who in their prior state had been serialized, atomized individuals, forge bonds of "fraternity" (the third of the three slogans of the French Revolutionaries after liberty and equality, as it will be recalled) which give them a new life, so to speak, in common. But he also goes out of his way to stress the dialectically necessary dark side of any pledge, which he calls "terror." Groups of the sort exemplified by the takers of the Bastille are typically born out of *violence*, as he has shown, and he contends that the effort to ensure against the destruction of their new life must entail a certain interiorization of that external violence within the group itself. He is right in noting that the most extreme forms of oaths (e.g., "blood brotherhoods") actually do involve expressions of a willingness to be killed if the oath-taker should ever betray the group, but it is also true that far softer forms exhibit some of the same dialectical pattern that Sartre dramatically calls "fraternity-terror." Most of us, for example, have no doubt experienced at least mild feelings of disappointment and disapproval when someone who was once as committed as we to a group to which we belong – be it even something as banal as a card club! – begins to lose interest and "drop out."

In the succeeding 100(–)plus pages of the *Critique*, from which for reasons of space we have taken no excerpts, Sartre explores various forms of *organization*, such as football teams and political parties, showing how diverse roles and functions develop as surviving, "statutory" groups may begin to move in the direction of full-fledged institutions. I say "may" because Sartre is certainly not insisting on any one inevitable trajectory, and wishes, as he says, to hold open the possibility of reversals of direction, or of skipping some stages of development, etc. But the very sequence of his analyses establishes, willy(-)nilly, a certain sense of direction, and the impression that this direction is not a positive one at least from the standpoint of the original group project is strongly conveyed in the next part of the text from which we have taken excerpts, in which the institutionalized group, or *institution*, is first introduced. Institutions, for Sartre, are characterized by hierarchy and by the pervasive internal exercise of *power*, as is well illustrated by that quintessential conformist institution, the army. "The institutional moment," he says here, " . . . corresponds to what might be called the systematic self-domestication of man by man." Freedom now disappears from view, and everyone in the group is "reified," or rendered thing-like. This part of Sartre's work constitutes an interesting anticipation of Michel Foucault's later focus on power, but there are important differences in tone and content between them: among other things, Foucault's analysis is far less radical and less resentful of the role played by power in social structures, as well as being much more detailed. Sartre rather quickly moves on to analyze one particular form of power, "a power over all powers and over all third parties," namely, *authority*.

Sovereignty, the Sovereign Individual, and the State

Although Sartre does not delve into the history of the notion of "sovereignty," it is interesting to recall in view of his own rather original, highly "deconstructive" treatment of it. In brief, "sovereignty" evolved from meaning simply the rule of a "sovereign" or monarch into the clearly defined concept, of utmost importance for both municipal and international law, with which we are familiar today in the early modern political philosophies first of Jean Bodin and then of Hobbes. Now, of course, we are witnessing its gradual erosion in the New World Order. Sartre appears to be annoyed, as it were, with any discussion of sovereignty and, by implication, of the so-called basis of political authority that treats these ideas as problematic or even somewhat mysterious. There could be only two possible sources for a sovereignty conceived as a mysterious bond existing among citizens, he says – God, or else some process internal to a society whereby it becomes a "totalized totality," a completely integrated whole – and both of these are illusions. In fact, the only real source of sovereignty, and in a significant sense the only real sovereign, is each individual human being as free. What happens is simply that as groups become increasingly institutionalized, with roles being allocated and functions assigned, the supreme power within them tends to devolve upon a single leader or "a unified subgroup." To be accurate, no sovereign, however powerful, ever exercises more than a *quasi*-sovereignty, because at any moment his soldiers or other enforcers could decide to refuse his commands. The exercise of sovereignty, as Sartre conceives it, is always a "top-down" procedure. Since no society as a whole can ever, realistically speaking, constitute a single group, but rather always consists of a number of (often overlapping) groups and series, the fact is that sovereign authority is always deployed by one or a few individuals over the vast mass of a society's members, who are passive in relation to that sovereign.

Having dealt dismissively with sovereign authority in a way that writers who see it in a more favorable light, such as Hannah Arendt, would find completely unacceptable, Sartre turns to its most important locus in the modern world, the State. His quite jaundiced views on this topic follow from what he has said previously: the State can never embody the wishes of a society as a whole or even of a majority, and the question of "legitimacy," such a central concern for political philosophers, especially Continental European political philosophers, from Jean-Jacques Rousseau to Jürgen Habermas, is more or less a "non-starter" for Sartre. That is, the State may indeed have legitimacy for the governing group that constitutes it, he says, but the State is neither legitimate nor necessarily illegitimate for the members of the collectives which are being governed, who have little to say about it. This is not to deny that something resembling *acceptance*, even widespread acceptance, of the State's rule may occur, but it is at best only a passive, acquiescent acceptance. As for the Marxist view that the State is the organ of the dominant class, Sartre agrees with it, but with an important reservation: the successful State must paradoxically present itself, at the same time, "as a deep negation of the class struggle." Finally, he insists that every group, in his somewhat technical sense of that word, must define itself either quite outside the sphere of the State or else in opposition to it.

A couple of comments about this Sartrean treatment of political philosophy's most sacred cows may be in order before we move to consider the dénouement of volume 1. First, by way of criticism, it could be said to have been too much influenced by the negative models which Sartre had most in mind. To begin with, his treatment of sovereignty seems, throughout much of the text, to be heavily weighted towards imagining the sovereignty of a single person, although he does admit the possibility of a small subgroup's exercising sovereignty. To some extent, he was thinking of ancient examples – at one point, not cited in our excerpts, he mentions "an Assyrian King", for instance – but above all he was thinking of Stalin's role as "incarnation" or embodiment of the sovereignty of the Russian people, which is the single most central theme of the unfinished volume 2. Had he gone on to complete volume 1, he once indicated, he would have dealt at equal or greater length with the still more complex case of the embodiment of sovereignty in a more democratic structure, as well as with the intermediate case of an aristocratic republic, of which Renaissance Venice would have been his case study. It is perhaps no wonder that he gave up trying to finish this task: even the very incomplete portion of volume 2 that we now have occupies more than 450 pages! In any case, his preoccupation with the case of Stalin, understandable as it is for someone whose most productive years coincided with the height of the Cold War, does somewhat skew the treatment of sovereignty and related subjects even here in volume 1.

But on a second, more positive note, I think that Sartre deserves more credit than he is usually accorded for sympathetically comprehending the deep malaise-*cum*-apathy of so many members of modern societies with respect to their governments, a common attitude which contrasts so strongly with the cheerleading for the glories of procedural democracy that one commonly finds in books on the topic, or with the impossibly idealistic expectations of consensus through communication that lie at the heart of Habermas's intellectual project. One need only consider the percentages of eligible voters who actually cast ballots wherever this is not mandatory, now even in countries of Eastern Europe where a few years ago there was so much talk about having a choice at last. Sartre takes the measure of polls (concerning which his text contains several interesting analyses which it has not been possible to include here) and elections alike, and shows us the vast gap between what they are supposed to mean and reality. Many have resented him for it: he was, in the words of the subtitle of John Gerassi's biography,[4] the "hated conscience of his century." On the other hand, there is today probably a more widespread awareness of the extent of the mystifications to which "popular opinion" is constantly being subjected than there was at the time at which the *Critique*, which is so relentless in identifying and debunking mystifications, was written.

With Sartre's account of sovereignty and the State, which also includes a discussion (not excerpted here) of bureaucracy and of the "cult of personality" that again draws heavily on the Soviet experience especially under Stalin, a sort of dialectical circle has been closed: that is, as he makes explicit what has become increasingly obvious in his account, the increasingly sclerosed groups that govern such regimes amount, in effect, to a return to seriality, Sartre's name for early, pre-group forms of social structure. It is at this point that, having finally attained, at least to his own satisfaction, the level of concrete social existence after nearly 700 pages of investigation of such structures, Sartre raises the question whether regrouping and petrification may not constantly recur in a perpetual cyclical movement. He responds to his own question by saying, rather disappointingly from the reader's point of view, that it doesn't matter, because in any case his goal has been the furthering of intelligibility, and he thinks that he has been successful in achieving it.

Dénouement

A large portion of the book's last 100(−)plus pages is devoted to class struggle as a concrete phenomenon, although these pages also contain an interesting analysis of racism and colonialism which, without mentioning him by name, shows indebtedness to Frantz Fanon's work on Algeria, and which anticipates later treatments of the so-called "Third World" by such philosophers as Enrique Dussel, himself greatly influenced by Sartre at a certain stage of his career. Sartre here combines a classical Marxian account of workers as commodities under capitalism with his own reflections on the Manichaean nature of the class struggle – the effort by capitalists, particularly in the nineteenth century, to define workers as "anti-human" or at any rate as lesser beings than themselves (the same type of mentality which today rationalizes, as entirely proper, the vast gap between CEO's salaries and perquisites and those of their employees), along with workers' concomitant refusal to accept this view and regard themselves as "evil." In place of the smooth intellectual defenses of the rightness of existing relations of class dominance, Sartre maintains, the very situation of being oppressed will, at the proper time and place, dialectically inspire workers to forge a new "truth" through collective action. After this moment of implicit exhortation, Sartre concludes volume 1 by returning to the theme of intelligibility or explanation as having been his principal objective.

The final paragraph of the book is meant to be an anticipation of volume 2, which was supposed to deal with "the real problem of History." It is Sartre's hope, as expressed in this paragraph, that it will eventually be possible to view History as being, in some very complex way, *one*, that is, as having followed a "totalizing" path through all the myriad smaller totalizations of particular historical developments, and as ultimately yielding, at least in principle, some intelligible truth about this path to historical investigators. (What we have of volume 2 bears the subtitle, "L'Intelligibilité de l'Histoire.") If we were to take the text of this paragraph in isolation, it might well be thought to justify postmodernists' concerns (and others' hopes) that Sartre was indeed posing as a new Hegel, with a totalistic or even, in a sense that is not overtly ideological but could nevertheless provoke fears and suspicions, *totalitarian* view of history. (In one sentence, he does actually use the word *totalitaire*.) His concluding words must at the very least be said to express a strong Sartrean *wish* for a radical "breakthrough" in this domain: to achieve new, comprehensive insights that have never before been attained, and that were in any event unattainable prior to the advent of our dawning "One World" after the failure of Stalinism. But it is hardly a philosophical "stretch" for me to observe that this wish appears extremely extravagant, to put it mildly, in light of all the possible ways, uncovered by Sartre himself in the course of his illuminating analyses, in which the most progressive sociopolitical projects may fail utterly and be succeeded by reactionary movements.

Moreover, if we leave the *Critique* for a moment and reflect on pronouncements made by Sartre in other famous texts, we will find a number, from both early and late in his career, in which he accepts the possibility that the historical future may turn out badly in terms of his own most fundamental political values, values which are perhaps most succinctly epitomized in the name of an intellectual Resistance group to which he belonged during World War II, "Socialism and Freedom." In the polemical open letter that constituted his break with Camus, occasioned by a negative review in *Les Temps Modernes* of the latter's book, *L'Homme Révolté* (*The Rebel*) and Camus' angry response, Sartre upbraided him for allegedly waiting to learn whether history has a meaning, rather than acting on the recognition that it is we who give it the meaning(s) we choose to give it. And in the shortest and most finished book-length work by Sartre among those that have been published posthumously, *Truth and Existence*, he makes much of the idea that each *generation* gives its own new meaning(s) to past history, and that there can never be a final, definitive summing-up because, when the human race ends, there will be no one present to "close humanity's eyes," as he colorfully puts it. Thus he repeatedly offered good reasons, throughout his career, for being highly skeptical of efforts to extract an ultimate meaning from history.

The theme from *Truth and Existence* concerning the generational relativity of humanity's understanding of its past suggests a useful way of taking the "final" measure of the significance of the *Critique* – though of course this cannot really be final, either, for the very same reason: this work will almost certainly be judged differently at a later time, just as I myself see it somewhat differently now from the way I looked at it when I first read it soon after its publication. Far more than most political philosophers, for whom the lure of sketching out imaginary ideal states of affairs – Republics, original positions, communicative speech situations, etc. – and/or sets of pure normative principles so often proves irresistible, Sartre tried very hard to ground his explanatory framework in concrete experience. Despite his sometimes annoying tendency to write more abstractly and to use more technical terms specific to this framework than may have been strictly necessary, he was often, in my view, quite successful, as for instance in his accounts of the bus queue and of the government-controlled radio broadcast. What he may be regarded as having accomplished best in the *Critique*, even though his most central trope, the taking of the Bastille, comes from the late eighteenth century, is to have conveyed a strong sense of both the extreme alienation and frustration and also the ever-recurring sense of hope for a radically different and brighter future that were characteristic of the time at which the book was published. A Leftist worldview heavily influenced by the philosophy of Marx but not dominated by simplistic, dogmatic Marxism-Leninism had wide currency in France and virtually worldwide (though least so in the Anglo-Saxon countries); the colonial empires were crumbling; resistance to hegemonic capitalist institutions and the profit-oriented consumerist values that they reinforce was still widely regarded as feasible; and there were still those who, taking some modicum of inspiration from the admittedly flawed but nevertheless potentially promising Yugoslav example, thought that institutional communism itself just might ultimately be corrigible in the long term. At the same time, the threat of a massive exchange of nuclear weapons between the USSR and the West, which could have been the ultimate resolution of the Cold War, was still considered very real by intelligent observers. (Its reality has been confirmed with certainty by recent revelations concerning the Cuba Missile Crisis of 1963.) This is the actual world of which Sartre's *Critique of Dialectical Reason* is redolent, even when at its most abstract.

It is no longer our world at the beginning of the new century. Marxism has of course returned to the status of being a spectre, many former colonies have become globalization's victims with lower living standards than those of decades ago, transnational capitalist consumerism is experiencing a triumphalist phase, ex-Yugoslavia is splintered and much of it is in ruins, and the old institutional communism survives, if at all, in Cuba and perhaps one or two other isolated outposts. (It does *not* survive in China, rhetoric to the contrary notwithstanding.) The threat of a nuclear war between superpowers has temporarily receded, if for no other reason than the fact that there is now only one superpower. Political processes have become sclerosed along lines anticipated in the latter half of the *Critique*, and neither "politics as usual" nor revolutionary politics occupies the public's attention to the degree that both did in Sartre's day. At the same time, his prediction in *Search for a Method* that the era of Marxism would be succeeded by that of a philosophy of freedom, with as yet indeterminable contours, has been falsified: freedom-talk nowadays concerns primarily the freedom of the markets, and in virtually all non-economic aspects of social life there is far greater emphasis on *control* and repression.

Not every reader will agree with these generalization about the present era, and there will no doubt be those who will point, optimistically, to the overcoming of past communicative "scarcities" by means of the Internet and other new media as the most important clue to charting the "true" direction that History will take in our "one world" . . . But at the same time no one can deny the many obvious ways in which these same media also dramatically increase the possibilities for near-total control by a powerful few over the rest. . . . But, again at the same time, the possibilities of large-scale, violent disruptions of the "Net" by hackers with anti–Establishment agendas have also increased. . . . And so on.

This point-counterpoint dialogue can be seen as illustrating, it seems to me, the two single most salient elements of the political philosophy of the *Critique* at its most basic level: the *dialectical* nature of political change, which is itself unending, and the unpredictability of future changes due to the role of *freedom* in human affairs. In emphasizing these elements and integrating them into an open-ended but comprehensive explanatory framework, Sartre has left us with an interesting, challenging alternative to standard analytic approaches to politics from within the tradition of political liberalism – approaches that appear to some of us increasingly irrelevant in a globalized and economically polarized world that is evolving as rapidly as ours is.

Notes

1 William L. McBride, *Sartre's Political Theory* (Bloomington and Indianapolis: Indiana University Press, 1991).
2 Wilfrid Desan, *The Marxism of Jean-Paul Sartre* (Garden City, NY: Doubleday, 1965).
3 Claude Lévi-Strauss, *The Savage Mind* (Chicago: University of Chicago Press, 1966), 245–69.
4 John Gerassi, *Jean-Paul Sartre: Hated Conscience of His Century* (Chicago: University of Chicago Press, 1989).

PART III

CRITICAL THEORY

LIBERAL DEMOCRACY AND THE DIALECTIC OF INDIVIDUAL AND COMMUNITY

5

THREE NORMATIVE MODELS OF DEMOCRACY

Jürgen Habermas

In what follows I refer to the idealized distinction between the "liberal" and the "republican" understanding of politics – terms which mark the fronts in the current debate in the United States initiated by the so-called communitarians. Drawing on the work of Frank Michelman, I will begin by describing the two polemically contrasted models of democracy with specific reference to the concept of the citizen, the concept of law, and the nature of processes of political will-formation. In the second part, beginning with a critique of the "ethical overload" of the republican model, I introduce a third, procedural model of democracy for which I propose to reserve the term "deliberative politics."

I

The crucial difference between liberalism and republicanism consists in how the role of the democratic process is understood. According to the "liberal" view, this process accomplishes the task of programming the state in the interest of society, where the state is conceived as an apparatus of public administration, and society is conceived as a system of market-structured interactions of private persons and their labor. Here politics (in the sense of the citizens' political will-formation) has the function of bundling together and bringing to bear private social interests against a state apparatus that specializes in the administrative employment of political power for collective goals.

On the republican view, politics is not exhausted by this mediating function but is constitutive for the socialization process as a whole. Politics is conceived as the reflexive form of substantial ethical life. It constitutes the medium in which the members of quasi-natural solidary communities become aware of their dependence on one another and, acting with full deliberation as citizens, further shape and develop existing relations of reciprocal recognition into an association of free and equal consociates under law. With this, the liberal architectonic of government and society undergoes an important change. In addition to the hierarchical regulatory apparatus of sovereign state authority and the decentralized regulatory mechanism of the market – that is, besides administrative power and self-interest – *solidarity* appears as a third source of social integration.

This horizontal political will-formation aimed at mutual understanding or communicatively achieved consensus is even supposed to enjoy priority, both in a genetic and a normative sense. An autonomous basis in civil society independent of public administration and market-mediated private commerce is assumed as a precondition for the practice of civic self-determination. This basis prevents political communication from being swallowed up by the government apparatus or assimilated to market structures. Thus, on the republican conception, the political public sphere and its base, civil society, acquire a strategic significance. Together they are supposed to secure the integrative power and autonomy of the communicative practice of the citizens.[1] The uncoupling of political communication from the economy has as its counterpart a coupling of administrative power with the communicative power generated by political opinion-and will-formation.

These two competing conceptions of politics have different consequences.

(a) In the first place, their concepts of the citizen differ. According to the liberal view, the citizen's status is determined primarily by the individual rights he or she has *vis-à-vis* the state and other citizens. As bearers of individual rights citizens enjoy the protection of the government as long as they pursue their private interests within the boundaries drawn by legal statutes – and this includes protection against state interventions that violate the legal prohibition on government interference. Individual rights are negative rights that guarantee a domain of freedom of choice within which legal persons are freed from external compulsion. Political rights have the same structure: they afford citizens the opportunity to assert their private interests in such a way that, by means of elections, the composition of parliamentary bodies, and the formation of a government, these interests are finally aggregated into a political will that can affect the administration. In this way the citizens in their political role can determine whether governmental authority is exercised in the interest of the citizens as members of society.[2]

According to the republican view, the status of citizens is not determined by the model of negative liberties to which these citizens can lay claim as private persons. Rather, political rights – preeminently rights of political participation and communication – are positive liberties. They do not guarantee freedom from external compulsion, but guarantee instead the possibility of participating in a common practice, through which the citizens can first make themselves into what they want to be – politically responsible subjects of a community of free and equal citizens.[3] To this extent, the political process does not serve just to keep government activity under the surveillance of citizens who have already acquired a prior social autonomy through the exercise of their private rights and prepolitical liberties. Nor does it act only as a hinge between state and society, for democratic governmental authority is by no means an original authority. Rather, this authority proceeds from the communicative power generated by the citizens' practice of self-legislation, and it is legitimated by the fact that it protects this practice by institutionalizing public freedom.[4] The state's *raison d'être* does not lie primarily in the protection of equal individual rights but in the guarantee of an inclusive process of opinion-and will-formation in which free and equal citizens reach an understanding on which goals and norms lie in the equal interest of all. In this way the republican citizen is credited with more than an exclusive concern with his or her private interests.

(b) The polemic against the classical concept of the legal person as bearer of individual rights reveals a controversy about the concept of law itself. Whereas on the liberal conception the point of a legal order is to make it possible to determine which individuals in each case are entitled to which rights, on the republican conception these "subjective" rights owe their existence to an "objective" legal order that both enables and guarantees the integrity of an autonomous life in common based on equality and mutual respect. On the one view, the legal order is conceived in terms of individual rights; on the other, their objective legal content is given priority.

To be sure, this conceptual dichotomy does not touch on the *intersubjective* content of rights that demand reciprocal respect for rights and duties in symmetrical relations of recognition. But the republican concept at least points in the direction of a concept of law that accords equal weight to both the integrity of the individual and the integrity of the community in which persons as both individuals and members can first accord one another reciprocal recognition. It ties the legitimacy of the laws to the democratic procedure by which they are generated and thereby preserves an internal connection between the citizens' practice of self-legislation and the impersonal sway of the law:

> For republicans, rights ultimately are nothing but determinations of prevailing political will, while for liberals, some rights are always grounded in a "higher law" of transpolitical reason or revelation.... In a republican view, a community's objective, common good substantially consists in the success of its political endeavor to define, establish, effectuate, and sustain the set of rights (less tendentiously, laws) best suited to the conditions and *mores* of that community. Whereas in a contrasting liberal view, the higher-law rights provide the transactional structures and the curbs on power required so that pluralistic pursuit of diverse and conflicting interests may proceed as satisfactorily as possible.[5]

The right to vote, interpreted as a positive right, becomes the paradigm of rights as such, not only because it is constitutive for political self-determination, but because it shows how inclusion in a community of equals is connected with the individual right to make autonomous contributions and take personal positions on issues:

> [T]he claim is that we all take an interest in each others' enfranchisement because (i) our choice lies between hanging together and hanging separately; (ii) hanging together depends on reciprocal assurances to all of having one's vital interests heeded by others; and (iii) in the deeply pluralized conditions of contemporary American society, such assurances are not attainable through virtual representation, but only by maintaining at least the semblance of a politics in which everyone is conceded a voice.[6]

This structure, read off from the political rights of participation and communication, is extended to *all* rights via the legislative process constituted by political rights. Even the authorization guaranteed by private law to pursue private, freely chosen goals simultaneously imposes an obligation to respect the limits of strategic action which are agreed to be in the equal interest of all.

(c) The different ways of conceptualizing the role of citizen and the law express a deeper disagreement about the nature of the political process. On the liberal view, politics is essentially a struggle for positions that grant access to administrative power. The political process of opinion- and will-formation in the public sphere and in parliament is shaped by the competition of strategically acting collectives trying to maintain or acquire positions of power. Success is measured by the citizens' approval of persons and programs, as quantified by votes. In their choices at the polls, voters express their preferences. Their votes have the same structure as the choices of participants in a market, in that their decisions license access to positions of power that political parties fight over with a success-oriented attitude similar to that of players in the market. The input of votes and the output of power conform to the same pattern of strategic action.

According to the republican view, the political opinion- and will-formation in the public sphere and in parliament does not obey the structures of market processes but rather the obstinate structures of a public communication oriented to mutual understanding. For politics as the citizens' practice of self-determination, the paradigm is not the market but dialogue. From this perspective there is a structural difference between communicative power, which proceeds from political communication in the form of discursively generated majority decisions, and the administrative power possessed by the governmental apparatus. Even the parties that struggle over access to positions of governmental power must bend themselves to the deliberative style and the stubborn character of political discourse:

> Deliberation...refers to a certain attitude toward social cooperation, namely, that of openness to persuasion by reasons referring to the claims of others as well as one's own. The deliberative medium is a good faith exchange of views – including participants' reports of their own understanding of their respective vital interests –...in which a vote, if any vote is taken, represents a pooling of judgements.[7]

Hence the conflict of opinions conducted in the political arena has legitimating force not just in the sense of an authorization to occupy positions of power; on the contrary, the ongoing political discourse also has binding force for the way in which political authority is exercised. Administrative power can only be exercised on the basis of policies and within the limits laid down by laws generated by the democratic process.

II

So much for the comparison between the two models of democracy that currently dominate the discussion between the so-called communitarians and liberals, above all in the US. The republican model has advantages and disadvantages. In my view it has the advantage that it preserves the radical democratic meaning of a society that organizes itself through the communicatively united citizens and does not trace collective goals back to "deals" made between competing private interests. Its disadvantage, as I see it, is that it is too idealistic in that it makes the democratic process dependent on the virtues of citizens devoted to the public weal. For politics is not concerned in the first place with questions of ethical self-understanding. The mistake of the republican view consists in an ethical foreshortening of political discourse.

To be sure, ethical discourses aimed at achieving a collective self-understanding – discourses in which participants attempt to clarify how they understand themselves as members of a particular nation, as members of a community or a state, as inhabitants of a region, etc., which traditions they wish to cultivate, how they should treat each other, minorities, and marginal groups, in what sort of society they want to live – constitute an important part of politics. But under conditions of cultural and social pluralism, behind politically relevant goals there often lie interests and value-orientations that are by no means constitutive of the identity of the political community as a whole, that is, for the totality of an intersubjectively shared form of life. These interests and value-orientations, which conflict with one another within the same polity without any prospect of consensual resolution, need to be counterbalanced in a way that cannot be effected by ethical discourse, even though the results of this nondiscursive counterbalancing are subject to the proviso that they must not violate the basic values of a culture. The balancing of interests takes the form of reaching a compromise between parties who rely on their power and ability to sanction. Negotiations of this sort certainly presuppose a readiness to cooperate, that is, a willingness to abide by the rules and to arrive at results that are acceptable to all parties, though for different reasons. But compromise-formation is not conducted in the form of a rational discourse that neutralizes power and excludes strategic action. However, the fairness of compromises is measured by presuppositions and procedures which for their part are in need of rational, indeed normative, justification from the standpoint of justice. In contrast with ethical questions, questions of justice are not by their very nature tied to a particular collectivity. Politically enacted law, if it is to be legitimate, must be at least in harmony with moral principles that claim a general validity that extends beyond the limits of any concrete legal community.

The concept of deliberative politics acquires empirical relevance only when we take into account the multiplicity of forms of communication in which a common will is produced, that is, not just ethical self-clarification but also the balancing of interests and compromise, the purposive choice of means, moral justification, and legal consistency-testing. In this process the two types of politics which Michelman distinguishes in an ideal- typical fashion can interweave and complement one another in a rational manner. "Dialogical" and "instrumental" politics can *interpenetrate* in the medium of deliberation if the corresponding forms of communication are sufficiently institutionalized. Everything depends on the conditions of communication and the procedures that lend the institutionalized opinion- and will-formation their legitimating force. The third model of democracy, which I would like to propose, relies precisely on those conditions of communication under which the political process can be presumed to produce rational results because it operates deliberatively at all levels.

Making the proceduralist conception of deliberative politics the cornerstone of the theory of democracy results in differences both from the republican conception of the state as an ethical community and from the liberal conception of the state as the guardian of a market society. In comparing the three models, I take my orientation from that dimension of politics which has been our primary concern, namely, the democratic opinion- and will-formation that issue in popular elections and parliamentary decrees.

According to the liberal view, the democratic process takes place exclusively in the form of compromises between competing interests. Fairness is supposed to be guaranteed by rules of compromise-formation that regulate the general and equal right to vote, the representative composition of parliamentary bodies, their order of business, and so on. Such rules are ultimately justified in terms of liberal basic rights. According to the republican view, by contrast, democratic will-formation is supposed to take the form of an ethical discourse of self-understanding; here deliberation can rely for its content on a culturally established background consensus of the citizens, which is rejuvenated through the ritualistic reenactment of a republican founding act. Discourse theory takes elements from both sides and integrates them into the concept of an ideal procedure for deliberation and decision making. Weaving together negotiations and discourses of self-understanding and of justice, this democratic procedure grounds the presumption that under such conditions reasonable or fair results are obtained. According to this proceduralist view, practical reason withdraws from universal human rights or from the concrete ethical life of a specific community into the rules of discourse and forms of argumentation that derive their normative content from the validity-basis of action oriented to reaching understanding, and ultimately from the structure of linguistic communication.[8]

These descriptions of the structures of democratic process set the stage for different normative conceptualizations of state and society. The sole presupposition is a public administration of the kind that emerged in the early modern period together with the European state system and in functional interconnection with a capitalist economic system. According to the republican view, the citizens' political opinion- and will-formation forms the medium through which society constitutes itself as a political whole. Society is centered in the state; for in the citizens' practice of political self-determination the polity becomes conscious of itself as a totality and acts on itself via the collective will of the citizens. Democracy is synonymous with the political self-organization of society. This leads to a polemical understanding of politics as directed against the state apparatus. In Hannah Arendt's political writings one can see the thrust of republican arguments: in opposition to the civic privatism of a depoliticized population and in opposition to the acquisition of legitimation through entrenched parties, the political public sphere should be revitalized to the point where a regenerated citizenry can, in the forms of a decentralized self-governance, (once again) appropriate the governmental authority that has been usurped by a self-regulating bureaucracy.

According to the liberal view, this separation of the state apparatus from society cannot be eliminated but only bridged by the democratic process. However, the weak normative connotations of a regulated balancing of power and interests stands in need of constitutional channeling. The democratic will-formation of self-interested citizens, construed in minimalist terms, constitutes just one element within a constitution that disciplines governmental authority through normative constraints (such as basic rights, separation of powers, and legal regulation of the administration) and forces it, through competition between political parties, on the one hand, and between government and opposition, on the other, to take adequate account of competing interests and value orientations. This state-centered understanding of politics does not have to rely on the unrealistic assumption of a citizenry capable of acting collectively. Its focus is not so much the input of a rational political will-formation but the output of successful administrative accomplishments. The thrust of liberal arguments is directed against the disruptive potential of an administrative power that interferes with the independent social interactions of private persons. The liberal model hinges not on the democratic self-determination of deliberating citizens but on the legal institutionalization of an economic society that is supposed to guarantee an essentially nonpolitical common good through the satisfaction of the private aspirations of productive citizens.

Discourse theory invests the democratic process with normative connotations stronger than those of the liberal model but weaker than those of the republican model. Once again, it takes elements from both sides and fits them together in a new way. In agreement with republicanism, it gives center stage to the process of political opinion-and will-formation, but without understanding the constitution as something secondary; on the contrary, it conceives the basic principles of the constitutional state as a consistent answer to the question of how the demanding communicative presuppositions of a democratic opinion- and will-formation can be institutionalized. Discourse theory does not make the success of deliberative politics depend on a collectively acting citizenry but on the institutionalization of corresponding procedures. It no longer operates with the concept of a social whole centered in the state and conceived as a goal- oriented subject writ large. But neither does it localize the whole in a system of constitutional norms mechanically regulating the interplay of powers and interests in accordance with the market model. Discourse theory altogether jettisons the assumptions of the philosophy of consciousness, which invite us either to ascribe the citizens' practice of self-determination to one encompassing macro-subject or to apply the anonymous rule of law to competing individuals. The former approach represents the citizenry as a collective actor which reflects the whole and acts for its sake; on the latter, individual actors function as dependent variables in systemic processes that unfold blindly because no consciously executed collective decisions are possible over and above individual acts of choice (except in a purely metaphorical sense).

Discourse theory works instead with the *higher-level intersubjectivity* of communication processes that unfold in the institutionalized deliberations in parliamentary bodies, on the one hand, and in the informal networks of the public sphere, on the other. Both within and outside parliamentary bodies geared to decision making, these subjectless modes of communication form arenas in which a more or less rational opinion- and will-formation concerning issues and problems affecting society as a whole can take place. Informal opinion-formation result in institutionalized election decisions and legislative decrees through which communicatively generated power is transformed into administratively utilizable power. As on the liberal model, the boundary between state and society is respected; but here civil society, which provides the social underpinning of autonomous publics, is as distinct from the economic system as it is from the public administration. This understanding of democracy leads to the normative demand for a new balance between the three resources of money, administrative power, and solidarity from which modern societies meet their need for integration and regulation. The normative implications are obvious: the integrative force of solidarity, which can no longer be drawn solely from sources of communicative action, should develop through widely expanded autonomous public spheres as well as through legally institutionalized procedures of democratic deliberation and decision making and gain sufficient strength to hold its own against the other two social forces – money and administrative power.

III

This view has implications for how one should understand legitimation and popular sovereignty. On the liberal view, democratic will-formation has the exclusive function of *legitimating* the exercise of political power. The outcomes of elections license the assumption of governmental power, though the government must justify the use of power to the public and parliament. On the republican view, democratic will-formation has the significantly stronger function of *constituting* society as a political community and keeping the memory of this founding act alive with each new election. The government is not only empowered by the electorate's choice between teams of leaders to exercise a largely open mandate, but is also bound in a programmatic fashion to carry out certain policies. More a committee than an organ of the state, it is part of a self-governing political community rather than the head of a separate governmental apparatus. Discourse theory, by contrast, brings a third idea into play: the procedures and communicative presuppositions of democratic opinion- and will-formation function as the most important sluices for the discursive rationalization of the decisions of a government and an administration bound by law and statute. On this view, *rationalization* signifies more than mere legitimation but less than the constitution of political power. The power available to the administration changes its general character once it is bound to a process of democratic opinion- and will-formation that does not merely retrospectively monitor the exercise of political power but also programs it in a certain way. Notwithstanding this discursive rationalization, only the political system itself can "act." It is a subsystem specialized for collectively binding decisions, whereas the communicative structures of the public sphere comprise a far-flung network of sensors that respond to the pressure of society-wide problems and stimulate influential opinions. The public opinion which is worked up via democratic procedures into communicative power cannot itself "rule" but can only channel the use of administrative power in specific directions.

The concept of *popular sovereignty* stems from the republican appropriation and revaluation of the early modern notion of sovereignty originally associated with absolutist regimes. The state, which monopolizes the means of legitimate violence, is viewed as a concentration of power which can overwhelm all other temporal powers. Rousseau transposed this idea, which goes back to Bodin, to the will of the united people, fused it with the classical idea of the self-rule of free and equal citizens, and sublimated it into the modern concept of autonomy. Despite this normative sublimation, the concept of sovereignty remained bound to the notion of an embodiment in the (at first actually physically assembled) people. According to the republican view, the at least potentially assembled people are the bearers of a sovereignty that cannot in principle be delegated: in their capacity as sovereign, the people cannot let themselves be represented by others. Constitutional power is founded on the citizens' practice of self-determination, not on that of their representatives. Against this, liberalism offers the more realistic view that, in the constitutional state, the authority emanating from the people is exercised only "by means of elections and voting and by specific legislative, executive, and judicial organs."[9]

These two views exhaust the alternatives only on the dubious assumption that state and society must be conceived in terms of a whole and its parts, where the whole is constituted either by a sovereign citizenry or by a constitution. By contrast to the discourse theory of democracy corresponds the image of a *decentered* society, though with the political public sphere it sets apart an arena for the detection, identification, and interpretation of problems affecting society as a whole. If we abandon the conceptual framework of the philosophy of the subject, sovereignty need niether be concentrated in the people in a concretistic manner nor banished into the anonymous agencies established by the constitution. The "self" of the self-organizing legal community disappears in the subjectless forms of communication that regulate the flow of discursive opinion- and will-formation whose fallible results enjoy the presumption of rationality. This is not to repudiate the intuition associated with the idea of popular sovereignty but rather to interpret it in intersubjective terms. Popular sovereignty, even though it has become anonymous, retreats into democratic procedures and the legal implementation of their demanding communicative presuppositions only to be able to make itself felt as communicatively generated power. Strictly speaking, this communicative power springs from the interactions between legally institutionalized will-formation and cul-turally mobilized publics. The latter for their part find a basis in the associations of a civil society distinct from the state and the economy alike.

The normative self-understanding of deliberative politics does indeed call for a discursive mode of socialization for the *legal community*; but this mode does not extend to the whole of the society in which the constitutionally established political system is *embedded*. Even on its own proceduralist self-understanding, deliberative politics remains a component of a complex society, which as a whole resists the normative approach of legal theory. In this regard, the discourse-theoretic reading of democracy connects with an objectifying sociological approach that regards the political system neither as the peak nor the center, nor even as the structuring model of society, but as just *one* action system among others. Because it provides a kind of surety for the solution of the social problems that threaten integration, politics must indeed be able to communicate, via the medium of law, with all of the other legitimately ordered spheres of action, however these may be structured and steered. But the political system remains dependent on other functional mechanisms, such as the revenue-production of the economic system, in more than just a trivial sense; on the contrary, deliberative politics, whether realized in the formal procedures of institutionalized opinion- and will-forma-tion or only in the informal networks of the political public sphere, stands in an internal relation to the contexts of a rationalized lifeworld that meets it halfway. Deliberatively filtered political communications are especially dependent on the resources of the lifeworld – on a free and open political culture and an enlightened political socialization, and above all on the initiatives of opinion-shaping associations. These resources emerge and regenerate themselves spontaneously for the most part – at any rate, they can only with difficulty be subjected to political control.

Notes

1   Cf. H. Arendt, *On Revolution* (New York, 1965); *On Violence* (New York, 1970).
2   Cf. F. I. Michelman, "Political Truth and the Rule of Law," *Tel Aviv University Studies in Law* 8 (1988): 283: "The political society envisioned by bumper-sticker republicans is the society of private rights bearers, an association whose first principle is the protection of the lives, liberties, and estates of its individual members. In that society, the state is justified by the protection it gives to those prepolitical interests; the purpose of the constitution is to ensure that the state apparatus, the government, provides such protection for the people at large rather than serves the special interests of the governors or their patrons; the function of citizenship is to operate the constitution and thereby to motivate the governors to act according to that protective purpose; and the value to you of your political franchise – your right to vote and speak, to have your views heard and counted – is the handle it gives you on influencing the system so that it will adequately heed and protect *your* particular, prepolitical rights and other interests."
3   On the distinction between positive and negative freedom see Ch. Taylor, "What is Human Agency?" in *Human Agency and Language: Philosophical Papers 1* (Cambridge, 1985), pp. 15–44.
4   Michelman, "Political Truth and the Rule of Law," p. 284: "In [the] civic constitutional vision, political society is primarily the society not of rights bearers, but of citizens, an association whose first principle is the creation and provision of a public realm within which a people, together, argue and reason about the right terms of social coexistence, terms that they will set together and which they understand as comprising their common good. . . . Hence, the state is justified by its purpose of establishing and ordering the public sphere within which persons can achieve freedom in the sense of self-government by the exercise of reason in public dialogue."
5   Michelman, "Conceptions of Democracy in American Constitutional Argument: Voting Rights," *Florida Law Review* 41 (1989): 446 ff. (hereafter "Voting Rights").
6   Michelman, "Voting Rights," p. 484.
7   Michelman, "Conceptions of Democracy in American Constitutional Argument: The Case of Pornography Regulation," *Tennessee Law Review* 291 (1989): 293.
8   Cf. J. Habermas, "Popular Sovereignty as Procedure," in *Between Facts and Norms*, trans. W. Rehg (1996), pp. 463–90.
9   Cf. *The Basic Law of the Federal Republic of Germany,* article 20, sec. 2.

ON THE INTERNAL RELATION BETWEEN THE RULE OF LAW AND DEMOCRACY

In academia we often mention law and politics in the same breath, yet at the same time we are accustomed to consider law, the rule of law, and democracy as subjects of different disciplines; jurisprudence deals with law, political science with democracy, and each deals with the constitutional state in its own way – jurisprudence in normative terms, political science from an empirical standpoint. The scholarly division of labor continues to operate even when legal scholars attend to law and the rule of law, on the one hand, and will-formation in the constitutional state, on the other; or when social scientists, in the role of sociologists of law, examine law and the constitutional state and, in the role of political scientists, examine the democratic process. The constitutional state and democracy appear to us as entirely separate objects. There are good reasons for this. Because political rule is always exercised in the form of law, legal systems exist where political force has not yet been domesticated by the constitutional state. And constitutional states exist where the power to govern has not yet been democratized. In short, there are legally ordered governments without constitutional institutions, and there are constitutional states without democratic constitutions. Of course, these empirical grounds for a division of labor in the academic treatment of the two subjects by no means imply that, from a normative standpoint, the constitutional state could exist without democracy.

In this paper I want to treat several aspects of this internal relation between the rule of law and democracy. This relation results from the concept of modern law itself (section 1) as well as from the fact that positive law can no longer draw its legitimacy from a higher law (section 2). Modern law is legitimated by the autonomy guaranteed equally to each citizen, and in such a way that private and public autonomy reciprocally presuppose each other (section 3). This conceptual interrelation also makes itself felt in the dialectic of legal and factual equality. It was this dialectic that first elicited the social- welfare paradigm of law as a response to the liberal understanding of law, and today this same dialectic necessitates a proceduralist self-understanding of constitutional democracy (section 4). In closing I will elucidate this proceduralist legal paradigm with the example of the feminist politics of equality (section 5).

1   Formal Properties of Modern Law

Since Locke, Rousseau, and Kant, a certain concept of law has gradually prevailed not only in philosophical thought but in the constitutional reality of Western societies. This concept is supposed to account simultaneously for both the positivity and the freedom-guaranteeing character of coercible law. The positivity of law – the fact that norms backed by the threat of state sanction stem from the changeable decisions of a political lawgiver – is bound up with the demand for legitimation. According to this demand, positively enacted law should guarantee the autonomy of all legal persons equally; and the democratic procedure of legislation should in turn satisfy this demand. In this way, an internal relation is established between the coercibility and changeability of positive law on the one hand, and a mode of lawmaking that engenders legitimacy on the other. Hence from a normative perspective there is a conceptual or internal relation – and not simply a historically, accidental relation – between law and democracy, between legal theory and democratic theory.

At first glance, the establishment of this internal relation has the look of a philosophical trick. Yet, as a matter of fact, the relation is deeply rooted in the presuppositions of our everyday practice of law. For in the mode of validity that attaches to law, the facticity of the state's legal enforcement is intermeshed with the legitimating force of a legislative procedure that claims to be rational in that it guarantees freedom. This is shown in the peculiar ambivalence with which the law presents itself to its addressees and expects their obedience: that is, it leaves its addressees free to approach the law in either of two ways. They can either consider norms merely as factual constraints on their freedom and take a strategic approach to the calculable consequences of possible rule-violations, or they can comply with legal statutes in a performative attitude, indeed comply out of respect for results of a common will-formation that claim legitimacy. Kant already expressed this point with his concept of "legality," which highlighted the connection between these two moments without which legal obedience cannot be reasonably expected: legal norms must be fashioned so that they can be viewed simultaneously in two ways, as coercive and as laws of freedom. These two aspects belong to our understanding of modern law: we consider the validity of a legal norm as equivalent to the explanation that the state can simultaneously guarantee factual enforcement and legitimate enactment – thus it can guarantee, on the one hand, the legality of behavior in the sense of average compliance, which can if necessary be compelled by sanctions; and, on the other hand, the legitimacy of the rule itself, which must always make it possible to comply with the norm out of respect for the law.

Of course, this immediately raises the question of how the legitimacy of rules should be grounded when the rules in question can be changed at any time by the political legislator. Constitutional norms too are changeable; and even the basic norms that the constitution itself has declared nonamendable share with all positive law the fate that they can be abrogated, say, after a change of regime. As long as one was able to fall back on a religiously or metaphysically grounded natural law, the whirlpool of temporality enveloping positive law could be held in check by morality. Situated in a hierarchy of law, temporalized positive law was supposed to remain *subordinate* to an eternally valid moral law, from which it was to receive its lasting orientations. But even aside from the fact that in pluralistic societies such integrating worldviews and collectively binding comprehensive doctrines have in any case disintegrated, modern law, simply by virtue of its formal properties, resists the direct control of a posttraditional morality of conscience, which is, so to speak, all we have left.

2   The Complementary Relation between Positive Law and Autonomous Morality

Modern legal systems are constructed on the basis of individual rights. Such rights have the character of releasing legal persons from moral obligations in a carefully circumscribed manner. By introducing rights that concede to agents the latitude to act according to personal preferences, modern law as a whole implements the principle that whatever is not explicitly prohibited is permitted. Whereas in morality an inherent symmetry exists between rights and duties, legal duties are a consequence of entitlements, that is, they result only from statutory constraints on individual liberties. This basic conceptual privileging of rights over duties is explained by the modern concepts of the "legal person" and of the "legal community." The moral universe, which is *unlimited* in social space and historical time, includes *all natural persons* with their complex life histories; morality itself extends to the protection of the integrity of fully individuated persons (*Einzelner*). By contrast, the legal community, which is always localized in space and time, protects the integrity of its members precisely insofar as they acquire the artificial status of *rights bearers*. For this reason, the relation between law and morality is more one of complementarity than of subordination.

The same is true if one compares their relative scope. The matters that require legal regulation are at once both narrower and broader in scope than morally relevant concerns: narrower inasmuch as legal regulation has access only to external, that is, coercible, behavior, and broader inasmuch as law, as an organizational form of politics, pertains not only to the regulation of interpersonal conflicts but also to the pursuit of political goals and the implementation of policies. Hence legal regulations touch not only on moral questions in the narrow sense, but also on pragmatic and ethical questions, and on forming compromises among conflicting interests. Moreover, unlike the clearly delimited normative validity claimed by moral norms, the *legitimacy* claimed by legal norms is based on various sorts of reasons. The legislative practice of justification depends on a complex network of discourses and bargaining, and not just on moral discourse.

The idea from natural law of a hierarchy of laws at different levels of dignity is misleading. Law is better understood as a functional complement to morality. As positively valid, legitimately enacted, and actionable, law can relieve the morally judging and acting person of the considerable cognitive, motivational, and organizational demands of a morality based entirely on individual conscience. Law can compensate for the weaknesses of a highly demanding morality that – if we judge from its empirical results – provides only cognitively indeterminate and motivationally unreliable results. Naturally, this does not absolve legislators and judges from the concern that the law be in harmony with morality. But legal regulations are too concrete to be legitimated solely through their compatibility with moral principles. From what, then, can positive law borrow its legitimacy, if not from a superior moral law?

Like morality, law too is supposed to protect the autonomy of all persons equally. Law too must prove its legitimacy under this aspect of securing freedom. Interestingly enough, though, the positive character of law forces autonomy to split up in a peculiar way, which has no parallel in morality. Moral self-determination in Kant's sense is a unified concept insofar as it demands of each person, *in propria persona*, that she obey just those norms that she herself posits according to her own impartial judgment, or according to a judgment reached in common with all other persons. However, the binding quality of legal norms does not stem solely from processes of opinion- and will- formation, but arises also from the collectively binding decisions of authorities who make and apply law. This circumstance makes it conceptually necessary to distinguish the role of authors who make (and adjudicate) law from that of addresses who are subject to established law. The autonomy that in the moral domain is all of a piece, so to speak, appears in the legal domain only in the dual form of private and public autonomy.

However, these two moments must then be mediated in such a way that the one form of autonomy does not detract from the other. Each form of autonomy, the individual liberties of the subject of private law and the public autonomy of the citizen, makes the other form possible. This reciprocal relation is expressed by the idea that legal persons can be autonomous only insofar as they can understand themselves, in the exercise of their civic rights, as authors of just those rights which they are supposed to obey as addressees.

3   The Mediation of Popular Sovereignty and Human Rights

It is therefore not surprising that modern natural law theories have answered the legitimation question by referring, on the one hand, to the principle of *popular sovereignty* and, on the other, to the *rule of law* as guaranteed by human rights. The principle of popular sovereignty is expressed in rights of communication and participation that secure the public autonomy of citizens; the rule of law is expressed in those classical basic rights that guarantee the private autonomy of members of society. Thus the law is legitimated as an instrument for the equal protection of private and public autonomy. To be sure, political philosophy has never really been able to strike a balance between popular sovereignty and human rights, or between the "freedom of the ancients" and the "freedom of the moderns." The political autonomy of citizens is supposed to be embodied in the self-organization of a community that gives itself its laws through the sovereign will of the people. The private autonomy of citizens, on the other hand, is supposed to take the form of basic rights that guarantee the anonymous rule of law. Once the issue is set up in this way, either idea can be upheld only at the expense of the other. The intuitively plausible co-originality of both ideas falls by the wayside.

Republicanism, which goes back to Aristotle and the political humanism of the Renaissance, has always given the public autonomy of citizens priority over the pre-political liberties of private persons. *Liberalism*, which goes back to John Locke, has invoked the danger of tyrannical majorities and postulated the priority of human rights. According to republicanism, human rights owed their legitimacy to the ethical self-understanding and sovereign self-determination achieved by a political community; in liberalism, such rights were supposed to provide, from the very start, legitimate barriers that prevented the sovereign will of the people from encroaching on inviolable spheres of individual freedom. In their concepts of the legal person's autonomy, Rousseau and Kant certainly aimed to conceive of sovereign will and practical reason as unified in such a way that popular sovereignty and human rights would reciprocally interpret one another. But even they failed to do justice to the co-originality of the two ideas; Rousseau suggests more of a republican reading, Kant more of a liberal one. They missed the intuition they wanted to articulate: that the idea of human rights, which is expressed in the right to equal individual liberties, must neither be merely imposed on the sovereign legislator as an external barrier, nor be instrumentalized as a functional requisite for legislative goals.

To express this intuition properly it helps to view the democratic procedure – which alone provides legitimating force to the lawmaking process in the context of social and ideological pluralism – from a discourse-theoretical standpoint. Here I assume a principle that I cannot discuss in detail, namely, that a regulation may claim legitimacy only if all those possibly affected by it could consent to it after participating in rational discourses. Now, if discourses – and bargaining processes as well, whose fairness is based on discursively grounded procedures – represent the place where a reasonable political will can develop, then the presumption of reasonability, which the democratic procedure is supposed to ground, ultimately rests on an elaborate communicative arrangement:

the presumption depends on the conditions under which one can legally institutionalize the forms of communication necessary for legitimate lawmaking. In that case, the desired internal relation between human rights and popular sovereignty consists in this: human rights themselves are what satisfy the requirement that a civic practice of the public use of communicative freedom be legally institutionalized. Human rights, which make the exercise of popular sovereignty legally possible, cannot be imposed on this practice as an external constraint. Enabling conditions must not be confused with such constraints.

Naturally, this analysis is at first plausible only for those political civil rights, specifically the rights of communication and participation, that safeguard the exercise of political autonomy. It is less plausible for the classical human rights that guarantee the citizens' private autonomy. Here we think in the first instance of the fundamental right to the greatest possible degree of equal individual liberties, though also of basic rights that constitute membership status in a state and provide the individual with comprehensive legal protection. These rights, which are meant to guarantee everyone an equal opportunity to pursue his or her private conception of the good, have an intrinsic value, or at least they are not reducible to their instrumental value for democratic will-formation. We will do justice to the intuition that the classical liberties are co-original with political rights only if we state more precisely the thesis that human rights legally enable the citizens' practice of self-determination. I turn now to this more precise statement.

4   The Relation between Private and Public Autonomy

However well-grounded human rights are, they may not be paternalistically foisted, as it were, on a sovereign. Indeed, the idea of citizens' legal autonomy demands that the addressees of law be able to understand themselves at the same time as its authors. It would contradict this idea if the democratic legislator were to discover human rights as though they were (preexisting) moral facts that one merely needs to enact as positive law. At the same time, one must also not forget that when citizens occupy the role of co-legislators they are no longer free to choose the medium in which alone they can realize their autonomy. They participate in legislation only as legal subjects; it is no longer in their power to decide which language they will make use of. The democratic idea of self-legislation *must* acquire its validity in the medium of law itself.

However, when citizens judge in the light of the discourse principle whether the law they make is legitimate, they do so under communicative presuppositions that must themselves be legally institutionalized in the form of political civil rights, and for such institutionalization to occur, the legal code as such must be available. But in order to establish this legal code it is necessary to create the status of legal persons who as bearers of individual rights belong to a voluntary association of citizens and when necessary effectively claim their rights. There is no law without the private autonomy of legal persons in general. Consequently, without basic rights that secure the private autonomy of citizens there is also no medium for legally institutionalizing the conditions under which these citizens, as citizens of a state, can make use of their public autonomy. Thus private and public autonomy mutually presuppose each other in such a way that neither human rights nor popular sovereignty can claim primacy over its counterpart.

   This mutual presupposition expresses the intuition that, on the one hand, citizens can make adequate use of their public autonomy only if, on the basis of their equally protected private autonomy, they are sufficiently independent; but that, on the other hand, they can arrive at a consensual regulation of their private autonomy only if they make adequate use of their political autonomy as enfranchised citizens.

   The internal relation between the rule of law and democracy has been concealed long enough by the competition between the legal paradigms that have been dominant up to the present. The liberal legal paradigm reckons with an economic society that is institutionalized through private law – above all through property rights and contractual freedom – and left to the spontaneous workings of the market. Such a "private law society" is tailored to the autonomy of legal subjects who as market participants more or less rationally pursue their personal life-plans. This model of society is associated with the normative expectation that social justice can be realized by guaranteeing such a negative legal status, and thus solely by delimiting spheres of individual freedom. The well-founded critique of this supposition gave rise to the social welfare model. The objection is obvious: if the free "capacity to have and acquire" is supposed to guarantee social justice, then an equality in "legal capacity" must exist. As a matter of fact, however, the growing inequalities in economic power, assets, and living conditions have increasingly destroyed the factual preconditions for an equal opportunity to make effective use of equally distributed legal powers. If the normative content of legal equality is not to be inverted, then two correctives are necessary. On the one hand, existing norms of private law must be substantively specified, and on the other, basic social rights must be introduced, rights that ground claims to a more just distribution of socially produced wealth and to more effective protection against socially produced dangers.

   In the meantime, of course, this *materialization* of law has in turn created the unintended side effects of welfare paternalism. Clearly, efforts to compensate for actual living conditions and power positions must not lead to "normalizing" interventions of a sort that once again restrict the presumptive beneficiaries' pursuit of an autonomous life-project. The further development of the dialectic of legal and factual equality has shown that both legal paradigms are equally committed to the productivist image of an economic society based on industrial capitalism. This society is supposed to function in such a way that the expectation of social justice can be satisfied by securing each individual's private pursut of his or her conception of the good life. The only dispute between the two paradigms concerns whether private autonomy can be guaranteed directly by negative liberties (*Freiheitsrechte*), or whether on the contrary the conditions for private autonomy must be secured through the provision of welfare entitlements. In both cases, however, the internal relation between private and public autonomy drops out of the picture.

5   An Example: The Feminist Politics of Equality

In closing, I want to examine the feminist politics of equality to show that policies and legal strategies oscillate helplessly between the conventional paradigms as long as they remain limited to securing private autonomy and disregard how the individual rights of private persons are related to the public autonomy of citizens engaged in lawmaking.

For, in the final analysis, private legal subjects cannot enjoy even equal individual liberties if they themselves do not jointly exercise their civic autonomy in order to specify clearly which interests and standards are justified, and to agree on the relevant respects that determine when like cases should be treated alike and different cases differently.

Initially, the goal of liberal policies was to uncouple the acquisition of status from gender identity and to guarantee to women equal opportunities in the competition for jobs, social recognition, education, political power, etc., regardless of the outcome. However, the formal equality that was partially achieved merely made more obvious the ways in which women were *in fact* treated unequally. Social welfare politics responded, especially in the areas of social, labor, and family law, by passing special regulations relating, for example, to pregnancy and child care, or to social hardship in the case of divorce. In the meantime feminist critique has targeted not only the unredeemed demands, but also the ambivalent consequences of successfully imple- mented welfare programs – for example, the higher risk of women losing their jobs as a result of compensatory regulations, the over-representation of women in lower wage brackets, the problematic issue of "what is in the child's best interests," and in general the progressive feminization of poverty. From a legal standpoint, one reason for this reflexively generated discrimination is found in the overgeneralized classifications used to label disadvantaged situations and disadvantaged groups of persons, because these "false" classifications lead to "normalizing" interventions into how people conduct their lives, interventions that transform what was intended as compensation for damages into new forms of discrimination. Thus instead of guaranteeing liberty, such over-protection stifles it. In areas of law that are of concern to feminism, welfare paternalism takes on a literal meaning to the extent that legislation and adjudication are oriented by traditional patterns of interpretation and thus serve to buttress existing stereotypes of sexual identity.

The classification of gender-specific roles and differences touches on fundamental levels of a society's cultural self-understanding. Radical feminism has only now made us aware of the fallible character of this self-understanding, an understanding that is essentially contested and in need of revision. It rightly insists that the appropriate interpretation of needs and criteria be a matter of public debate in the political public sphere. It is here that citizens must clarify the aspects that determine which differences between the experiences and living situations of (specific groups of) men and women are relevant for an equal opportunity to exercise individual liberties. Thus, this struggle for the equal status of women is a particularly good example of the need for a change of the legal paradigm.

The dispute between the two received paradigms – whether the autonomy of legal persons is better secured through individual liberties for private competition or through publicly guaranteed entitlements for clients of welfare bureaucracies – is superseded by a *proceduralist conception of law*. According to this conception, the democratic process must secure private and public autonomy at the same time: the individual rights that are meant to guarantee to women the autonomy to pursue their lives in the private sphere cannot even be adequately formulated unless the affected persons themselves first articulate and justify in public debate those aspects that are relevant to equal or unequal treatment in typical cases. The private autonomy of equally entitled citizens can be secured only insofar as citizens actively exercise their civic autonomy.

6

CAN PROCEDURAL DEMOCRACY
BE RADICAL?

Simone Chambers

There was a time when the Frankfurt School held out the last hope for radical politics on the Continent. The critique of the Enlightenment and instrumental reason along with the attack on a mass culture created by advertising and driven by degrading consumerism appeared to contain a transformative potential that could move Western society beyond liberalism. Looking at Jürgen Habermas's work today, however, one might ask whatever happened to that hope? This question is often taken up on two related but distinct levels. On one level, people ask if Habermas's embrace of Anglo-American philosophy, his clear affinities with John Rawls, and his apparent rejection of a Hegelian/Marxist paradigm have purged the Continental out of his thought. Hor-kheimer and Adorno are now vague memories, leaving little or no trace on the philosophical method and argumentation of their most famous student. At another level this question is raised as a direct political challenge to Habermas. Where has the political and social radicalism gone? Where, if at all, can we see the legacy of Marx and the possibility of emancipatory politics? Is Habermas just another liberal constitutional-ist? Like his embrace of Anglo-American philosophy, has he also become so enamored with an idealized American constitutional model that he has turned his back on the radical critique of liberalism that gave the Frankfurt School its name?

Ironically, one of the reasons Habermas moved away from the Continental tradition of the Frankfurt School is that he is haunted by the same fear that overshadowed Horkheimer and Adorno. Despite Habermas's "Americanization" it is Germany's experience with Nazism that stands behind all of his work and puts some of the big shifts in perspective. For Habermas, the potential dangers lurking in group solidarity will always outweigh those inherent in individualism. And the infusion of the American constitutional tradition into the German experience in 1949 will always represent the turning away from a dangerous path. Thus, the irony here is that Habermas's rejection of a certain form of Continentalism (Hegelian Marxism to be precise) is essentially a Continental phenomenon. What we see emerging from this experience is a fusion between liberal moral philosophy and Critical Theory method. Habermas is a liberal, there is no doubt. But he has developed a liberal paradigm that offers a unique critical perspective on liberalism. Thus, in the tradition of the Frankfurt School, he offers an imminent critique of liberalism. Not, however, with a view of transcending liberalism, but rather, with a view to boot-strapping our way to a more adequate liberalism.

In what follows, I investigate Habermas's critical liberalism, via an exposition of the main features of Habermas's political theory and a survey of some criticisms that this theory has attracted. I argue that certain features of his critical liberalism dictate a trade off between two types of political philosophy and two types of radicalism. At the philosophical level this is a divide between substantive and procedural theories and at the political level this translates into a divide between theories of justice and theories of democracy. Habermas has chosen the procedural route for reasons I elaborate below. This means he has opted for a theory of radical democracy. The cost is that he does not appear to be able to say very much about substantive questions of justice. As a thorough-going democrat he leaves questions of justice up to the people to decide. He feels that it is presumptuous of philosophers to speak for the people. Such philosophical modesty, from the standpoint of political radicalism, may entail a great cost, however: the abandonment of a truly transformative model of politics.

The Political Philosophy

In his long career Habermas has produced a distinct and seminal political philosophy. Habermas himself distinguishes it from other contemporary theories such as liberalism or republicanism by the designation deliberative politics or deliberative democracy. Deliberative democracy is very much in vogue these days. Many thinkers, not all of them followers of Habermas, consider themselves advocates of this type of democratic theory. Nevertheless, it is safe to say that Habermas is the father of deliberative democracy. For although it is only in the last ten years that a full articulation of his political theory has emerged, he has been building the foundations for over forty years in his theory of communication. In hindsight one can identify the main features of deliberative democracy as early as 1962 in the publication of his dissertation, *Struktürwandel der Öffentlichkeit*.[1] Despite the impressive consistency of his communicative message, Habermas's work stretches over the full length and breadth of the social sciences and humanities. He has waded into debates in the fields of history, psychology, literary criticism, sociology, political science, philosophy, ethics, and anthropology. I cannot offer a full survey of all these various contributions. Instead I start with the components of his theory of deliberative democracy and then work backwards, if you will, filling in only those philosophical presuppositions and arguments necessary to make sense of his political theory and its distinctiveness within the contemporary debate.

Deliberative democracy

Habermas positions his political theory on middle ground between liberalism and republicanism.[2] Liberals answer the question "what is politics?" by reference to the aggregation and balance of private and group interests. The state's job is to pursue a collective good understood as a fair compromise between competing interests. Republicanism, on the other side, is an essentially communitarian view where politics is all about the creation of a solidaristic whole that can express a collective interest. There-fore, the state's job is to respond to, implement, and sometimes embody the vision of this collective solidarity and to create the conditions that nurture its growth. Habermas employs a rough and somewhat simplistic depiction of the liberal versus communitarian divide, not because any liberal or communitarian thinker actually fits this description in any detail, but simply as a foil for elaborating the main features of deliberative politics.

The liberal view is essentially instrumental in that it envisions the democratic relation between citizens to be one of bargaining, compromise, and competition. Politics is understood on a market model. Governments have two functions, first to create fair conditions for citizens to compete for goods and second, in situations where that is not possible, to sometimes distribute goods themselves. The first job is embodied in the protection of rights and the second in a legislative agenda that is determined by the competition and compromise between various interests. By contrast, republicanism is based on a "dialogic" model. Citizens come together not as competitors in a zero sum game but as fellow citizens interested in articulating a shared identity and set of goals and goods. It is a cooperative vision that sees the state as facilitator of this conversation and then executor of its results. This vision refocuses the most important political activity not so much in battles between representatives hashing out comprises in national assemblies, but in civil society and the public sphere.

If all one knew about Habermas was that he was a student of the Frankfurt School, one might think that an instrumentalization of politics would pose the most serious danger in his eyes. Furthermore, that republicanism is often depicted as dialogical would also lead one to suppose that Habermas would have more affinities with a republican model than a liberal one. And indeed he does nod at times to such an affinity.[3] On closer reading, however, this does not appear to be the case. Liberalism and republican-ism do not pose the same sorts of dangers when they go wrong. The crucial divide here is on the question of rights. Liberalism, for all its instrumentalization of politics and citizenship, has at its core the protection of individual rights. Although contemporary republican thinkers all endorse rights, rights simply do not have the same central role as in liberalism. And indeed, one of the major claims of republicanism is that liberalism has made rights too central and we have left other (equally) important values to languish.[4]

The real problem with republicanism for Habermas, however, could be called the Aristotelian dilemma: when it is good it is very good but when it goes bad it is the worst sort of regime. The danger in republicanism is that in promoting the common good it could promote exclusionary and dangerous ideas of a collective subject – a "people" or a "nation." In an important passage Habermas notes: "discourse theory does not make the success of deliberative politics depend on a collectively acting citizenry but on the institutionalization of corresponding procedures."[5] The basic principles of a liberal constitutional state are a "consistent answer" to the question of what is an appropriate institutionalization of corresponding procedures. Over and over again Habermas stresses that deliberation is "subjectless," "anonymous," and even "anarchic." A communitarian utopianism that lies at the center of republicanism frightens Habermas more than the atomization that haunts liberalism. It is no accident that as a philosopher, Habermas appears more interested in engaging Rawls and Ronald Dworkin in debate than Michael Sandel or Charles Taylor. Rawls and Dworkin occupy the theoretical space Habermas wishes to colonize. While as a citizen on the Continent, where he is engaged as a combatant, he is ever vigilant against any attempt by the German right to reinvent or rejuvenate an ethnic collective identity.[6]

The first picture of deliberative politics to emerge is the following: take the liberal state as it stands now in most Western liberal democracies; expand the public sphere in such a way as to involve citizens in a process of public opinion and will formation. The idea is to take citizens out of the narrow competitive model of politics so often found in Western democracies and into a deliberative politics where their opinions are formed in critical concert with others. Although deliberation and debate in the public sphere will be "free wheeling" we can identify three types of discourses that can help us categorize the nature of the talk. These are moral, pragmatic, and ethical.[7] Moral discourse deals with questions of justice and ideally concludes with generally valid moral principles. Pragmatic discourse concentrates on means/ends issues. What, for example, are the most efficient ways to promote the economy? Ethical discourse involves a hermeneutically oriented conversation delving into questions of self-understanding both of individuals and groups. Here we must ask other questions such as, what does it mean to be a Québécois? Or what values do Americans care most about? All three types of discourse are governed by the rules of equality, freedom, and fair play. All are directed at mutual understanding through the power of reasoned argument. However, only moral discourse sets itself the high standard of rational consensus.

Democratic deliberation entails all three types of discourse. In addition, Habermas now acknowledges that democratic politics must also contain non-discursive methods of conflict resolution such as bargaining. Bargaining is legitimate if it proceeds under fair conditions and if there is a general (meaning discursively justifiable) agreement that bargaining is appropriate in that particular circumstance.[8] The more the issue under public discussion involves deep foundational issues of justice, however, the more important rational consensus becomes. We may also try to reach agreement on questions of the best means to achieve a desired end or on who we are and what we want. But these agreements, when reached, are more closely tied to contingent problems or particular ways of life than the search for just principles. In most cases, however, agreement will not be possible. Mass democracies require decision rules that call for something less than unanimity. Habermas is well aware of the constraints of real politics as well as its inherent messiness, and envisions a process of debate that goes back and forth between the three types of discussions. Questions of justice always raise issues of feasibility, not to mention ethical questions of identity. Conversely, questions like "What is the most efficient way to promote the economy?" always contain an unstated moral premise: What is the most efficient and *fair* way to promote the economy. His main point is that understanding that politics involves all three types of contestations and debates makes a deliberative conception a more complete conceptualization of politics.[9]

Deliberative democracy is a two-tier model of democracy. The relatively formal institutions of representative democracy form one tier; the informal interactions of a public forming their opinion in a well ordered public sphere forms the other. I postpone for the moment the question of what would constitute a well ordered public sphere. As I mentioned earlier, it is very important to Habermas to stress that public deliberation is anonymous. By this he means that unlike some communitarian views, when citizens come together to deliberate they do not create a supra subject, even in a metaphorical sense. Habermas again is very concerned to distance himself not so much from liberal individualism as from theories of strong democracy that seek a higher collective identity. Habermas's concern is that higher level subjectivities will always encounter dissent and so will always be exclusionary. In his effort to distance himself from even the hint that he might be proposing another form of collectivism, Habermas has even begun to embrace some language of his critics and talk about publics in the plural rather than one public.[10] He wants a strong theory of popular sovereignty minus the dangers of radical Rousseauianism.

Public opinion and will formation are anonymous and informal. The informal nature of public opinion and will formation means that it does not "rule" directly. Such formation generates a kind of communicative power that underpins the established "rulers," that is, the system of representative democracy. Communicative power, if unleashed under the proper and healthy democratic conditions, gives content to legislative agendas, limits those agendas, and stands as a permanent publicity test for those agendas. "The public opinion which is worked up via democratic procedures into communicative power cannot itself 'rule' but can only channel the use of administrative power in specific directions."[11] The relationship between deliberatively formed public opinion and representative institutions has been characterized as a relationship between two types of publics: weak and strong.[12] Strong publics issue authoritative decisions; they rule. Weak publics, although they deliberate, do not issue authoritative decisions, so do not rule. Although this has become a common way of talking about the two-tier model, I think it is misleading. It implies that weak publics are incomplete and require strong publics to have any efficacy. As I will argue in the concluding section, Habermas's conception of informal opinion and will formation does not, as some have thought, limit the power of public deliberation to an ability to influence parliaments. If that was all that he was saying then there really would not be anything new here.

Public and private autonomy

What exactly does Habermas think this theory of deliberative democracy adds to contemporary political theory? Liberals and republicans do not only argue about what democracy should look like. They also argue about deep questions of justification. Habermas believes that liberal democracy has been caught in a fruitless conceptual struggle between rights fundamentalists and deep popular sovereigntists. Rights fundamentalists hold that rights are the ultimate trump card in liberal democracies and are neither justified by nor subject to the popular will of the people. The problem that rights fundamentalists raise is, if our consent does not justify rights, what does? Habermas feels that ultimately they will have to fall back on some form of natural law theory that could not be generally accepted today. By contrast, popular sovereignty fundamentalists, while not denying the importance of rights, argue that the ultimate justification for political arrangements is the will and consent of the people. The problem here, of course, is what limits the empirical will of the people. History has shown democracy to be a poor safeguard of fundamental rights.

Habermas answers this dilemma by appealing to the interdependence of individual and public autonomy.[13] Individual autonomy corresponds to the liberal notion of individual freedom safeguarded, for the most part, through a system of rights. Public autonomy refers to notions of popular sovereignty. Public autonomy can be understood in very abstract terms as in liberal contract theory or in more concrete terms as in theories of strong democracy. Habermas argues that, on the one hand, authentic public autonomy is impossible without private autonomy and, on the other, private autonomy can only be justified through public autonomy.

Public autonomy is impossible without private autonomy because without strong guarantees of individual freedom in the private sphere our democratic outcomes would be suspect. For example, no one was under the illusion that the votes taken in the Supreme Soviet of the USSR represented authentic democracy. These votes were suspect because there was no corresponding system of rights and protections that could give us confidence that individuals had been able to develop and express their true interests or opinions. Similarly, contract theories only make sense given the assumption that the parties are free and equal. Thus, authentic and healthy democracy requires a system of wide guarantees in civil society. Without those wider guarantees we would have no confidence that the opinions brought to the public (or the choice to remain silent) are authentic and autonomous.

From the opposite angle, Habermas takes up the argument that private autonomy can only be justified through public autonomy. Because we can no longer rely on God, or Nature, or self-evident truth as a shared justification for rights, some version of public autonomy (Rawls's original position or Habermas's discursive democracy are two such versions) must be introduced to justify and legitimize the institutions of private rights. Rights are justified along two lines in Habermas: (1) as necessary preconditions of democracy and deliberation and, and (2) as the outcomes of deliberation. We can be confident that rights are "valid" both because citizens would endorse them in a discourse of all affected and because they are a necessary condition of a discourse of all affected. I address the obvious circularity introduced here under "Substantive versus Procedural Theory."

In answer to the liberal objection that deliberative democracy privileges the people's will over rights, and to the democrat's objection that it privileges rights over the people's will, Habermas defends the "co-originality" (*Gleichursprünglichkeit*) of rights and popular sovereignty: the chicken and the egg cannot be prioritized.[14] There is no people's will to speak of without rights and there are no rights without some theory of consent.

The relationship between private and public autonomy mirrors the relationship between law and democracy. Habermas is trying to solve the riddle posed by Rousseau: "Man was born free, and he is everywhere in chains." How can we both be free, that is the authors of our own lives, and at the same time be governed, that is limited by coercive laws? The answer, of course, is to be both the author as well as addressee of the law. These two roles are interdependent. We are authors only to the extent that we are legal persons under the law. We are legal persons protected by rights only to the extent that we are authors of those laws.

Legitimacy and rationality

Habermas not only defends deliberative democracy on the grounds that it stands between liberalism and republicanism, incorporating the best of both. Neither does he defend it solely on the grounds that such a positioning allows deliberative democracy to resolve the inherent tension between democracy and rights. There is clearly something missing. What makes the outcomes of deliberation legitimate or right? Here is the most characteristic part of Habermas's contribution to political theory – the theory of communication that underpins his political theory.

One way to understand the procedures of deliberative democracy is as a democratic reformulation of Kant's principle of publicity. Publicity reconciles the requirements of right (justice/general interest) with the requirements of politics (obedience/stability).[15] The idea of public right finds expression in the following principle: "all actions affecting the rights of other human beings are wrong if their maxim is not compatible with their being made public."[16] The idea is that the sovereign is the guardian of the general interest and therefore should have no reason to fear public debate on the legitimacy of his actions. Indeed, surviving public debate and scrutiny is an indicator that the sovereign's actions are just, that is, in the public interest.

In addition to serving as a negative test for the justness of laws, publicity also serves as a means of gaining obedience while respecting each citizen as an autonomous moral agent capable of making rational judgements: "There must be a *spirit of freedom*, for in all matters concerning universal human rights, each individual requires to be convinced by reason that the coercion which prevails is lawful, otherwise he would be in contradiction with himself." Thus, by making public the grounds for state action and subjecting these grounds to the critical force of "independent and public thought," one can ensure that the state has just reasons for its actions as well as that citizens believe that these reasons are just.[17]

When we join Kant's idea of publicity with modern notions of democracy, we arrive at a deliberative theory of democratic legitimacy. Rather than pure consent, this theory stresses the deliberative processes that lead to consent and the reasons which underpin consent. The central idea is that citizens should be "convinced by reason" that the institutions and norms of their community are in the general interest. Conversely, the institutions and norms of the community are not in the public interest when citizens cannot be convinced by reason that they are such.

But what does it mean to be "convinced by reason"? Here is where the theory of communicative action enters. Habermas has spent a lifetime investigating what it means for two people to understand each other. We already have a pretty good idea what it means for two people to coerce each other or influence each other through incentives or threats. This instrumental model of motivation and rationality has a long pedigree. Habermas, by contrast, has been interested in a more mysterious process: what is going on when two (or more) people come to agree about something, that is, really see eye to eye? How does the activity of convincing someone of something, differ from the activity of influencing them to behave a certain way? This project involves nothing less than developing an alternative conception of rationality, again intended to stand between two alternatives. Western philosophy has been dominated by two models of rationality. On the one hand, there are substantive views, for example found in Aristotle and Natural Law, that point to objective human goods. On the other hand, with modernity we see the eclipsing of such views in favor of an instrumental view of rationality with no moral content. Communicative rationality stands between these two. While not stipulating human goods, it is not devoid of moral content.

This is not the place to reconstruct Habermas's complete theory of communicative action and rationality. Instead, I concentrate on the meaning of agreement embedded in the theory. I formulate the question in the negative: what would lead us to doubt that a so-called agreement was really an agreement? The first thing that would undermine our confidence is if we thought that coercion had been used. Habermas, for example, notes that "should one party make use of privileged access to weapons, wealth or standing, in order to wring agreement from another party through the prospects of sanctions and rewards, no one involved will be in doubt that the presuppositions of argumentation are no longer satisfied."[18] Something has gone wrong when we talk about *wringing* agreement out of someone. Consent under duress does not usually count as real consent; the use of deception and fraud to gain agreement is normally thought illegitimate. Introducing threats, bribes, blackmail, pressure tactics, and so on, can often void agreements. We tend to doubt the authenticity of agreements if we have reason to believe that force or deception was used or if we think that participants were in a situation of inequality.

Habermas takes these intuitions and formalizes them into a set of rules designed to gurantee discursive equality, freedom, and fair play: no one with the competency to speak and act may be excluded from discourse; everyone is allowed to question and/or introduce any assertion as well as express her attitudes, desires, and needs; no one may be prevented, by internal or external coercion, from exercising these rights.[19] When these rules are in place we can be confident that authentic communication has a chance to flourish and that participants are swayed by the merits of the arguments and nothing else. These then become the conditions of rationality because everything except rational persuasion has been expunged from the process.

Habermas's communicative theory issues in a general principle of validity, the discourse-principle: "Just those action norms are valid to which all possible affected persons could agree as participants in rational discourse."[20] This then is given political content in a democratic-principle: "only those statutes can claim legitimacy that can meet with the assent (*Zustimmung*) of all citizens in a discursive process of legislation that in turn has been legally constituted."[21] As I have already noted, "discursive process" includes all types of discourse including ones that have strategic content. The idea of deliberative democracy and democratic legitimacy that emerges from discourse theory can be defended on three overlapping grounds.

Agreements reached under these conditions have the power to legitimize institutions and political principles in a way that the simple aggregation of votes does not. Agreements reached under the egalitarian and fair conditions of discourse ensure that consent is free and reasonable. Under these conditions we can be confident that arguments rather than inducements sway participants. Here deliberative politics is defended as a better embodiment of our already existing intuitions regarding popular sovereignty. Citizens in liberal democracies generally believe that legitimacy rests on the consent of the governed; discourse theory offers an intuitively compelling account of authentic or autonomous consent.

In addition to "consent of the governed," a deliberative model of politics also corresponds to intuitions regarding the quality of public opinion. Democratic theory champions "informed" consent. Deliberative democracy offers a model of informed consent. We can value deliberation even when, as in most cases, full agreement is not reached. A discursively formed public opinion can represent a process of *Bildung* or education in which citizens build better foundations to their opinions through discursive interaction. Through discursive interaction on various issues from "who are we?" to the best means of promoting the economy, citizens become more informed about the issues, they become aware of what others think and feel, they reevaluate their positions in light of criticism and argument, in short, by defending their opinions with reason their opinions become more reasoned. There is such a thing as reasonable disagreement, and deliberation conceived discursively is one way to achieve it.

Finally, outcomes of deliberative democracy are defended on epistemological grounds as being rational. Although fallible and corrigible, outcomes of discourse can claim a certain warranted acceptability because if the conditions have been met, then outcomes have been subjected to a rigorous process of criticism and debate. The reasons why we might support a proposal have to withstand challenge from many different quarters. Using a Popperian analogy, one can say that, just as rigorous attempts to falsify scientific truth strengthen our confidence in the soundness of our findings, so too rigorous attempts to criticize and challenge norms and policies especially from the point of view of marginalized voices, strengthen their claim to express a generalizable interest. Such a process gives us confidence that policies and principles are backed by the best possible reasons. These then are the grounds for saying outcomes are rational.

Substantive versus Procedural Theory

Deliberative democracy is a pure procedural theory of law and democracy.[22] What this means is that outcomes are evaluated solely on the grounds of the processes that brought them about. There is no independent method of deriving outcomes against which we test democratic outcomes. We can only say whether an outcome is right, or valid, or legitimate with a view to whether or not certain procedural standards are met. A number of theorists have found serious problems with this type of approach. In the second half of this essay I review some of these criticisms and ask how damaging they are to the deliberative project that Habermas sets for himself.

The problem of "bad" outcomes

Outside of the Habermasian paradigm, Amy Gutmann and Dennis Thompson are the two most prominent proponents of deliberative democracy. It is worth considering how they distinguish their approach from Habermas's. They take issue with pure procedural views of deliberative democracy. They argue that these theories – and they have Habermas in mind as the leading example – attempt to define all outcomes with reference to process only. This severely limits the theory and opens it up to some serious dangers. In particular they see two problems with a purely procedural approach. The first is that at the end of the day, when we need to justify a decision, reference to procedure alone is not enough. In order to persuade everyone that justice has truly been done it is not enough to say participants followed the rules to the letter; one must also be able to give substantive reasons for the justness of the outcome. The second argument is that only by including substantive principles that can be defended independent of process can we assert, when necessary, that "what the majority decides, even after full deliberation, is wrong."[23]

Gutmann and Thompson appeal to a medical ethics case to illustrate their first point. They evaluate the deliberation of the National Institute for Clinical Excellence (NICE) on whether the National Health Service in Britain should fund a particular anti-flu drug, Relenza. I am not so much interested in the merits of the case as the general point about democratic process that Gutmann and Thompson make using this example. They believe that all in all NICE was a pretty good example of deliberation at work. It was an open public forum designed to canvas public opinion and deliberate about important principles of health care and then advise the NHS based on results. The idea was to take health-care decisions out of the hidden hands of bureaucrats and subject them to some form of publicity test. Gutmann and Thompson argue that one could not fault NICE on procedural grounds. But when it came time to justify their decision to the public, they could not simply stand up and say, "we followed respected democratic procedures therefore the outcome is valid." They needed to appeal to substantive arguments. They defended their chosen policy preference by saying "the decision not to fund Relenza would not adversely affect the basic life chances of any citizen."[24] Thus, they appealed to a substantive principle in defending the legitimacy of the outcome and not simply process.

Habermas would not disagree with Gutmann and Thompson on this point. He is very much aware that we all do use and indeed must use substantive arguments within discourse and deliberation. We could not really have discourse without substantive arguments. The process of defending the justness of a something, whether it be a proposal within a debate or the outcome of a debate, always involves substantive arguments.

When we do come to an agreement we often (but not always) come to that agreement for the same reason. Thus it is perfectly appropriate to include the reason for the agreement in the justification of the outcome. Proceduralism enters as a presupposed background condition. That the decision "would not adversely affect the life chances of any citizen" was a justificatory reason because (presumably) participants were persuaded by it in a free and open debate. Habermas sometimes implies that a really successful deliberation that ends in agreement will also end in participants agreeing for the same reason.[25] This is a problematic assumption. It makes more sense, and Habermas at times appears to agree with this, to assume that deliberative agreement may be based on a number of overlapping reasons so that I might agree for Kantian reasons, and you might agree for religious reasons. But even in this case, when the decision is to be justified to others we appeal to the substantive reasons in *that* conversation as in any other justificatory conversation. There is nothing in a pure procedural theory to say we ought not to make such appeals.

A persistent critic might insist that for a true proceduralist it is not really the substantive reasons that justify outcomes but the procedures. At a very abstract level this might be true, but not on the day-to-day level of real deliberations. One cannot thematize or question every assumption in debate. Take, for example, appeal to the principle that all people should have equal basic life chances. We could perhaps think of a number of historical contexts in which such an appeal would have been thought controversial and even odd – fourth-century Athens comes to mind. Appeal to such a reason in this context would not justify a decision. Within our context, even if not every single individual believes that we all deserve equal life chances, it is very widely shared and not in need of justification. Nevertheless, we assume or at least act as if we assume that such a principle could be defended in discourse. Because we do not engage in infinite justificatory regress in every deliberation, but instead appeal to widely shared substantive principles, it does not mean that a hypothetical or assumed procedure does not stand behind these appeals. Actual debate proceeds by appeal to substantive principles. Outcomes are justified by appeal to the same principles or those that prove the most persuasive. This fact about the way we argue does not undermine the procedural claim that "persuasiveness" should be understood along procedural lines. Thus Gutmann's and Thompson's first argument does not really hit the mark with regard to Habermas. The second criticism, however, is somewhat more problematic.

Gutmann and Thompson argue that one advantage of "a theory that does not limit itself to procedural principles is that it has no problem with asserting that what the majority decides, even after full deliberation, is wrong."[26] They begin with certain fundamental substantive principles, for example, a prohibition on racial discrimination. With these in hand they are able to criticize outcomes without having to go back and look at the procedure. Habermas cannot use this type of failsafe mechanism. Gutmann and Thompson do point to a weakness in the Habermasian model, but it is not quite the weakness they imagine. Proceduralism stipulates that the validity of outcomes cannot be determined by reference to principles or values given independently of the procedure. But many people have wondered if this is really possible. When we see democratic outcomes that, say, flirt with racial discrimination, what alerts us that something is wrong? It is, as Gutmann and Thompson suppose, that outcomes do not fit with our considered judgments. It is very difficult not to evaluate substantive outcomes against other possible substantive outcomes. We do not need to know anything about the procedure to know that racially discriminatory outcomes are wrong and, furthermore, Gutmann and Thompson want to add that we want to be able to say that such outcomes would be wrong even if procedures were perfectly adhered to. Habermas, in contrast, wants to say that this outcome would never happen if procedures were perfectly adhered to.

It is important to remember that empirical discourse is always less than perfect. Therefore, the very idea that we could reach "full deliberation" under existing conditions is impossible. This means that all outcomes are provisional, fallible, and criticizable. Deliberative democracy, like all other conceptions of democracy designed for mass society, must confront the problem of less than ideal conditions. One such condition is the need to use majoritarian decision rule. Majoritarianism always raises the possibility of bad outcomes. But we can at least compare majority decisions with hypothetical outcomes of idealized deliberation. From this point of view the racial discrimination example is an easy case. It would be difficult to imagine racial minorities agreeing to this principle if they participated in a full deliberation.

This method of criticism, however, is very limited. It is plausible to argue that it is unlikely that racial minorities would agree to their own discrimination. But there just are not that many such clear examples. One of the drawbacks of Habermas's pure proceduralism is that it is impossible to deduce specific outcomes from the procedure and very difficult to speculate except in very general terms about what would be the likely outcome of deliberation. There are too many variables to take into account (millions upon millions if we think of a nationwide deliberation on some fundamental matter). The use of hypothetical thought experiments as a test for the validity of outcomes is very limited. Furthermore, we do not want to say that all majority decisions are suspect simply because a minority did not in fact agree with the decision. Hypothetical thought experiments which speculate what all affected might or might not agree to are only appropriate for issues of justice where we want to hold out the high standard of consensus as the regulative ideal. For most democratic decisions this is not necessary.

Even in situations where consensus is not required for legitimacy, deliberation is appropriate. Deliberation lends a stronger legitimacy to majority decisions because majorities must be accountable to minorities even while they can out-vote minorities. It is not reasonable to say something like "vote for this policy because it benefits us and we are numerically stronger than you." Majorities need to find arguments that at least appear to appeal to generalizable interests.[27] And such appeals can be publicly challenged and questioned, forcing majorities to find more reasonable policy options or lose even their own supporters through a loss of credibility. As many theorists of deliberative democracy have pointed out, the argumentative dynamic of deliberative accountability has a logic of its own that can push even cynical and deceptive participants toward either persuasive arguments or exposure as cynical and deceptive.[28] The more robust deliberation, in the sense of maintaining conditions of equality and accessibility and encouraging participation, publicity, and cooperation, the more accountable majorities will be to minorities and the more decisions based on majority rule will reflect reasonable policy. Reasonable policy here means that the policy is backed by reasons that have been scrutinized and defended in light of minority objections.

Coherent majoritarianism requires that it is not simply the most votes that signals a legitimate outcome, it is the most votes produced by the best arguments.[29] Dewey captured this point well when he said:

> Majority rule, just as majority rule, is as foolish as its critics charge it with being. But it is never merely majority rule.... The means by which a majority comes to be a majority is the important thing: antecedent debates, the modification of views to meet the opinions of minorities.... The essential need, in other words, is the improvement of the methods and conditions of debate, discussion, and persuasion.[30]

The more the outcome under consideration touches on questions of justice, the more we can invoke counterfactual consensus as a standard against which to criticize outcomes. The more the issues under discussion fall away from or do not touch upon moral questions, the more we need to look at the quality of debate. Gutmann and Thompson are clearly concerned with the former and not the latter. It is difficult to talk about bad outcomes in a non-moral sense except in terms either of being based on factual error or unsound reasoning. This is not what worries Gutmann and Thompson.

Counterfactual consensus, as I mentioned, is a limited tool of criticism because, although we can eliminate some obvious candidates as being unlikely outcomes, we cannot deduce positive outcomes. There is, however, another way to criticize outcomes. Bad outcomes like racial discrimination are criticizable within the Habermasian framework because such outcomes would be self-defeating. Outcomes are legitimate to

the extent that the process is fair but this particular outcome, that is racial discrimination, would undermine the fairness of the process and therefore undermine the
legitimacy of outcomes. It is this type of argument that Gutmann and Thompson really
want to take issue with. They feel that it is important to be able to say racial discrimination is wrong in and of itself and not because its presence would jeopardize some other
(presumably more important) principle like democratic citizenship: "democratic theorists should be able to object that racial discrimination . . . is not justified even if democratic citizenship or no other process values are at stake" (p. 9).

First, to repeat a point I made earlier, each one of us may believe that racial
discrimination is unjust in and of itself independent of democratic procedures. Habermasian discourse theory does not require that we all exchange our particular substantive
and often comprehensive views for purely procedural views. Second, Habermas has a
broader notion of the conditions of discourse than democratic citizenship. As I described in the section on private and public autonomy, Habermas wants to argue that an
extensive system of individual rights is a prerequisite for authentic public autonomy.
This would include for example a defense of certain ideas of privacy. Now it is not
immediately clear why we need privacy in order to exercise democratic citizenship. But
it is clear why we might need privacy to develop individual autonomy and the basis of
self-respect. Only within a system that allows for individual autonomy will we have the
proper preconditions for democracy. Habermas's arguments should not be equated with
the legal tradition that places democratic citizenship at the center of rights talk. In this
tradition, rights are justified by showing that they directly enhance citizenship opportunities.[31] For Habermas, the connection is much broader. We must have a legal order
that protects our autonomy, an autonomy that might include, for example, the choice
not to exercise our citizenship. Gutmann and Thompson worry that tying anti-discrimination principles to democratic citizenship devalues anti-discrimination. That is, it
implies that we only value racial integration to the extent that it promotes democracy.
But Habermas has tied anti-discrimination to the conditions of developing individual
autonomy. This makes anti-discrimination a necessary condition, not just for a particular political arrangement, but a necessary condition for a democratic way of life.[32]

Gutmann and Thompson imply that this way of putting it makes the difference
between proceduralist and substantive "definitional" and, therefore, not very interesting. That is, what Gutmann and Thompson call substantive principles, Habermas simply
calls preconditions. But the issue is not simply definitional. Their contrasting approaches
means that Gutmann and Thompson are faced with a different set of justificatory
problems than Habermas. For Gutmann and Thompson the question is what justifies
these substantive principles if not procedure? Is it natural law, context-specific intuitions,
considered judgments, or Rawlsian first principles? Habermas's talk of presuppositions
raises a different set of problems. The co-originality of rights and democracy introduces a
circularity to Habermas's justificatory project that some have thought to be devastating.

The problem of circularity

Frank Michelman investigates the contrast between substantive and procedural views of
law and democracy via a comparison of Ronald Dworkin and Habermas. Michelman
describes the two approaches in the following words:

In the substantive view of constitutional democracy, the question of a given regime's democratic character depends only on what its fundamental or constitutive laws prescribe and not at all on how they came to prescribe it. . . . On the procedural view, in contrast, the regime is not democratic, no matter the democratic nicety of its fundamental-legal prescriptive content, unless the country's people at all times retain appropriate joint control over the content, too.[33]

Michelman describes the circularity problem faced by Habermas using hate speech as an example. The legal regulation of hate speech is valid only to the extent that it is the outcome of fair democratic procedures; however, it appears as if valid hate speech regulation is also a condition of fairness in the first place. As Michelman puts it:

We cannot decide whether the conditions of debate were adequately democratic without first deciding whether democracy requires, permits, or excludes the regulation of hate speech. Presuppositional to proper democracy, it seems, is a set of institutionally supported norms – one may as well call them, as Dworkin does, "constitutive rights" . . . Habermasian validity, in short, requires the presence on the scene of individuals already constituted by fundamental laws as free and equal; yet only they can validly decide what content is required for the fundamental laws that thus constitute them.[34]

The circularity just described raises two separate types of problems. The first is a jurisprudential one: can we make sense of a procedural legal theory when the legitimacy of enacting fundamental law depends on a prior establishment of fundamental law? The second problem is more of a political or pragmatic problem: are citizens likely to enact laws enhancing the conditions of deliberative democracy if those very conditions are not already in place? Michelman and Dworkin are concerned with the jurisprudential problem. I take up the pragmatic political problem in the concluding section.

Michelman's example of hate speech does not, in fact, raise the problems he suggests it raises. Hate speech is regulated differently in different places. This is in keeping with the idea that deliberative democracy offers a procedure the content of which will vary from context to context. Principles that can claim purely moral validity, and not legal validity, are principles that we could imagine receiving universal assent. Candidates are few and far between and are of necessity very general. Furthermore, because we must rely on hypothetical conversation, results are fallible and corrigible. Certain human rights come to mind as candidates of principles about which we might say that they would be agreed to by all affected, in an ideal discourse. This argument could be partially tested by looking at actual debates and levels of agreement that exist in the world today. Once we talk about enacting principles into law then we move to a level of specificity that requires that the legally enforced principles meet with the agreement of the citizens who will live under the law.[35]

Specific legalization of general principles will vary from context to context. So, for example, we might postulate that some guarantee of freedom of speech is both a precondition of authentic democracy as well as a likely outcome of practical discourse. Different contexts will enact this in different ways. Thus, in Canada, for example, certain types of hate speech are not protected as they are in the United States. It is not obvious that one or the other has put the presuppositions of the democratic process into question. What this means is that the legal embodiment of discursive presuppositions falls within a wide range which can only be determined within a given political and legal culture. Which in turn means that it is misleading of Michelman to say that "we cannot decide whether the conditions of debate were adequately democratic without first deciding whether democracy requires, permits, or excludes the regulation of hate speech."[36] First, all three of these options are possible and within the realm of the legitimate. Given their varying cultural and institutional histories it is not obviously problematic that Germany requires the regulation of hate speech, Canada permits it, and the USA excludes such regulation. Furthermore, it is possible to imagine a popular deliberation aimed at changing how hate speech is regulated under the old system of regulation. So, for example, Germany, as it moves away from its twentieth-century history, might very well engage in a public debate about "deregulating" hate speech where the fact that it was regulated at the time of debate would not necessarily undermine the outcome.

Perhaps Michelman's point is good but his example is bad. Let us take a more fundamental question, for example, free speech itself. It would indeed be difficult to imagine a genuine and thus legitimating deliberation about free speech, under conditions that severely limited free speech, especially conditions that silenced advocates of liberalizing free speech. But this points to a different problem than identified by Michelman, namely transition from non-liberal systems to liberal ones. I fully grant that deliberative democracy does not have answers to transitional questions. Here the circularity appears insurmountable under normal conditions. We cannot look to the democratic voice of the people because the conditions are not present to guarantee that there is a democratic voice. And the conditions are not likely to be in place until there is a democratic voice. These circumstances call for extraordinary forms of politics, revolution, and transitional activism, that can have as their end a deliberative form of politics but cannot be conducted as deliberative politics.

Habermas is the first to admit that his theory presupposes already constituted individuals: "deliberative politics . . . stands in an internal relation to the contexts of a rationalized lifeworld that meets it halfway."[37] What this means is that the institutions of liberal democracy develop at the same time as a culture of liberal democracy. Deliberative democracy reflects an internal and already existing relationship between a liberal democratic culture and liberal democratic institutions. Here the "circle" indicates a process of back and forth — a boot-strapping, if you will — between rules and outcomes. We can argue about the limits of the First Amendment and even perhaps improve on our present understanding of those limits without undermining conditions of democracy. As long as liberalism and the rule of law have some foothold, we improve and reevaluate liberalism as we go. Such boot-strapping poses no problem in principle, although as we will see there may be some problems in practice.

Dualist democracy

Before turning to the more damaging form of circularity, I want to take up one more criticism introduced by Michelman. He argues that due to the incoherent circularity of the co-originality thesis, one side of the democracy/rights relationship must come out on top. In order to break the circle something must give and "what gives way, to a degree, is fundamental lawmaking by the people." Here Michelman challenges Habermas's two-tier democracy for being a not particularly strong institutional model of democracy. He goes so far as to say that "for many democrats, surely, this will be a dispiriting meltdown of popular sovereignty."[38]

For William Scheuerman, two-tier democracy is indeed a dispiriting meltdown of popular sovereignty.[39] He, among others, has raised some serious questions regarding Habermas's model of democracy. Although Habermas talks about communicative power steering authoritative decisions, and deliberatively formed opinion and will formation constituting the legitimating force behind modern law, what Habermas actually says about the relationship between informal opinion and will formation and formal legislative bodies is very vague. He talks about the "interplay" between weak and strong publics, but is very insistent in stressing that communicative power does not rule but only "influences" or countersteers. Scheuerman argues that Habermas is simply too vague about the relationship between the communicative power generated in informal citizen deliberation.[40] Although there is a smattering of radical democratic rhetoric, if we look closely at what he does say about institutions it is not clear that what he has in mind is that different from normal politics as it pretty much stands today and nobody is likely to say that contemporary liberal democracies are pushing the envelope in democratic experimentation. The implication here is that Habermas's decentering of democracy into civil society, while retaining the basic institutional structure of existent parliamentary systems, in fact disempowers communication rather than empowers it.

Habermas has a partial answer to this. Concurring with theorists like Jean Cohen and Andrew Arato, Habermas might say that people who look at the direct influence of weak publics on strong publics have missed an important aspect of the radical nature of a deliberative model of democracy.[41] The dualist nature of deliberative democracy does not refer to the two tiers (weak and strong) so much as the two functions undertaken by the "weak" political movements in civil society. The radicalness of the theory is not so much seen in radical policies adopted by state actors in response to communicative power. Many critics appear to be caught in a state-centered view of transformation. They are looking to see the clear points of pressure where civil society and communicative power influence and shape state policy. The transformative potential of deliberative politics is more indirect and resides in the way in which activity within informal venues changes and expands the potential of those venues.

The contrast is between mere "users" of the public sphere, who pursue their political goals within already existing forums and with little or no interest in the procedures themselves, and "creators" of the public sphere who are interested in expanding democracy as they pursue their more particularist goals. Habermas observes that

> actors who support the public sphere are distinguished by the *dual orientation* of their political engagement: with their programs, they directly influence the political system, but at the same time they are also reflexively concerned with revitalizing and enlarging civil society and the public sphere as well as with confirming their own identities and capacities to act.[42]

Habermas, along with Cohen and Arato, identifies new social movements as the actors who have most characteristically taken on this dual role. Cohen and Arato identify this dualism as offensive and defensive strategies. Offensively, groups set out to influence the state and economy. So, for example, environmental movements are intent on influencing legislation, shaping public opinion, and containing economic growth. But at the same time the environmental movement has consciously contributed to the expansion of associational life, to the encouragement of grassroots participation, to the development of new and innovative forms of involvement, and to the extension of public forums of debate and deliberation. This sort of activity empowers citizens within civil society, helps maintain autonomy, and expands and strengthens democracy by giving citizens effective means of shaping their world. Thus to the complaint that Habermas has not given enough institutional detail about what a well-ordered delib- erative democracy might look like, we might respond that that too must be up to participants. They must expand the civil society and the public sphere in creative and empowering ways. That is part of the process. It is certainly the case that Habermas appears to think that radical democracy really only comes on the scene in moments of crisis or at extraordinary times. Normal politics is not directly influenced or only influenced in an uninteresting way by communicative power. However, these moments of crisis leave public spheres expanded and citizen potential greater. Thus feminism has not just induced the state to enact legislation guaranteeing gender equality, feminism has brought millions of women into the public sphere, spawned thousands of activist and civil society groups, and introduced new and innovative ways to understand and practice politics. In short, feminism's contribution has been to help reshape civil society and the public sphere into more democratic and empowering venues.

Democracy versus justice and the problem of vanguards

There is a second and perhaps more damaging component to Scheuerman's criticisms. Habermas acknowledges that a well ordered deliberative democracy would have to address social inequality. Social inequality is a serious barrier to the ideal that all members of the political community are able to participate in the generation of political power. Although Habermas appears to acknowledge this fact, he does not address it. "My concern," says Scheuerman "is merely that *Between Facts and Norms* has nothing adequately *systematic* in character to say about social asymmetries of power, let alone how we might go about counteracting them."[43] Scheuerman feels that Habermas has failed to follow through on the radical potential of deliberative democracy. That potential lies in spelling out the ways in which the capitalist system, globalization, and consumerism are undermining authentic democratic participation. Habermas has a real problem here. His own radical democratic bent has boxed him into a corner.

Is it possible to have equal participation in a world full of inequalities? Nancy Fraser suggests that it is not possible.[44] She argues that Habermas's model of discourse, in asking participants to "bracket" inequalities, does not take this problem seriously enough. Communicating "as if" we were all equal, when in fact we are not, simply will not be enough to immunize discourse from the distorting affects of economic inequality. I agree that bracketing inequalities and pretending they do not exist will not be enough. However, the alternative that she proposes is also problematic. She argues that "a necessary condition for participatory parity is that systemic social inequalities be eliminated."[45] Although not specific about what such an elimination would entail, it is clear that it would involve a radical restructuring of the economy. The problem with this argument is that it does not really solve the difficulty.

Distribution questions are questions of justice. These are properly the subject matter of discourse. In calling for a redistribution of wealth, Fraser must be understood as a participant in discourse and offering a proposal for general consideration. The argument or reason for such a proposal is that it will enhance democracy and equal citizenship. If sincerely committed to democracy, then Fraser must be committed to persuading citizens to reevaluate the relationship between the economy and politics along social-democratic lines. But such a reevaluation must start from within the existing system in which systematic inequalities have not yet been eliminated. In other words, we must find a way of talking with each other as equals about the elimination of systemic inequality before we can eliminate it. Those who challenge Habermas on this issue must answer the vanguard question. They appear to preempt deliberation and debate by saying that we cannot take democratic voices seriously until we have the right conditions.

Habermas is faced with the opposite problem, again eerily reminiscent of early Marxist dilemmas. Habermas is not simply a committed proceduralist; he is a committed empirical proceduralist. Procedures must be undertaken in the real world and philosophers cannot preempt them. Thus, one of his ongoing criticisms of Rawls is that in deducing outcomes to the original position, Rawls in preempting real debate. Habermas cannot predict with any degree of detail what would be agreed to in a full democratic debate. He could speculate broad boundaries of outcomes. As I mentioned before we might be able to presume that certain outcomes would be unlikely (for example, racial inequality), but that does not get very far. We might even be able to presume that an authentic deliberation would be likely to come up with a more egalitarian scheme than we presently have. But we could not go any further than that. A theory of deliberative democracy does not yield a principle of distribution like Rawls's procedure. It is ultimately left up to us, to citizens. But then again we have the problem of circularity, only now in a pragmatic form.

What if it is the case that the present–day social economic conditions are such that the public sphere is stacked against any egalitarian outcome? Perhaps those likely to make the most persuasive arguments in favor of egalitarianism are severely handicapped by existing conditions. Or conversely, perhaps those most likely to distort the economic facts have the most access to the public sphere. Campaign financing is a good example, even if it only touches the tip of the iceberg. As long as the people who benefit from the system are in power then we will never change the system, but we will never get other people in power until we change the system.

While people like Scheuerman and Michelman worry that Habermas is not enough of a democrat, one might take the opposite tack. He is too much of a democrat. In his unwillingness to speak for the people in fear of preempting their own deliberation, he is unable to offer any substantive principles of social justice. By being a radical procedural democrat he is unable to be a radical social democrat, at least while he is acting the philosopher and social theorist.

Habermas's stand is admirable if not unproblematic. Despite what looks like grand theory building in the tradition of Hegel, he actually makes very modest claims on behalf of philosophy. Philosophy cannot tell us what the world ought to look like. It can offer some guiding rules that ought to apply as we go about the business of figuring out how the world should be. But ultimately it is not as philosophers and academics that we will change the world: it is as activists, citizens, and participants in the hurly-burly of politics. Habermas's unwillingness to go beyond proceduralism is a call to philosophers to step out of that role and enter the fray. On the one hand, he is trying to retain a certain claim to objectivity on the part of philosophy and even jurisprudence; on the other hand, he is questioning those who think that philosophers enjoy a special status within normative debates.

Nevertheless, we might still want to say that he is maddeningly vague when it comes to the details of deliberative democracy. It is one thing to refuse to defend clear redistributive principles. It is another to refuse to elaborate institutional venues of deliberation. Again, he would insist that a *theory* of deliberative politics cannot determine the details of institutions because these must fit the context, be discussed, shaped, and adopted by a particular group of people with a particular cultural and political history. Nevertheless, it would not be too much to ask Habermas to describe the universe of possibilities. I assume he simply does not see this as his job. And indeed, there are many political theorists who are undertaking such a task.[46] It is important to remember, however, that in elaborating possible and specific institutional reform, one has stepped over a line from the philosopher to the participant. To paraphrase Feuerbach, one is no longer interpreting the world but changing it, which is, after all, the point.

Notes

1 Jürgen Habermas, *Struktürwandel der Öffentlichkeit* (Darmstadt: Luchterhand, 1962). Translated as *The Structural Transformation of the Public Sphere* (Cambridge, MA: MIT Press, 1998).

2 Habermas often writes as if Americans were his primary audience. So, for example, he self-consciously discusses his "deliberative politics" within "the current debate in the United States initiated by the so called communitarians." Jürgen Habermas, *The Inclusion of the Other: Studies in Political Theory* (Cambridge, MA: MIT Press, 1998) (p. 151, this volume).

3 Ibid, p. 154, this volume.

4 Michael Sandel, *Democracy's Discontent: America in Search of a Public Philosophy* (Cambridge, MA: Harvard University Press, 1996) and Mary Ann Glendon, *Rights Talk: The Impoverishment of Political Discourse* (New York: Free Press, 1991).

5 Habermas, *The Inclusion of the Other*, p. 157, this volume.

6 See Charles S. Maier, *The Unmasterable Past: History, Holocaust, and German National Identity* (Cambridge, MA: Harvard University Press, 1988).

7 Jürgen Habermas, *Between Facts and Norms: Contributions to a Discourse Theory of Law and Democracy*, trans. William Rehg (Cambridge, MA: MIT Press, 1996), 163–8 (henceforth, BFN).

8 Habermas, BFN, pp. 108, 304.

9 How hard and fast Habermas conceives these divisions is an issue of contention among his critics. It appears particularly problematic with regard to Habermas's insistence on a strong division between moral and ethical questions, the former being open in principle to universal validity while the latter only to lifeworld-specific justification. I will not enter that debate at the moment. I will only say that with regard to politics Habermas acknow-

ledges that these distinctions are interpretive tools and are not perfectly reflected in the hurly-burly of democratic politics. See Seyla Benhabib, *Situating the Self: Gender, Community and Postmodernism in Contemporary Ethics* (New York: Routledge, 1992), 23–67. Thomas McCarthy, "Legitimacy and Diversity: Dialectical Reflections on Analytical Distinctions," in *Habermas on Law and Democracy: Critical Exchanges*, ed. Michel Rosenfeld and Andrew Arato (Berkeley: University of California Press, 1998), 115–53.

10   Nancy Fraser, "Rethinking the Public Sphere: A Contribution to the Critique of Actually Existing Democracy," in *Habermas and the Public Sphere*, ed. Craig Calhoun (Cambridge, MA: MIT Press, 1993), 109–42.

11   Habermas, *The Inclusion of the Other*, p. 158, this volume.

12   First used by Nancy Fraser then adopted by Habermas in BFN, p. 306. Nancy Fraser, "Rethinking the Public Sphere," p. 134.

13   Habermas, BFN, pp. 84–118.

14   Ibid, p. 104.

15   Immanuel Kant, "Perpetual Peace," in *Kant's Political Writings*, ed. Hans Reiss (Cambridge: Cambridge University Press, 1970), 130.

16   Ibid, p. 126.

17   Immanuel Kant, "On the Common Saying: 'This May Be True in Theory, But It Does Not Apply in Practice'," in *Kant's Political Writings*, p. 85.

18   Jürgen Habermas, "A Reply to my Critics," in *Habermas: Critical Debates*, ed. John B. Thompson and David Held (Cambridge, MA: MIT Press, 1982), 272–3.

19   Jürgen Habermas, *Moral Consciousness and Communicative Action*, trans. Christian Lenhardt and Shierry Weber Nicholsen (Cambridge, MA: MIT Press, 1990), 89. Examples of external coercion are things like threats and bribes; examples of internal coercion are things like psychological pressure, rhetorical manipulation and deception.

20   Habermas, BFN, p. 107.

21   Ibid, p. 110.

22   The term "pure procedural justice" was introduced by John Rawls and used in contrast to perfect procedural justice. See John Rawls, *Political Liberalism* (New York: Columbia University Press, 1993), 70–1.

23   Amy Gutmann and Dennis Thompson, "Deliberative Democracy Beyond Process." Prepared for Fellows Seminar, University Center for Human Values, Princeton University, April, 2000, p. 8.

24   Ibid.

25   Habermas, BFN, p. 119.

26   Gutmann and Thompson, "Deliberative Democracy Beyond Process," p. 8.

27   Bernard Manin makes this argument in "On Legitimacy and Political Deliberation" in *Political Theory* 15 (August 1987): 349.

28   I have tried to trace this dynamic in Simone Chambers. *Reasonable Democracy: Jürgen Habermas and the Politics of Discourse* (Ithaca, NY: Cornell University Press, 1996), 212–27.

29   Habermas, BNF, p. 179. See Amy Gutmann, "How Not to Resolve Moral Conflicts in Politics," *Ohio State Journal of Dispute Resolution*, vol. 15 (1999), no. 1, p. 5.

30   John Dewey, "The Public and Its Problems," in *The Later Works*, vol. 2 (Carbondale: University of Southern Illinois Press, 1988), 365.

31   Alexander Meiklejohn, *Political Freedom: The Constitutional Powers of the People* (New York: Harper, 1960) and John Hart Ely, *Democracy and Distrust: A Theory of Judicial Review* (Cambridge, MA: Harvard University Press, 1980).

32   Autonomous identity formation plays a central role in Habermas. He avoids the most obvious communitarian criticism by offering an intersubjective communicative idea of autonomous identity formation.

33 Frank Michelman, "Democracy and Positive Liberty," http://bostonreview.mit.edu/
    BR21.5/. p. 2

34 Ibid, p. 7. Many commentators have a difficult time accepting the co-originality of rights
    and democracy and insist that Habermas comes down on one side or the other. But
    commentators appear to be evenly split about which side he comes down on. Some, like
    Michelman, say he is a closet rights fundamentalist, while others, like William Rehg, say
    that in the end the democratic/discourse principle is the trump card. See William Rehg,
    "Against Subordination: Morality, Discourse, and Decision in the Legal Theory of Jürgen
    Habermas," in Rosenfeld and Arato, Habermas on Law and Democracy, pp. 257–71.

35 As universal human rights declarations become more enforced in the international arena
    there will be a corresponding need for real discourse and democracy at the international
    level.

36 Michelman, "Democracy and Positive Liberty," p. 7.

37 Habermas, BFN, p. 252.

38 Michelman, "Democracy and Positive Liberty," p. 8.

39 William E. Scheuerman, "Between Radicalism and Resignation: Democratic Theory in
    Habermas's Between Facts and Norms," in Habermas: A Critical Reader, ed. Peter Dews
    (Oxford: Blackwell Publishers, 1999), 153–77.

40 Melissa Williams makes the same point in "The Deliberative Transformation of Social
    Meanings: The Case of Sexual Harassment." Prepared for presentation at the Annual
    Meeting of the American Political Science Association, Washington, DC, 2000.

41 See Jean Cohen and Andrew Arato, Civil Society and Political Theory (Cambridge, MA: MIT
    Press, 1992) and Andrew Arato, "Procedural Law and Civil Society: Interpreting the
    Radical Democratic Paradigm," in Rosenfeld and Arato, Habermas on Law and Democracy,
    pp. 26–36.

42 Habermas, BFN, p. 370.

43 Scheuerman, "Between Radicalism and Resignation," p. 161.

44 Nancy Fraser, "Rethinking the Public Sphere: A Contribution to the Critique of Actually
    Existing Democracy," in Calhoun, Habermas and the Public Sphere, pp. 109–42.

45 Ibid, p. 121.

46 See, for example, James Bohman, Public Deliberation: Pluralism, Complexity, and Democracy
    (Cambridge, MA: MIT Press, 1996).

PART IV

POSTSTRUCTURALISM

MODERN POLITICAL VIRTUE AND THE DIALECTIC OF GOVERNANCE AND RESISTANCE

7

WHAT IS CRITIQUE?

Michel Foucault

Henri Gouhier[1]   Ladies and Gentlemen, I would first like to thank Mr. Michel Foucault for having made time in his busy schedule this year for this session, especially since we are catching him, not the day after, but only about two days after his long trip to Japan. This explains why the invitation for this meeting was rather terse. Since Michel Foucault's paper is in fact a surprise and, as we can assume, a good surprise, I will not have you wait any longer for the pleasure to hear it.

Michel Foucault   I thank you very much for having invited me to this meeting before this Society. I believe that about ten years ago I gave a talk here on the subject entitled *What is an author?*[2]

For the issue about which I would like to speak today, I have no title. Mr Gouhier has been indulgent enough to say that the reason for this was my trip to Japan. Truthfully, this is a very kind attenuation of the truth. Let's say, in fact, that up until a few days ago, I had hardly been able to find a title; or rather there was one that kept haunting me but that I didn't want to choose. You are going to see why: it would have been indecent.

Actually, the question about which I wanted to speak and about which I still want to speak is: *What is critique?* It might be worth trying out a few ideas on this project that keeps taking shape, being extended and reborn on the outer limits of philosophy, very close to it, up against it, at its expense, in the direction of a future philosophy and in lieu, perhaps, of all possible philosophy. And it seems that between the high Kantian enterprise and the little polemical professional activities that are called critique, it seems to me that there has been in the modern Western world (dating, more or less, empirically from the fifteenth to the sixteenth centuries) a certain way of thinking, speaking and acting, a certain relationship to what exists, to what one knows, to what one does, a relationship to society, to culture and also a relationship to others that we could call, let's say, the critical attitude. Of course, you will be surprised to hear that there is something like a critical attitude that would be specific to modern civilization, since there have been so many critiques, polemics, etc. and since even Kant's problems presumably have origins which go back way before the fifteenth and sixteenth centuries. One will be surprised to see that one tries to find a unity in this critique, although by its very nature, by its function, I was going to say, by its profession, it seems to be condemned to dispersion, dependency and pure heteronomy. After all, critique only exists in relation to something other than itself: it is an instrument, a means for a future or a truth that it will not know nor happen to be, it oversees a domain it would want to police and is unable to regulate. All this means that it is a function which is subordinated in relation to what philosophy, science, politics, ethics, law, literature, etc., positively constitute. And at the same time, whatever the pleasures or compensations accompanying this curious activity of critique, it seems that it rather regularly, almost always, brings not only some stiff bit of utility it claims to have, but also that it is supported by some kind of more general imperative – more general still than that of eradicating errors. There is something in critique which is akin to virtue. And in a certain way, what I wanted to speak to you about is this critical attitude as virtue in general.

There are several routes one could take to discuss the history of this critical attitude. I would simply like to suggest this one to you, which is one possible route, again, among many others. I will suggest the following variation: the Christian pastoral, or the Christian church inasmuch as it acted in a precisely and specifically pastoral way, developed this idea – singular and, I believe, quite foreign to ancient culture – that each individual, whatever his age or status, from the beginning to the end of his life and in his every action, had to be governed and had to let himself be governed, that is to say directed towards his salvation, by someone to whom he was bound by a total, meticulous, detailed relationship of obedience. And this salvation-oriented operation in a relationship of obedience to someone, has to be made in a triple relationship to the truth: truth understood as dogma, truth also to the degree where this orientation implies a special and individualizing knowledge of individuals; and finally, in that this direction is deployed like a reflective technique comprising general rules, particular knowledge, precepts, methods of examination, confessions, interviews, etc. After all, we must not forget what, for centuries, the Greek church called *technè technôn* and what the Latin Roman church called *ars artium*. It was precisely the direction of conscience; the art of governing men. Of course, this art of governing for a long time was linked to relatively limited practices, even in medieval society, to monastic life and especially to the practice of relatively restricted spiritual groups. But I believe that from the fifteenth century on and before the Reformation, one can say that there was a veritable explosion of the art of governing men. There was an explosion in two ways: first, by displacement in relation to the religious center, let's say if you will, secularization, the expansion in civil society of this theme of the art of governing men and the methods of doing it; and then, second, the proliferation of this art of governing into a variety of areas – how to govern children, how to govern the poor and beggars, how to govern a family, a house, how to govern armies, different groups, cities, States and also how to govern one's own body and mind. *How to govern* was, I believe, one of the fundamental questions about what was happening in the fifteenth or sixteenth centuries. It is a fundamental question which was answered by the multiplication of all the arts of governing – the art of pedagogy, the art of politics, the art of economics, if you will – and of all the institutions of government, in the wider sense the term government had at the time.

So, this governmentalization, which seems to me to be rather characteristic of these societies in Western Europe in the sixteenth century, cannot apparently be dissociated from the question "how not to be governed?" I do not mean by that that governmentalization would be opposed in a kind of face-off by the opposite affirmation, "we do not want to be governed, and we do not want to be governed *at all*." I mean that, in this great preoccupation about the way to govern and the search for the ways to govern, we identify a perpetual question which would be: "how not to be governed *like that*, by that, in the name of those principles, with such and such an objective in mind and by means of such procedures, not like that, not for that, not by them." And if we accord this movement of governmentalization of both society and individuals the historic dimension and breadth which I believe it has had, it seems that one could approximately locate therein what we could call the critical attitude. Facing them head on and as compensation, or rather, as both partner and adversary to the arts of governing, as an act of defiance, as a challenge, as a way of limiting these arts of governing and sizing them up, transforming them, of finding a way to escape from them or, in any case, a way to displace them, with a basic distrust, but also and by the same token, as a line of development of the arts of governing, there would have been something born in Europe at that time, a kind of general cultural form, both a political and moral attitude, a way of thinking, etc. and which I would very simply call the art of not being governed or better, the art of not being governed like that and at that cost. I would therefore propose, as a very first definition of critique, this general characterization: the art of not being governed quite so much.

You will tell me that this definition is both very general and very vague or fluid. Well, of course it is! But I still believe that it may allow us to identify some precise points inherent to what I try to call the critical attitude. These are historical anchoring points, of course, which we can determine as follows:

(1) First anchoring point: during a period of time when governing men was essentially a spiritual art, or an essentially religious practice linked to the authority of a Church, to the prescription of a Scripture, not to want to be governed like that essentially meant finding another function for the Scriptures unrelated to the teaching of God. Not wanting to be governed was a certain way of refusing, challenging, limiting (say it as you like) ecclesiastical rule. It meant returning to the Scriptures, seeking out what was authentic in them, what was really written in the Scriptures. It meant questioning what sort of truth the Scriptures told, gaining access to this truth of the Scriptures in the Scriptures and maybe in spite of what was written, to the point of finally raising the very simple question: were the Scriptures true? And, in short, from Wycliffe to Pierre Bayle, critique developed in part, for the most part, but not exclusively, of course, in relation to the Scriptures. Let us say that critique is biblical, historically.

(2) Not to want to be governed, this is the second anchoring point. Not to want to be governed like that also means not wanting to accept these laws because they are unjust because, by virtue of their antiquity or the more or less threatening ascendancy given them by today's sovereign, they hide a fundamental illegitimacy. Therefore, from this perspective, confronted with government and the obedience it stipulates, critique means putting forth universal and indefeasible rights to which every government, whatever it may be, whether a monarch, a magistrate, an educator or a pater familias, will have to submit. In brief, if you like, we find here again the problem of natural law.

Natural law is certainly not an invention of the Renaissance, but from the sixteenth century on, it took on a critical function that it still maintains to this day. To the question "how not to be governed?" it answers by saying: "What are the limits of the right to govern?" Let us say that here critique is basically a legal issue.

(3) And finally "to not to want to be governed" is of course not accepting as true, here I will move along quickly, what an authority tells you is true, or at least not accepting it because an authority tells you that it is true, but rather accepting it only if one considers valid the reasons for doing so. And this time, critique finds its anchoring point in the problem of certainty in its confrontation with authority.

The Bible, jurisprudence, science, writing, nature, the relationship to oneself; the sovereign, the law, the authority of dogmatism. One sees how the interplay of governmentalization and critique has brought about phenomena which are, I believe, of capital importance in the history of Western culture whether in the development of philological sciences, philosophical thought, legal analysis or methodological reflections. However, above all, one sees that the core of critique is basically made of the bundle of relationships that are tied to one another, or one to the two others, power, truth and the subject. And if governmentalization is indeed this movement through which individuals are subjugated in the reality of a social practice through mechanisms of power that adhere to a truth, well, then! I will say that critique is the movement by which the subject gives himself the right to question truth on its effects of power and question power on its discourses of truth. Well, then!: critique will be the art of voluntary insubordination, that of reflected intractability. Critique would essentially ensure the desubjugation of the subject in the context of what we could call, in a word, the politics of truth.

I would have the arrogance to think that this definition, however empirical, approximate and deliciously distant its character in relation to the history it encompasses, is not very different from the one Kant provided: not to define critique, but precisely to define something else. It is not very far off in fact from the definition he was giving of the *Aufklärung*. It is indeed characteristic that, in his text from 1784, *What is the Aufklärung?*, he defined the *Aufklärung* in relation to a certain minority condition in which humanity was maintained and maintained in an authoritative way. Second, he defined this minority as characterized by a certain incapacity in which humanity was maintained, an incapacity to use its own understanding precisely without something which would be someone else's direction, and he uses *leiten*, which has a religious meaning, well-defined historically. Third, I think that it is telling that Kant defined this incapacity by a certain correlation between this excess of authority which maintains humanity in this minority condition, the correlation between this excess of authority and, on the other hand, something that he considers, that he calls a lack of decision and courage. And consequently, this definition of the *Aufklärung* is not simply going to be a kind of historical and speculative definition. In this definition of the *Aufklärung*, there will be something which no doubt it may be a little ridiculous to call a sermon, and yet it is very much a call for courage that he sounds in this description of the *Aufklärung*. One should not forget that it was a newspaper article. There is much work to be done on the relationship between philosophy and journalism from the end of the eighteenth century on, a study.... Unless it has already been done, but I am not sure of that.... It is very interesting to see from what point on philosophers intervene in newspapers in order to say something that is for them philosophically interesting and which, nevertheless, is inscribed in a certain relationship to the public which they intend to mobilize. And finally, it is characteristic that, in this text on the *Aufklärung*, Kant precisely gives religion, law and knowledge as examples of maintaining humanity in the minority condition and consequently as examples of points where the *Aufklärung* must lift this minority condition and in some way majoritize men. What Kant was describing as the *Aufklärung* is very much what I was trying before to describe as critique, this critical attitude which appears as a specific attitude in the Western world starting with what was historically, I believe, the great process of society's governmentalization. And in relation to this *Aufklärung* (whose motto you know and Kant reminds us is "*sapere aude*," to which Frederick II countered: "Let them reason all they want to as long as they obey") in any case, in relation to this *Aufklärung*, how will Kant define critique? Or, in any case, since I am not attempting to recoup Kant's entire critical project in all its philosophical rigor . . . I would not allow myself to do so before such an audience of philosophers, since I myself am not a philosopher and barely a critic . . . in terms of this *Aufklärung*, how is one going to situate what is understood by *critique*? If Kant actually calls in this whole critical movement which preceded the *Aufklärung*, how is one going to situate what *he* understands as critique? I will say, and these are completely childish things, that in relation to the *Aufklärung*, in Kant's eyes, critique will be what he is going to say to knowledge: do you know up to what point you can know? Reason as much as you want, but do you really know up to what point you can reason without it becoming dangerous? Critique will say, in short, that it is not so much a matter of what we are undertaking, more or less courageously, than it is the idea we have of our knowledge and its limits. Our liberty is at stake and consequently, instead of letting someone else say "obey," it is at this point, once one has gotten an adequate idea of one's own knowledge and its limits, that the principle of autonomy can be discovered. One will then no longer have to hear the *obey*; or rather, the *obey* will be founded on autonomy itself.

I am not attempting to show the opposition there may be between Kant's analysis of the *Aufklärung* and his critical project. I think it would be easy to show that for Kant himself, this true courage to know which was put forward by the *Aufklärung*, this same courage to know involved recognizing the limits of knowledge. It would also be easy to show that, for Kant, autonomy is not at all opposed to obeying the sovereign. Nevertheless, in his attempt to desubjugate the subject in the context of power and truth, as a prolegomena to the whole present and future *Aufklärung*, Kant set forth critique's primordial responsibility, to know knowledge.

I would not like to insist any further on the implications of this kind of gap between *Aufklärung* and critique that Kant wanted to indicate. I would simply like to insist on this historical aspect of the problem which is suggested to us by what happened in the nineteenth century. The history of the nineteenth century offered a greater opportunity to pursue the critical enterprise that Kant had in some way situated at a distance from the *Aufklärung*, than it did for something like the *Aufklärung* itself. In other words, nineteenth century history – and, of course, twentieth-century history, even more so – seem to have to side with Kant or at least provide a concrete hold on this new critical attitude, this critical attitude set back from the *Aufklärung*, and which Kant had made possible.

This historical hold, seemingly afforded much more to Kantian critique than to the courage of the *Aufklärung*, was characterized very simply by the following three basic features: first, positivist science, that is to say, it basically had confidence in itself, even when it remained carefully critical of each one of its results; second, the development of a State or a state system which justified itself as the reason and deep rationality of history and which, moreover, selected as its instruments procedures to rationalize the economy and society; and hence, the third feature, this stitching together of scientific positivism and the development of States, a science of the State, or a statism, if you like. A fabric of tight relationships is woven between them such that science is going to play an increasingly determinant part in the development of productive forces and, such that, in addition, state-type powers are going to be increasingly exercised through refined techniques. Thus, the fact that the 1784 question, *What is Aufklärung?*, or rather the way in which Kant, in terms of this question and the answer he gave it, tried to situate his critical enterprise, this questioning about the relationships between *Aufklärung* and *Critique* is going to legitimately arouse suspicion or, in any case, more and more skeptical questioning: for what excesses of power, for what governmentalization, all the more impossible to evade as it is reasonably justified, is reason not itself historically responsible?

Moreover, I think that the future of this question was not exactly the same in Germany and in France for historical reasons which should be analyzed because they are complex.

Roughly, one can say this: it is less perhaps because of the recent development of the beautiful, all-new and rational State in Germany than due to a very old attachment of the universities to the *Wissenschaft* and to administrative and state structures, that there is this suspicion that something in rationalization and maybe even in reason itself is responsible for excesses of power, well, then!: it seems to me that this suspicion was especially well-developed in Germany and let us say to make it short, that it was especially developed within what we could call the Germany Left. In any case, from the Hegelian Left to the Frankfurt School, there has been a complete critique of positivism, objectivism, rationalization, of *technè* and technicalization, a whole critique of the relationships between the fundamental project of science and techniques whose objective was to show the connections between science's naive presumptions, on one hand, and the forms of domination characteristic of contemporary society, on the other. To cite the example presumably the most distant from what could be called a Leftist critique, we should recall that Husserl, in 1936, referred the contemporary crisis of European humanity to something that involved the relationships between knowledge and technique, from *épistèmè* to *technè*.

In France, the conditions for the exercise of philosophy and political reflection were very different. And because of this, the critique of presumptuous reason and its specific effects of power do not seem to have been directed in the same way. And it would be, I think, aligned with a certain kind of thinking on the Right, during the nineteenth and twentieth centuries, where one can again find this same historical indictment of reason or rationalization in the name of the effects of power that it carries along with it. In any case, the block constituted by the Enlightenment and the Revolution has no doubt prevented us in a general way from truly and profoundly questioning this relationship between rationalization and power. Perhaps it is also because the Reformation, that is to say, what I believe was a very deeply rooted, first critical movement of the art of not being governed, the fact that the Reformation did not have the same degree of expansion and success in France as it had in Germany, clearly shows that in France this notion of the *Aufklärung*, with all the problems it posed, was not as widely accepted, and moreover, never became as influential a historical reference as it did in Germany. Let us say that in France, we were satisfied with a certain political valorization of the eighteenth-century philosophers even though Enlightenment thought was disqualified as a minor episode in the history of philosophy. In Germany, on the contrary, the *Aufklärung* was certainly understood, for better or worse, it doesn't matter, as an important episode, a sort of brilliant manifestation of the profound destination of Western reason. In the *Aufklärung* and in the whole period that runs from the sixteenth to the eighteenth century and serves as the reference for this notion of *Aufklärung*, an attempt was being made to decipher and recognize the most accentuated slope of this line of Western reason whereas it was the politics to which it was linked that became the object of suspicious examination. This is, if you will, roughly the chasm between France and Germany in terms of the way the problem of the *Aufklärung* was posed during the nineteenth and the first half of the twentieth century.

I do believe that the situation in France has changed in recent years. It seems to me that in France, in fact (just as the problem of the *Aufklärung* had been so important in German thought since Mendelssohn, Kant, through Hegel, Nietzsche, Husserl, the Frankfurt School, etc. . . .), an era has arrived where precisely this problem of the *Aufklärung* can be reapproached in significant proximity to the work of the Frankfurt School. Let us say, once again to be brief — and it comes as no surprise — that the question of what the *Aufklärung* is has returned to us through phenomenology and the problems it raised. Actually, it has come back to us through the question of meaning and what can constitute meaning. How it is that meaning could be had out of nonsense? How does meaning occur? This is a question which clearly is the complement to another: how is it that the great movement of rationalization has led us to so much noise, so much furor, so much silence and so many sad mechanisms? After all, we shouldn't forget that *La Nausée* is more or less contemporaneous with the *Krisis*. And it is through the analysis, after the war, of the following, that meaning is being solely constituted by systems of constraints characteristic of the signifying machinery. It seems to me that it is through the analysis of this fact whereby meaning only exists through the effects of coercion which are specific to these structures that, by a strange short-cut, the problem between *ratio* and *power* was rediscovered. I also think (and this would definitely be a study to do) that — analyzing the history of science, this whole problematization of the history of the sciences (no doubt also rooted in phenomenology which, in France, by way of Cavaillès, via Bachelard and through Georges Canguilhem, belongs to another history altogether) — the historical problem of the historicity of the sciences has some relationships to and analogies with and echoes, to some degree, this problem of the constitution of meaning. How is this rationality born? How is it formed from something which is totally different from it? There we have the reciprocal and inverse problem of that of the *Aufklärung*: how is it that rationalization leads to the furor of power?

So it seems that whether it be the research on the constitution of meaning with the discovery that meaning is only constituted by the coercive structures of the signifier or analyses done on the history of scientific rationality with the effects of constraint linked to its institutionalization and the constitution of models, all this, historical research has done, I believe, is break in like a ray of morning light through a kind of narrow academic window to merge into what was, after all, the deep undertow of our history for the past century. For all the claim that our social and economic organization lacked rationality, we found ourselves facing I don't know if it's too much or too little reason, but in any case surely facing too much power. For all the praises we lavished on the promises of the revolution, I don't know if it is a good or a bad thing where it actually occurred, but we found ourselves faced with the inertia of a power which was maintaining itself indefinitely. And for all our vindication of the opposition between ideologies of violence and the veritable scientific theory of society, that of the proletariat and of history, we found ourselves with two forms of power that resembled each other like two brothers: Fascism and Stalinism. Hence, the question returns: what is the *Aufklärung*? Consequently, the series of problems which distinguished the analyses of Max Weber is reactivated: where are we with this rationalization which can be said to characterize not only Western thought and science since the sixteenth century, but also social relationships, state organizations, economic practices and perhaps even individual behaviors? What about this rationalization with its effects of constraint and maybe of obnubilation, of the never radically contested but still all massive and ever-growing establishment of a vast technical and scientific system?

This problem, for which in France we must now shoulder the responsibility, is this problem of what is the *Aufklärung*? We can approach it in different ways. And the way in which I would like to approach this – you should trust me about it – is absolutely not evoked here to be critical or polemical. For these two reasons I am seeking nothing else than to point out differences and somehow see up to what point we can multiply them, disseminate them, and distinguish them in terms of each others, displacing, if you will, the forms of analyses of this *Aufklärung* problem, which is perhaps, after all, the problem of modern philosophy.

In tackling this problem which shows our fellowship with the Frankfurt School, I would like, in any case, to immediately note that making the *Aufklärung* the central question definitely means a number of things. First, it means that we are engaging a certain historical and philosophical practice which has nothing to do with the philosophy of history or the history of philosophy. It is a certain historical–philosophical practice, and by that I mean that the domain of experience referred to by this philosophical work in no way excludes any other. It is neither inner experience, nor the fundamental structures of scientific knowledge. It is also not a group of historical contents elaborated elsewhere, treated by historians and received as ready-made facts. Actually, in this historical–philosophical practice, one has to make one's own history, fabricate history, as if through fiction, in terms of how it would be traversed by the question of the relationships between structures of rationality which articulate true discourse and the mechanisms of subjugation which are linked to it. This is evidently a question which displaces the historical objects familiar to historians towards the problem of the subject and the truth about which historians are not usually concerned. We also see that this question invests philosophical work, philosophical thought and the philosophical analysis in empirical contents designed by it. It follows, if you will, that historians faced with this historical or philosophical work are going to say: "yes, of course, yes, maybe." In any case, it is never exactly right, given the effect of interference due to the displacement toward the subject and the truth about which I was speaking.

And even if they don't take on an air of offended guinea-fowls, philosophers generally think: "philosophy, in spite of everything, is something else altogether." And this is due to the effect of falling, of returning to an empiricity which is not even grounded in inner experience.

Let us grant these sideline voices all the importance they deserve, and it is indeed a great deal of importance. They indicate at least negatively that we are on the right path, and by this I mean that through the historical contents that we elaborate and to which we adhere because they are true or because they are valued as true, the question is being raised: "what, therefore, am I," I who belong to this humanity, perhaps to this piece of it, at this point in time, at this instant of humanity which is subjected to the power of truth in general and truths in particular? The first characteristic of this historical–philosophical practice, if you will, is to desubjectify the philosophical question by way of historical contents, to liberate historical contents by examining the effects of power whose truth affects them and from which they supposedly derive. In addition, this historical–philosophical practice is clearly found in the privileged relationship to a certain period which can be determined empirically. Even if it is relatively and necessarily vague, the Enlightenment period is certainly designed as a formative stage for modern humanity. This is the *Aufklärung* in the wide sense of the term to which Kant, Weber, etc. referred, a period without fixed dates, with multiple points of entry since one can also define it by the formation of capitalism, the constitution of the bourgeois world, the establishment of state systems, the foundation of modern science with all its correlative techniques, the organization of a confrontation between the art of being governed and that of not being quite so governed. Consequently, this is a privileged period for historical–philosophical work, since these relationships between power, truth and the subject appear live on the surface of visible transformations. Yet it is also a privilege in the sense that one has to form a matrix from it in order to transit through a whole series of other possible domains. Let us say, if you will, that it is not because we privilege the eighteenth century, because we are interested in it, that we encounter the problem of the *Aufklärung*. I would say instead that it is because we fundamentally want to ask the question, *What is Aufklärung?* that we encounter the historical scheme of our modernity. The point is not to say that the Greeks of the fifth century are a little like the philosophers of the eighteenth or that the twelfth century was already a kind of Renaissance, but rather to try to see under what conditions, at the cost of which modifications or generalizations we can apply this question of the *Aufklärung* to any moment in history, that is, the question of the relationships between power, truth and the subject.

Such is the general framework of this research I would call historical–philosophical. Now we will see how we can conduct it.

I was saying before that I wanted in any case to very vaguely trace possible tracks other than those which seemed to have been up till now most willingly cleared. This in no way accuses the latter of leading nowhere or of not providing any valid results. I would simply like to say and suggest the following: it seems to me that this question of the *Aufklärung*, since Kant, because of Kant, and presumably because of this separation he introduced between *Aufklärung* and *critique*, was essentially raised in terms of knowledge (*connaissance*), that is, by starting with what was the historical destiny of knowledge at the time of the constitution of modern science. Also, by looking for what in this destiny already indicated the indefinite effects of power to which this question was necessarily going to be linked through objectivism, positivism, technicism, etc., by connecting this knowledge with the conditions of the constitution and legitimacy of all possible knowledge, and finally, by seeing how the exit from legitimacy (illusion, error, forgetting, recovery, etc.) occurred in history. In a word, this is the procedure of analysis that seems to me to have been deeply mobilized by the gap between *critique* and *Aufklärung* engineered by Kant. I believe that from this point on, we see a procedure of analysis which is basically the one most often followed, an analytical procedure which could be called an investigation into the legitimacy of historical modes of knowing (*connaître*). It is in this way, in any case, that many eighteenth-century philosophers understood it, it is also how Dilthey, Habermas, etc. understood it. Still, more simply put: what false idea has knowledge gotten of itself and what excessive use has it exposed itself to, to what domination is it therefore linked?

Well, now! Rather than this procedure which takes shape as an investigation into the legitimacy of historical modes of knowing, we can perhaps envision a different procedure. It may take the question of the *Aufklärung* as its way of gaining access, not to the problem of knowledge, but to that of power. It would proceed not as an investigation into legitimacy, but as something I would call an examination of "*eventualization*" (*événementialisation*). Forgive me for this horrible word! And, right away, what does it mean? What I understand by the procedure of eventualization, whilst historians cry out in grief, would be the following: first, one takes groups of elements where, in a totally empirical and temporary way, connections between mechanisms of coercion and contents of knowledge can be identified. Mechanisms of different types of coercion, maybe also legislative elements, rules, material set-ups, authoritative phenomena, etc. One would also consider the contents of knowledge in terms of their diversity and heterogeneity, view them in the context of the effects of power they generate in as much as they are validated by their belonging to a system of knowledge. We are therefore not attempting to find out what is true or false, founded or unfounded, real or illusory, scientific or ideological, legitimate or abusive. What we are trying to find out is what are the links, what are the connections that can be identified between mechanisms of coercion and elements of knowledge, what is the interplay of relay and support developed between them, such that a given element of knowledge takes on the effects of power in a given system where it is allocated to a true, probable, uncertain or false element, such that a procedure of coercion acquires the very form and justifications of a rational, calculated, technically efficient element, etc.

Therefore, on this first level, there is no case made here for the attribution of legitimacy, no assigning points of error and illusion.

And this is why, at this level, it seems to me that one can use two words whose function is not to designate entities, powers (*puissances*) or something like transcendentals, but rather to perform a systematic reduction of value for the domains to which they refer, let us say, a neutralization concerning the effects of legitimacy and an elucidation of what makes them at some point acceptable and in fact, had them accepted. Hence, the use of the word knowledge (*savoir*) that refers to all procedures and all effects of knowledge (*connaissance*) which are acceptable at a given point in time and in a specific domain; and secondly, the term power (*pouvoir*) which merely covers a whole series of particular mechanisms, definable and defined, which seem likely to induce behaviors or discourses. We see right away that these two terms only have a methodological function. It is not a matter of identifying general principles of reality through them, but of somehow pinpointing the analytical front, the type of element that must be pertinent for the analysis. It is furthermore a matter of preventing the perspective of legitimation from coming into play as it does when the terms knowledge (*connaissance*) or domination are used. It is also important, at every stage in the analysis, to be able to give knowledge and power a precise and determined content: such and such an element of knowledge, such and such a mechanism of power. No one should ever think that there exists *one* knowledge or *one* power, or worse, *knowledge* or *power* which would operate in and of themselves. Knowledge and power are only an analytical grid. We also see that this grid is not made up of two categories with elements which are foreign to one another, with what would be from knowledge on one side and what would be from power, on the other – and what I was saying before about them made them exterior to one another – for nothing can exist as an element of knowledge if, on one hand, it does not conform to a set of rules and constraints characteristic, for example, of a given type of scientific discourse in a given period, and if, on the other hand, it does not possess the effects of coercion or simply the incentives peculiar to what is scientifically validated or simply rational or simply generally accepted, etc. Conversely, nothing can function as a mechanism of power if it is not deployed according to procedures, instruments, means, and objectives which can be validated in more or less coherent systems of knowledge. It is therefore not a matter of describing what knowledge is and what power is and how one would repress the other or how the other would abuse the one, but rather, a nexus of knowledge–power has to be described so that we can grasp what constitutes the acceptability of a system, be it the mental health system, the penal system, delinquency, sexuality, etc.

In short, it seems that from the empirical observability for us of an ensemble to its historical acceptability, to the very period of time during which it is actually observable, the route goes by way of an analysis of the knowledge–power nexus supporting it, recouping it at the point where it is accepted, moving toward what makes it acceptable, of course, not in general, but only where it is accepted. This is what can be characterized as recouping it in its positivity. Here, then, is a type of procedure which, unconcerned with legitimizing and consequently, excluding the fundamental point of view of the law, runs through the cycle of positivity by proceeding from the fact of acceptance to the system of acceptability analyzed through the knowledge–power interplay. Let us say that this is, approximately, the *archeological* level.

Secondly, one sees right away from this type of analysis that there are several dangers which cannot fail to appear as its negative and costly consequences.

These positivities are ensembles which are not at all obvious in the sense that whatever habits or routines may have made them familiar to us, whatever the blinding force of the power mechanisms they call into play or whatever justifications they may have developed, they were not made acceptable by any originally existing right. And what must be extracted in order to fathom what could have made them acceptable is precisely that they were not at all obvious, that they were not inscribed in any *a priori*, nor contained in any precedent. There are two correlative operations to perform: bring out the conditions of acceptability of a system and follow the breaking points which indicate its emergence. It was not at all obvious that madness and mental illness were superimposed in the institutional and scientific system of psychiatry. It was not a given either that punishment, imprisonment and penitentiary discipline had come to be articulated in the penal system. It was also not a given that desire, concupiscence and individuals' sexual behavior had to actually be articulated one upon the other in a system of knowledge and normality called sexuality. The identification of the acceptability of a system cannot be dissociated from identifying what made it difficult to accept: its arbitrary nature in terms of knowledge, its violence in terms of power, in short, its energy. Hence, it is necessary to take responsibility for this structure in order to better account for its artifices.

The second consequence is also costly and negative for these ensembles are not analyzed as universals to which history, with its particular circumstances, would add a number of modifications. Of course, many accepted elements, many conditions of acceptability may have a long history, but what has to be recovered in some way through the analysis of these positivities are not incarnations of an essence, or individualizations of a species, but rather, pure singularities: the singularity of madness in the modern Western world, the absolute singularity of sexuality, the absolute singularity of our moral–legal system of punishment.

There is no foundational recourse, no escape within a pure form. This is, without a doubt, one of the most important and debatable aspects of this historical–philosophical approach. If it neither wants to swing toward the philosophy of history, nor toward historical analysis, then it has to keep itself within the field of immanence of pure singularities. Then what? Rupture, discontinuity, singularity, pure description, still tableau, no explanation, dead-end, you know all that. One may say that the analysis of positivities does not partake in these so-called explicative procedures to which are attributed causal value according to three conditions:

1   causal value is only recognized in explanations targeting a final authority, valorized as a profound and unique agency; for some, it is economics; for others, demography;
2   causal value is only recognized for that which obeys a pyramid formation pointing towards the cause or causal focus, the unitary origin;
3   and, finally, causal value is only recognized for that which establishes a certain unavoidability, or at least, that which approaches necessity.

The analysis of positivities, to the degree that these are pure singularities which are assigned not to a species or an essence, but to simple conditions of acceptability, well then, this analysis requires the deployment of a complex and tight causal network, but presumably of another kind, the kind which would not obey this requirement of being saturated by a deep, unitary, pyramidal and necessary principle. We have to establish a network which accounts for this singularity as an effect. Hence there is a need for a multiplicity of relationships, a differentiation between different types of relationships, between different forms of necessity among connections, a deciphering of circular interactions and actions taking into account the intersection of heterogeneous processes. There is, therefore, nothing more foreign to such an analysis than the rejection of causality. Nevertheless, what is very important is not that such analyses bring a whole group of derived phenomena back to a cause, but rather that they are capable of making a singular positivity intelligible precisely in terms of that which makes it singular.

Let us say, roughly, that as opposed to a genesis oriented towards the unity of some principal cause burdened with multiple descendants, what is proposed instead is a *genealogy*, that is, something that attempts to restore the conditions for the appearance of a singularity born out of multiple determining elements of which it is not the product, but rather the effect. A process of making it intelligible but with the clear understanding that this does not function according to any principle of closure. There is no principle of closure for several reasons.

The first is that this singular effect can be accounted for in terms of relationships which are, if not totally, at least predominantly, relationships of interactions between individuals or groups. In other words, these relationships involve subjects, types of behavior, decisions and choices. It is not in the nature of things that we are likely to find support. Support for this network of intelligible relationships is in the logic inherent to the context of interactions with its always variable margins of non-certainty.

There is also no closure because the relationships we are attempting to establish to account for a singularity as an effect, this network of relationships must not make up one plane only. These relationships are in perpetual slippage from one another. At a given level, the logic of interactions operates between individuals who are able to respect its singular effects, both its specificity and its rules, while managing along with other elements interactions operating at another level, such that, in a way, none of these interactions appears to be primary or absolutely totalizing. Each interaction can be resituated in a context that exceeds it and conversely, however local it may be, each has an effect or possible effect on the interaction to which it belongs and by which it is enveloped. Therefore, schematically speaking, we have perpetual mobility, essential fragility or rather the complex interplay between what replicates the same process and what transforms it. In short, here we would have to bring out a whole form of analyses which could be called *strategics*.

In speaking of archeology, strategy and genealogy, I am not thinking of three successive levels which would be derived, one from the other, but of characterizing three necessarily contemporaneous dimensions in the same analysis. These three dimensions, by their very simultaneity, should allow us to recoup whatever positivities there are, that is, those conditions which make acceptable a singularity whose intelligibility is established by identifying interactions and strategies within which it is integrated. It is such research accounting for ... [*a few sentences are missing here where the tape was turned over*] ... produced as an effect, and finally *eventualization* in that we have to deal with something whose stability, deep rootedness and foundation is never such that we cannot in one way or another envisage, if not its disappearance then at least, identifying by what and from what its disappearance is possible.

I was saying before that instead of defining the problem in terms of knowledge and legitimation, it was necessary to approach the question in terms of power and eventualization. As you see, one does not have to work with power understood as domination, as mastery, as a fundamental given, a unique principle, explanation or irreducible law. On the contrary, it always has to be considered in relation to a field of interactions, contemplated in a relationship which cannot be dissociated from forms of knowledge. One always has to think about it in such a way as to see how it is associated with a domain of possibility and consequently, of reversibility, of possible reversal.

Thus you see that the question is no longer through what error, illusion, oversight, or illegitimacy has knowledge come to induce effects of domination manifested in the modern world by the hegemony of [*inaudible*]. The question instead would be: how can the indivisibility of knowledge and power in the context of interactions and multiple strategies induce both singularities, fixed according to their conditions of acceptability, and a field of possibles, of openings, indecisions, reversals and possible dislocations which make them fragile, temporary, and which turn these effects into events, nothing more, nothing less than events? In what way can the effects of coercion characteristic of these positivities not be dissipated by a return to the legitimate destination of knowledge and by a reflection on the transcendental or semi-transcendental that fixes knowledge, but how can they instead be reversed or released from within a concrete strategic field, this concrete strategic field that induced them, starting with this decision not to be governed?

In conclusion, given the movement which swung critical attitude over into the question of critique or better yet, the movement responsible for reassessing the *Aufklärung* enterprise within the critical project whose intent was to allow knowledge to acquire an adequate idea of itself – given this swinging movement, this slippage, this way of deporting the question of the *Aufklärung* into critique – might it not now be necessary to follow the opposite route? Might we not try to travel this road, but in the opposite direction? And if it is necessary to ask the question about knowledge in its relationship to domination, it would be, first and foremost, from a certain decision-making will not to be governed, the decision-making will, both an individual and collective attitude which meant, as Kant said, to get out of one's minority. A question of attitude. You see now why I could not, did not dare, give a title to my conference since if I had, it would have been: "What is the *Aufklärung*?"

Gouhier I thank Michel Foucault very much for having given us such a well-coordinated group of reflections which I would call philosophical, although he said *not being a philosopher myself*. I have to say right away that after having said "not being a philosopher myself," he added "barely a critic," that is to say, anyway, a bit of a critic. And after his presentation I wonder if being a bit of a critic is not being very much a philosopher.

Noël Mouloud I would like to make, perhaps, two or three remarks. The first is the following: Mr Foucault seems to have confronted us with a general attitude of thought, the refusal of power or the refusal of the constraining rule which engenders a general attitude, a critical attitude. He went from there to a problematics that he presented as an extension of this attitude, an actualization of this attitude. These are problems which are presently raised concerning the relationships of knowledge, technology and power. I would see, in a way, localized critical attitudes, revolving around certain core problems with, that is to say, to a great extent, sources or, if you will, historical limits. We first have to have a practice, a method which reaches certain limits, which posits problems, which ends up at certain impasses, in order for a critical attitude to emerge. And thus, for example, there are the successful methodologies of positivism which, notwithstanding the difficulties raised, have elicited the well-known critical reactions that appeared a half-century ago, that is to say, logicist reflection and criticist reflection. I am thinking of the Popperian school or Wittgensteinian school on the limits of a normalized scientific language. Often, in these critical periods, we see a new resolution appear, the search for a renewed practice, for a method which itself has a regional aspect, an aspect of historical research.

Foucault You are absolutely right. It is very much in this way that the critical attitude got started and developed its consequences in a privileged manner in the nineteenth century. I would say that this is precisely the Kantian channel, that the strong period, the essential phase of critical attitude should be the problem of questioning knowledge on its own limits or impasses, if you like, which it encounters in its primary and concrete exercise.

Two things struck me. On one hand, if you like, this Kantian use of critical attitude – and to tell the truth, in Kant, the problem is very explicitly posed – did not prevent critique from asking this question. (We can argue whether or not this is a fundamental issue.) This question is: what is the use of reason, what use of reason can carry its effects over to the abuses of the exercise of power, and consequently, to the concrete destination of liberty? I think that this problem was far from being ignored by Kant and that there was, especially in Germany, a whole movement of reflection around this theme. If you like, generalizing it some, it displaced the strict critical problem that you cited towards other regions. You cite Popper, but after all, excesses of power were also a very fundamental problem for him.

On the other hand, what I wanted to point out is that – and please forgive me for the sketchiness in all this – the history of the critical attitude, as it unfolds specifically in the West and in the modern Western world since the fifteenth to sixteenth centuries – must have its origin in the religious struggles and spiritual attitudes prevalent during the second half of the Middle Ages, precisely at the time when the problem was posed: how should one be governed, is one going to accept being governed like that? It is then that things are at their most concrete level, the most historically determined: all the struggles around the pastoral during the second half of the Middle Ages prepared the way for the Reformation and, I think, were the kind of historical limit upon which this critical attitude developed.

Henri Birault I do not wish to play the upset guinea-fowl here! I completely agree with the way in which the question of the *Aufklärung* was explicitly taken over by Kant in order to simultaneously undergo a decisive theoretical restriction in terms of the moral, religious and political imperatives, etc., which are characteristic of Kant's philosophy. I think that we are in total agreement on this point.

Now, concerning the more directly positive part of the exposition, when it was a matter of studying the crossfire between knowledge and power, on the ground level, somehow on the level of the event, I wonder if there still is not some space there all the same for an underlying question and, let us say, one which is more essentially or traditionally philosophical and would be a backdrop to this precious and minute study of the interplay between knowledge and power in different areas. This metaphysical and historical question might be formulated in the following way: can we not say that at a point in our history and in a certain region of the world, knowledge in and of itself, knowledge as such, took on the form of a power (*pouvoir*) or a potency (*puissance*) while on the side of power, always defined as a *savoir-faire*, a certain way of knowing how to take or how to take on something finally manifested the properly dynamic essence of the noetic? It comes as no surprise that this had to be so and that Michel Foucault is then able to find and disentangle the networks or multiple relations established between knowledge and power since at least from a certain period on, knowledge is down deep a power, and power down deep a knowledge, knowledge and power of the same will, of the same will I must call a will to power.

Foucault   Would your question be about the generality of this type of relationship?

Birault   Not so much its generality as its radicality or occult foundation this side of the duality of the two terms knowledge–power. Is it not possible to rediscover a sort of common essence of knowledge and power, knowledge defining itself as knowledge of power and power defining itself as knowledge of power (to then carefully explore the multiple meaning of this double genitive)?

Foucault   Absolutely. I was insufficiently clear about this very point, in as much as what I would like to do, what I was suggesting, is above or below a kind of description. Roughly, there are intellectuals and men in power, there are scientists and the requirements of industry, etc. In fact, we have an entirely interwoven network. Not only with elements of knowledge and power; but for knowledge to function as knowledge it must exercise a power. Within other discourses of knowledge in relation to discourses of possible knowledge, each statement considered true exerts a certain power and it creates, at the same time, a possibility. Inversely, all exercise of power, even if it is a question of putting someone to death, implies at least a *savoir-faire*. And, after all, to savagely crush an individual is also a way of taking something on. Therefore, if you will, I completely agree and this is what I was trying to bring out: there is a kind of shimmering under the polarities which, to us, seem very distinct from those of power. . . .

Mouloud   I return to our common reference, for both Mr Birault and myself: Popper. One of Popper's intentions is to show that in the constitution of spheres of power, whatever their nature, that is, dogmas, imperative norms, paradigms, it is not knowledge itself which is active and responsible, but a deviant rationality which is no longer truly knowledge. Knowledge – or rationality, inasmuch as it is formative, itself stripped of paradigms, stripped of recipes. On its own initiative it questions its own assurances, its own authority and engages in a "polemics against itself." It is precisely for this reason that it is indeed rationality, and the methodology Popper conceives of is to separate these two behaviors, to decide between them in order to make any confusion or mixture impossible between the use of recipes, the management of procedures and the invention of reasons. And I would wonder, although it is more difficult, if in the human, social, historical domain, social sciences as a whole are not equally and primarily responsible for this opening; yet, it is a very difficult situation because social sciences are, in fact, allied with technology. Between a science and the powers that use it, there is a relationship which is not truly essential; although important, it remains "contingent" in a certain way. The technical conditions for the use of knowledge are in a more direct relationship with the exercise of a power, a power which dodges exchange or examination, rather than the conditions of knowledge itself. And it is in this sense that I do not altogether understand the argument. Otherwise, Mr Foucault made some enlightening remarks which he will surely develop. But I ask myself the question: is there a really direct link between the obligations or requirements of knowledge and those of power?

Foucault   I would be thrilled if one could do it like that, that is, if one could say: there is a good science, one which is both true and does not partake of nasty power; and then obviously the bad use of science, either in its opportunistic application or in its errors. If you can prove to me that this is the case, then, well! I will leave here happy.

Mouloud   I am not saying as much. I recognize that the historical connection, the factual link is strong. But I observe several things: that new scientific investigations (those in biology, the social sciences) are again putting man and society in a situation of non-determination, opening up inroads to liberty for them, and thus constraining them, to put it this way, to once again making decisions. Besides that, oppressive powers rarely rely on scientific knowledge, but prefer to rely on non-knowledge, a science which has first been reduced to a "myth." Racism founded on a "pseudo-genetics" or political pragmatism founded on a neo-Lamarckian deformation of biology are familiar examples. And finally, I also understand very well that a science's positive information calls for the distance of critical judgment. Yet it seems to me – and this was approximately my argument – that humanist critique, which assumes cultural and axiological criteria, cannot be entirely developed or succeed without the support that knowledge brings to it, criticizing its bases, its presuppositions and its antecedents. This especially concerns explanations provided by the human sciences and history. And it seems to me that Habermas, in particular, includes this analytic dimension in what he calls the critique of ideologies, even of those very ones engendered by knowledge.

Foucault   I think that this is precisely the advantage of critique!

Gouhier   I would like to ask you a question. I completely agree with your historical distinctions and the importance of the Reformation. But it seems to me that throughout all of Western tradition, there is a critical ferment due to Socratic thought. I wanted to ask you if the word *critique* as you defined it and used it, could not be an appropriate term with which to call what I would provisionally label a critical ferment of Socratism in Western thought, which played a role in the sixteenth and seventeenth centuries with the return to Socrates?

Foucault   You confront me with a more difficult question. I will say that the return to Socratism (we feel it, identify it, see it historically, it seems, between the sixteenth and seventeenth centuries) was only possible in the context of these, for me far more important, issues which were the pastoral struggles and this problem of governing men, using the term government in the very full and broad meaning that it had at the end of the Middle Ages. To govern men was to take them by the hand and lead them to their salvation through an operation, a technique of precise piloting, which implied a full range of knowledge concerning the individual being guided, the truth towards which one was guiding. . . .

Gouhier   Would you be able to do your analysis all over again if you were giving a paper on Socrates and his times?

Foucault   This indeed is the real problem. Here again, I am responding rapidly to something rather difficult. It seems to me that fundamentally when one investigates Socrates like that, or rather – I dare not say it – I wonder if Heidegger investigating the Presocratics doesn't do it . . . no, not at all, it is not at all a matter of resorting to anachronism and of projecting the eighteenth century on the fifth. . . . But this question of the *Aufklärung* which is, I think, quite fundamental for Western philosophy since Kant, I wonder if it is not a question which somehow scans all possible history down to the radical origins of philosophy. In this light, the trial of Socrates can, I think, be investigated in a valid manner, without any anachronism, but starting with a problem which is and which was, in any case, perceived by Kant as the problem of the *Aufklärung*.

Jean-Louis Bruch   I would like to ask a question about an expression which is central to your presentation, but which was formulated in two ways which seemed different to me. At the end, you spoke of "the decision-making will not to be governed" as a foundation or a reversal of the *Aufklärung* which was the subject of your talk. In the beginning, you spoke of "not being governed *like that*," of "not being governed so much," of "not being governed at such a price." In one case, the expression is absolute, in the other, it is relative, and according to what criteria? Is it because of having felt the abuse of governmentalization that you come to the radical position, "the decision-making will not to be governed?" I am asking this question, and finally, doesn't this last position need to be in turn the object of an investigation, a questioning that would, in essence, be philosophical?

Foucault   Two good questions. On the point you raise about the variations in the expressions: I do not think that the will not to be governed at all is something that one could consider an originary aspiration. I think that, in fact, the will not to be governed is always the will not to be governed thusly, like that, by these people, at this price. As for the expression of not being governed *et al*, I believe it is the philosophical and theoretical paroxysm of something that would be this will not to be relatively governed. And when at the end I was saying "decision-making will not to be governed," then there, an error on my part, it was not to be governed thusly, like that, in this way. I was not referring to something that would be a fundamental anarchism, that would be like an originary freedom, absolutely and wholeheartedly resistant to any governmentalization. I did not say it, but this does not mean that I absolutely exclude it. I think that my presentation stops at this point, because it was already too long, but also because I am wondering . . . if one wants to explore this dimension of critique that seems to me to be so important because it is both part of, and not a part of, philosophy. If we were to explore this dimension of critique, would we not then find that it is supported by something akin to the historical practice of revolt, the non-acceptance of a real government, on one hand, or, on the other, the individual experience of the refusal of governmentality? What strikes me in particular – but I am perhaps haunted by this because I am working on it a lot right now – is that, if this matrix of critical attitude in the Western world must be sought out in religious attitudes and in connection with the exercise of pastoral power in the Middle Ages, all the same it is surprising that mysticism is seen as an individual experience while institutional and political struggles are viewed as absolutely unified, and in any case, constantly referring to one another. I would say that one of the first great forms of revolt in the West was mysticism. All the bastions of resistance to the authority of the Scriptures, to mediation by the pastor, were developed either in convents or outside convents by the secular population. When one sees that these experiences, these spiritual movements have very often been used as attire, vocabulary, but even more so as ways of being, and ways of supporting the hopes expressed by the struggle that we can define as economic, popular, and in Marxist terms as the struggle between the classes, I think we have here something that is quite fundamental.

In following the itinerary of this critical attitude whose history seems to begin at this point in time, should we not now investigate what the will not to be governed thusly, like that, etc., might be both as an individual and a collective experience? It is now necessary to pose the problem of will. In short, you will say that this is obvious, one cannot confront this problem, sticking closely to the theme of power without, of course, at some point, getting to the question of human will. It was so obvious that I could have realized it earlier. However, since this problem of will is a problem that Western philosophy has always treated with infinite precaution and difficulties, let us say that I tried to avoid it as much as possible. Let us say that it was unavoidable. Here I have given you some considerations on my work in progress.

André Sernin To which side do you lean more? Would it be towards August Comte, schematically speaking, who rigorously separates spiritual from temporal power or, on the contrary, towards Plato who said that things would never go well until philosophers were themselves made the leaders of temporal power?

Foucault Do I really have to choose?

Sernin No, you don't have to choose between them, but which one would you tend to lean to more?

Foucault I would try to inch my way out from between them!

Pierre Hadji-Dimou You have successfully presented us with the problem of critique in its connection to philosophy and you have arrived at the relationships between power and knowledge. I wanted to contribute a little clarification on the subject of Greek thought. I think that the problem was already formulated by our President. "To know" (*connaître*) is to have *logos* and *mythos*. I think that with the *Aufklärung*, we are not able "to know." Knowledge is not only rationality, it is not only *logos* in historical life, there is a second source, *mythos*. If we refer to the discussion between Protagoras and Socrates, when Protagoras is asking the question about the right of the *Politeia* to punish, about its power, he says that he will specify and illustrate his thought about *mythos*. *Mythos* is linked to *logos* because there is rationality: the more it teaches us, the more beautiful it is. Here is the question I wanted to add: is it in suppressing a part of thought, irrational thought which arrives at *logos*, that is to say, is it by suppressing the *mythos* that we are able to know the sources of knowledge, the knowledge of power which also has a mythic sense to it?

Foucault I agree with your question.

Sylvain Zac I would like to make two remarks. You said, and rightly so, that critical attitude could be considered a virtue. In fact, there is a philosopher, Malebranche, who studied this virtue: it is freedom of spirit. On one hand, I do not agree with you about the relationships you establish in Kant between his article on the *Enlightenment* and his critique of knowledge. The latter obviously assigns limits, but does not itself have any limit; it is total whereas when one reads the article on the *Enlightenment*, one sees that Kant makes a very important distinction between public use and private use. In the case of public use, this courage must disappear. Which means that . . .

Foucault It's the opposite, since what he calls public use is . . .

Zac When someone has, for example, a tenured position in a philosophy department at a university, there, he can speak publicly and he must not criticize the Bible: on the other hand, in private, he can do so.

Foucault It's quite the contrary and that is what is so very interesting. Kant says: "there is a public use of reason which must not be limited." What is this public use? It is what circulates from scholar to scholar, appears in newspapers and publications, and appeals to everyone's conscience. These uses, these public uses of reason must not be limited, and curiously what he calls private use is, in some way, the government employee's use of reason. And the functionary or government employee, the officer, he says, does not have the right to tell his superior: "I will not obey you and your order is absurd." Curiously, what Kant defines as private use is each individual's obedience, inasmuch as he is a part of the State, to his superior, to the Sovereign or his representative.

Zac   I agree with you. I made a mistake. Nevertheless, the result is that there are limits to the manifestation of courage in this article. And these limits, I found them all over, in all the *Aufklärer*, obviously in Mendelssohn. There is a good deal of conformist writing in the German *Aufklärung* movement which we do not find in the French *Enlightenment* of the eighteenth century.

Foucault   I agree completely. I don't exactly see how this challenges what I said.

Zac   I do not believe that there is an intimate historical link between the *Aufklärung* movement that you have given as a central focus and the development of critical attitude, of the attitude of resistance, from either the political or the intellectual point of view. Don't you think that we could admit this point?

Foucault   I do not think, on the one hand, that Kant felt like a stranger to the *Aufklärung* which was for him his actuality and within which he was getting involved, not only through the article on the *Aufklärung*, but also in many other affairs...

Zac   The word *Aufklärung* is found again in *Religion According to the Limits of Simple Reason*, but then it is applied to the purity of sentiments, to something internal. An inversion occurred, as with Rousseau.

Foucault   I would like to finish up what I was saying. . . . Therefore, Kant feels perfectly connected to this present that he calls the *Aufklärung* and that he attempts to define. And regarding this movement of the *Aufklärung*, it seems to me that he introduces a dimension we can consider as more specific or, to the contrary, more general and more radical which is this: the first bold move that one must make when it is a matter of knowledge and knowing is to know what it is that one can know. This is the radicality and for Kant, moreover, the universality of his enterprise. I believe in this kinship, whatever limits, of course, the boldness of the *Aufklärer* has. I do not see how the fact that the *Aufklärer* were timid would in any way change anything in this kind of movement that Kant went through and of which, I believe, he was relatively conscious.

Birault   I think that critical philosophy represents a movement which both restricts and radicalizes *Aufklärung* in general.

Foucault   But its link to the *Aufklärung* was the question everyone was asking at that time. What are we saying, what is this movement that immediately preceded us and to which we still belong called the *Aufklärung*? The best proof is that it was in a newspaper that the series of articles by Mendelssohn and Kant were published. . . . It was a current event. A little like how we ourselves might ask the question: what is the present crisis in values?

Jeanne Dubouchet   I would like to ask you what material you place within knowledge. Power, I believe I understood, since it was a matter of not being governed: but what kind of knowledge?

Foucault   If I use that word it is once again essentially to neutralize everything that might either legitimize or simply hierarchize values. If you like, for me – as scandalous as this may be and must seem to be in the eyes of a scientist or a methodologist or even a historian of sciences – for me, between a statement by a psychiatrist and a mathematical operation, when I am speaking of knowledge, for now, I make no distinction between them. The only point through which I would introduce differences is to know which are the effects of power, if you like, of induction – not in the logical sense of the term – that this proposition can have, on one hand, within the scientific domain in which it is formulated – mathematics, psychiatry, etc. – and, on the other, what are the non-discursive, non-formalized, not especially scientific networks of institutional power to which it is linked as soon as it is being circulated. This is what I would call knowledge (*savoir*): elements of knowledge (*connaissance*) which, whatever their value in relation to us, in relation to a pure spirit, exercise effects of power inside and outside their domain.

Gouhier   It is my honor to thank Michel Foucault for having provided us with such an interesting session which is certain to become an especially important publication.

Foucault   Thank you.

Translated by Lysa Hochroth

Notes

1   Henri Gouhier is an historian of philosophy and a specialist in Malebranche and Bergson. Although part of the academic establishment, he remained open to new ideas (he directed Lucien Goldmann's dissertation). The discussion which follows Foucault's lecture involved various specialists in philosophy: Mouloud (aesthetics); Bruch (Kant): Zac (Spinoza); Birault (Heidegger); etc.

2   "What is an Author," first published in the *Bulletin de la Societe française de philosophie*, was translated from the French by Josue V. Harari in *Textual Strategies: Perspectives in Post-Structuralist Criticism*, edited by Josue V. Harari (Ithaca, NY: Cornell University Press, 1979). It was reprinted in *Foucault Reader*, ed. Paul Rabinow (New York: Pantheon Books, 1984).

8

WHAT IS CRITIQUE? AN ESSAY ON FOUCAULT'S VIRTUE

Judith Butler

What is it to offer a critique? This is something that, I would wager, most of us understand in some ordinary sense. But matters become move vexing if we attempt to distinguish between a critique of this or that position and critique as a more generalized practice, one that might be described without reference to its specific objects. Can we even ask such a question about the generalized character of critique without gesturing toward an essence of critique? And if we achieved the generalized picture, offering something which approaches a philosophy of critique, would we then lose the very distinction between philosophy and critique that operates as part of the definition of critique itself? Critique is always a critique *of* some instituted practice, discourse, episteme, institution, and it loses its character the moment in which it is abstracted from its operation and made to stand alone as a purely generalizable practice. But if this is true, this does not mean that no generalizations are possible or that, indeed, we are mired in particularisms. On the contrary, we tread here in an area of constrained generality, one which broaches the philosophical, but must, if it is to remain critical, remain at a distance from that very achievement.

The essay I offer here is about Foucault, but let me begin by suggesting what I take to be an interesting parallel between what Raymond Williams and Theodor Adorno, in different ways, sought to accomplish under the name of "criticism" and what Foucault sought to understand by "critique." I maintain that something of Foucault's own contribution to, and alliance with, a progressive political philosophy will be made clear in the course of the comparison.

Raymond Williams worried that the notion of criticism has been unduly restricted to the notion of "fault-finding"[1] and proposed that we find a vocabulary for the kinds of responses we have, specifically to cultural works, "which [do] not assume the habit (or right or duty) of judgment." And what he called for was a more specific kind of response, one that did not generalize too quickly: "what always needs to be understood," he wrote, "is the specificity of the response, which is not a judgment, but a practice." I believe this last line also marks the trajectory of Foucault's thinking on this topic, since "critique" is precisely a practice that not only suspends judgment for him, but offers a new practice of values based on that very suspension.

So, for Williams, the practice of critique is not reducible to arriving at judgments (and expressing them). Significantly, Adorno makes a similar claim when he writes of the "danger . . . of judging intellectual phenomena in a subsumptive, uninformed and administrative manner and assimilating them into the prevailing constellations of power which the intellect ought to expose."[2] So, the task of exposing those "constellations of power" is impeded by the rush to "judgment" as the exemplary act of critique. For Adorno, the very operation of judgment serves to separate the critic from the social world at hand, a move which deratifies the results of its own operation, constituting a "withdrawal from praxis." Adorno writes that the critic's "very sovereignty, the claim to a more profound knowledge of the object, the separation of the idea from its object through the independence of the critical judgment threatens to succumb to the thing-like form of the object when cultural criticism appeals to a collection of ideas on display, as it were, and fetishizes isolated categories." For critique to operate as part of a praxis, for Adorno, is for it to apprehend the ways in which categories are themselves instituted, how the field of knowledge is ordered, and how what it suppresses returns, as it were, as its own constitutive occlusion. Judgments operate for both thinkers as ways to subsume a particular under an already constituted category, whereas critique asks after the occlusive constitution of the field of categories themselves. What becomes especially important for Foucault in this domain, is to try to think the problem of freedom and, indeed, ethics in general, beyond judgment: critical thinking constitutes this kind of effort.

In 1978 Foucault delivered a lecture entitled, "What is Critique?",[3] a piece that prepared the way for his more well-known essay, "What is Enlightenment?" (1984). He not only asks what critique is, but seeks to understand the kind of question that critique institutes, offering some tentative ways of circumscribing its activity. What remains perhaps most important about that lecture, and the more developed essay that followed, is the question form in which the matter is put. For the very question "what is critique?" is an instance of the critical enterprise in question, and so the question not only poses the problem – what is this critique that we supposedly do or, indeed, aspire to do? – but enacts a certain mode of questioning which will prove central to the activity of critique itself.

Indeed, I would suggest that what Foucault seeks to do with this question is something quite different from what we have perhaps come to expect from critique. Habermas made the operation of critique quite problematic when he suggested that a move beyond critical theory was required if we are to seek recourse to norms in making evaluative judgments about social conditions and social goals. The perspective of critique, in his view, is able to call foundations into question, denaturalize social and political hierarchy, and even establish perspectives by which a certain distance on the naturalized world can be had. But none of these activities can tell us in what direction we ought to move, nor can they tell us whether the activities in which we engage are realizing certain kinds of normatively justified goals. Hence, in his view, critical theory had to give way to a stronger normative theory, such as communicative action, in order to supply a foundation for critical theory, enabling strong normative judgments to be made,[4] and for politics not only to have a clear aim and normative aspiration, but for us to be able to evaluate current practices in terms of their abilities to reach those goals. In making this kind of criticism of critique, Habermas became curiously uncritical about the very sense of normativity he deployed. For the question "what are we to do?" presupposes that the "we" has been formed and that it is known, that its action is possible, and the field in which it might act is delimited. But if those very formations and delimitations have normative consequences, then it will be necessary to ask after the values that set the stage for action, and this will be an important dimension of any critical inquiry into normative matters.

And though the Habermasians may have an answer to this problem, my aim today is not to rehearse these debates nor to answer them, but to mark the distance between a notion of critique that is characterized as normatively impoverished in some sense, and another, which I hope to offer here, which is not only more complex than the usual criticism assumes but which has, I would argue, strong normative commitments that appear in forms that would be difficult, if not impossible, to read within the current grammars of normativity. Indeed, in this essay, I hope to show that Foucault not only makes an important contribution to normative theory, but that both his aesthetics and his account of the subject are integrally related to both his ethics and politics. Whereas some have dismissed him as an aesthete or, indeed, as a nihilist, I hope to suggest that the foray he makes into the topic of self-making and, by presupposition, into poeisis itself is central to the politics of desubjugation that he proposes. Paradoxically, self-making and desubjugation happen simultaneously when a mode of existence is risked which is unsupported by what he calls the regime of truth.

Foucault begins his discussion by affirming that there are various grammars for the term, "critique," distinguishing between a "high Kantian enterprise" called critique as well as "the little polemical activities that are called critique." Thus, he warns us at the outset that critique will not be one thing, and that we will not be able to define it apart from the various objects by which it itself is defined. "By its function," he writes "[critique] seems to be condemned to dispersion, dependency and pure heteronomy." "It only exists in relation to something other than itself."

Thus, Foucault seeks to define critique, but finds that only a series of approximations are possible. Critique will be dependent on its objects, but its objects will in turn define the very meaning of critique. Further, the primary task of critique will not be to evaluate whether its objects – social conditions, practices, forms of knowledge, power, and discourse – are good or bad, valued highly or demeaned, but to bring into relief the very framework of evaluation itself. What is the relation of knowledge to power such that our epistemological certainties turn out to support a way of structuring the world that forecloses alternative possibilities of ordering? Of course, we may think that we need epistemological certainty in order to state for sure that the world is and ought to be ordered a given way. To what extent, however, is that certainty orches-trated by forms of knowledge precisely in order to foreclose the possibility of thinking otherwise? Now, one might wisely ask, what good is thinking otherwise, if we don't know in advance that thinking otherwise will produce a better world? If we do not have a moral framework in which to decide with knowingness that certain new possibilities or ways of thinking otherwise will bring forth that world whose betterness we can judge by sure and already established standards? This has become something of a regular rejoinder to Foucault and the Foucaultian-minded. And shall we assume that the relative silence that has greeted this habit of fault-finding in Foucault is a sign that his theory has no reassuring answers to give? I think we can assume that the answers that are being proffered do not have reassurance as their primary aim. This is, of course, not to say what withdraws reassurance is, by definition, not an answer. Indeed, the only rejoinder, it seems to me, is to return to a more fundamental meaning of "critique" in order to see what may well be wrong with the question as it is posed and, indeed, to pose the question anew, so that a more productive approach to the place of ethics within politics might be mapped. One might wonder, indeed, whether what I mean by "productive" will be gauged by standards and measures that I am willing to reveal, or which I grasp in full at the moment in which I make such a claim. But here I would ask for your patience since it turns out that critique is a practice that requires a certain amount of patience in the same way that reading, according to Nietzsche, required that we act a bit more like cows than humans and learn the art of slow rumination.

Foucault's contribution to what appears as an impasse within critical and post-critical theory of our time is precisely to ask us to rethink critique as a practice in which we pose the question of the limits of our most sure ways of knowing, what Williams referred to as our "uncritical habits of mind" and what Adorno described as ideology (where the "unideological thought is that which does not permit itself to be reduced to 'operational terms' and instead strives solely to help the things themselves to that articulation from which they are otherwise cut off by the prevailing language.") One does not drive to the limits for a thrill experience, or because limits are dangerous and sexy, or because it brings us into a titillating proximity with evil. One asks about the limits of ways of knowing because one has already run up against a crisis within the epistemological field in which one lives. The categories by which social life are ordered produce a certain incoherence or entire realms of unspeakability. And it is from this condition, the tear in the fabric of our epistemological web, that the practice of critique emerges, with the awareness that no discourse is adequate here or that our reigning discourses have produced an impasse. Indeed, the very debate in which the strong normative view wars with critical theory may produce precisely that form of discursive impasse from which the necessity and urgency of critique emerges.

For Foucault, critique is "a means for a future or a truth that it will not know nor happen to be, it oversees a domain it would not want to police and is unable to regulate." So critique will be that perspective on established and ordering ways of knowing which is not immediately assimilated into that ordering function. Significantly, for Foucault, this exposure of the limit of the epistemological field is linked with the practice of virtue, as if virtue is counter to regulation and order, as if virtue itself is to be found in the risking of established order. He is not shy about the relation here. He writes, "there is something in critique that is akin to virtue." And then he says something which might be considered even more surprising: "this critical attitude [is] virtue in general."

There are some preliminary ways we can understand Foucault's effort to cast critique as virtue. Virtue is most often understood either as an attribute or a practice of a subject, or indeed a quality that conditions and characterizes a certain kind of action or practice. It belongs to an ethics which is not fulfilled merely by following objectively formulated rules or laws. And virtue is not only a *way* of complying with or conforming with preestablished norms. It is, more radically, a critical relation to those norms, one which, for Foucault, takes shape as a specific stylization of morality.

Foucault gives us an indication of what he means by virtue in the introduction to *The Use of Pleasure: The History of Sexuality, Volume Two*.[5] At this juncture he makes clear that he seeks to move beyond a notion of ethical philosophy that issues a set of prescriptions. Just as critique intersects with philosophy without quite coinciding with it, so Foucault in that introduction seeks to make of his own thought an example of a non-prescriptive form of moral inquiry. In the same way, he will later ask about forms of moral experience that are not rigidly defined by a juridical law, a rule or command to which the self is said mechanically or uniformly to submit. The essay that he writes, he tells us, is itself the example of such a practice, "to explore what might be changed, in its own thought, through the practice of a knowledge that is foreign to it." Moral experience has to do with a self-transformation prompted by a form of knowledge that is foreign to one's own. And this form of moral experience will be different from the submission to a command. Indeed, to the extent that Foucault interrogates moral experience here or elsewhere, he understands himself to be making an inquiry into moral experiences that are not primarily or fundamentally structured by prohibition or interdiction.

In the first volume of *The History of Sexuality*[6] he sought to show that the primary interdictions assumed by psychoanalysis and the structuralist account of cultural prohibitions cannot be assumed as historical constants. Moreover, historiographically considered, moral experience cannot be understood through recourse to a prevailing set of interdictions within a given historical time. Although there are codes to be studied, these codes must always be studied in relation to the modes of subjectivation to which they correspond. He makes the claim that the juridification of law achieves a certain hegemony within the thirteenth century, but that if one goes back to Greek and Roman classical cultures, one finds practices, or "arts of existence" which have to do with a cultivated relation of the self to itself.

Introducing the notion of "arts of existence," Foucault also reintroduces and reemphasizes "intentional and voluntary actions," specifically, "those actions by which men not only set themselves rules of conduct, but also seek to transform themselves in their singular being, and to make their life into an oeuvre." Such lives do not simply conform to moral precepts or norms in such a way that selves, considered preformed or ready-made, fit themselves into a mold that is set forth by the precept. On the contrary, the self fashions itself in terms of the norm, comes to inhabit and incorporate the norm, but *the norm is not in this sense external to the principle by which the self is formed*. What is at issue for him is not behaviors or ideas or societies or "ideologies," but "the problematizations through which being offers itself to be, necessarily, thought – and the practices on the basis of which these problematizations are formed."

This last claim is hardly transparent, but what it suggests is that certain kinds of practices which are designed to handle certain kinds of problems produce, over time, a settled domain of ontology as their consequence, and this ontological domain, in turn, constrains our understanding of what is possible. Only with reference to this prevailing ontological horizon, itself instituted through a set of practices, will we be able to understand the kinds of relations to moral precepts that have been formed as well as those that are yet to be formed. For instance, he considers at length various practices of austerity, and he ties these to the production of a certain kind of masculine subject. The practices of austerity do not attest to a single and abiding prohibition, but work in the service of crafting a certain kind of self. Or put in a more precise way, the self, incorporating the rules of conduct that represent the virtue of austerity, creates itself as a specific kind of subject. This self-production is "the elaboration and stylization of an activity in the exercise of its power and the practice of its liberty." This was not a practice that opposed pleasure pure and simple, but a certain practice of pleasure itself, a practice of pleasure in the context of moral experience.

Thus, in section 3 of that same introduction, Foucault makes clear that it will not suffice to offer a chronicled history of moral codes, for such a history cannot tell us how these codes were lived and, more specifically, what forms of subject-formation such codes required and facilitated. Here he begins to sound like a phenomenologist. But there is, in addition to the recourse to the experiential means by which moral categories are grasped, a critical move as well, for the subjective relation to those norms will be neither predictable nor mechanical. The relation will be "critical" in the sense that it will not comply with a given category, but rather constitute an interrogatory relation to the field of categorization itself, referring at least implicitly to the limits of the epistemo-logical horizon within which practices are formed. The point will not be to refer practice to a pregiven epistemological context, but to establish critique as the very practice that exposes the limits of that epistemological horizon itself, making the contours of the horizon appear, as it were, for the first time, we might say, in relation to its own limit. Moreover, the critical practice in question turns out to entail self-transformation in relation to a rule of conduct. How, then, does self-transformation lead to the exposure of this limit? How is self-transformation understood as a "practice of liberty," and how is this practice understood as part of Foucault's lexicon of virtue?

Let us begin first by understanding the notion of self-transformation at stake here, and then consider how it is related to the problem called "critique" which forms the focus of our deliberations here. It is, of course, one thing to conduct oneself in relation to a code of conduct, and it is another thing to form oneself as an ethical subject in relation to a code of conduct (and it will be yet another thing to form oneself as that which risks the orderliness of the code itself). The rules of chastity provide an important example for Foucault. There is a difference, for instance, in not acting on desires that would violate a precept to which one is morally bound and developing a practice of desire, so to speak, which is informed by a certain ethical project or task. The model according to which submitting to a rule of law is required would involve one in not acting in certain ways, installing an effective prohibition against the acting out of certain desires. But the model which Foucault seeks to understand and, indeed, to incorporate and exemplify, takes moral prescription to participate in the forming of a kind of action. Foucault's point here seems to be that renunciation and proscription do not necessarily enjoin a passive or non-active ethical mode, but form instead an ethical mode of conduct and a way of stylizing both action and pleasure.

I believe this contrast that Foucault lays out between a command-based ethics and the ethical practice which centrally engages the formation of the self sheds important light on the distinction between obedience and virtue that he offers in his essay, "What is Critique?" Foucault contrasts this yet to be defined understanding of "virtue" with obedience, showing how the possibility of this form of virtue is established through its difference from an uncritical obedience to authority.

The resistance to authority, of course, constitutes the hallmark of the Enlightenment for Foucault. And he offers us a reading of the Enlightenment which not only establishes his own continuity with its aims, but reads his own dilemmas back into the history of the Enlightenment itself. The account he provides is one that no "Enlightenment" thinker would accept, but this resistance would not invalidate the characterization at hand, for what Foucault seeks in the characterization of the Enlightenment is precisely what remains "unthought" within its own terms: hence, his is a critical history. In his view, critique begins with questioning the demand for absolute obedience and subjecting every governmental obligation imposed on subjects to a rational and reflective evaluation. Although Foucault will not follow this turn to reason, he will nevertheless ask what criteria delimits the sorts of reasons that can come to bear on the question of obedience. He will be particularly interested in the problem of how that delimited field forms the subject and how, in turn, a subject comes to form and reform those reasons. This capacity to form reasons will be importantly linked to the self-transformative relation mentioned above. To be critical of an authority that poses as absolute requires a critical practice that has self-transformation at its core.

But how do we move from understanding the reasons we might have for consenting to a demand to forming those reasons for ourselves, to transforming ourselves in the course of producing those reasons (and, finally, putting at risk the field of reason itself)? Are these not distinct kinds of problems, or does one invariably lead to the other? Is the autonomy achieved in forming reasons which serve as the basis for accepting or rejecting a pregiven law the same as the transformation of the self that takes place when a rule becomes incorporated into the very action of the subject? As we shall see, both the transformation of the self in relation to ethical precepts and the practice of critique are considered forms of "art," stylizations and repetitions, suggesting that there is no possibility of accepting or refusing a rule without a self who is stylized in response to the ethical demand upon it.

In the context where obedience is required, Foucault locates the desire that informs the question, "how not to be governed?" This desire, and the wonderment that follows from it, forms the central impetus of critique. It is of course unclear how the desire not to be governed is linked with virtue. He does make clear, however, that he is not posing the possibility of radical anarchy, and that the question is not how to become radically ungovernable. It is a specific question that emerges in relation to a specific form of government: "how not to be governed *like that*, by that, in the name of those principles, with such and such an objective in mind and by means of such procedures, not like that, not for that, not by them."

This becomes the signature mark of "the critical attitude" and its particular virtue. For Foucault, the question itself inaugurates both a moral and political attitude, "the art of not being governed or, better, the art of not being governed like that and at that cost." Whatever virtue Foucault here circumscribes for us will have to do with objecting to that imposition of power, to its costs, to the way in which it is administered, to those who do that administering. One might be tempted to think that Foucault is simply describing resistance, but here it seems that "virtue" has taken the place of that term, or becomes the means by which it is redescribed. We will have to ask why. Moreover, this virtue is described as well as an "art," the art of not being governed "quite so much," so what is the relation between aesthetics and ethics at work here?

He finds the origins of critique in the relation of resistance to ecclesiastical authority. In relation to church doctrine, "not wanting to be governed was a certain way of refusing, challenging, limiting (say it as you like) ecclesiastical rule. It meant returning to the Scriptures . . . it meant questioning what kind of truth the Scriptures told." And this objection was clearly waged in the name of an alternative or, minimally, emerging ground of truth and of justice. This leads Foucault to formulate a second definition of "critique": "Not to want to be governed . . . not wanting to accept these laws because they are unjust because . . . they hide a fundamental illegitimacy."

Critique is that which exposes this illegitimacy, but it is not because critique has recourse to a more fundamental political or moral order. Foucault writes that the critical project is "confronted with government and the obedience it stipulates" and that what "critique means" in this context is "putting forth universal and indefeasible rights to which every government, whatever it may be, whether a monarch, a magistrate, an educator or a pater familias, will have to submit." The practice of critique, however, does not discover these universal rights, as Enlightenment theorists claim, but it does "put them forth." However, it does not put them forth as positive rights. The "putting forth" is an act which limits the power of the law, an act which counters and rivals the workings of power, power at the moment of its renewal. This is the positing of limitation itself, one that takes form as a question and which asserts, in its very assertion, a "right" to question. From the sixteenth century on, the question "how not to be governed" becomes specified as "What are the limits of the right to govern?" " 'To not want to be governed' is of course not accepting as true . . . what an authority tells you is true, or at least not accepting it because an authority tells you that it is true, but rather accepting it only if one considers valid the reasons for doing so." There is of course a fair amount of ambiguity in this situation, for what will constitute a ground of validity for accepting authority? Does the validity derive from the consent to accept authority? If so, does consent validate the reasons offered, whatever they are? Or is it rather the case that it is only on the basis of a prior and discoverable validity that one offers one's consent? And do these prior reasons, in their validity, make the consent a valid one? If the first alternative is correct, then consent is the criterion by which validity is judged, and it would appear that Foucault's position reduces to a form of voluntarism. But perhaps what he is offering us by way of "critique" is an act, even a practice of freedom, which cannot reduce to voluntarism in any easy way. For the practice by which the limits to absolute authority are set is one that is fundamentally dependent on the horizon of knowledge effects within which it operates. The critical practice does not well up from the innate freedom of the soul, but is formed instead in the crucible of a particular exchange between a set of rules or precepts (which are already there) and a stylization of acts (which extends and reformulates that prior set of rules and precepts). This styliza-tion of the self in relation to the rules comes to count as a "practice."

In Foucault's view, following Kant in an attenuated sense, the act of consent is a reflexive movement by which validity is attributed to or withdrawn from authority. But this reflexivity does not take place internal to a subject. For Foucault, this is an act which poses some risk, for the point will not only be to object to this or that governmental demand, but to ask about the order in which such a demand becomes legible and possible. And if what one objects to are the epistemological orderings that have estab-lished the rules of governmental validity, then saying "no" to the demand will require departing from the established grounds of its validity, marking the limit of the validity, which is something different and far more risky than finding a given demand invalid. In this difference, we might say, one begins to enter a critical relation to such orderings and the ethical precepts to which they give rise. The problem with those grounds that Foucault calls "illegitimate" is not that they are partial or self-contradictory or that they lead to hypocritical moral stands. The problem is precisely that they seek to foreclose the critical relation, that is, to extend their own power to order the entire field of moral and political judgment. They orchestrate and exhaust the field of certainty itself. How does one call into question the exhaustive hold that such rules of ordering have upon certainty without risking uncertainty, without inhabiting that place of wavering which exposes one to the charge of immorality, evil, aestheticism? The critical attitude is not moral according to the rules whose limits that very critical relation seeks to interrogate. But how else can critique do its job without risking the denunciations of those who naturalize and render hegemonic the very moral terms put into question by critique itself?

Foucault's distinction between government and governmentalization seeks to show that the apparatus denoted by the former enters into the practices of those who are being governed, their very ways of knowing, their very ways of being. To be governed is not only to have a form imposed upon one's existence, but to be given the terms within which existence will and will not be possible. A subject will emerge in relation to an established order of truth, but it can also take a point of view on that established order that retrospectively suspends its own ontological ground.

> If governmentalization is . . . this movement through which individuals are subjugated in the reality of a social practice through mechanisms of power that adhere to a truth, well, then! I will say that *critique is the movement by which the subject gives himself the right* [*le sujet se donne le droit*] *to question truth on its effects of power and question power on its discourses of truth.* (my emphasis)

Note here that the subject is said to "give himself that right," a mode of self-allocation and self-authorization that seems to foreground the reflexivity of the claim. Is this, then, a self-generated movement, one which shores up the subject over and against a countervailing authority? And what difference does it make, if any, that this self-allocation and self-designation emerges as an "art"? "Critique," he writes, "will be the art of voluntary insubordination, that of reflected intractability [*l'indocilité réfléchie*]." If it is an "art" in his sense, then critique will not be a single act, nor will it belong exclusively to a subjective domain, for it will be the stylized relation to the demand upon it. And the style will be critical to the extent that, as style, it is not fully determined in advance, it incorporates a contingency over time that marks the limits to the ordering capacity of the field in question. So the stylization of this "will" will produce a subject who is not readily knowable under the established rubric of truth. More radically, Foucault pronounces: "Critique would essentially insure the desubjugation [*désassujetiisement*] of the subject in the context [*le jeu*] of what we could call, in a word, the politics of truth."

The politics of truth pertains to those relations of power that circumscribe in advance what will and will not count as truth, which order the world in certain regular and regulatable ways, and which we come to accept as the given field of knowledge. We can understand the salience of this point when we begin to ask: What counts as a person? What counts as a coherent gender? What qualifies as a citizen? Whose world is legitimated as real? Subjectively, we ask: Who can I become in such a world where the meanings and limits of the subject are set out in advance for me? By what norms am I constrained as I begin to ask what I may become? And what happens when I begin to become that for which there is no place within the given regime of truth? Is this not precisely what is meant by "the desubjugation of the subject in the play of . . . the politics of truth" (my translation)?

At stake here is the relation between the limits of ontology and epistemology, the link between the limits of what I might become and the limits of what I might risk knowing. Deriving a sense of critique from Kant, Foucault poses the question that is the question of critique itself: "Do you know up to what point you can know?" "Our liberty is at stake." Thus, liberty emerges at the limits of what one can know, at the very moment in which the desubjugation of the subject within the politics of truth takes place, the moment where a certain questioning practice begins that takes the following form: "'What, therefore, am I', I who belong to this humanity, perhaps to this piece of it, at this point in time, at this instant of humanity which is subjected to the power of truth in general and truths in particular?" Another way of putting this is the following: "What, given the contemporary order of being, can I be?" If, in posing this question, liberty is at stake, it may be that staking liberty has something to do with what Foucault calls virtue, with a certain risk that is put into play through thought and, indeed, through language where the contemporary ordering of being is brought to its limit.

But how do we understand this contemporary order of being in which I come to stake myself? Foucault chooses here to characterize this historically conditioned order of being in a way that links him with the critical theory of the Frankfurt School, identifying "rationalization" as the governmentalizing effect on ontology. Allying himself with a Left critical tradition post-Kant, Foucault writes,

> From the Hegelian Left to the Frankfurt School, there has been a complete critique of positivism, rationalization, of techne and technicalization, a whole critique of the rela-tionships between the fundamental project of science and techniques whose objective was to show the connections between science's naive presumptions, on one hand, and the forms of domination characteristic of contemporary society, on the other.

In his view, rationalization takes a new form when it comes into the service of bio-power. And what continues to be difficult for most social actors and critics within this situation is to discern the relationship between "rationalization and power." What appears to be a merely epistemic order, a way of ordering the world, does not readily admit of the constraints by which that ordering takes place. Nor does it eagerly show the way in which the intensification and totalization of rationalizing effects leads to an intensification of power. Foucault asks, "How is it that rationalization leads to the furor of power?" Clearly, the capacity for rationalization to reach into the tributaries of life not only characterizes modes of scientific practice, "but also social relationships, state organizations, economic practices and perhaps even individual behaviors?" It reaches its "furor" and its limits as it seizes and pervades the subject it subjectivates. Power sets the limits to what a subject can "be," beyond which it no longer "is," or it dwells in a domain of suspended ontology. But power seeks to constrain the subject through the force of coercion, and the resistance to coercion consists in the stylization of the self at the limits of established being.

One of the first tasks of critique is to discern the relation "between mechanisms of coercion and elements of knowledge?" Here again we seem confronted with the limits of what is knowable, limits which exercise a certain force without being grounded in any necessity, limits which can only be tread or interrogated by risking a certain security within an available ontology:

> Nothing can exist as an element of knowledge if, on the one hand, it . . . does not conform to a set of rules and constraints characteristic, for example, of a given type of scientific discourse in a given period, and if, on the other hand, it does not possess the effects of coercion or simply the incentives peculiar to what is scientifically validated or simply rational or simply generally accepted, etc.

He then continues to show that knowledge and power are not finally separable, but work together to establish a set of subtle and explicit criteria for thinking the world: "It is therefore not a matter of describing what knowledge is and what power is and how one would repress the other or how the other would abuse the one, but rather, a nexus of knowledge-power has to be described so that we can grasp what constitutes the acceptability of a system."

The critic thus has a double task, to show how knowledge and power work to constitute a more or less systematic way of ordering the world with its own "conditions of acceptability of a system," but also "to follow the breaking points which indicate its emergence." So not only is it necessary to isolate and identify the peculiar nexus of power and knowledge that gives rise to the field of intelligible things, but also to track the way in which that field meets its breaking point, the moments of its discontinuities, the sites where it fails to constitute the intelligibility for which it stands. What this means is that one looks both for the conditions by which the object field is constituted, but also for the limits of those conditions, the moments where they point up their contingency and their transformability. In Foucault's terms, "schematically speaking, we have perpetual mobility, essential fragility or rather the complex interplay between what replicates the same process and what transforms it."

Indeed, another way to talk about this dynamic within critique is to say that rationalization meets its limits in desubjugation. If the desubjugation of the subject emerges at the moment in which the episteme constituted through rationalization exposes its limit, then desubjugation marks precisely the fragility and transformability of the epistemics of power.

Critique begins with the presumption of governmentalization and then with its failure to totalize the subject it seeks to know and to subjugate. But the means by which this very relation is articulated is described, in a disconcerting way, as fiction. Why would it be fiction? And in what sense is it fiction? Foucault refers to "an historical–philosophical practice [in which] one had to make one's own history, fabricate history, as if through fiction [de faire comme par fiction], in terms of how it would be traversed by the question of the relationships between structures of rationality which articulate true discourse and the mechanisms of subjugation which are linked to it." There is thus a dimension of the methodology itself which partakes of fiction, which draws fictional lines between rationalization and desubjugation, between the knowledge–power nexus and its fragility and limit. We are not told what sort of fiction this will be, but it seems clear that Foucault is drawing on Nietzsche and, in particular, the kind of fiction that genealogy is said to be.

You may remember that although it seems that for Nietzsche the genealogy of morals is the attempt to locate the origins of values, he is actually seeking to find out how the very notion of the origin became instituted. And the means by which he seeks to explain the origin is fictional. He tells a fable of the nobles, another about a social contract, another about a slave revolt in morality, and yet another about creditor and debtor relations. None of these fables can be located in space or time, and any effort to try to find the historical complement to Nietzsche's genealogies will necessarily fail. Indeed, in the place of an account that finds the origin of values or, indeed, the origin of the origin, we read fictional stories about the way that values are originated. A noble says something is the case and it becomes the case: the speech act inaugurates the value, and becomes something like an atopical and atemporal occasion for the origination of values. Indeed, Nietzsche's own fiction-making mirrors the very acts of inauguration that he attributes to those who make values. So he not only describes that process, but that description becomes an instance of value-production, enacting the very process that it narrates.

How would this particular use of fiction relate to Foucault's notion of critique? Consider that Foucault is trying to understand the possibility of desubjugation within rationalization without assuming that there is a source for resistance that is housed in the subject or maintained in some foundational mode. Where does resistance come from? Can it be said to be the upsurge of some human freedom shackled by the powers of rationalization? If he speaks, as he does, of a will *not* to be governed, how are we to understand the status of that will?

In response to a query along these lines, he remarks,

> I do not think that the will not to be governed at all is something that one could consider an originary aspiration [*je ne pense pas en effet que la volonté de n'etre pas gouverné du tout soit quelque chose que l'on puisse considérer comme une aspiration originaire*]. I think that, in fact, the will not to be governed is always the will not to be governed thusly, like that, by these people, at this price.

He goes on to warn against the absolutizing of this will that philosophy is always tempted to perform. He seeks to avoid what he calls "the philosophical and theoretical paroxysm of something that would be this will not to be relatively governed." He makes clear that accounting for this will involves him in a problem of the origin, and he comes quite close to ceding the terrain, but a certain Nietzschean reluctance prevails. He writes,

> I was not referring to something that would be a fundamental anarchism, that would be like an originary freedom [*qui serait comme la liberté originaire*], absolutely and wholeheart-edly [*absolument et en son fond*] resistant to any governmentalization. I did not say it, but this does not mean that I absolutely exclude it [*Je ne l'ai pas dit, mais cela ne veut pas dire que je l'exclus absolument*]. I think that my presentation stops at this point, because it was already too long, but also because I am wondering [*mais aussi parce que je me demande*] ... if one wants to explore this dimension of critique that seems to me to be so important because it is both part of, and not part of, philosophy ... it is supported by something akin [*qui serait*

ou] to the historical practice of revolt, the non-acceptance of a real government, on one hand, or, on the other, the individual refusal of governmentality.

Whatever this is that one draws upon as one resists governmentalization will be "*like an originary freedom*" and "something *akin to* the historical practice of revolt" (my emphasis). Like them, indeed, but apparently not quite the same. As for Foucault's mention of "originary freedom," he offers and withdraws it at once. "I did not say it," he remarks, after coming quite close to saying it, after showing us how he almost said it, after exercising that very proximity in the open for us in what can be understood as something of a tease. What discourse nearly seduces him here, subjugating him to its terms? And how does he draw from the very terms that he refuses? What artform is this in which a nearly collapsible critical distance is performed for us? And is this the same distance that informs the practice of wondering, of questioning? What limits of knowing does he dare to broach as he wonders out loud for us? The inaugural scene of critique involves "*the art* of voluntary insubordination," and the voluntary or, indeed, "originary freedom" is given here, but in the form of a conjecture, in a form of art that suspends ontology and brings us into the suspension of disbelief.

Foucault finds a way to say "originary freedom," and I suppose that it gives him great pleasure to utter these words, pleasure and fear. He speaks them, but only through staging the words, relieving himself of an ontological commitment, but releasing the words themselves for a certain use. Does he refer to originary freedom here? Does he seek recourse to it? Has he found the well of originary freedom and drunk from it? Or does he, significantly, post it, mention it, say it without quite saying it? Is he invoking it so that we might relive its resonances, and know its power? The staging of the term is not its assertion, but we might say that the assertion is staged, rendered artfully, subjected to an ontological suspension, precisely so it might be spoken. And that it is this speech act, the one which for a time relieves the phrase "originary freedom" from the epistemic politics within which it lives which also performs a certain desubjugation of the subject within the politics of truth. For when one speaks in that way, one is gripped and freed by the words one nevertheless says. Of course, politics is not simply a matter of speaking, and I do not mean to rehabilitate Aristotle in the form of Foucault (although, I confess, that such a move intrigues me, and I mention it here to offer it as a possibility without committing myself to it at once). In this verbal gesture toward the end of his lecture, a certain freedom is exemplified, not by the reference to the term without any foundational anchor, but by the artful performance of its release from its usual discursive constraints, from the conceit that one might only utter it knowing in advance what its anchor must be.

Foucault's gesture is oddly brave, I would suggest, for it knows that it cannot ground the claim of original freedom. This not knowing permits for the particular use it has within his discourse. He braves it anyway, and so his mention, his insistence, becomes an allegory for a certain risk-taking that happens at the limit of the epistemological field. And this becomes a practice of virtue, perhaps, and not, as his critics profess, a sign of moral despair, precisely to the extent that the practice of this kind of speaking posits a value which it does not know how to ground or to secure for itself, posits it anyway, and thereby shows that a certain intelligibility exceeds the limits on intelligibility that power–knowledge has already set. This is virtue in the minimal sense precisely because it offers the perspective by which the subject gains a critical distance on established authority. But it is also an act of courage, acting without guarantees, risking the subject at the limits of its ordering. Who would Foucault be if he were to utter such words? What desubjugation does he perform for us with this utterance?

To gain a critical distance from established authority means for Foucault not only to recognize the ways in which the coercive effects of knowledge are at work in subject-formation itself, but to risk one's very formation as a subject. Thus, in "The Subject and Power,"[7] Foucault will claim "this form of power [that] applies itself to immediate, everyday life which categorizes the individual, marks him by his own individuality, attaches him to his own identity, imposes a law of truth on him which he must recognize and which others have to recognize in him." And when that law falters or is broken, the very possibility of recognition is imperiled. So when we ask how we might say "originary freedom," and say it in the wondering, we also put into question the subject who is said to be rooted in that term, releasing it, paradoxically, for a venture which might actually give the term new substance and possibility.

In concluding, I would simply return to the introduction to *The Use of Pleasure* where Foucault defines the practices that concern him, the "arts of existence," as having to do with a cultivated relation of the self to itself. This kind of formulation brings us closer to the strange sort of virtue that Foucault's anti-foundationalism comes to represent. Indeed, as I wrote earlier, when he introduces the notion of "arts of existence" Foucault also refers to such arts of existence as producing subjects who "seek to transform themselves in their singular being, and to make their life into an oeuvre." We might think that this gives support to the charge that Foucault has fully aestheticized existence at the expense of ethics, but I would suggest only that he has shown us that there can be no ethics, and no politics, without recourse to this singular sense of poeisis. The subject who is formed by the principles furnished by the discourse of truth is not yet the subject who endeavors to form itself. Engaged in "arts of existence," this subject is both crafted and crafting, and the line between how it is formed, and how it becomes a kind of forming, is not easily, if ever drawn. For it is not the case that a subject is formed and then turns around and begins suddenly to form itself. On the contrary, the formation of the subject is the institution of the very reflexivity that indistinguishably assumes the burden of formation. The "indistinguishability" of this line is precisely the juncture where social norms intersect with ethical demands, and where both are produced in the context of a self-making which is never fully self-inaugurated.

Although Foucault refers quite straightforwardly to intention and deliberation in this text, he also lets us know how difficult it will be to understand this self-stylization in terms of any received understanding of intention and deliberation. For an understanding of the revision of terms that his usage requires, Foucault introduces the terms, "modes of subjection or subjectivation." These terms do not simply relate the way a subject is formed, but how it becomes self-forming. This becoming of an ethical subject is not a simple matter of self-knowledge or self-awareness; it denotes a "process in which the individual delimits that part of himself that will form the object of his moral practice." The self delimits itself and decides on the material for its self-making, but the delimi-tation that the self performs takes place through norms which are, indisputably, already in place. Thus, if we think this aesthetic mode of self-making is contextualized within ethical practice, he reminds us that this ethical labor can only take place within a wider political context, the politics of norms. He makes clear that there is no self-forming outside of a mode of subjectivation, which is to say, there is no self-forming outside of the norms that orchestrate the possible formation of the subject.

We have moved quietly from the discursive notion of the subject to a more psychologically resonant notion of "self," and it may be that for Foucault the later term carries more agency than the former. The self forms itself, but it forms itself within a set of formative practices that are characterized as modes of subjectivations. That the range of its possible forms is delimited in advance by such modes of subjectivation does not mean that the self fails to form itself, that the self is fully formed. On the contrary, it is compelled to form itself, but to form itself within forms that are already more or less in operation and underway. Or, one might say, it is compelled to form itself within practices that are more or less in place. But if that self-forming is done in disobedience to the principles by which one is formed, then virtue becomes the practice by which the self forms itself in desubjugation, which is to say that it risks its deformation as a subject, occupying that ontologically insecure position which poses the question anew: who will be a subject here, and what will count as a life, a moment of ethical questioning which requires that we break the habits of judgment in favor of a riskier practice that seeks to yield artistry from constraint.

Notes

This essay was originally delivered, in shorter form, as the Raymond Williams Lecture at Cambridge University in May of 2000. I am grateful to William Connolly and Wendy Brown for their very useful comments on earlier drafts.

1 Raymond Williams, *Keywords* (New York: Oxford University Press, 1976), 75–6.
2 Theodor W. Adorno, "Cultural Criticism and Society," in *Prisms* (Cambridge, MA: MIT Press, 1984), 30.
3 Michel Foucault, "What is Critique?" in *The Politics of Truth*, ed. Sylvère Lotringer and Lysa Hochroth (New York: Semiotext(e), 1997), transcript by Monique Emery, revised by Suzanne Delorme, et al., translated into English by Lysa Hochroth. This essay was originally a lecture given at the French Society of Philosophy on 27 May 1978, subsequently published in *Bulletin de la Société française de la philosophie* 84: 2 (1990), 35–63. See chapter 7, this volume.
4 For an interesting account of this transition from critical theory to a theory of communicative action, see Seyla Benhabib, *Critique, Norm, and Utopia: A Study of the Foundations of Critical Theory* (New York: Columbia University Press, 1986), 1–13.
5 Michel Foucault, *The Use of Pleasure: The History of Sexuality, Volume Two* (New York: Pantheon Press, 1985).
6 Michel Foucault, *The History of Sexuality, Volume One* (New York: Random House, 1978).
7 Michel Foucault, "The Subject and Power," in Hubert L. Dreyfus and Paul Rabinow, eds., *Michel Foucault: Beyond Structuralism and Hermeneutics* (Chicago: University of Chicago Press, 1982), 208–28.

PART V

POSTMODERNISM

TOTALITARIANISM AND THE DIALECTIC OF IDENTITY AND DIFFERENCE

9

MEMORANDUM ON LEGITIMATION

Jean-François Lyotard

I would like to approach the question of totalitarianism from the apparently narrow perspective of the language of legitimation. I believe this is a more radical approach than any other (politicological, sociological, or historical) in that it does not appeal to received, often unquestioned, entities like power, society, the people, or tradition. Furthermore, it seems to me that such an approach can help us to distinguish between different states of totalitarianism, while the term, itself somewhat totalizing, tends to conceal or confuse them.

I will begin by reminding you of a distinction made by Kant (who thus attaches himself to the political philosophy of the critical Enlightenment) without explaining my decision to resort to it here. In *Perpetual Peace* (second section, first article), Kant distinguishes between the *forma imperii*, the form according to which supreme authority is exercised, and the form of government (*forma regiminis*), the principle according to which the state makes use of its power. The first of these, the form of sovereignty (*Beherrschung*), consists in the delegation of supreme power: either to a single person (autocracy) or to several people (aristocracy) or to everybody (democracy). The second, the form of government (*Regierung*), is either despotic or republican, depending on whether or not executive and legislative powers are combined. Kant is quick to add that the democratic form, that is, the mode of sovereignty that directly confers the exercise of public power upon all citizens without the mediation of representative instances, calls for a form of government that is necessarily despotic. This is because the people as sovereign is at the same time both legislator and executor of its own decisions. Conversely, according to Kant, an autocrat like Frederick II of Prussia can exercise his authority in a manner that is analogous to republicanism (in terms of government).

The question of legitimacy is not, as you know, treated directly in this passage from *Perpetual Peace*. I would like, however, to graft it onto the distinction between despotic and republican governments in the following way.

We could call the subject of the normative phrase its legitimating instance. A phrase is termed normative when it gives the force of law to its object, a prescriptive phrase. For the prescription *it is obligatory for x to perform action* a, the normative phrase would be *it is a norm decreed by* y *that it is obligatory for* x *to perform action* a. In this formulation the normative phrase designates, here in the name of *y*, the instance that legitimates the prescription addressed to *x*. The legislative power is held by *y*. The despotism and republicanism described by Kant can easily be located within this little complex of phrases.

If we now ask who *y* could be to command such legislative authority, we soon find ourselves slipping into the usual aporias. We encounter the vicious circle: *y* has authority over *x* because *x* authorizes *y* to have it; the *petitio principii*: the authorization authorizes the authority (i.e., it is the normative phrase that authorizes *y* to set the norm); the infinite regress: *x* is authorized by *y*, who is authorized by *z*, and so on; the paradox of the idiolect (in Wittgenstein's sense): God, Life, or any big A designates *y* to exercise authority, but *y* is the only witness to this revelation.

I would argue that, at least in the framework of a reflection on totalitarianism, there are two primary procedures of language that come to mask the logical aporia of authorization (or fill the ontological gap) that such a reflection would disclose. Both of these procedures make recourse to narration; that is, on the surface at least, they both disperse this absence, spreading the theoretical problem along the diachronic axis. But that is the only thing they have in common. For while one procedure directs this dispersion upstream, toward an origin, the other directs it downstream, toward an end. In very simple terms (which you will have to excuse), one of these narrations shapes those mythic narratives that are essential to traditional communities, while the other shapes the narratives of emancipation (which I called metanarratives in *The Postmodern Condition*).

At this point I would like to clarify their respective functions – without losing sight of the question of totalitarianism.

To be completely clear, I should really begin by setting out the questions of language that form the basis for my argument in this memorandum. I cannot do that here, so I will make do with a quick summary. Language is the object of an Idea. It is not like a box of tools that "speakers" (human, in general) dip into when they want to communicate or express themselves. If we free ourselves of this functionalist approach, we will notice that the only *givens* are phrases, in their hundreds and thousands. We see that these phrases do not simply convey meanings: however unassuming and ephemeral (or silent) they may be, they situate, within the universe they present, an addressor, an addressee, and a referent. We see that we can distinguish different families or regimes of phrases from one another, since it is impossible to convert one phrase into another without modifying what I will simply call the pragmatic situation of the instances I have just mentioned (referent, addressee, addressor). *The door is closed* is a descriptive phrase. In the universe it presents, the question is whether or not the door is closed: it is therefore governed by the criterion of truth or falsity. *Close the door* is a prescriptive phrase, and the question it raises hinges on the justice of the order given to the addressee and on the execution of the act it prescribes. As we can see, the regime governing a normative phrase is completely different from the regime governing a prescriptive phrase. The same is true of interrogative, performative (in the strict sense), and exclamatory phrases.

The other point underlying my argument, and one that I think is essential for an understanding of totalitarianism, is that each phrase, no matter how ordinary, arrives as an event. I am not saying that each phrase is exceptional, sensational, or unprecedented, but that what it contains is never necessary. It is necessary *that* something happens (the event), but *what* happens (the phrase, its meaning, object, interlocutors) is never necessary – the necessity of contingency or, if you like, the being of nonbeing. The linkage between phrase and phrase is not, as a rule, predetermined. *Genres of discourse clearly exist*: exposition (like the present one), the genre of dialectics (which we call discussion), the genre of comedy, the genre of tragedy, satire (the genre of genres), the essay, the diary, and so forth. These genres of discourse set rules for the linking of phrases to ensure that the discourse proceeds toward its generically assigned end: to convince, to persuade, to inspire laughter or tears, and so forth. Respecting these rules thus allows the linking of phrases toward a generic end. But, as you would know, these rules of linking are seldom (if ever) respected outside of classical poetics and rhetoric. Modern writers and artists continually break these rules, precisely because they set a greater value on questioning the event than on worrying about imitation or conformity. Like Auerbach, I would put Augustine among modern writers, next to Rabelais, Montaigne, Shakespeare, Sterne, Joyce, and Stein. What is interesting about these modern infractions is not that they are transgressive, as Bataille thought, but that they constantly open the question of nothingness, the question of the event. This is demonstrated by Benjamin with regard to Baudelaire, and by Barthes with his theory of the text and writing.

Let us now return to our reflection on the narrative of legitimation and totalitarianism. First, mythic narration.

The old question – is myth originary or origin mythic? – goes back to Schelling. Freud struggled with the same question. (Your mother has written an impressive study on this subject.) The corpus of narratives of a traditional ethnic group – the Cashinahua as studied by André Marcel d'Ans – together with its ritual of transmission, is composed of narratives of origin, myths in the strict sense, and also little stories, tales, and legends. The important thing for our question seems to me to be the pragmatics of narration itself rather than the analysis of narrative contents. To *hear* a Cashinahua narrative, one has to be an adult male or a girl prior to puberty, and one must have a Cashinahua name (as does the anthropologist). To *recount* a narrative, one has to be a man and have a Cashinahua name. Finally, every Cashinahua without exception can *form the object* of one of these narratives. In this sense, the transmission of narratives is subject to constraints. These constraints are used to effect the separation of the community into kinship groups governing exogamous unions: among the Cashinahua there are two masculine and two feminine "moieties," with two age groups in each moiety – eight kinship groups in all. And, as the ethnologist notes, "exogamous unions have the explicit function of transmitting *names*." The constraints acting on the pragmatics of narration should be understood as rules for the authentication and conservation of narratives, and therefore of the community itself, through the repetition of names.

The ethnologist confirms this, noting that every narration opens with a set formula: "Here is the story of... as I've always heard it. I am, in turn, going to tell it to you. Listen!" He adds that the recitation invariably closes with another formula: "Here ends the story of... He who told it to you is... (Cashinahua name), known to the whites as... (Spanish or Portuguese name)." Each time the story is told, this narrative ritual fastens it to the names of the three instances (the narrator, his listener, and the hero) and thus legitimates the story by inscribing it in the world of Cashinahua names.

The effect of this is a process characteristic of historical time. Each narrator declares that he is telling the story as he has "always heard" it. He was a listener to this story and the narrator he heard it from was, in his turn, also once a listener. It is the same all the way along the chain of transmission. It follows that the heroes themselves must have been the first narrators. The time of the diegesis, when the action described takes place, and the time of the actual narration that describes this action, communicate without interruption. Two operations ensure such a panchrony: the permanence of names (which are finite in number and bestowed on individuals by a system independent of time) and the permutability of named individuals across the three narrative instances (narrator, listener, hero), which is governed by ritual on each occasion.

I believe this apparatus of language exemplifies our first *forma regiminis*, the form of government, or regime, that Kant called despotism, and the legitimation of the normative instance corresponding to that form. Names, or what Kripke calls "rigid designators," define a world, a world of names – the cultural world. This world is finite because in it the number of available names is finite. This world has forever been the same. Each human comes into this world with a place, that is, with a name that will determine his or her relationship to other names. This place in effect controls the sexual, economic, social, and linguistic exchanges that one has the right or the duty to have (or not to have) with others who bear names. An event (there we are) can only be introduced into the tradition when it is framed within a story – a story subject to the rules of naming as much in what it tells (its referents: heroes, places, times) as in the manner of its telling (its narrator, its audience). So the void that in principle separates two phrases, and makes the phrase into an event, is filled by narrative, itself subordinate to the repetition of the world of names and to the permutation of names across the instances. In this way the Cashinahua identity, the *we* that draws together the three narrative instances, escapes the vertigo of contingency and nothingness. And as narrative has an intrinsic capacity to collect, arrange, and transmit descriptions, as well as prescriptions, evaluations, and feelings (exclamatory and interrogative phrases, for example), this tradition transmits obligations attached to names, along with prescriptions for particular situations, and legitimates them simply by placing them under the authority of the Cashinahua name.

The Cashinahua call themselves "the true men." Whatever stands outside this tradition – any event, natural or human, for which there is no name – is *not*, for it is not authorized (not "true"). Authority is not *represented* in the modern sense of the term: the Cashinahua people legislate through the transmission of their narratives and, in performing them (since names create all sorts of obligations), exercise executive power. So there is certainly a kind of politics at play in this narrative practice, but it is immersed in the totality of life instituted by the narratives and could, in this sense, be said to be "totalitarian."

I am conscious that my description is somewhat simplistic. An ethnologist would have little trouble refuting my conclusions – by showing how my analysis flows from the ancient desire of the West to discover in the exotic the figure of what it has lost, as Plato did long ago in Egypt and Atlantis. I completely agree with this criticism. Our vision of myth is itself probably mythic; what we do with Cashinahua stories is evidently far less amusing than what the Cashinahua do themselves. Yet for the problematic that concerns us here, modern totalitarianism, this tendency to exaggerate the value of narrative as archaic legitimation is interesting in itself. It is even essential.

This overvaluation, still prevalent in attitudes and still potentially active, may explain why Nazism could be successful in resorting to myth when it pitted its own despotic authority against the republican authority that defined modern political life in the West, initially against the Weimar. Nazism put the Aryan name in the place occupied by the Idea of the citizen. Abandoning the modern horizon of cosmopolitanism, it grounded its legitimacy in the saga of the Nordic peoples. The reason it could succeed was that it released in the sovereign people, "democratically" in Kant's sense, a desire to "return to the source," a desire only mythology could satisfy. Nazism provided the people with names and narratives that permitted them to identify exclusively with Germanic heroes and heal the wounds inflicted by the event of defeat and crisis. Xenophobia and chronophobia are necessarily implicated in this use of language as an apparatus of legitimation. I will come back to this.

Republicanism is more than the separation of powers: it demands the fission, even the disintegration, of popular identity. It is not just about representation: from the perspective of language, it is an organization of regimes of phrases and genres of discourse that relies on their dissociation, thus allowing a "play" between them or, if you prefer, preserving the possibility of accounting for the event in its contingency. This organization I will call *deliberative*.

As we have seen, in traditional narration the combination of multiple stakes – converting, informing, convincing, persuading, and so on – is concealed by the homogeneity of the story's unfolding. The organic and (I would say) totalizing character of narrative does not lend itself to analysis. On the other hand, it is easy to dismantle the arrangement of genres of discourse and regimes of phrases in deliberative politics. A simple, even naive description of the moments of the deliberative process will make this easy to understand:

1   The highest end is formulated in a canonical phrase (let's call it the stake) that is an interrogative prescriptive: *What ought we to be?* The phrase is full of possible meanings: *happy, wise, free, equal, rich, powerful, artistic, American?* The answers are examined in the philosophies of history; in the political arena they are scarcely discussed, though they are present in the phrase "kindred spirits."

2   To the *What ought we to be?* is linked a *What ought we to do in order to be that?* In this way, one moves from a pure, almost ethical prescription to a hypothetical imperative, such as: If you want to be this, then do that.

3   The previous question calls for an inventory of the means to attain this end: an analysis of the situation, a description of the resources available to both allies and adversaries, and a definition of their respective interests. This is a completely different genre of discourse in that it is properly cognitive – it is the discourse of specialists, experts, advisers, and consultants, put to use in inquiries, reports, polls, indexes, statistics, and the like.

4   Once this information has been collected – as comprehensively as the nature of the enterprise will permit – a new genre of discourse is needed, where the stake is *What might we do?* Here Kant would see an idea of the imagination (intuition without

concept), and Freud would see free association; we call it simulation, or montage of scenarios. Narrations of the unreal.

5 Deliberation in the strict sense of the term is concerned with these scenarios. It is subject to the regime of argumentation. Each party to the deliberation sets out to prove the other wrong, and show why. This is the genre Aristotle calls dialectics. Rhetoric is also involved. *Logoi*, or arguments, combine with *topoi*, or the classical steps of persuasion. The aim is not only to refute the other but to persuade a third party (a judge, president, or electoral body in a democracy).

6 Then comes the moment of decision, that is, the moment of judgment: the most enigmatic of phrases, as Kant thought, the phrasing of the event *par excellence*. It can take the form of resolutions, programs, ballots, or arbitrations.

7 The judgment must be legitimated. This is the role of normative discourse (does one have the right to decide in this way?). Then it must be rendered executory (decrees, orders, laws, notices), and infractions must be punished.

This arrangement, despite appearances, is paradoxical in its linkages because of the heterogeneity of its components: how can a prescriptive phrase (*We ought to do this*) be deduced from a descriptive phrase (*This is what we can do*)? How can one link onto the prescription a normative phrase that will legitimate it? So, in this sense, there is a kind of fragility in the deliberative apparatus. The important role played by knowledge in this apparatus (technoscience at the service of politics) – when knowledge is itself subject to the continual deliberation of scientists – makes it still more fragile. But above all, the unity of the heterogeneous genres at play in this organization lies solely in the answer given to the first question: *What ought we to be?* This organization of the deliberative process is able to resist the separation of its elements only because it is a flow chart of the free will, of pure practical reason.

In the republic there is, by definition, a prevailing uncertainty about ends – an uncertainty about the identity of the *we*. As we have seen, the question of a final identity does not arise in the narrative tradition: the Cashinahua narrative always says that we ought to be what we are – Cashinahua. (And the Aryan narrative says the same thing.) In the republic, there are many narratives because many final identities are possible; in despotism, there is only one because there is only one origin. The republic inspires not belief but reflection and judgment. It wills itself.

The grand narratives it needs are narratives of emancipation – they are not myths. Like myths, they fulfill a legitimating function: they legitimate social and political institutions and practices, forms of legislation, ethics, modes of thought, and symbolics. Yet unlike myths, they ground this legitimacy not in an original "founding" act, but in a future to be brought about, that is, in an Idea to realize. This Idea (of freedom, "enlightenment," socialism, general prosperity) has legitimating value because it is universal. It gives modernity its characteristic mode: the *project*, that is, the will directed toward a goal.

To elaborate this question, we would need to go back to Kant's historicopolitical opuscules; not just *An Answer to the Question: What Is Enlightenment?* but *Perpetual Peace, Idea for a Universal History within a Cosmopolitan Plan*, and especially the second *Conflict of the Faculties*, the conflict between philosophy and the faculty of law. I cannot do that here. The general sense we can draw from them is that the narrative of the universal history of humanity cannot be affirmed in mythical form; it must remain suspended from an Ideal of practical reason (freedom, emancipation). It cannot be verified by empirical proofs but only by indirect signs, *analoga*, which signal in experience that this ideal is present in people's minds. So any discussion of this history is "dialectical" in the Kantian sense, which is to say, without conclusion. The ideal is not presentable to the sensibility; the free society is no more demonstrable than the free act. And in the same way, there will always be a profound tension between what one ought to be and what one is.

Only one thing is certain: right cannot be de facto; real society draws legitimacy not from itself but from a community that is not properly nameable, merely required. One cannot deduce what a people ought to be from what it is today, nor can one deduce the concept of the universal citizen from its French or American name – only the reverse is possible. This is why, as I remarked earlier, the ferment and decomposition of the real community are inscribed in the principle of republicanism and in the history it develops. Sovereignty belongs not to the people but to the Idea of the free community. History simply marks the tension of this lack. The republic invokes freedom against security.

These brief reflections should make it possible, I think, to come to a better understanding of what the term totalitarianism implies. Evidently we ought to distinguish between the totalitarianism that turns its back on modern legitimation through the Idea of freedom and the totalitarianism that, on the contrary, issues from that Idea. Power can only draw its authority from a national or ethnic name (inscribed within a more or less fabulous corpus of stories, like the Germanic, Celtic, or Italic sagas) if it has completely broken with the legacy of the Declaration of Rights of 1789. It is not a case of "abandoning" the project of modernity, as Habermas has said with regard to postmodernity, but of the "liquidation" of that project. With this annihilation, an irreparable suspicion is engraved in European, if not Western, consciousness: that universal history does not move inevitably "toward the better," as Kant thought, or rather, that history does not necessarily have a universal finality. The authority of the proper name derives from the pragmatics of narration described above: I, Aryan, tell you Aryans the story of our Aryan ancestors as it was handed down to us. Listen to it, pass it on, execute it. This organization implies what I will call the exception. Aryans are the true men – the only ones. That which is not Aryan lives only because of a failure in the functioning of the vital principle. It is already dead. All that remains is to finish it off. The Nazi wars are sanitary operations, purifications. Nothing could be more foreign to republican legitimacy and the deliberative organization of discourse it demands, or, finally, to the idea of history it develops.

But things are not quite this simple. In the case of republicanism, the question of what the community ought to be and the answer given in the ideal of freedom do not deny that this community is already real. Rather they presuppose that it is, that it can name itself and honor this name in heroism, in "beautiful deaths." If we are to be citizens of the world, it is because we continue to be only French. We will always be French. This imbrication of authority with tradition and authority with the Idea can be clearly seen in an analysis of the Preamble to the Declaration of the Rights of Man of 1789, for example. Who, what y, could have the authority to declare the rights of man?

There is an aporia of authorization. It is nonetheless surprising to find the name of an Assembly that represents a particular people, the French people, in the position of the legitimating instance, even though it places the declaration under the auspices of the Supreme Being. Why would the affirmation of a universal normative instance have universal value if a singular instance makes the declaration? How can one tell, afterward, whether the wars conducted by the singular instance in the name of the universal instance are wars of liberation or wars of conquest?

Equally, in the case of totalitarianism, the opposition to republicanism is not absolutely distinct. Nazism maintains the facade of a deliberative organization – parties, parliament – and it can even employ the republican epic of revolutionary wars to dress up the ethnocentrism of its conquests. (Hitler, with great ceremony, returned the ashes of Napoleon II [*l'Aiglon*] to the Invalides.) These things are parodies, of course. But what is their motive? To mask the reversal of legitimation. Despotism in this way recognizes the audience for republicanism. And indeed it needs that audience. A certain universalism persists in the logic of the exception when this logic is extended to include the whole of humanity.

The heart of this equivocation lies in the idea of the people. We are aware of the great value Nazism attached to it. The name of the people encompasses at once the singularity of a contingent community and the incarnation of a universal sovereignty. When one says *people*, it is impossible to tell exactly which identity one is talking about. When one puts the people, *das Volk*, in the place of the normative instance, it is impossible to tell whether the authority being invoked is despotic – summoning the tradition of an originary narrative – or if it is republican and appeals to the systematic institution of deliberation drawn to an Idea of freedom.

The peculiar importance Nazi politics placed in the mise-en-scène has often been noted. The aesthetics elaborated by postromanticism and Wagner (especially that of the "total work of art"), in which opera and cinema are privileged as "complete" arts, is put to the service of despotism, undermining the whole economy of the Schillerian project. Far from educating humanity and making it more receptive to Ideas, the sensible representation of the people to itself encourages it to identify itself as an exceptional singularity. Whether monumental or familiar in scale, the Nazi "festivals" exalt the Germanic identity by making symbolic figures from Aryan mythology sensible to the ear and eye. What is at work here is an art of persuasion that can only make a place for itself by eliminating the avant-gardist tendencies drawn to reflection.

This attempt at orthopedic figuration, elaborated and deployed by Nazism from the very beginning, only bore fruit because the German community was in the grip of a severe crisis of identity. This crisis, itself the culmination of the defeat of 1918, the settlement at Versailles, and the great socioeconomic depression of the 1930s, is often taken to be the cause of Nazism. But in any event, the idea of a cause is inappropriate in such matters. For our purposes, it is more interesting to remember that the identity crisis Nazism sought to cure – and which it merely succeeded in spreading to the rest of humanity – is potentially contained in the republican principle of legitimacy.

In *The Phenomenology of Spirit*, Hegel described the negativism of the modern ideal of freedom as a power capable of decomposing every concrete, singular objectivity, notably that of traditional institutions, and, I would add, that of every despotic community in Kant's sense – those communities that find the legitimacy of their modes of life in their name and their past. The dialectic of the particular and the universal, which Hegel gives the title of absolute freedom, can, he claims, end only in terror. For the ideal of absolute freedom, which is empty, any given reality must be suspected of being an obstacle to freedom. It has not been willed. Here I would say that the sole normative instance, the sole source of law, the sole y, is pure will – which is never this or that, never determined, but simply the potential to be all things. So it judges any particular act, even when it is prescribed by law and executed according to the rules, as failing to match up to the ideal. Terror acts on the suspicion that nothing is emancipated enough – and makes it into a politics. Every particular reality is a plot against the pure, universal will. Even the individual who occupies the position of the normative instance is contingent in the light of this ideal, and therefore suspect. Robespierre could have no objection to his own execution, unless it was that his judges were no less suspect than he was. " 'In whose name' is the army being called in against the Assembly?" he asks Couthon on the eve of his death. The suppression of reality through the death of suspects satisfies a logic that sees reality as a plot against the Idea. And terror in this way plunges the real community into despair about its identity. The French no longer deserve the name of citizens when they recoil in fear before the enormity of the crime by which they sought to institute republican legitimacy. But in wanting to be only French, the French renounce deliberation and universal history, and renounce the ideal of freedom. The Popular Front spreads fear across the land (and among the Left), and the anti-Dreyfusard and Pétainist state brings shame to the republicans (even the moderates).

As I see it, there should, in principle, be no confusion between a politics of terror and the possible consequences of despotic government, even though most of the time it is not easy to make this distinction in historical reality. But you only have to consider this: the normative instance has to remain empty; any singularity (individual, family, party) intending to occupy this place will be suspected of being merely a usurper or impostor. The y who authorizes the order and makes it law does not have a name – it is pure will, unaffected by any determination and without ties to any singularity. On whatever scale – a small Puritan community like Salem or the French nation – such an arrangement is highly likely to give rise to a politics of terror. And a politics of terror, far from dispensing with deliberation and its institutional organization, in fact demands it. For this organization alone carries to the limit the responsibility each person (as both representative and represented) has regarding each of the genres of discourse necessary for a political decision. What people put on the line in these deliberations is not only, and perhaps not essentially, their lives: it is their judgment, their responsibility in the face of the event. We should remember that, in principle, a complex deliberative organization leaves open the way that one phrase or genre of discourse is linked to another. This is true at every step in the process of the will.

The republic is, in its very constitution, attentive to the event. What we call freedom is this alertness to what can happen, which must be judged outside of any rule. Terror is one way of accounting for the indeterminacy of what is happening. Philosophy is another. The difference between them lies in the time set aside for collecting information and making judgments. Philosophy takes its time, as they say. Urgency hastens republican decision making – and political decision making generally.

Totalitarianism would consist in subjecting institutions legitimated by the Idea of freedom to legitimation by myth. Although clearly despotic in the Kantian sense, it borrows its universalizing power from republicanism. It is not simply *Let us become what we are – Aryans*, but *Let the whole of humanity be Aryan*. Once named, the singular *we* then has the pretension of imparting its name to the end pursued by human history. In this sense totalitarianism is modern. It needs not only the people, but the decomposition of the people into "masses" in search of an identity by means of parties authorized by the republic. If it is to overturn the republic, totalitarianism needs democracy's equivocation.

I would also distinguish Nazi totalitarianism from Stalinist totalitarianism. The Stalinist mode of legitimation is, in principle, still republican. Socialism is one version of the narrative of universal emancipation born of the Declaration of the Rights of Man. The First International takes its authority from a declaration of the rights of the universal worker. Communism is a philosophy of human history. Its internationalism plainly meant that it would never recognize the legitimacy of any local powers, which, being particular, – are necessarily despotic. An enormous effort was made to give the universal proletariat a reality beyond that of working classes still bound to national traditions and differential claims. That this effort failed, that Bolshevism, like Stalinism, was to become the very incarnation of chauvinism, does not mean that the mode of legitimation of Soviet power was ever in principle a slogan like *Let us be Russian* or *Let humanity be Russian*. Again in principle, the idea of the people was itself subject to a radical critique in Marxism, in the concept of class struggle. Marxism thus significantly accelerated the decomposition of the particular nominal community, and did so in the spirit of workers' republicanism.

The question I am asking is whether Stalinism is not a politics of despotism so much as a politics of terror. The analyses sketched out here lead me to just this conclusion. The very decomposition of Russian civil society by the Stalinist and post-Stalinist apparatus supports this hypothesis. It has no equivalent in Nazism. Nazism, on the contrary, provided a solid and durable structure to accommodate the modes of life and socioeconomic reality of Germany, in conformity with the despotic principle – and this is what has in Germany engendered a feeling of guilt unknown in communist nations. The Stalinist terror was able to decieve people as long as it did because it seemed to be working toward the realization of the socialist republic. Its authority came from Bolshevism, the Marxist cousin of Enlightenment Jacobinism. It has taken almost half a century for this imposture to be exposed. In those nations that have, as a result of imperialism, suffered an identity crisis analogous to Germany's in the 1930s, it has still not exhausted its powers of deception. And it is still the case that in every so-called communist country the normative instance authorizes the law only by setting it against those to whom it applies. The normative instance cannot invoke the life of the people or the conservation of people's origins and identity. It cannot rule by true despotism, the despotism of singularity. But conversely, it can no longer claim to take its authority from an infinite process of emancipation without provoking the laughter or tears of those it oppresses – it has been a long time since its terror was republican. People in these countries know what bureaucratic power is – the delegitimation of the legislator.

I have said nothing about capitalism. There is just one thing I would like to suggest to you. The principle that *any* object and *any* action are acceptable (permitted) so long as they can enter into economic exchange is not totalitarian in a political sense. But in terms of language it is, since it calls for the complete hegemony of the economic genre of discourse. The simple canonical formula of this genre is: *I will let you have this, if you in return can let me have that.* Among its other attributes, this genre always calls for new *thises* to enter into exchange (today, for example, technoscientific knowledge) and uses payment as a means of neutralizing their power as events. Evidently market expansion has nothing to do with the universality of republicanism. Capital does not need deliberation either politically or economically. But socially it does, because it needs civil society in order to repeat its cycle. Society is for capital the indispensable moment of the destruction (consumption) of singular *thises* or *thats.*

An examination of the present status of capitalism from the point of view of totalitarianism would be extremely useful. Capitalism accommodates the republican institution, but cannot cope with terror (which destroys the market). It gets along well with despotism (as we saw with Nazism). It is hardly bothered by the decline of the grand narratives of universality (including the liberal narrative of humanity's increasing prosperity). Capital, it could be said, does not need legitimation: it prescribes nothing, in the strict sense of obligation, and consequently has no need to cite an instance to make a prescription normative. Capital is present everywhere, but as necessity rather than finality. We can, I think, understand why it seems like necessity if we analyze the canonical formula of the genre of discourse peculiar to it. We would see that behind this appearance there is still a hidden finality: gaining time. Is this a universally valid end?

10

DEMOCRACY IN THE ERA OF IDENTITY POLITICS: LYOTARD ON POSTMODERN LEGITIMATION

David Ingram

How does one begin to assess the political implications of a philosopher whose theory – if one can call it that – is firmly cemented in the present while forever remaining *au courant* – fashionable but elusive? Clearly, Lyotard's is a philosophy so obsessed with its own modernity as to defy summary description; for what is modernity but the ceaseless questioning of all fixed dogmas and determinations, this self-surpassing we call the *post-modern*?

The Dilemma of Modern Democracy

Rereading Lyotard's essay "Memorandum on Legitimation" after a twelve-year hiatus has again reminded me how frightfully relevant and disturbing his diagnosis of modern political rationality is for contemporary theorists of democratic inclusion.[1] Since its first publication in 1986, esteemed thinkers from Rawls to Habermas have weighed in on its central dilemma: the modern fragmentation of political community into opposed religious, ethnic, racial, and ideological groups – a "postmodern" condition (as Lyotard puts it) more familiarly referred to in academic circles as "identity politics." What makes this fragmentation a dilemma for theorists of democracy is its threat to the rational consensus supporting universal respect for basic rights and impartial procedures. If nations (groups, persons, etc.) disagree about these fundamentals, how can they be expected to live together in peace, let alone cooperate in solving common problems?

A sampling of cases involving group rights suffices to illustrate this dilemma. The first concerns international disputes over human rights, the other three, domestic disagreements about democratic power-sharing.

Example 1: In an era noted for its rapacious capitalism, those who urge global democracy in resolving the world's most pressing economic and environmental problems can only be disheartened by continuing disagreements over what constitutes basic rights. While the US State Department continues to insist that civil, property, and political rights have priority over economic, social, and cultural rights, signatories to the Bangkok Declaration and many other developing countries disagree. And, while the State Department proudly trumpets the superiority of American-styled democracy, with its multiparty, money-driven competition for power (the essence of "free speech," so we are told), the leadership of single-party socialist regimes extols the virtues of democratic centrism with a nod toward worker-and community-managed cooperatives.

Example 2: In what has since become a textbook case regarding the limits of federalism, French Canadian Nationalists insisted that Francophone Québécois were at a cultural, economic, and political disadvantage with respect to English-speaking Canadians. Hence the federal government was persuaded to allow Quebec to require French in business and educational settings. Their critics pointed out that this requirement violates the universal right, guaranteed by the Canadian Charter, that business owners and parents have over their businesses and children's education.

Example 3: In other cases involving federal power-sharing, indigenous people living on tribal reservations in the US and Canada demand as a matter of treaty right special exemptions – from civil suits, gambling prohibitions, environmental regulations, common law strictures regulating property, liberal notions of democratic governance, and even drug laws. Their critics charge that such exemptions clash with the idea of universal citizenship, which implies an equal sharing of legal burdens regardless of differences. As for tribal sovereignty, reservation counsels (many dominated exclusively by men) have come under increasing attack for discriminating against women and dissenters.

Example 4: In a controversial attempt to urge the US Department of Justice to embark on a policy of proportional group representation, African Americans, Latinos, and other ethnic minorities sought the creation of legislative districts wherein they would be empowered as majorities. This policy, which enabled minorities to elect substantial numbers of representatives of their choice for the first time since Reconstruction, was curtailed by the conservative majority on the Supreme Court beginning in 1993 on the grounds that it mirrors a similar policy, adopted by Southern whites during the 1960s, that empowered *them* as majorities. In both instances, the Court argued, race-conscious redrawing of legislative districts has had the effect of *disempowering* racial minorities within the districts in question (in the former case whites; in the latter case blacks).[2]

Outline of the Argument

"Memorandum" tells us that no resolution of these dilemmas will ever be forthcoming. If its argument is correct, both sides in these disputes appeal to conflicting interpretations of democratic fairness that are equally implausible. For one side, rational impartiality bestows the blessings of liberty on all equally and on no one in particular. It is impartial with respect to group differences. Yet (queries the other side) who commands these blessings of liberty if not particular persons representing distinct groups? If *non*-group-specific rights apply to individuals as instantiations of universal personhood – in virtue, one supposes, of impartial reason itself – then group-specific rights apply to particular peoples who enact these rights, differentially, for themselves.

Affirming the indeterminacy of the democratic ideal in this manner – as at once universally and particularly specified – amounts to denying what we take to be central to the democratic rule of law: consensus on the rules of fair play. The rule of law assumes that law, which defines the duties and rights that constitute our collective identity as citizens, treats everyone impartially, without regard to differences in gender, race, ethnicity, nationality, religion, and class. Furthermore, it assumes that citizens believe this to be so. They freely obey the law because it affirms their values, their interests, in short, their universal identity as "reasonable and rational persons" (as John Rawls puts it). Accordingly, they trust that others do likewise for the same reasons.

That the legitimacy of law (its moral authority to command voluntary obedience) resides in its expressing a universal identity or will is the hallmark of modern theories of democracy from Rousseau to Rawls and Habermas. Yet, as "Memorandum" incisively notes, this "will" is dangerously ambiguous. On one hand it refers to a transcendent norm of reason. To the extent that different groups of persons reason the same way, they do so as citizens of the world, without regard to particular legal jurisdictions and identities. Suppose that all reasonable and rational citizens agree in the abstract that each must be respected and tolerated. Agreeing on this vague generality won't go very far in resolving disputes over who should be tolerated how much and when. So the "will" that underwrites "our" consensus on basic rights and procedures will remain indeterminate and open to contestation.

On the other hand, because this "will" is indeterminate, its concrete exercise in any given instance will necessarily take the form of a particular command. Different nations – and different subgoups within nations – will reason differently about such "rational" ideas as "equal respect and liberty for all," in a manner that reflects their particular economic and sociocultural circumstances. The legitimating basis for law in universal consensus will be lacking, with the meaning of law itself becoming a site of ceaseless political contestation among different nations. And, within any given nation, some persons will insist that rights must apply to each citizen in exactly the same way (in accordance with their uniform rational agency), while others will insist otherwise, in deference to the particular circumstances in which each group or person finds itself.

Where does this leave the postmodern theorist? In his "Memorandum" Lyotard dismisses democratic theorists' appeal to reason in legitimating law. Indeed, he finds this appeal dangerously "totalitarian" in its practical implications, which can lead all too easily to the suppression of foreign states and domestic groups that dissent from the dominant order. But just as appeal to "universal human rights" can lead to the suppression of groups whose identities are perceived to be unreasonable and irrational by the powers that be, so appeal to group identities can lead to the suppression of dissident individuals whose identities are perceived to be deviant *vis-à-vis* the group.

As we shall see, the dangers posed by identity politics in all its varieties present Lyotard with unhappy choices. On one hand, the threat of majoritarian tyranny inherent in the modern notion of universal citizenship leads him to advocate on behalf of developing nations, domestic minorities, and other marginalized groups. Group-specific rights that strengthen the bargaining position of weaker parties are just, he believes, because they aim to reduce existing harms to those parties. This conception of identity politics accords with recent arguments on behalf of rights – ranging from multicultural respect for traditional and communitarian societies at the global level to schemes allowing proportional group representation for minorities and women at the domestic level – that guarantee a more just basis for democratic cooperation. On the other hand, because this conception of identity politics presumes that all individuals within a subgroup share the same political identity, the earlier concern about totalitarianism resurfaces. In advocating on behalf of "double minorities" (or members of a minority group that dissent from the dominant identity of the group), Lyotard attacks any conception of identity as potentially repressive.

"Memorandum" drives home the attack on identity politics with singular tenacity. However, its postmodern critique of democracy is of a piece with modern political rationality. Modern political rationality presumes that persons who have reflected on who they are will have critically detached themselves from any parochial, fixed and predetermined, group-based identity simply as a condition for voluntarily *reattaching* themselves to a universal citizen-based identity. This is because legitimate legal authority under conditions of modern pluralism depends upon the *shared* voluntary consent of reasonable and rational citizens. But now that all political identities have been theorized as universal citizen-based identities, what remains to be represented by democratic politics? Whose "will," "identity," or "interest" is to be legislated once citizenship has been reduced to a vapid abstraction? Universal sameness is not a recipe for democratic legislation, but totalitarian administration. Democratic legislation, however, involves a collective determination of the indeterminate; it requires that citizens interpret the meaning of their citizenship in conformity with their ever-changing, ever diversifying beliefs and circumstances. But then how does one link the particular will embodied in a determinate law or command and executed by a particular person, group, or people to this universal but inherently indeterminate locus of rational normativity? How does one legitimate *inclusive* forms of democratic law that allow all persons, groups, and peoples fair representation and participation once it is conceded that procedural norms underwriting fair competition are unavoidably biased by dint of being legislated?

As we shall see, Habermas and other stalwart defenders of democratic legitimation have a partial response to these questions. More often than not, they prefer to take the easier path of reversing the charges, criticizing in turn what they regard as the conservative implications of Lyotard's own deconstruction of democratic legitimation.[3] Isn't the rejection of rational consensus (citizenship identity) as a basis for legitimation an endorsement of unrestrained power politics in which the most numerous or wealthy group prevails? If all we are left with after the dissolution of universal citizenship is just an assortment of groups – or worse, a mass of mutually repelling atoms – then why worry about the under-representation of oppressed women, nations, and domestic minorities? But then why assume that persons grouped together share anything in common meriting representation?

I'm not sure that anyone, let alone Lyotard, has an adequate response to all these questions. However, I do think that Lyotard's theory can be useful for thinking about the advantages and disadvantages of different conceptions of democracy. Rational impartiality means more than simply treating individuals the same way. It means including individuals and groups within a process of equitable power-sharing. Tolerance and inclusion can assume the form of multicultural cooperation based on what Rawls calls "overlapping consensus," or what Lyotard dubs "an agreement to disagree."[4] This form is especially compatible with group identities and group rights, because it acknowledges that membership in particular cultural groups is essential for cultivating and exercising rational subjective choice. Such choice can lead to switching or modifying our group-based identities; we can learn new languages, discard old gender roles, and rethink what it means to be racially identified. But we cannot by choice transcend our identification with and involvement in particular languages, cultural practices, and solidaristic groups.

Inclusion can also assume the contrary form of transformative dialogue based on what Habermas calls a "communicative consensus." This form is somewhat less compatible with group identities and group rights, because it holds that we do transcend our particular identifications and involvements as we learn to expand our horizons to encompass universal humanity. Such horizon expanding is less a matter of subjective choice than it is of open and undistorted communication with others. But once it is achieved, we are in a position to exercise our subjective discretion in choosing who and how we want to be. Rather than being predefined by a group, we become just ourselves, open to the entreaties of others and willing to change (endlessly, if need be) for the sake of reaching mutual understanding and agreement with them – all free from the rigid routines of traditional prejudice and habit.

At this point the dialectic of reason and democracy comes back to haunt us. Who and what determines democratic legislation, once our emancipated identities as cosmopolitan citizens have burst free from any and all parochial constraint? If this freedom is at best relative and willing the particular is in some sense rational and necessary, does there still remain a logical chain of command linking what universal reason counsels, on one side, and what founders of states constitute, what "the people" want, what legislators prescribe, and what judges and officers decide, on the other? If not, does this impugn the prospect for legitimation or just Lyotard's peculiar diagnosis of it? Finally, do our answers to these questions ultimately hinge on whether we accept a transformative conception of democratic deliberation?

Despotism versus Democracy

"Memorandum" begins, curiously enough, with a theme that, at first glance, seems far removed from any discussion of democracy: totalitarianism. This theme is less arbitrary than one might imagine, however, since on Lyotard's reading, totalitarianism is not the antithesis of democracy, but one of its extreme possibilities. More precisely, it is what democracy degenerates into when it fails to resolve its legitimation crisis. At the far end of democracy's inability to manage ethnic and racial diversity or class conflict stands the zero-point of utter homogeneity. Totalitarianism replaces both identity politics and universal citizenship with something that is neither and both: a rapacious nationalism whose limits are as universal as they are indeterminate.

Drawing on Kant's distinction between "despotism" and "republicanism," Lyotard argues that totalitarianism is distinguished by its total identification of political functions and powers that, in any modern "republican" government, are rightfully thought to be conceptually distinct.[5] For Kant, despotism collapses law and politics by reducing law – whose impartiality ought to be grounded solely in universal reason – to the partial, arbitrary decisions of particular persons. On this reading, democracy can become despotic if it permits the majority to legislate according to its own particular advantage.

Conversely, autocracy can be legitimate and lawful if the ruler commands only what pure reason legislates.

Lyotard finds Kant's distinction between despotism and republicanism useful because it underscores a basic difference in the way in which totalitarian and so-called liberal-democratic regimes legitimate their legal authority. Totalitarian regimes – specifically fascist ones – legitimate their authority by returning to a premodern, mythic narrative that identifies the identity of each individual citizen with the specific identity of a primordial group, or people. This group understands itself to be naturally sovereign and self-determining (recall the Nazis' exaltation of the primordial destiny of the Aryan people). Its legitimating narrative accordingly identifies the unitary will of the people with the unitary will of the fascist leader. The entire chain of identifications and determinations is thus so total that it escapes even Kant's anachronistic definition of despotism; for what we have here is no politicization of law, but the annihilation of politics and law.

Liberal-democratic regimes, by contrast, legitimate their authority by appeal to a distinctly modern "metanarrative" of universal political emancipation. Unlike its totalitarian counterpart, this modern narrative claims to be rationally enlightened. However, it is so in name only. For, as we shall see, in order for it to do its legitimating work, it would have to smooth over the logical breaks in its complex web of argumentation in a manner similar to premodern mythic discourse. This recourse is denied it.

Lyotard does not hesitate to draw what he takes to be the anarchic implications of this crisis. Being logically underdetermined by any prior legitimating ground (origin or foundation), the "rule of law" cannot but descend into the partial but ever open-ended play of political forces. Contrary to Kant, this is not despotism, but something closer to the anarchic "terror" of a permanent, revolutionary turn-over (overthrow) of all settled law, all settled political identity. In the words of Lyotard, it is *freedom* to contest any *particular* (determinate) procedure or law as contrary to what *universal* (indeterminate) reason demands. Unfortunately, such freedom as this cannot be tolerated long by those who depend upon the regularity of law, which includes most of us but especially members of the business class. Hence the pathos of Lyotard's conclusion: those who seek order will turn to totalitarianism.

Languages of Legitimation

I hinted above that the emancipatory metanarratives of the Enlightenment contain logical gaps in their legitimating arguments. Indeed, it is reason itself, or logic, that compels us to recognize them as gaps rather than enthymemes. Now, Lyotard proceeds to illustrate these gaps by turning to the founding documents of liberal democracy (the French and American *Declarations*), as well as to constitutionally established processes of democratic deliberation. However, instead of appealing to formal logic to make his case, he appeals to the pragmatic logic of everyday language use.

According to Lyotard, spoken utterances (*phrases*) not only convey meanings, but they specify an addressee, an addressor, and a referent. We have already noted the importance of addressee, addressor, and referent in discussing the logic of identification in mythic narrative. In myth, the narrator (addressor) purports to be telling a story that was first recounted by the hero (referent) of his story and that will be repeated endlessly in the same way by each person (addressee) who hears it. Citing Andre Marcel d'Ans' studies of the myths of one traditional ethnic group, the Cashinahua, Lyotard adds that these narratives simultaneously perform both legislative and executive functions, thereby effecting a kind of totalitarian (or in Kant's terms, despotic) regimentation of social roles and privileges with respect to age, gender, and kinship. Because each person's name is identical to the name of some mythic hero, his or her specific power to execute commands is directly transmitted from the primordial normative source to which it is nominally identified.[6] Nazi myths effect the same kind of circular (cyclical) repetition and closure of authorization by collapsing the descent of each authentic German (established by surname) into the great saga of the Nordic peoples, whose sovereign destiny is then linked to the particular will of a single leader.

The seamless, circular identification of addressor, addressee, and referent characteristic of mythic narrative finds no logical equivalent in modern legitimating metanarratives. That proves to be their downfall. A quick glance at the American *Declaration of Independence* (1776) and the French *Declaration of the Rights of Man* (1789) confirms that these documents are deeply question-begging. Both attempt to bridge over the logical gap separating the divine legislation of inalienable rights and the political legislation of contingent rights.

For example, Article 16 of the French *Declaration* asserts that "The representatives of the French People, organized in National Assembly . . . have resolved to set forth in solemn declaration the natural, inalienable rights of man." This assertion, Lyotard maintains, is patently question-begging because it conflates a finite group of individuals ("representatives of the French People, organized in National Assembly") with the Divine power that legislates for all of humanity. Its tacit conflation of addressor (delegates to the National Assembly), addressee (the French People), and referent (God, Nature, Reason, or Humanity) suggests a logic of identification similar to that found in myth, but one that is expressly forbidden by its own rational disjunction between universal normative foundation and particular political act. From within the logic of rational metanarrative, the determinate, historically specific prescriptions of right and wrong conduct legislated by the politician (addressor) do not necessarily follow from the indeterminate, universal norm of freedom.

The danger of equating a particular nation's determinate institutionalization of freedom with what is universally right for all of humanity is obvious: the nation in question – be it the United States in the year 2000 or France in 1789 – will be strongly tempted to impose its will and identity on the rest of the world.

> The splitting of the addressee of the Declaration into two entities, French nation and human being, corresponds to the *equivocation* of the declarative phrase: it presents a philosophical universe and copresents a historical–political universe. The revolution in politics that is the French Revolution comes from this *impossible* passage from one universe to another. Thereafter it will no longer be known whether the law thereby declared is French or human, whether the violence exerted under the title of freedom is repressive or pedagogical (progressive), whether those nations which are not French ought to be French or become human by endowing themselves with Constitutions that conform to the Declaration, be they anti-French. (my italics)[7]

Thanks to its equivocation, the Declaration of Rights set in motion a world revolution whose effects are still being felt two hundred years later. But were the revolutionary wars that continued through the Napoleonic era wars of liberation (attempts to extend the blessings of divinely sanctioned freedom to all of humanity) or were they wars of imperial expansion (attempts to extend the dominion of the French government over its neighbors)? The same question applies to the colonization of Asia and Africa by Europe, the domination of Latin America by the United States, the hegemony of NATO in Europe, and the current influence of the World Trade Organization and the World Bank on the economies and polities of countless developing countries. Do we not have, as Enrique Dussel has argued, a form of cultural imperialism that masks itself under the guise of human progress and freedom?[8]

To be sure, the founding documents mentioned above do not appeal exclusively to transcendent (divine or rational) authority in legitimating their historical enactments. Seemingly less hegemonic and imperialistic legitimating strategies were available to their authors. The signers of the American *Declaration*, for instance, state that they are "acting in the name and by the authority of the good people of these colonies" in declaring that "these united colonies... ought to be free."

Leaving aside the exclusion of slaves, Native Americans, and Loyalists in its conception of "the good people of these colonies," this narrative, like its rationalist counterpart, also effects a quasi-mythic identification of addressor and addressee: the signers declare and thereby constitute the free, independent normative authority ("these united colonies") that supposedly authorizes their own declaration. In Lyotard's opinion, this attempt to link an arbitrary political declaration to a preexisting source of normative legitimacy is viciously circular. The one who authorizes (addressor) and the one who is authorized (addressee) cannot be identical, otherwise the constraints imposed by the former on the latter would no longer be constraints. Self-authorizing power is unlimited despotic power, not limited legitimate power.[9] That explains why so many slaves, Native Americans, and Loyalists regarded the revolutionaries as usurpers and (to use Kant's phrase) despots, whose brand of democracy portended more, not less, oppression for them.

Lyotard's linguistic analysis of legitimating narratives extends well beyond his discussion of the founding documents of democracy. His analysis of democratic deliberation takes up yet another dimension of his speech act theory. For our purposes what is most important is his theory of phrasal *regimes*. According to this theory, utterances can be classified into different sorts of language games (*regimes*) that are governed by different rules. For example, "The door is closed" is a descriptive phrase whose meaning and pragmatic acceptability are largely governed by the criterion of truth or falsity. By contrast, "Close the door!" is a prescription, or command, whose meaning and pragmatic acceptability is governed by the criterion of normative rightness, or justice.

The important thing to note is that utterances belonging to different regimes occur together in more complex language games, such as storytelling, debating, and legitimating. These *genres* of discourse "set rules for the linking of phrases to ensure that the discourse proceeds towards its generically assigned end: to convince, to persuade, to inspire laughter or tears, and so forth."

As we have seen, legitimating discourses fall into two main genres: myth and metanarrative. In myth, something's being assigned a name automatically bestows upon it descriptive truth (reality), normative legitimacy, and prescriptive (executive) power *simultaneously*. Hence, descriptions, normative injunctions, and prescriptive commands follow one another seamlessly. The same, however, does not hold true for modern metanarratives. Their Enlightenment pedigrees tacitly commit them to rational distinctions between types of phrases that resist logical connection. Thus, normative injunctions asserting that something general *ought* to be done (like respecting each individual's inalienable freedom) do not necessarily follow from descriptions asserting that something *is* true. Likewise, *particular* executive commands and prescriptions that a *specific* person, or people, are permitted or forbidden a certain behavior do not necessarily follow from *universal* normative injunctions addressed to what humanity at large ought to aspire to.

Notwithstanding logical prohibitions against inferences of this sort, modern metanarratives succeed in convincing their addressees only by fallaciously implying that a particular legal prescription (declaration) follows from a general principle of right which in turn follows from a metaphysical description about what is rational, natural, and necessary. That the American and French Declarations commit such fallacies stands to reason.[10] But Lyotard has in mind a target that is more central to our concerns: democratic deliberation.

I will not bother with the details of Lyotard's analysis of democratic deliberation except to note that the complex chains of reasoning involving different regimes and genres of discourse, on one side, and different agents who are authorized to speak and listen, on the other, present multiple possibilities for injustices. These injustices (or *differends*, to use Lyotard's word) typically involve linkages between phrases that are both necessary and impossible. This dilemma encourages the suppression of one type of discourse in favor of another.

For instance, the normative questions guiding democratic deliberation ("What ought we to be?") cannot be answered without reference to descriptive assertions about what we can in fact be. Suppose we answer that we ought to be reasonably and rationally tolerant of others. The norm of reasonable and rational tolerance cannot be left undefined and unlimited in scope, otherwise we end up tolerating criminals, bigots, and fascists. So we turn to descriptions about what we can and do tolerate. While we might all agree that reasonable and rational people do not and cannot tolerate criminals, we will not agree that they do not and cannot tolerate bigots and fascists. So, taken alone, these facts do not themselves imply anything about what we ought to do.

Because of the wide variation in our descriptions about what we do and can do with regard to toleration, the question about who to tolerate, how much, and when, remains underdetermined. Since our deliberation must be conclusive (if even only temporarily), we allow a particular group of persons (legislators, judges, administrators, etc.) to decide the matter for us. In deciding the question in a particular way, they invariably favor one group's description of the facts over another's. But they also thereby reduce (in a manner that can only be described as fallacious) the normative question about what universal reason demands in the way of ideal justice to the factual question about what the existing system, as viewed by one group, demands for its efficient management. We let, for example, the Chairman of the Federal Reserve Board set interest rates that are most conducive to maintaining stable, non-inflationary growth as a way of deciding who should get laid off and who should profit.

We can effect the reduction in reverse order as well; instead of suppressing the normative question behind the factual (or functional) one, we can suppress the factual question behind the normative one. For instance, we can describe the system as one in which each individual is absolutely and equally free to act on what is in his or her best interest (conservative ideologues tell us that we are individually responsible for choosing our own destiny). We can then infer (again fallaciously) that what reason demands in the way of justice is a *laissez-faire* market economy that tolerates extreme inequalities.

Although Lyotard has devoted much attention to discussing how both technocracy and ideology (not to mention the peculiar totalitarianism of techno-capitalism) threaten democracy,[11] in "Memorandum" he is mostly concerned with the dangers of political ideology. For Lyotard, the problem of ideology is implicit in the conflation of universal normativity (Reason, Humanity, or God) and a particular power of command (party, people, nation) that claims to issue orders on its behalf. The temptation to commit this fallacy is inherent in all modern legitimating narratives, although doing so entails prematurely closing off political debate in a manner that can only be described as totalitarian.

Strictly speaking, modern narratives enjoin the radical self-determination of agents who, identifying with the indeterminate universality of moral reason, critically free themselves from the fixed identities (or dogmatic authorities) transmitted to them by particular groups. Accordingly, Lyotard shares Hegel's assessment of the *terroristic* "negativism of the modern ideal of freedom as a power capable of decomposing every concrete, singular objectivity, notably that of traditional institutions, and...that of every despotic community in Kant's sense."

The permanent incapacity to resolutely decide who "we" are generates a permanent identity crisis in democratic deliberation that in turn calls forth a permanent revolution in "our" thinking about democratic procedure and law. I say "we" and "our," but for Lyotard the rational responsibility to continually rethink one's identity is destructive of all factual community, all political consensus:

> Only one thing is certain: right cannot be de facto; real society draws legitimacy not from itself but from a community that is not properly nameable, merely required.... That is why... the ferment and decomposition of the real community are inscribed in the principle of republicanism and in the history it develops. Sovereignty belongs not to the people but to the Idea of the free community. History simply marks the tension of this lack. The republic invokes freedom against security.

Republicanism can be dangerously revolutionary, as the example of Stalinist terror well illustrates. Eliminating class-based inequalities for the sake of extending freedom to all requires concerted government intervention in the marketplace. Controlling or eliminating markets, in turn, requires a partisan politicization of legal institutions that can lead to a total undermining of legal predictability and certainty. At the point of extreme anarchy, the rule of law ceases to exist and only the terror imposed by a succession of leaders – or single-party revolutionary movements masquerading as democratic centrist regimes – remains to maintain order. Here, at the zero point of radical democratic populism, not much remains to distinguish democracy from totalitarianism, except perhaps the former's invocation of reason.

Political Implications of Postmodern Democratic Theory

Postmodern political theory holds that any attempt to legitimate democracy by appeal to moral reason or any other consensual basis is futile. Given the fragmentation of the political landscape, legitimation by way of democratic consensus is also not to be expected. Attempts to impose consensus – or even to encourage it – are therefore totalitarian. As Lyotard puts it, "majority does not mean large number, but great fear."[12] But simply letting things be is no more an option for Lyotard than it is for Habermas. For both believe that economic models of democracy which reduce politics to interest-group bargaining (threats), market mechanisms for distributing government largesse based on effective demand (political bribes), or procedures for aggregating utilities (top-down administrative choices based on vote tabulations), are morally repugnant if not totalitarian.

Unfortunately, these economic models all too closely approximate the way things are in Western-style democracies. However, far from rejoicing in this Hobbesian night-mare, Lyotard steadfastly criticized it, insisting on justice as a condition for legitimation.

Now, anyone knowledgeable in the ways of Lyotard will doubtless smile with irony upon reading this. For it is well known that Lyotard seldom wavered from defending postmodern casuistry, shifting his sense of justice from context to context. Let us begin with one notorious – albeit negative – formulation. *Injustice*, he tells us in one passage from *The Differend* (1983), occurs "whenever a plaintiff is deprived of the means of arguing and by this fact becomes a victim." This happens, for instance, where the settling of a conflict between two parties "is made in the idiom of one of them in which the wrong suffered by the other signifies nothing."[13] Lyotard illustrates this injustice (or *differend*) with the example of workers who are forced to define their laboring power in the contractual language of capitalism (as remunerable exchange value) instead of the political language of mutual social contribution. Defining labor as a commodity ex-changeable in a private transaction implies no political right to participate as an equal in the democratic management of the workplace, but defining labor as social contribution (source of value) does.

The examples mentioned at the outset of this essay also illustrate injustices. When developing socialist countries are ostracized and sanctioned for refusing to adopt Western-style economic and political institutions (whose democracy is but a guise for oligarchy), they suffer an injustice. Conversely, when dissidents in these countries are suppressed for lobbying on behalf of more extensive, diverse, and freer forms of democratic participation, they too suffer an injustice. When Québécois are constrained by the English-speaking majority to conduct business transactions in English instead of French, this puts them at a certain economic disadvantage (and they suffer an injustice). When Native Americans are forced to defend their territorial claims in the alien language of property and contract bequeathed to them from English common law, they are prevented from convincing others that their land designates a spiritual locus of communal identity (and they suffer an injustice). And when African Americans are forced to defend redistricting proposals that empower them to elect representatives of their choice in the "color-blind" language of formal voting rights, they are prevented from fully articulating the sense in which democracy depends on empowering disadvantaged groups as much as guaranteeing individuals the right to vote (and they suffer an injustice).

The injustice perpetrated in requiring all rational speakers to speak the same language and mean the same thing by the words they use exposes a serious weakness in the Habermasian model of an ideal speech situation. On this model, it is assumed that speakers will satisfy the formal logical requirement of semantic consistency. But now we see that, in practice, the requirement sometimes works to suppress subaltern minority voices. By academic standards of conversational civility and rationality, noisy street demonstrations, personal narratives, rhetorical bombast, and simple silence do not rate as acceptable "reason-giving." As in the above examples, uses of language that deviate from the dominant norm are suppressed or simply penalized. Superior command of academic English enables the better educated to conduct conversations toward outcomes they desire. This happens regardless of whether each interlocutor has been formally vested with an equal opportunity to speak, because (as Foucault has shown us) power is exercised indirectly and anonymously, through the exclusions, entitlements, and rhetorical strategies made available through the dominant discourse.

In order to mitigate these injustices, courts, Lyotard reasons, would have to intervene on behalf of the weaker party. This "partiality," be it noted, violates the ideal of conversational reciprocity and symmetry implicit in Habermas's ideal speech situation. It also redefines the concept of rights and equal treatment by taking into account the different (unequal) circumstances of particular groups. This apparent qualification of "universal rights" by "group-specific goods" is not an endorsement of any particular, hegemonic good (as communitarians are wont to have it); for Lyotard insists that "politics cannot have for its stake the good, but would have to have the least bad,"[14] where "the least bad" is equivalent to a "justice of multiplicities."[15] On this reading, Lyotard's views about justice and legitimation do not appear to be fundamentally different from similar views espoused by Charles Taylor and Will Kymlicka, who defend the idea of according cultural and racial minorities group-specific rights as a way of treating them with equal respect and concern.[16]

But there is another conception of justice and legitimation that crops up in Lyotard's writings that seems to have radically different implications. "Legitimation by paralogy," as Lyotard puts it, satisfies "both the demand for justice and the desire for the unknown," by encouraging the breakdown of any and all hegemonic identities.[17] What drives this destruction of identity in all its forms is critical self-reflection, reason's indeterminate imperative to free the "self" from all particular, dogmatic limiting conditions. As democracy becomes ever more inclusive, it becomes imperative that each and every citizen be rational and open-minded. Dialogue between persons sharing opposed comprehensive doctrines and group identities requires that they assume an eccentric, critical standpoint with respect to their own doctrines and identities. The certainty and fixed determinacy attached to such doctrines and identities must be surrendered, so that they can be critically evaluated and changed in "transformative dialogue," as Habermas puts it.

In sum, with Lyotard we find two competing postmodern models of broad participatory democracy. The first model, which finds support in liberal doctrines of toleration and multicultural doctrines of group rights, assumes that persons are entitled to their comprehensive doctrines and identities without having to render public account for them, so long as they exercise due tolerance of opposing doctrines and identities. Inclusion here means tolerance, and tolerance means legal protection, which can sometimes involve the use of group-specific rights. For example, guaranteeing freedom of religion for the Amish in Wisconsin may require exempting them from having to send their children to high schools; guaranteeing Native Americans freedom to define their tribal lands collectively and spiritually may require exempting them from civil actions and a host of other regulations; and so on.

What makes this democracy "inclusive," according to Rawls and others, is that each group can support a more general constitutional framework of mutual tolerance and cooperation by appealing to its own particular values, its own particular identity, rather than to some transcendent citizenship identity. Constitutional consensus is "overlapping" rather than dialogical. Consensus-oriented dialogue between groups sharing incommensurable doctrines and identities is still possible, but only so long as each group is willing to exercise "public civility" and "conversational restraint" by refraining from appealing to those aspects of its identity that are peculiar to it.[18] In the field of international law, this will require respecting non-democratic, illiberal "peoples," at least so long as they incorporate what Rawls calls a procedure for "reasonable hierarchical consultation" and exercise toleration with respect to minorities. To demand, as Habermas does, that a socialist state or Islamic theocracy adopt liberal democratic institutions (and perhaps a particular model of liberal democracy) as a condition for participating as an equal member in global democratic governance thus seems undemocratic, according to the model of overlapping consensus.[19]

The second, communicative model of broad participatory democracy, by contrast, appeals to an *ideal* of rational autonomy that refuses to protect the integrity of groups by insulating them from the demands of public accountability. In comparison to the first model, this model seems less tolerant of deviations from liberal democracy and less sympathetic to group-specific rights than the first. Accordingly, we find Habermas differing with Rawls on international law and rejecting Taylor's defense of Quebec's language laws. International law, Habermas believes, should focus on protecting the rights of individuals to immigrate freely and secure themselves against environmental and economic exploitation. This change in priorities – from "peoples" to "individuals" – reflects Habermas's belief that reason itself is exercised principally through open dialogue. While multicultural migration and communication undermine the homogeneous cultural integrity of "peoples," the power and wealth of global financial institutions and multinationals undermine the sovereignty of nation-states.

My purpose in highlighting the difference between Habermas and Rawls with regard to international law is to raise, once again, the question of how our contextual understanding of social realities influences our conception of legal procedure. Both Rawls and Habermas insist that their own respective interpretation of procedural justice (impartiality) constitutes a more realistic reconstruction of what practical reason urges upon us. Without trying to resolve their "differend," it seems plain that the kind of impartiality implicit in practical reason is – as Lyotard would say – indeterminate with respect to their competing reconstructions of it. If so, what determines our preferences for one or the other reconstruction will hinge on personal assessment of social realities. If shared concerns about terrorism and environmental destruction urge peaceful coexistence between peoples who do not all subscribe to liberal-democratic principles, then the procedure of overlapping consensus might seem most compelling. If shared concerns about immigrants and the economic destitution of individuals urge a global redistribution of resources, then the procedure of communicative consensus might be better recommended. Which concerns we prefer to emphasize will determine our choice of procedure.

Global realities pose serious challenges to the implementation of broad participatory democracy, no matter its procedural form. At the very least, they suggest that, at the international level especially, adjudication and legislation will have to confront a growing mass of complications, linguistic and procedural "differends," that will render the meaning of law more indeterminate than ever before. And, this indeterminacy – which is scarcely compassed by even the United Nations or the European Parliament – will continue to affect our differing interpretations of broad partcipatory democracy.

Here again, the problematic impact of cross-cultural communication and economic complexity on determining the proper balance between group rights and individual rights finds parallel expression at the domestic level. The disagreement between Habermas and Taylor over Quebec's language laws (which Taylor supported) illustrates the problem well. Habermas's belief that individuals rather than peoples (or states) ought to be the proper subjects and beneficiaries of international law resonates with his claim that Quebec's language laws inhibit individual freedom of speech.

> Even if such group rights could be granted in a constitutional democracy, they would be not only unnecessary but questionable from a normative point of view. For in the last analysis, the protection of forms of life and traditions in which identities are formed is supposed to foster the recognition of their members; it does not represent a kind of preservation of species by administrative means.... The constitutional state can make this hermeneutical achievement of the cultural reproduction of worlds possible, but it cannot guarantee it. For to *guarantee* survival would necessarily rob the members of the freedom to say yes or no, which nowadays is crucial if they are to remain able to appropriate and preserve their cultural heritage. When a culture has become reflexive, the only traditions and forms of life that can sustain themselves are those that *bind* their members, while at the same time allowing members to subject the traditions to critical examination and leaving later generations the *option* of learning from other traditions or converting and setting for other shores.[20]

According to Habermas, rights that protect groups from cultural contamination by inhibiting freedom of speech also inhibit the free, undistorted formation of identities. Applied to the context of tribal and religious autonomy, it means that traditional ways of life and their corresponding "mythic" legitimations ought not to be shielded from the partially disintegrative effects of rational ideas. Even Kymlicka, who defends group-specific rights for aboriginals, concedes that traditional groups should abandon their ethnocentrism and transform their collectivist identities to accommodate modern ideas of individual freedom and equality. Racial groups, too, would have to cease thinking of themselves as "solidaristic" communities of interest that merit guaranteed "racial" representation. For multicultural and multiracial integration – not to mention the overlapping intersection of many communities of interest – have rendered both group and personal identities highly complex, fluid, and indeterminate. The implications of this postmodern deconstruction of collective identity for the defense of proportional group representation are clearly spelled out by Lani Guinier:

> A racial group identity should be represented to the extent that its members in fact act collectively. Mere assumptions about alleged uniformity should be insufficient to justify measures to ensure group representation. This approach acknowledges that one's racial group is not the only club to which one belongs. Collective group preferences might be measured by using innovative electoral schemes like cumulative voting and proportional representation. In this view, unity is defined as collaboration rather than as sameness.[21]

Like her conservative opponents on the Supreme Court, Guinier objects to racial redistricting schemes that impose a racial group identity on a community of individuals in an illegitimate, top-down fashion. Unlike them, however, she defends the importance of representing interests and perspectives that African Americans as individuals largely share. Current racial redistricting schemes, she believes, frustrate the representation of African American perspectives as well as the satisfaction of African American interests by marginalizing African American representatives who are elected from these districts. In her judgment, a more effective way of increasing the number of African American representatives *and* satisfying African American interests would be to replace small, single-seat districts with larger, more demographically diverse, multi-seat districts. By giving voters in these districts the opportunity to cast multiple ballots for as many candidates as they choose, voters would have a better chance of getting their various interests and perspectives represented in proportion to their groups' numbers. Just as important, it would force candidates and voters to enter into coalitions with different racial groups, thereby encouraging transformative interracial dialogue.[22]

Concluding Remarks: Assessing Postmodern Theory

Both models of postmodern democratic inclusion have strengths and weaknesses. The liberal model, which guarantees toleration and group rights for minorities, is more impartial with respect to traditional groups and more respectful of traditional forms of geographically based conceptions of community. The price it pays for its tolerance is a frank agnosticism with respect to its own deeper and more comprehensive philosophical truth; for political liberalism stands or falls to the extent that it is supported by an overlapping consensus among many competing truths. By contrast, the radical model is possibly more coherent and better suited to grounding principles of justice. For this reason, it will be especially attractive to postmodern theorists of broad participatory democracy who are looking to tame modernity's legitimation crisis.

The liberal model clearly does a better job of acknowledging the right of traditional groups to practice their religious convictions – which by reason's own "burden of proof" (as Rawls puts it) ought to be matters of private conscience – without having to be publicly accountable for them. By contrast, the radical model is hardly impartial; indeed, as Rawls notes, idealistic and perfectionist conceptions of liberalism and democracy of Kantian or Millian provenance represent a kind of religious faith (or existential choice) all their own, on a par with other particular comprehensive doctrines and identities.

Contrary to what Lyotard might have us believe, rational autonomy as he under-stands it – requiring as it does the relentless criticism of all particular, dogmatic beliefs and identities – does indeed designate a *particular* identity, lifestyle, and faith alongside and relative to other "traditional" identities. The fact (however ironic) that it is also critical of particular identities, lifestyles, and faiths yields an additional reason for *not* ascribing it to *universal* reason. At least, this is the conclusion that seems to follow from Lyotard's (and Rawls's) concern about totalitarian (and imperialistic) hegemony. The liberal model, by contrast, advances a much weaker but (arguably) more universally acceptable conception of autonomy in its notion of reasonable uncertainty and toler-ance of particular identities.[23] Given our postmodern condition – that the free exercise of reason generates as much dissensus as consensus – we cannot hope to persuade all reasonable persons in the deeper philosophical truth of liberal tolerance. And so liberals like Rawls can only speculate that underlying our "reasonable pluralism" in philosoph-ical belief is an overlapping consensus that happens to converge on this principle.

The liberal model also harmonizes somewhat better with traditional, geographically based conceptions of democratic sovereignty and representation. Religious, ethnic, and racial groups are often concentrated in relatively segregated enclaves. So long as these conditions obtain, the best way to protect their interests against the tyranny of the majority will be to ensure their right to local self-governance coupled with some kind of guaranteed representation in governing bodies at municipal, state, and federal levels. Opening up the geographical boundaries defining legislative districts in the manner recommended by Guinier would be preferable, of course, if the minorities in question were geographically dispersed or if they possessed sufficient resources for competing with more powerful majorities for political influence. In that case, geographically based mechanisms of representation might be dispensed with, or at least supplemented with non-geographically based systems of proportional representation[24] or even computer-ized participatory democracy (a favorite of Lyotard's).[25]

That said, the radical model does a better job of theoretically mitigating the "incom-mensurabilities" between groups and their interests that generate problems for advocates of broad participatory democracy. In short, it explains how rational indeterminacy can be reduced by explaining how consensus emerges out of dissention. When combined with a non-deductive, dialogical model of democratic deliberation, it even vindicates democratic self-determination as a non-vicious circle of authorizations.

Let me expand upon these points by first addressing the problem of incommensur-ability. Lyotard has frequently been criticized for exaggerating the "incommensurabil-ity" between particular groups and their respective ways of talking. However, if "incommensurability" is taken to mean (as Lyotard apparently intends) that items in one language cannot be translated into another language, then, as Donald Davidson and others have convincingly shown, the thesis of radical incommensurability refutes itself. We could not know that expressions in two different languages were incapable of being translated into each other unless we had succeeded in translating them both into our own language, which in effect would render them commensurable.[26] But if there is no reason to believe that the worldviews and languages of particular groups (e.g., Japanese Buddhists and Anglican Catholics) are incommensurable, there is no reason to believe that rational consensus is impossible (in which case we might end up with more Anglican Catholic Trappist monks, like Thomas Merton). The only way that could be known would be if different groups engaged in consensus-oriented dialogue. Engaging in dialogue would constrain the parties to transform their beliefs so that they might agree. But contrary to Lyotard's fears about totalitarian consensus, the transformative effects of consensus-oriented dialogue could just as likely foster dissensus (on talking with you about something we both agree on, I now discover reasons to change my mind). So transformative dialogue is itself indeterminate with respect to possible outcomes (consensus or dissensus).

This takes us to our second concern. Granting that transformative democracy is indeterminate with respect to outcomes, I submit that it has at least as good a chance of mitigating postmodern indeterminism as liberal democracy. Assumptions about cultural incommensurability and dissensus have long persuaded liberal democrats on the virtues of tolerance and group rights. Given these assumptions, they have sought consensus on the principles governing tolerance and mutual freedom in the nether regions of abstract reason. This appeal seems futile, however, since reason so construed is largely indeterminate, or without prescriptive meaning and force.

Liberals, of course, have struggled mightily with this dilemma. Rawls's notion of an "overlapping consensus" attempts to mitigate this indeterminacy without abandoning the thesis of incommensurability and dissensus. By postulating that each group affirms the principles of tolerance and mutual freedom in its own particular way, it tries to have its cake and eat it too. But this solution only ends up reintroducing indeterminacy at the national level, where each group will fight to have its own interpretation of these principles embedded in law. So, even if Rawls is right that philosophers would be better off abandoning the attempt to ground principles of political liberalism in comprehensive philosophical truths that everyone will find convincing, it would still be irresponsible for us not to at least engage others in conversations about these multiple efforts as a way of moderating our conflicting interpretations.

The kind of consensus generated by transformative democracy, by contrast, does not consist of overlapping positions that remain in a state of contentious isolation. Dialogic consensus is forged out of shareable reasons that have emerged in the course of each group's transformation of its original, contentious position. Because these reasons are not held in abstraction from any group's determinate system of beliefs and values, the resulting consensus is likewise determinate.[27]

No political example testifies better to the possibilities of transformative consensus than alliance building.[28] While alliances can take many forms, ranging from a *modus vivendi* based on strategic compromise and temporary convenience to an overlapping consensus based on moral principles (however incommensurable they might be), the most stable and enduring forms occur whenever the partners in alliance alter their identities to incorporate each other's differing perspectives. Just thirty years ago a labor/environmental alliance in the US would have been unheard of. But last year's demonstration against the World Trade Organization in Seattle showed that such an alliance was indeed possible. Both sides realized that the important issue revolved around neither losing jobs (to environmental protection) nor sacrificing ecological integrity (to job growth) but losing both to unregulated global trade. They did so because they realized that global capitalism creates uneven and wasteful development, which in turn results in the environmental degradation and impoverishment of the most vulnerable sectors of the labor force. Finally, both sides concluded that more democratic forms of technological development and industrial organization were the key to combating underemployment as well as environmental degradation.

By trumpeting the positive alliances born of transformative democracy I don't mean to underestimate the existence of trenchant disagreement. Social conflicts manage to insinuate themselves in the highest echelons of law, and nothing bears this out better than the continuing exacerbation of class conflict. Focusing on the intersection of class, gender, and racial conflicts, Critical Legal Studies scholars have devoted much energy to demonstrating alleged contradictions between competing legal paradigms (classical liberal versus social democratic, formalist versus substantivist, etc.). However, far from conceding their argument, I think it likely (as legal philosophers from Dworkin and Ackerman to Habermas have shown) that such legal antinomies are not hopelessly unresolvable.[29] Still, reducing social inequalities, extending the principles of broad participatory democracy into the workplace, empowering women and minorities, and allowing greater multicultural flexibility in the formulation of legal concepts, are all changes that will have to be made before law can become rationally coherent.

Recognizing that principles and procedures of justice are partially determined (or in Hegel's words, "mediated") by the concrete rationales generated in transformative democracy does not, therefore, eliminate the need for administrative decision. Lyotard's point still stands: there necessarily exists a logical gap between the weakly normative meaning of any general principle and the strongly prescriptive meaning of a concrete command. In this sense, particular laws, judicial verdicts, and executive decrees remain partly underdetermined by both constitutional principles and public opinion, and are to that extent subject to administrative discretion.

Some might find this sad confirmation of Sartre's and Arendt's pessimistic diagnoses of popular revolutionary movements; having emerged out of a radical break with tradition and institution, anarchic freedom born of popular existential self-annihilation cannot but return to the atomistic, alienated, but infinitely more sustainable form of institutional self-determination, in which appointed bureaucrats fix our identities and freedoms for us. However, this characterization paints a picture of modern political life that is too bleak. Even administrative and judicial decision-making is susceptible to degrees of popular influence. So the fact of unavoidable decision-making only generates a legitimation crisis if we adopt, as Lyotard does, a deductive model of democratic deliberation, a model that virtually no legal philosopher (excepting a few positivists and formalists) accepts as descriptively or normatively valid.[30]

Let me elaborate. In transformative democracy, laws, judicial verdicts, and executive decrees are subject to collective, dialogic interpretation in the same way that principles are. In effect, they interpret and give concrete meaning to these principles. This means, too, that the legislation, adjudication, and executive actions that define constitutional procedure are in turn authorized and limited by it. This is not a vicious circle of legitimation, as Lyotard sometimes suggests. For the agents and powers specified by the procedures for amending the procedures will not be identical (for example, those responsible for drawing up a constitution are not those empowered to amend it).

As Habermas reminds us, the republican principle that mandates a separation of powers renders the circuitous process of legitimation harmless by interrupting it with checks and balances. It also renders the revolutionary trajectory of legitimation less unpredictable and terrifying. Certainly transformative democracy continually calls into question its own legitimacy – there is no end to its progressive attempts at realizing its own indeterminate idea. But the revolutionary circle of reform is not terroristic or anarchic. Being interrupted by countless checks and balances and constrained by the arc of its own trajectory, reform is predictable where it matters most: in its procedural determinations.

Not everyone will participate (equally or otherwise) at every step in this revolutionary project, as Habermas calls it. Fully inclusive deliberation should be encouraged in public forums responsible for generating the opinions that guide legislators in setting policy agendas. Less inclusive but fully accountable deliberation should obtain in parliaments, courts, and government bureaucracies, where specialized expertise is required. Needless to say, some individual discretion by legislators, judges, and government bureaucrats in interpreting the public's will as set forth in public opinion, law, and so on can scarcely be dispensed with.

Concern about the abuse of discretionary power raises a final question about the legal, political, economic, and social–psychological languages that legitimate power. As I remarked earlier, citizens must come to understand how the effects of power and domination insinuate themselves into technical expertise no less than everyday vernacular. These effects distort the very linguistic medium in which democratic discussion occurs. It may well be, as Foucault ceaselessly reminded us, that no language is free from these effects, none neutral or impartial in articulating all possible interests. However, the mere fact that no language is entirely innocent is hardly cause for despair. Differends and other linguistic biases can be exposed in inclusive dialogue with those who feel victimized by the dominant discourse. True, the struggle to create a language more adequate to the expression of diverse experiences (cultural, racial, class, etc.) is never-ending. That is why alliances between heterogeneous groups are so difficult to forge and maintain. But without embracing the risk of radical self-transformation presented by broad participatory democracy, we stand to lose more than just our freedom; we stand to lose the world.

Notes

1 J.-F. Lyotard, "Memorandum on Legitimation," in *The Postmodern Explained: Correspondence 1982–85* (Minneapolis: University of Minnesota Press, 1993), 39–60. See chapter 9, this volume.

2 For a more detailed discussion of the legal issues involved in international human rights, treaty rights, racial redistricting, and Quebec's sovereignty, see David Ingram, *Group Rights: Reconciling Equality and Difference* (Lawrence: University Press of Kansas, 2000), chs. 3, 5, 9, and 10; and *Reason, History, and Politics: The Communitarian Grounds of Reason in the Modern Age* (Albany: State University of New York Press, 1995), 143–8.

3 J. Habermas, "Modernity: An Unfinished Project," in David Ingram and Julia Simon-Ingram, eds., *Critical Theory: The Essential Readings* (New York: Paragon House, 1991), 342–56. For a more detailed discussion of the debate between Habermas and Lyotard, see Ingram, *Reason, History, and Politics*, ch. 7.

4 J.-F. Lyotard, *Le Différend* (Paris: Les Editions de Minuit, 1983), 243. Translated into English by Georges Van den Abbeele as *The Differend: Phrases in Dispute* (Minneapolis: University of Minnesota Press, 1988).

5 I. Kant, "Perpetual Peace," in *Political Writings*, ed. Hans Reiss (Cambridge: Cambridge University Press, 1970), 99–102.

6 Elsewhere, in *The Postmodern Condition: A Report on Knowledge* (Minneapolis: University of Minnesota Press, 1984), Lyotard argues that myths and perhaps other "small narratives" (*petit récits*) that circulate in everyday life in modern societies are distinguished from scientific and Enlightenment "metanarratives" in being prediscursive. Unlike metanarratives, the utterances that make up myth cannot be formulated as abstract propositions – descriptions, prescriptions, etc. – that can be logically identified, analyzed, grounded (argumentatively deduced), and criticized (p. 65). Instead of conveying propositional meaning and knowledge, the utterances that comprise oral recitations convey a kind of pragmatic know-how. Their status is more like that of rituals that get legitimated through repetition and imitation, or (as Lyotard puts it) "by the simple fact that they do what they do" (pp. 18–23).

7 Lyotard, *The Differend*, p. 147.

8 E. Dussel, *Philosophy of Liberation* (Maryknoll, NY: Orbis Books, 1980).

9 Cf. *Le Differend*, p. 206. For a critical analysis of Jacques Derrida's similar deconstruction of the American *Declaration of Independence* ("Declarations of Independence," *New Political Science* 15, pp. 7–15), see Ingram, *Reason, History, and Politics*, ch. 8.

10 Derrida's deconstruction of the American *Declaration* (*supra*) closely parallels Lyotard's in its use of speech act theory. According to Derrida, the *Declaration* conflates constative (descriptive) and performative (prescriptive) utterances. I argue, to the contrary, that this conclusion is somewhat overdrawn, since (as John Searle has argued), given an appropriately institutionalized background of normative expectations (or constitutive rules), prescriptions such as "Smith ought to pay Jones five dollars," logically follow from descriptions such as "Smith promised to pay Jones five dollars." Stated differently, although commands do not follow from norms and norms do not follow from facts, commands do follow from a combination of norms and facts taken together (see Ingram, *Reason, History, and Politics*, pp. 351ff.).

11 As Lyotard notes, capitalism requires predictable economic institutions, so democratic reform (intervention in the market to secure substantive freedom and equality for all) is threatening to it. At the same time, he notes that capitalism does not require anything like a liberal rule of law (it happily accommodates despotism and even fascist totalitarianism). Does it, then, require any normative foundation (legitimation)? Lyotard equivocates. Economic exchange is not a form of political governance requiring legitimation. If anything, it is opposed to political governance. Those who wish to limit the regulatory and redistributive freedom of democratic communities in its name are advocating the impersonal rule of unrestricted global markets – not the rule of law – over people. If this threatens a kind of totalitarianism (the subjugation of humanity to the relentless machine of capital, as Marx would say), it is a totalitarianism that is nonetheless *non-political*. But because capitalism practically needs the support of the masses and the state (as guarantor of private property), it must counter the political legitimations offered by democratic socialism (or social democracy) with those of its own (such as its unparalleled success in increasing long-term prosperity). Yet, as Lyotard notes, its sheer ubiquity and apparent necessity are enough to resign most people to its fateful logic.

12 J.-F. Lyotard and J.-L. Thebaud, *Au Juste* (Paris: Christian Bourgeois, 1979), 188. Translated into English by Wlad Godzich as *Just Gaming* (Minneapolis: University of Minnesota Press, 1985).

13 Lyotard, *Le Differend*, pp. 24–5.

14 Ibid, p. 203.

15 Lyotard and Thebaud, *Au Juste*, p. 182.

16 Charles Taylor, *Multiculturalism and the Politics of Recognition: An Essay by Charles Taylor* (Princeton, NJ: Princeton University Press, 1992); and Will Kymlicka, *Multicultural Citizenship* (Oxford: Oxford University Press, 1995).

17 Lyotard, *Postmodern Condition*, pp. 65–7.

18 J. Rawls, *Political Liberalism* (New York: Columbia University Press, 1993). For a more detailed discussion of Rawls's position, see Ingram, *Reason, History, and Politics*, ch. 3; and Ingram, *Group Rights*, ch. 1.

19 J. Rawls, "The Law of Peoples," in *Collected Papers* (Cambridge, MA: Harvard University Press, 1999), 544–51; and David Ingram, "Rawls and Habermas on Global Justice," in *Nation States, Multinational States, and Supranational Organizations*, ed. Michel Seymour (Montreal, McGill University Press,2002).

20 J. Habermas, *The Inclusion of the Other: Studies in Political Theory* (Cambridge, MA: MIT Press, 1998), 203–36.

21 Lani Guinier, "[E]racing Democracy: The Voting Rights Cases," *Harvard Law Review* 108/109 (1994): 131–2.

22 For a detailed discussion of Guinier's views, see Ingram, *Group Rights*, ch. 9.

23 Rawls may well be right that Habermas's own Kantian conception of radical democracy represents a particular "comprehensive doctrine." However, I'm inclined to extend this charge to Rawls himself, who, while openly recognizing the comprehensive status of his earlier *Theory of Justice* (1971), overlooks the comprehensive nature of his later *Political Liberalism* (1993). Not only is the kind of tolerance specified by Rawls's political liberalism not extendible to illiberal regimes, but its peculiar distinction between reasonable and unreasonable comprehensive doctrines is not even accepted by all reasonable liberals.

24 For a detailed discussion of the complexities of racial redistricting in the US, see Ingram, *Group Rights*, ch. 9.

25 Lyotard recognizes the ambiguous impact of computer technology on encouraging or hindering the development of "virtual" democratic spaces. On one hand, such technology can "aid groups discussing metaprescriptives by supplying them with the information they usually lack for making knowledgeable decisions" (*The Postmodern Condition*, p. 67). Recent use of computer technology by college students protesting sweatshops and globalization exemplifies this potential. On the other hand, computer technology can be used to undermine face-to-face interaction and (in a more sinister scenario) concentrate information in the hands of powerful elites. Lyotard's call to "give the public free access to the memory and data banks" is powerfully defended by Andrew Feenberg in *Questioning Technology* (New York: Routledge, 1999), 105–6, 136–43). Feenberg's optimism about the use of computer democracy in organizing global labor and environmental struggles, however, is not shared by everyone. For a more pessimistic appraisal, see Matt Hern and Stu Chaulk, "Roadgrading Community Culture: Why the Internet is so Dangerous to Real Democracy," in *Democracy and Nature*, vol. 6, no. 1 (2000): 111–20.

26 Donald Davidson, "On the Very Idea of a Conceptual Scheme," in *Inquiries into Truth and Interpretation* (Oxford: Oxford University Press, 1985).

27 For a good defense of dialogical consensus (transformative democracy) versus overlapping consensus (political liberalism), see J. Habermas, *The Inclusion of the Other*, chs. 2 and 3. My attempt to strike a balance between these positions is developed in *Group Rights*, ch. 1, and *Reason, History, and Politics*, ch. 3.

28 For excellent discussions of the potential for alliance building within a transformative postmodern setting, see Ernesto Laclau and Chantal Mouffe, *Hegemony and Socialist Strategy: Toward a Radical Democratic Politics* (London: Verso, 1985); and Steven Best and Douglas Kellner, *The Postmodern Turn* (New York: Guilford, 1997), esp. pp. 270ff.

29 I discuss Dworkin's and Habermas's neo–Kantian responses to postmodern and pragmatist accounts of legal reasoning (frequently associated with the Critical Legal Studies Movement, the Law and Economics Movement, and American Legal Realism) in ch. 6 of *Reason, History, and Politics* and in "The Sirens of Pragmatism Versus the Priests of Proceduralism: Habermas and American Legal Realism," in *Habermas and Pragmatism*, ed. Mitchel Aboulafia and Catherine Kemp (New York: Routledge, 2001).

30 For defenses of interpretative and dialogical models of legal reasoning, see R. Dworkin, *Laws Empire* (Cambridge, MA: Harvard University Press, 1986); J. Habermas, *Between Facts and Norms: Contributions to a Discourse Theory of Law and Democracy* (Cambridge, MA: MIT Press, 1996). For critiques of them, see Ingram, *Reason, History, and Politics*, chs. 5 and 6.

PART VI

POSTCOLONIALISM

PLANETARY POLITICS AND THE DIALECTIC OF LIFE AND LIBERATION

11

SIX THESES TOWARDS A CRITIQUE OF POLITICAL REASON: THE CITIZEN AS POLITICAL AGENT

Enrique Dussel

We will briefly articulate six theses, which are general hypotheses, for a future political philosophy. They are six moments, or constitutive determinations (one may also say general principles) of all possible political action. For now they open up a space of reflection which will form part of a *Critique of Political Reason* which I am currently elaborating.

Introduction: The Reductionist Formalist Fallacy

It was the goal of Aristotle's politics of the *tó koinón agathón* (the common good), Aquinas's *bonum commune*, Hegel's organic state as *Sittlichkeit* (ethical life), Max Scheler's theory of the actualization of values, and even the more recent idea and practice of the *Welfare State*, to link up *material*[1] contents with politics. These projects have met with severe criticism. Contemporary political philosophy, in fact, can be read as an attempt to uncouple substantive ethical orientations from the practice and formulation of political justice. In more recent times, the difficulty of grounding political philosophy on *material* content has been met with by both liberal (such as that of John Rawls or Robert Nozick) and procedural discursive (such as that of Jürgen Habermas or Karl-Otto Apel) political philosophy with the rejection of all *material* politics. Both have rejected all material politics because this has been seen as either particularistic or non-generalizable, and thus a detriment to the exercising of a pluralist and tolerant democracy; or because it can be seen as conflating political action with economics. Upon eradicating the economic and ecological level (what is material) *ratio politica* may only move within the exclusive space of formal democratic validity of the legitimate structures of political systems, or of law, or of contractual (Rawls) or discursive (Habermas) participation within the public sphere.

This could be acceptable in countries experiencing late capitalism, countries which practice the *Rule of Law*, and which due to their level of development guarantee the survival all of their citizens. Within these type of societies, legitimate is that which complies with the procedural requirements of the democratic system, of the exercise of communicative power and of the system of laws. But this appears to be insufficient for a political philosophy that reflects out of and upon the real situation of our planet, from the impoverished and peripheral underdeveloped countries, which make up 85 per cent of the world's population. Since 1989 the *Rule of Law* in Latin America, Africa, and Asia is in a precarious state, and mere survival is in no way guaranteed for the majority of the populations in many nations in these continents. It is from this context that we discover the necessity for *critical* reflection within contemporary political philosophy.

1   Fundamental Politics

In this first part we will sketch the first three moments of political philosophy's architectonic, that is, its foundational principles.

Thesis 1. Ratio politica is complex precisely because it exercises different types of rationality. It has as its foundational content the imperative to produce, reproduce, and develop human life within a community, and in the last instance of humanity in general in the long run. Therefore, the practical–political claim to *truth* is universal. In this sense political reason is *practical and material*.

This first moment is so obvious that it has remained in the background, hidden away from political philosophy. I would like to give four well-known examples, and I cite them precisely because they are familiar, so as to indicate how obvious the point is. Speaking from the rationalism of a hegemonic Amsterdam, Spinoza posits in his *Theologico-Political Treatise* (1670), chapter 16, that:

> When we reflect that men without mutual help, or the aid of reason, must needs live most miserably . . . we shall plainly see that men must necessarily come to an agreement to live together as securely and well as possible if they are to enjoy as a whole the rights which naturally belong to them as individuals.[2]

It is reason, in effect, which serves as the medium which conserves the secure and peaceful life, and "there exists no one who does not desire *to live* safely, without fear, which cannot happen if each person *lives* according to their own caprices." The argument is based on the need to move away from a naturally chaotic state (because of our passions or inclinations, that is our animal nature) in order to pass into a state of civil or political order which, according to reason, secures *life*. John Locke is even more explicit in his *Two Treatises of Government*, when he writes in the second treatise, chapter 2 ("The state of nature"):

> Though this be a *State of Liberty*, yet it is *not a State of Licence*, though Man in that State have an uncontrollable Liberty, to dispose of this Person or Possessions, yet he has not Liberty to destroy himself, or so much as any Creature in his Possession, but where some nobler use, than its bare Preservation calls for it. The *State of Nature* has a Law of Nature to govern it, which obliges evry one: And Reason, which is that Law, teaches all Mankind, who will

but consult it, that being all equal and independent, no one ought to harm another in his Life, Health, Liberty, or Possessions. . . . Every one as he is *bound to preserve himself. . . to preserve the rest of Mankind.*[3]

Following Hooker's line of thought, Locke shows that in the "state of nature" we are incapable of securing for ourselves the essentials needed in order to "live according to our human dignity." The state of nature is akin to a "state of war" in which the adversary may easily take our life away. And because human beings do not have power over their own lives, they cannot dispose of power so as to end their own lives. The transition to private property, in the same way, is established for being the most advantageous to life. In the first place, it is true that natural reason teaches us that once born, humans have the right to preserve their life, which entails eating, drinking, and other activities which naturally secure our survival. But, in second place, it is through our work that we make the earth useful and available for life, and:

> The same Law of nature, that does by this means give us Property, does also *bound* that *Property* too. . . . As much as any one can make use of to any advantage *of life* before it spoils; so much he may by his labour fix a Property in.[4]

Until here Locke's argument is based always on human life. Suddenly, however, thanks to money, great possessions may be accumulated, which permit the exchange of truly useful goods and articles. Once money enters the fore the meaning of Locke's discourse changes, beginning with chapter 6 of the *Second Treatise*, and he no longer employs life as his fundamental argument. The primary end of political or civil society now becomes the defense of property. Life definitively loses its significance.

Similarly, Jean-Jacques Rousseau writes in book 1, chapter 6 of his *Social Contract*:

> I suppose men to have reached the point at which the obstacles in the way of their preservation in the state of nature show their power of resistance to be greater than the resources at the disposal of each individual for his maintenance in that state. That primitive condition can then subsist no longer; and the human race would perish unless it changed its manner of existence.[5]

In order to avoid extinction, in order to preserve life, it is necessary to move to a higher "form of association." Life is once again the basis of the argument.

I would now like to refer to two contemporary philosophers who have suffered persecution firsthand. The first one is Hans Jonas, a Jewish philosopher who lived through the Nazi persecution and exiled himself in the United States, and who developed an ethics of life as responsibility. The other is Ignacio Ellacuría, a Christian philosopher who was assassinated by the military dictatorship orchestrated by the Pentagon and the CIA for his political commitments in El Salvador. One is a philosopher of the struggle for life in the first part of the twentieth century, and the other in the second part. For humanity, since its origin, human life was a non-problematic natural event. It was death which always appeared as enigmatic. Biology was still a science, devoid of any ethical obligations. When the "Club of Rome" first exposed the "limits of growth" in 1972, life began to appear problematic, not just theoretically but ethically pressing and anguishing. The vulnerability, limitation, precariousness, and even the beginning of extinction of life in the planet is now seen as the possible collective suicide of humanity:

> Take, for instance, . . . the critical vulnerability of nature to man's technological interven-
> tion – unsuspected before it began to show itself in damage already done. This discovery,
> whose shock led to the concept and nascent science of ecology, alters the very concept of
> ourselves as a causal agency in the larger scheme of things. It brings to light, through the
> effects, that the nature of human action has *de facto* changed, and that an object of an
> entirely new order -no less than the whole biosphere of the planet – has been added to
> what we must be responsible for because of our power over it.[6]

Which is put more pointedly later on in the following way:

> Bacon's formula says that knowledge is power. Now the Baconian program by itself, that
> is, under its own management, has at the height of its triumph revealed its insufficiency in
> the lack of control over itself, thus the impotence of its power to save not only man from
> himself but also nature from man . . . power has become self-acting, while its promise has
> turned into threat, its prospect of salvation into apocalypse. Power over the power is
> required now before the halt is called by catastrophe itself – the power to overcome that
> impotence over against the self-feeding compulsion of power to its progressive exercise.[7]

Illustrating the fundamental constitution of the "materiality of history," and after analyzing the presence, materiality, spatiality, and temporality of historical being, Ellacuría arrives at the "biological basis of history." He writes:

> Even though society is not an organism . . . different human groups are those which
> biologically see themselves as forced to make history. Many of the natural as well as
> optional realizations are due to fundamentally biological determinants. . . . Even more so
> when we attend to the riches and plenitude of the necessities and the biologically
> considered life powers.[8]

Unlike the two philosophers aforementioned, Franz Hinkelammert situates himself more decidely within the strict sense of "human life," and advances the importance of material content in its economic aspect, which includes the ecological dimension. This is best illustrated in his work, *Democracy and Totalitarianism*:

> Certainly, one cannot assure the material reproduction of human life without at the same
> time assuring the reproduction of material nature. Since the process of production is a
> transformation of material nature into items which satisfy the necessities based on work
> processes, the exploitation of nature will always mean the destruction of human life.[9]

The task of *ratio politica*, therefore, insofar as it is practical–material reason, is to deal with the production, reproduction, and the development of human life in community. Macro-politics manages the stated imperative at the level of humanity as a whole, in the "long run," and takes political responsibility for the production and reproduction of the biosphere (ecology), thereby working as the systems of the division of labor, production, distribution, and exchange (economy). When we say "in the long run," we refer to the next five thousand years, for example. Approximately five thousand years ago the planet, with sufficiently mature civilizations like those of Mesopotamia and Egypt, was populated by 60–100 million human beings. At the end of the twentieth century, humanity will have almost multiplied its demographic occupation by a hundred-fold. Overpopulation, the finitude of non-renewable resources, global warming, the hole in the ozone layer at the South Pole, all demonstrate that, materially, "planetary macro-politics" should adopt new criteria for the production, reproduction, and development of human life, or life will soon disappear. In economic production, the politician should implement criteria which would lower the rate at which non-renewable resources (petroleum, for example) are used; increase the use of recyclable fixed resources (iron or copper); increase the use of renewable resources (solar or hydraulic power, wood, synthetic plastics, alcohol combustion, etc.). From Aristotle to Rawls, never did politics have to occupy itself with these duties. *Materially* speaking, it has now become an absolute priority. But it is the end of modern politics as advanced by figures such as Machiavelli in the Renaissance, Locke in capitalism, Bacon in the scientific revolution. Political philosophy still has not subsumed this dimension. The green parties, knowing little political economy, are the products of a material newness, and will play a major role in the third millennium.

The carrying out of other ecological–economic activities on the international, national, regional, ethnic planes of practico-material political reason are partial, fragmentary aspects, specific to this fundamental criterion of political truth, which is at the same time an ethico-political material principle. This concerns the political duty of production, reproduction, and development of human life for all humanity, and as its condition of possibility, also the preservation of the biosphere. This "duty" is the fundamental deontic material principle of all politics that may be possible. And this is because the citizen is a living corporeality, a needing subjectivity, and a self-reflexive subject who has human life in its charge (its, as well as that of all humanity in the last instance). In a lucid, and convincing manner, Hinkelammert writes:

> The material reproduction of human life is the ultimate instance of all human life and its liberty [a point we will discuss in the second thesis]: the dead man, or the man threatened by death, ceases to be free, independently from the social context in which he lives.[10]

The material aspects of power still remain to be examined. In fact, since Schopenhauer being or reality is seen as Will (*Willen*). In our case it translates to "Will to Live" (*Willen zum Leben*) which registers in Nietzsche as the "Will to Power" (*Wille zur Macht*), which could rightly be interpreted as mobilizing and actualizing "power" which arises from life so as to create life, and thus even as the ultimate basis for such a Power. But this material question of politics should be more rigorously treated in a lengthier project. It is also the citizen's "Will to Live" which serves as the ultimate basis of the material conception (not solely procedural–formal) of legitimacy, as we will indicate further on.

Thesis 2. Ratio politica should discursively, procedurally, or democractically achieve validity (formal legitimacy) through the effective, symmetrical, and democratic public participation of all the affected, who are citizens as autonomous subjects, and who exercise the complete autonomy of the political community of communication. It is this political community of communication, as the intersubjective community of popular sovereignty, that then serves as the source and destination of law. Its decisions therefore have a *validity* claim or universal political *legitimacy*. In this sense, *ratio politica* is *practical–discursive political reason.*

We now enter a much more traveled terrain. It deals with the discursive moment of the consensus, of autonomy, freedom, popular sovereignty, which could be called, according to Jürgen Habermas, "Democracy-Principle"[11] (if we keep in mind that the principle enunciated in thesis 1 could have been called the "Life-Principle"). The material principle of the exercise of political reason cannot constitute itself, nor can it wield power without the mediation of the political–discursive reason. In other words, if we pose the question: "How do we politically produce human life in community?" The only answer would be "It can only be decided democratically or discursively according to the laws institutionalized by public legitimacy or validity!" In other words: demo-cratically!

All the hypothetical theory of modern contractualism is based on the moral and political exigencies of that which is *normative*, which in turn originates in the free and symmetrical participation of those affected. Upon reading Rousseau's formulation in *The Social Contract*, which treats the problem of originary consensus, we find that it is necessary

> to find a form of association which will defend and protect with the whole common force the person and goods of each associate, and in which each, while uniting himself with all, may still obey himself alone, and remain as free as before.[12]

Or as Spinoza defines it:

> A body politic of this kind is called a Democracy, which may be defined as a society which wields all its power as a whole. The sovereign power is not restrained by any laws, but everyone is bound to obey it in all things.[13]

All contractualist theories, including John Rawls's and Robert Nozick's, fall into an inevitable aporia due to their metaphysical individualism (and in some cases quasi-anarchical, in terms of the intrinsic perverseness of the state as institution). Given that a human is an individual and free being by nature, all "institution" inevitably produces a certain repression, discipline, constraint which is contrary to nature. Leftist anarchy – such as proposed by Bakunin – also holds that all "institution" is perverse, because it "represses" pristine and communitarian human liberty. Bakunin proposes to destroy institutions by means of direct action; Nozick proposes to reduce them to the most "minimal" influence possible. Kant clearly posed the question in his *The Metaphysic of Morals*:

> One can locate the concept of right directly in the possibility of connecting universal reciprocal coercion with the freedom of everyone. That is to say, just as right generally has as its object only what is external in action, so strict right, namely that which is not mingled with anything ethical, requires only external grounds for determining choice.[14]

Law as the external factor imposes itself upon the faculties of desire (material, always egotistical), on all individuals by "coercion" (*Zwang*), because "law is linked to the right to use coercion." Action according to law is not ethical ("that which is not mingled with anything ethical," as we copied above) and so it does not have any normativity, but mere external legality. The dilemma has grown in magnitude: individual morality has been excised from the coercive, external legality of law.

Karl-Otto Apel and Jürgen Habermas have solved this aporia by departing from a "discursive *community*," thus overcoming metaphysical individualism: it is the community which behaves without unnatural constraint, as both the *source* of law (giving unto itself the laws), with discursive equality, liberty, and autonomy, and as the *destination* of the law (it needs to obey itself). Theoretically, the one who is affected has been the symmetrical participant in the determination of the very regulations that will affect her/him. It is for this reason that the decisions that affect all are valid for all, and since they have been mediated by "the democratic principle," which regulates the institutionalization of all mediations, may then be considered legitimate. The concept of popular sovereignty, whereby the community is both the origin and destination of the law, exercised by a historico-discursive community, thus resolves the aporia. The democratic principle, moreover, is not only a merely formal, external, and legal proceedure. Instead, it has a normative basis, since it means the application of the "discursive principle" to the public political level. Habermas's contribution is formally a great advancement in the delimitation of "politico-discursive reason," and should be subsumed into a detailed political philosophy. However, once he negates the material level he inevitably falls into reductive formalism. According to Habermas, legitimacy is established in a purely discursive and formal level. He does not comprehend that a political system "*loses* legitimacy" once it does not acceptably treat and thereby maintain human life for its citizens. One must bring to bear the material aspect of human life and interaction when treating the concept of legitimacy, so as to enrich the purely formal or procedural conception of political justice. In postcolonial, peripheral, and poor countries, economic production is an essential political dimension of legitimacy. For example, in the present, the impoverishment of many nations due to neoliberal economic policies has entailed the delegitimation of many governments which have formally complied with the democratic principle, but have materially neglected the process of legitimization. Here, it concerns knowing how to articulate John Rawls's first principle along with the second (socioeconomic) principle, a topic poorly analyzed in his *Theory of Justice*. Furthermore, it is for this reason that his application of the "overlapping consensus" remains only at the politico-cultural level, thereby leaving behind the crucial ecological–economic and social levels.

The material principle of politics (the reproduction of human life) and the formal principle (the democratic principle) are mutually articulated in the constitution of objects proper to them, in the fluctuations of its process, thereby implicating itself within the application. Nothing pertaining to the development of human life in community can be politically decided without the mediation of the formal levels which achieve public validity or legitimacy that the discursive principle confers. But all that is democratically discussed should be *oriented* by the claim to practical truth of the first material principle of the imperative, abstractly and universally formulated in the prohibition of a maxim that is unable to be universalized – as Wellmer puts it: "Thou shall not kill!" It is not democratically legitimate to decide upon a collective suicide; as Wittgenstein wrote: "If suicide is permitted, everything is permitted."

In this case the citizen is a member of an intersubjective, linguistic, rational, democratic community. In other words, the citizen forms part of the democratic participation secured by popular sovereignty; which is in turn the origin and destination of law, power, and all subsequent subsystems.

Thesis 3. Ratio politica, in its dimension of strategic or instrumental feasibility, should consider the logical, empirical, ecological, economic, social, historical, etc., conditions of *real possibility* of the implementation of a maxim, norm, law, acts, institution, or political system. This will grant the maxim, norm, law, action, institution, subsystem, etc., political success and efficacy. In this case it concerns a strategic, or even instrumental, political reason, which is positively subsumed within the ethical complexity of political reason.

All that has been indicated in this *thesis 3* should operate inside of the parameters determined by the two principles treated in the previous theses. In this strict sense it shall be called *strategic*, or even instrumental, *political reason*.

Max Weber distinguished between formal and material reason. The first stems from "empirical judgments" which may be developed through science; the second operates with "value judgments" which are subjective, like taste judgments, and therefore cannot be inserted into scientific discourse. The two types of rationality aforementioned in theses 1 and 2 are unknown to Weber. This inevitably places him in the reductionism of "instrumental reason," which was so thoroughly criticized by the first Frankfurt School (Horkheimer, Adorno, or Marcuse). Formal rationality is subject to quantification and calculation, and is aimed at ends already in place in the existing system (whether they be political, economic, technological, etc.). There exists no possibility of positing or judging ends. The ethical and political problem of strategic reason consists, precisely, in becoming aware of the compatibility of the ends of action (that is, with reference to formal rationality; for example, the goals or ends of the bureacratic system or capitalist firm) with the possibility of maintaining human life (the truth of the end), and its legitimate democratic determination (the validity of the end). An action will be integrally political if it complies with the three principles: material–practical, formal rationality of truth, and validity of the end.

Thus, the entire problem of forms of government is not situated exactly at the level of the three enunciated principles, because these are universal, abstract conditions, even when generally speaking of feasibility.[15] The democratic principle, for example, must operate in a certain discursive universal manner (such as arriving at a valid decision by means of rational arguments with the democratic participation of those affected, in a public and institutionalized way as guaranteed by law), but as such it does not necessarily stipulate a concretely determined form of government. Universal and confidential suffrage is democratic; but such suffrage is not the only possible democratic type. The democratic principle is not an ideal type of government, but rather an ethical–political, universal principle (at level A, to use Apel's distinction.)[16] The types of democratic government, or models by means of which democracy may be exercised, are situated already at the level of political feasibility, at the level of mediation (level B, in Apel's terminology). Political philosophy, at the abstract level (A), analyzes the criteria and principles and still studies the criteria of the specific types of government (level B); political science forms part of its particular, more theoretical, sociological, historical studies. Singular political action (level C) determines concretely the principles and criteria of forms of political organization; through it they are either executed or transformed *de facto*.

Machiavellianism means the creation of an absolutely autonomous space where political strategic reason has no normative frames. Its end is political success, and is wont to surmount conflicts which test the effectiveness of the existing political order. Such an end justifies the means. On the contrary, political normative feasibility does not deny strategic reason, the success of political action, but subsumes it, thereby enframing it inside the exigencies of the first two principles, which in their negative universal formulation could be reduced to two prohibitions expressed by two maxims that are not universalizable. To cite Wellmer once more: "Thou shall not kill!" and "Thou shall neither exclude nor negate symmetry to anyone affected by that about which a concrete decision is being made!"

In this case the citizen acts as agent, situated within conditions of feasibility of the means–ends, and should thereby arrive at success by means of strategic action.

Corollary 1. Only the norm, law, action, institution, or system which complies with the indicated principles can make a claim to *political justice* (the ethical–political) within the established order.

The three theses are universal and abstract (level A). They are ethical–political requirements actualized in strategic action and concrete tactics (level B). It is here where science and political experience (*politiké* and political *frónesis*) bring together their contributions. *Practical truth* (the reproduction of human life, although now in concrete, within different fronts such as the ecological, economic, educational, etc.) is here articulated with *political validity* (with types of concrete government, with division of powers, with objective systems of laws, rights, institutions, which are the mediations of the democratic principle) and *practical feasibility* (that takes into consideration concrete conditions at all possible empirical levels, of historical space and time, of social, technological possibilities, etc.). It is political–strategic reason that manages all the complexity of this concrete level (B), which is frequently defined as political reason as such; but in this case one could not make its strategic action compatible with the requirements of human life and the validity of popular sovereignty which it supposedly serves.

In this case the citizen is a member of a ruling political order in which she/he can carry on with a certain standard of living, participate legitimately and sovereignly within political society, through necessary institutional mediations. There exists here a simultaneous claim to both political justice and efficacious strategy. But strategic reason must be equally responsible for the effects of its action, in the short run as well as in the long run, especially when the effects of political action are *negative* (I will call victims all those who suffer such negative effects), and not when they are positive (when these effects are positive they are readily transformed into merits of political success). Such responsibility in turn brings about other types of political rationality: critical political rationality as public principle for the development of human life and for the struggle for the recognition of needed new rights (new spaces of future validity and legitimacy).

2 Critical Politics

The discourse of political philosophy enters into a second moment. It is now necessary to take charge of current and future effects of political action. The positive effects rightly confirm the effectiveness of measures taken and success of existing structures. Only when *negative* effects turn preponderant, and thus intolerable and unacceptable, does reflection over the actions or systems which produced them arise. Such reflection, or "*critical* politics," serves to critique political structures which produce ecologically destructive effects or human victims. Both negative effects warn us about the need to rectify the causes of political action. Black Americans, Hispanics, feminist movements, ecologists, senior citizens, postcolonial countries oppressed by the globalization process, exploited classes, excluded populations, the marginalized, poor immigrants, ethnic groups, and so many other social groups victimized by the present political systems, become the objects of liberation or *critical* politics.

Thesis 4. *Ratio politica* is transformed into *critical* political reason insofar as it ought to assume responsibility for the *negative* effects of decisions, laws, actions, or institutions. It should struggle for political recognition of victims of political actions, past or present. Ethical, political critique proposes to disclose what is not true, not legitimate, what is not efficacious about a decision, norm, law, action, institution, or political order. *Critical political reason* is thus defined in this sense.

John Locke, that bourgeois "revolutionary" whom we have seen justify property as the end of political society, will propose negatively, at the end of *The Second Treatise of Government*, in chapter 19, "Of the Dissolution of Government," a position akin to Max Horkheimer's in *Critical Theory*, when he writes:

> For when the *People* are made *miserable*, and find themselves *exposed to the ill usage of Arbitrary Power*, cry up their Governours, as much as you will for Sons of *Jupiter*, let them be Sacred and Divine, descended or authoriz'd from Heaven.... *The People generally ill treated*, and contrary to right, will be ready upon any occasion to ease themselves of a burden that sits heavy upon them.[17]

In the same vein, Horkheimer writes in "Traditional and Critical Theory":

> Traditional theory may take a number of things for granted: its positive role in a functioning society, an admittedly indirect and obscure relation to the satisfaction of general needs, and participation in the self-renewing life process. But all these exigencies about which science need not trouble itself because their fulfillment is rewarded and confirmed by the social position of the scientist, are called into question in critical thought [*kritischen Denken*]. The goal at which the latter aims, namely the rational state of society, is forced upon him by present distress [*Not der Gegenwart*]. The theory which projects such a solution to the distress does not labor in the service of an existing reality but only gives voice to the mystery of that reality.[18]

Material negativity serves as the point of departure for political criticism. In this case the citizen is the victim unjustly repressed or excluded from the current political order, barred from the possibility of participation, and from the possibility of the reproduction of his/her life. The state is then considered anti-democratic and thereby illegitimate. The three principles enunciated in the first part are here dealt with in a negative manner. In taking the victim's perspective, political criticism initiates "a scientific diagnosis of the State's pathologies," as Hermann Cohen advanced.[19] It becomes evident that self-preservation is the end of a political system when it starts to produce an intolerable number of victims, repressed, "disciplined," and alienated members of society. The "self-preservation of the political system" (for example, the existence of slavery alongside Athenian democracy in Aristotle's time) is advanced as ultimate criterion against the very reproduction of human life itself. For this reason, who places his trust in life is criticized from the perspective of the "self-preservation of the existing system." The "valorization of value" (the ultimate criterion of capital) puts in question the reproduction of life (of the worker), but this last one should supersede the former. The critique of the self-reproduction of the system from the perspective of the development of the human life of the victim is the fundamental criterion for all critical politics, the criterion of all necessary political "transformation." Marx's political econ-omy and the ontology of Emmanuel Levinas both concur. It is already given that the agent of political, institutional transformation cannot be only the state, even when there exists a certain possibility for internal transformation of the state. It is the "new social movements" of civil society, which with a renewed claim to political justice, transform the state. From here arises the interest in a structural critique of "micro-power," from the standpoint of Difference, as was proposed by Michel Foucault. Those excluded from the political order (the insane, prisoners, homosexuals, etc.) corroborate through the "disciplinary" punishments inflicted upon them the existence of the ruling system. The mere reality of the victim (marginalized minorities, the homeless, feminists, homosexuals, etc.) serves as social, critical criterion. The question has yet to be adequately formulated and examined in contemporary political philosophy.

Thesis 5. Ratio politica, inasmuch as it is critique, should discursively and democratically, from the standpoint of excluded and stigmatized social actors, assume responsibility for (a) negatively judging the political order as "cause" of its victims, (b) it should then organize necessary new social movements so as to (c) positively propose alternatives to the existing political, legal, economic, educational, etc., systems. It is thus that from the struggles for the recognition of those excluded there emerge new systems of rights. These critical social movements have a growing claim to *legitimacy* (critical validity) before the decreasing legitimacy of the political order in power. Transversally they also claim universality. It is in this sense that political reason is *critical–discursive political reason*.

The excluded, victimized citizen now changes him/herself into an agent of trans-formation as a member of a "critical community" who struggles for the recognition of rights in civil society, in hopes of institutionalizing her/his demands within political society, the state, in the future. In the *Theses on Feuerbach* Marx's materialism, juxtaposed against the individual, cognitivistic, static, and functional materialism of Feuerbach, is shown in all its anthropological dimensions (with respect to living corporeality), as well as in all of its critical or negative, practical, and social aspects (for it is concerned with a subject who is immersed in "social relations"). Marx speaks of "human activity" that is carried out by the community of victims itself:

> The coincidence of the transformation of circumstances and of human activity or self-transformation can be conceived and rationally understood only as *revolutionary practice*.[20]

One should refer back to thesis 2 when studying this precise level; a level which is not that of a solipsistic and merely theoretical subject, but rather which is the level of practical or strategic subjects, in *critical* position, and whose own transformative praxis within the system which excludes and dominates them is the very condition of possibility of the enunciation of a critical judgment (objective truth):

> The question whether objective truth can be attributed to human thinking is not a question of theory but is a *practical* question. Man must prove the *truth*, i.e., the reality and power, the this-sidedness of his thinking in practice.[21]

Marx discovered the "point of departure" of praxis (the critical community of victims, the proletariat in its moment and specific perspective), upon affirmatively responding to the ethical interpellation of the victims themselves, who in turn liberate themselves.

When discussing the organization of a community of victims we should not forget the genius of Rosa Luxemburg, whose praxis made explicit the convergence of *strategic* praxis and *principles* (which should be distinguished from theory, even though Luxemburg does not explicitly do so). Upon criticizing the opportunists or reformists of the German Social Democratic Party, she asks herself: What distinguishes them from revolutionaries? She then answers:

> A certain hostility to "theory." This is quite natural, for our "theory," that is, the principles of scientific socialism, impose clearly marked limitations to practical activity – insofar as it concerns the aims of this activity, the means used in attaining these aims, and the method employed in this activity. It is quite natural for people who run after immediate "practical" results to want to free themselves from such limitations and to render their practice independent of our "theory."[22]

As one may observe, theory (which Luxemburg places within quotation marks) is something more when considered in its entirety: for the moment it may be described as a *series of principles*. These principles are the ones already elaborated. These principles, ethical and political conditions of possibility of the law, norms, actions, subsystems, political institutions, and limits which enframe such possibilities, are those which "impose strict parameters upon political activity" in Luxemburg's analysis. In other words, it is not possible to exercise "any political action" nor use any means, nor choose any political end, etc. One may only discursively decide "those actions which are possible" within the strictly defined parameters circumscribed by said principles. In a startlingly precise manner, in terms of strategic organization, Luxemburg indicates that the "principles" limit and contain criteria for decision "with reference to (a) the ends to be achieved, (b) the *means* for struggle which are applied, and (c) finally the *modes* of struggle." These three levels of strategic–instrumental political reason define the horizon of mediations. Our great intellectual politician clearly describes the ways in which strategic reason should be articulated alongside a democratic, material reason, otherwise known as *strategic–critical political reason*. It has now become possible to understand that political–material and democratic–formal critical reason "posit" the *ends* of strategic – critical political reason. It is from these posited ends that we may discover means (not "any" means is acceptable, just as not "any" end will do), and utilizes tactical methods for a concrete actualization that does not contradict the aforementioned principles. For this reason, not just any method is possible, since all of these remain enframed inside the political possibilities permitted (or dictated) by the enunciated principles.

A strategic–critical political reason is not a strategic reason which simply intends to realize ends imposed by tactics or circumstances. This would be Max Weber's position, for whom "ends" are inevitably those of the given culture, or the ruling tradition, and that as such should be accepted – a conservative yet irrational stance, since reasons cannot be given, based on practical principles, in favor of or against existing ends. Strategic–critical political reason, on the contrary, only allows for efficacious endeavors compliant with ethical macro–politics and critical politics. If one tries to liberate the victims, success will then depend on compliance with the conditions of possibility of that liberation, and in order to comply, the citizen cannot separate "praxis" from "theory."

Difference, as manifest in new social movements, should be affirmed through democratic practices that nonetheless open themselves up to the universality (transversality) of political society as a whole. The struggle for recognition of such Difference is, at the same time, a struggle for the universal development of human life in general.

Thesis 6. Ratio politica, as "ratio liberationis," should strategically organize and actualize the efficacious process of transformation, whether it be (a) negative or destructive (that is *de-constructive*) of the unjust structures of the current system, (b) whether it be *constructive* of aspects of the political order, or at the level of the system of rights and law, the economy, ecology, education, and so on. These maxims, norms, actions, institutions raise a strategic claim to be *possible* transformations (liberation as critical feasibility. This is the whole question of the possible utopia, real although not present). This is what is called *critical–strategic political reason.*

In this case the citizen is the subject of liberation, within the intersubjectivity of a movement which has initiated an activity of efficacious transformation. This was clearly the case with George Washington struggling for the emancipation of his country, which transformed New England into the Unites States of America. It is this very same liberating *ratio politica* that also drove Miguel Hidalgo to act against Spain in order to convert New Spain into Mexico, and Martin Luther King among Black Americans, or the feminists within *machista* political orders, or Fidel Castro to stand against the empire of the day.

What we have thus far indicated architectonically is, strictly, an introduction to Marx's famous formulation in his eleventh *Theses on Feuerbach*:

> The philosophers have only *interpreted* the world, in various ways; the point is to *transform* it.[23]

In this aphorism Marx does not reject philosophy, as Korsch thought, but rather signals that philosophy should cease to be mere hermeneutical theory, so that it may develop as a critical discourse which would enable real and practical transformation of the world. Such philosophical discourse cannot but be a practical philosophy, a *Politics of*

Transformation, a non–reformist Politics of Liberation. The Western Marxist tradition, since Lukács, derailed itself by turning to fields such as ontology, the critique of ideology, aesthetics, mere political economy, but it never attempted to develop a politics as "first and practical philosophy" that would analyze the criteria and principles that would ground the necessary "transformation of the world." The Ethics of Liberation has attempted this in diverse ways, since the 1960s.

Corollary 2. Only that maxim, norm, law, action, or institution which complies with the six indicated conditions of possibility may *claim* to be able to build fair political structures, as legitimate transformations of the established order, through the mediation of the creation of *new* norms, laws, institutions, or political order.

The objective of the liberating political act is to create a new political order which responds to the victims' demands. The person who acts according to responsibility for the Other and in compliance with the indicated conditions, may make a claim to be able to establish a more just order. History will judge whether or not such an order was indeed effective. Overall, honest political conscience intended to realize with strategic feasibility that new order with the symmetrical participation of all affected. In other words, such a transformative process can claim validity because it was attempted while being guided by the democratic principle, and as such it may claim to be a renewed political justice. History, as advanced by Walter Benjamin and the Ethics of Liberation, is a *justicia semper renovanda*, as is called for in the clamor of all victims, and by new social movements in civil society.

Translated by Christina Lloyd and Eduardo Mendieta

Notes

1 *Material* here is retained, even if it is not the most elegant English and a more appropriate term would be *content* (*Inhalt*), because by now it has become common to take this term as an antonym of *formal*. *Material* means value–content, and refers to a substantive ethical view or value, in opposition to *formal* which refers to procedures or universal rules for the determination of maxims and norms. The dichotomy material/formal parallels the opposition between procedural universalism (Kant) and contextual, hermeneutical, historical substantive ethical theories (Aristotle, Hegel). [Translators' note]

2 Benedict de Spinoza, *A Theologico-Political Treatise*, trans. R. H. M. Elwes (New York: Dover, 1951), 202.

3 John Locke, *Two Treatises of Government* (New York: New American Library, 1965), 311. Italics in original.

4 Ibid, p. 332.

5 Jean-Jacques Rousseau, *The Social Contract and Discourses*, trans. G. D. H. Cole (London: Everyman's Library, 1973), 173.

6 Hans Jonas, *The Imperative of Responsibility: In Search of an Ethics for the Technological Age* (Chicago: Chicago University Press, 1979), 6–7.

7 Ibid, p. 141.

8 Ignacio Ellacuría, *Filosofía de la realidad histórica* (Madrid: Editorial Trotta, 1991), 79.

9 Franz Hinkelammert, *Democracia y totalitarismo* (San José, Costa Rica: DEI, 1990), 31.

10 Ibid, p. 8.

11 Jürgen Habermas, *Between Facts and Norms*, trans. William Rehg (Cambridge, MA: MIT Press, 1996).

12 Rousseau, *The Social Contract*, p. 174.

13 Spinoza, *A Theologico-Political Treatise*, p. 205.

14 Immanuel Kant, *The Metaphysics of Morals*, in *Practical Philosophy* (Cambridge: Cambridge University Press, 1996), 389.

15 See Norbert Bobbio, *La teoría de las formas de gobierno en la historia del pensamiento político* (Mexico: FCE, 1989).

16 See my article "Principles, Mediations, and the 'Good' as Synthesis: (From 'Discourse Ethics' to 'Ethics of Liberation')" (forthcoming in *Philosophy Today*).

17 Locke, *Two Treatises of Government*, p. 463.

18 Max Horkheimer, *Critical Theory: Selected Essays*, trans. Matthew J. O'Connell, et al. (New York: Continuum, 1982), 216–17.

19 Hermann Cohen, *Religion of Reason out of the Sources of Judaism*, trans. Simon Kaplan (New York: Ungar Publishing, 1972 [1919]), 23.

20 Karl Marx, *Early Writings*, trans. Rodney Livingston and Gregor Benton (London: Penguin Books, 1975), 422. Translation slightly altered.

21 Ibid, italics added.

22 Rosa Luxemburg, *Reform or Revolution* (New York: Pathfinder, 1970), 59.

23 Marx, *Early Writings*, p. 423, translation slightly altered.

12

POLITICS IN AN AGE OF PLANETARIZATION: ENRIQUE DUSSEL'S CRITIQUE OF POLITICAL REASON

Eduardo Mendieta

Solamente el que puede desear la libertad, la liberación del Otro que es el pobre, desde él y no desde la totalidad, es quien realmente puede instaurar una política de justicia.

Dussel (1979a)

Introduction

The canon of political thought is not exempt from the identity crises that besiege all other similar practices of giving shape and continuity to a cultural identity. This means that like the religious, literary, legal, and philosophical canons that identify a culture, the political canon is at the mercy of the forces that shape history, while also contributing to the thrust of that history. This also means that canons serve as registers for the struggles that have catalyzed social transformations, and as such they also serve as large compendia of social memory. It is for this reason that they are the focus of so much attention and the locus of much contestation.

Very much like during the times of the Magna Carta, the Declaration of American Independence, the French Revolution, the Russian Revolution, the defeat of the Axis powers in 1945, and the fall of the Berlin Wall, in these years of the dawning of a new century, we also face a series of unprecedented political challenges that require innovative and forward-looking political thought, but also a rethinking of the key figures and concepts in our political canon. Globalization has become the shibboleth that points in the direction of these challenges. Unfortunately, at the same time, this term has become an excuse to glide over the immensity of the challenges, and has thus in turn become a crystallization of ideology. It is for this reason that many thinkers have reacted viscerally to the term, dismissing it as useless, as a mere gimmick. These thinkers see this term as the latest version of colonization, neocolonization, modernization, and the expansion of Western financial markets. Others have attempted to circumvent its coopting by reinscribing it within a different etymology, like mundalization or planetarization.

There is a third group of thinkers that have neither dismissed it nor attempted to refunction the term in a different grammar. This group, instead, can be said to have been thinking about the processes, forces, institutions, concepts, and challenges that are associated with globalization for at least the last three decades. This group has been thinking about this phenomenon we call globalization, although naming it differently, and thinking it from and through different categories. In fact, this has been one of their main contributions, namely to call for a rethinking of the fundamental concepts of political and social thought. This group, for instance, has been talking about the obsolescence of the classical nation-state; the planetary reach of the ecological crisis, which is just a general name for the demographic explosion of humanity and the concomitant problems this exponential growth means for the eco-systems on which all forms of life on our planet depend (erosion, deforestation, drying up of fresh-water sources, bioversity erosion, along with the introduction of genetically altered foods, more damaging herbicides, and the proliferation of luxury crops to feed the wealthy industrialized nations of the North); the need for a planetary ethic that supersedes the stalemate of Aristotelian communitarianisms and Kantian universalism; the need for supra-national mechanisms to legislate, arbitrate, and enforce global laws and human rights. Although some of these thinkers do not share the same political allegiances and beliefs, they can all be considered as members of this third group because of the consistency and acuity with which they have thought the thoroughness and immensity of the challenges globalization entails for humanity, and among them we might list: Karl-Otto Apel, Niklas Luhmann, Anthony Giddens, Immanuel Wallerstein, Benjamin Barber, Ulrich Beck, Daniel Bell, Zygmut Bauman, Jürgen Habermas, Vandana Shiva, and Enrique Dussel. It is against this background and in this company that Enrique Dussel's thought must be introduced and considered.

Enrique Dussel is unquestionably one of the most important Latin American philosophers of the last half a century. As one of the founders of the study of the history of the Latin American church, a prolific historian of religious ideas, and a philosopher of religion, he is well known to theologians in general and Latin Americanists in particular. He is perhaps less well known by philosophers, although his extensive *oeuvre* is beginning to receive the attention it deserves. His contributions to political theory are certainly scarcely known by political theorists and philosophers. Such unfamiliarity is understandable, since most of Dussel's work on political philosophy and theory has not been translated, and, as with most systematic thinkers, his observations on the political are nested within an expansive philosophical system that encompases ethics, history, theoretical philosophy, and so on. In the following, therefore, I will begin by giving a general overview of his thought and its evolution. In the last section, I will focus on the contribution to this volume and what it means for political thought in an age of planetarization.

Thinking From and About the "Third World"

Enrique Dussel was born in Argentina in 1934. After receiving his BA. in philosophy he traveled to Europe, where he proceeded to receive advanced degrees in philosophy, history, and theology. He studied in France and Germany, and lived in Israel for a year, earning his living as a day laborer.[1] He has lived in Mexico since 1975, when he arrived there as an exile from Argentina. An intellectual itinerary that spans half a century, several continents, and many national crises (or as he puts it, the crises of the small – Argentina – and large – Latin America – fatherlands), as well as global crises, cannot have failed to have undergone several and severe transformations. Dussel's thought has traversed at least six stages, all of them determined by biographical factors: studies, travel abroad, return to the homeland, the discovery of Latin American political reality, and the challenges to philosophy, exile, and so on (Alcoff and Mendieta 2000). For the purposes of our analysis and presentation, however, I would like to suggest that there are three significant intellectual stages or periods in Enrique Dussel's thought. Each stage is characterized by a quest or philosophical project. In this sense, Dussel's work has been marked with a conceptual and philosophical restlessness, albeit tempered by an ethical pertinacity.

The first stage is circumscribed by the trajectory from ontology to metaphysics. This stage covers the earliest years of Dussel's philosophical production, the decade of the 1960s Dussel was trained in Europe, mostly in France and Germany. There he came under the influence of Ricoeur and Heidegger. Dussel's early work therefore was deeply influenced by hermeneutics and phenomenology. He related to them less as traditions and more as forms of philosophical analysis which he proceeded to deploy in the discovering and forging of a Latin American philosophical project. From Heidegger, Dussel derived the idea that all worldviews are manifestations of existential attitudes. In other words, ideas are not absolute and abstract categories, but rather they are coagulations of existential experience. Existence entails certain pre-understandings. We cannot comprehend the world without already having some pre-experience of it. Conversely, certain forms of existence, or forms of social relations to put it in the language of sociology, entail certain conceptual schemas, or ways of making sense of the world. Our way of being with others and in relationship to the world result in particular ways of viewing those persons and things we are in relation with. Concepts and worldview are extensions of a web of existential relations. Another way of putting this would be to say that mind and world, ideas and things, consciousness and its other, are not ontologically different, but are part of a continuum.

From Ricoeur, Dussel learned that this continuum is always a circle of meaning: interpreted meaning and interpreting meaning. Everything is a crystallization of acts of interpretation. If we approach culture oriented by these intuitions, then culture is to be treated like a geological sediment, accumulations of layers of meaning. With these two methods in hand, Dussel set out to discover and recover the symbolics of Latin American culture which would yield to his investigations the layers of meaning accumulated by centuries of a unique Latin American existential experience. Ontology, however, is totalizing, as is already intimated by the correspondences established by Heidegger's ontology: mind and world, consciousness and its other, I and Thou. In this ontological circle, the other of both myself and my consciousness (or self-consciousness) can only be but a shadow of the already same. The other is a prefigured in the same, the I, the self-enclosed hermeneutical world. There is no other, merely a refracted version of what an ontological horizon contains within itself.

In the late 1960s and 1970s, challenged by the pedagogical inappropriateness of the methods he had learned in Europe, and urged on by the revolutionary fervor in Latin

America, and by the rise of populism in Argentina in particular, Dussel came to realize that existentially, hermeneutically, and culturally, Latin America occupied a place in world history that could not be assimilated to the European models of development, or even explanation.[2] Biographically, the context was of political and cultural turmoil and ferment, as was the case for most world thinkers around the momentous years of the late 1960s and early 1970s. Philosophically, as Dussel undertook a massive philosophical work of ethics, *Towards an Ethics of Latin American Liberation* (*Para una ética de la liberación latinoamericana*, 1973), he discovered the work of the great Jewish thinker Emmanuel Levinas, in particular *Totality and Infinity* (1969). This work produced in Dussel a "subversive disorientation" (Dussel and Guillot 1975, 7) that challenged all of his understandings, in particular his Heideggerianism. The discovery of Levinas allowed Dussel to develop his own unique philosophical methodology, one which he considered more appropriate to the task of the recovery of a Latin American symbolics and hermeneutics. This method he calls the analectical method, sometimes also the anadialectical method (Dussel 1973a). Analectics, which comes from the Greek root *ano* (beyond), takes as its point of departure the unmitigated transcendence of the other. The other is never the mere shadow, faulty, incomplete image or realization of the same, the I, the one. The other is beyond the horizon of what is already experienced and comprehended. The method of the self-mirroring and self-projection of the same is dialectics, and it is this method that has ruled all of Western philosophy, at least since the pre-Socratics (Parmenides and Heraclitus). But dialectics is war, the war of the same and the I to affirm itself in and through the other, and to wrest from the other what makes the other inassimilable alterity. The horizon of comprehension and existence of the I is a totality. Dialectics is the production of the totality. The other is an exteriority that is irreducible to the totality of the self-same. As long as we subscribe to an ontological approach, the otherness of the other will remain inscrutable alterity. To open ourselves to the other requires that we destroy ontology and in its place institute a metaphysical approach, one which sets out from the fundamental principle that the truth of the world is always beyond what is never exhausted by the given. To put it formulaically, ontology is to dialectics as metaphysics is to analectics. The former is mobilized by exclusion and war, the latter by expectant openness and solidarity.

In Dussel's works from the 1970s, then, Western thought is seen as the succession of dialectically produced and maintained totalities, whose very constitution and preservation has been predicated on the exclusion of an abject alterity: a vilified, despised, exploited, annihilated other. Thus, the totality of the polis was predicated on the exclusion of women, slaves, and barbarians (those who did not speak Greek); the totality of Christendom was predicated on the exclusion of women, the infidel, the atheist, the heterodox; the totality of modern Europe was predicated on the exclusion of the other of civilization and culture, namely the Amerindian, the African, and Asian cultures. Every hermeneutical and existential, or *ontologological* (epitomized in Hegel, the high priest of self-referential totalities), totality is totalitarian, belligerent, and martial. And as long as we approach them dialectically, we will remain within the domain of their domination. To brake free of their coercion and subjugation, we must open ourselves to the other from the standpoint of the other. We must think, hear, see, feel, and taste the world from the standpoint of the other. This is the analectical moment. Thus, if dialectics is conditioned by magnanimity, analectics is conditioned by humility; if the one is conditioned by erotic love, the other by compassionate solidarity; if one is conditioned by quid pro quos, the other is conditioned by expectant solicitude; if one is about production and profit, the other is about service and gift. We approach the other in a reverent attitude, disposed to service and to empathic solidarity. The alternative is war, dispossession, occlusion, exclusion, and genocide. A philosophy that tries to think this alternative, from the standpoint of the alterity of the other, is a philosophy of liberation, and not just simply a radical hermeneutics or phenomenology. Philosophy at the service of liberation, and produced by the experience of liberation, of and about. It is this philosophy which Dussel has been working on since the late 1960s and early 1970s.[3]

Politics, looked at from a metaphysical point of view, and dealt with by the analectical methods, yields the insight that there is a politics of the totality, and a politics of the other.[4] The former is the politics of the status quo, of the established and ruling totality. This is a politics of fetishization and divinification, of enthronement and intolerant homogenization. In fact, ontological politics turns into the science of the smooth functioning of the machine of power that assimilates otherness to the self-same, and excludes the indissoluble alterity of the other. Politics becomes the craft of the production and concentration of power with the telos of the control of the other within and outside the totality.

A political totality divides into the master and its oppressed, as oppressed within that particular system, and the other of the totality, as political alterity. Every totality has its interior and exterior others. The politics of the other, then, is an anti-politics, a politics of delegitimation, of subversion and contestation. It is a politics that challenges the established hierarchies and legal verities that justify and legitimize enforced exclusions. The politics of the other, the anti-politics of alterity, proclaims the injustice and illegitimacy of the present system, not in the name of chaos or lawlessness, but in the name of a new legality, a new lawfulness, one which will be generalized, more universalized, where these two terms refer to the point of view of the abjected and excluded other. In Dussel's view, then, metaphysical politics, the politics of the other, the anti-politics of alterity, is energized and made dynamic by the struggles of the excluded, exploited, and disenfranchised. Its determining virtues are neither equality nor justice, but respect and solidarity. At the core of the politics of anti-politics is the fundamental insight that all power struggles are predicated on asymmetries, and what mobilizes us to shift the scales is not justice, which remains within the outlook of the totality which grants to similars the same, but respect and solidarity for him/her or it, whose interpellation remains incomprehensible lest we opt for utter gratuitous solidarity with they who clamor. The suffering of the other raises as a cry. This turns into an interpellation that challenges the verities and principles of the extant legal and political system. The more reticent a system is to the interpellation of its others, the more totalitarian, belligerent, and intolerant it turns. The intolerant homogenizing totalitarian totality is the ontological version of the annihilating terrorist state of the concentration camp, what Eugene Kogon called the *SS-Staat* (Kogon 1960). This dual view of politics will remain a constant in Dussel's thought.

The second stage in Dussel's philosophical itinerary is circumscribed by the trajectory from metaphysics to Marxism. This stage overlaps partially with Dussel's exile in

Mexico, which begins in 1975. Philosophically, Dussel is confronted with the challenge of the increasing importance of a historically specific analysis of the systematic exclusion, not just of a group within a nation (class and *pueblo*, for instance), but of an entire continent within a world totality, more specifically Western culture.[5] Evidently, such a historically specific analysis took Dussel to a critique of capitalism, which at that time was seen as the only cause of the increasing impoverishment of the Latin American people. This critique could only be executed with the tools of Marxism. At the same time, however, this Marxism had to be wrested away from the entrenched and already solidified dogmatism of the Eastern bloc nations.

Notwithstanding the shift from ontology to metaphysics we described above, Dussel had continued to read Marx as another functionary of the totality. As a child and follower of Hegel, Marx was a thinker of the totality and an executor of dialectics. During the middle 1970s Dussel began to revise his reading of Marx, but already skeptical of Western, and in particular European philosophical readings, he realized that traditional approaches are insufficient for the task of the appropriation of Marx in a Latin American context. In fact, he realized that he must read Marx himself, and this meant reading the manuscripts that were being made available, too slowly for Dussel's interest and agenda, as the complete works of Marx and Engels were being published by the Marx–Lenin Institutes in Berlin and Moscow. Dussel immerses himself in a reading of the four redactions of *Capital*, as well as other manuscripts produced by Marx towards the end of his life. Out of this archival work there emerged a three-volume commentary and analysis of the process and evolution of Marx's categories (see Dussel 1985, 1988, 1990a).[6]

Dussel's reading of Marx distinguishes itself by at least the following four unique aspects. First, Dussel's reading of Marx is based on an unparalleled and unprecedented knowledge of the trajectory of Marx's own intellectual development. Dussel not only read the recently published works, but also the preparatory notes, and different drafts Marx worked on as he began to elaborate his *Capital*, of which he only saw through print volume one. Second, insofar as Dussel has studied, exegeted, and reconstructed for us an immense unknown corpus of theoretical productivity, Dussel not only discovered a Marx that was relevant to the project of Latin American liberation; he also discovered a hitherto unknown Marx that has made it indispensable to begin a critical assessment of Marx's reception in the twentieth century. To this extent, Dussel may have discovered a Marx for the twenty-first century.

Third, Dussel's careful reconstruction of the emergence of certain key categories in the *Grundrisse* and *Capital*, lead Dussel to conclude that Marx in fact was not just a left Hegelian, but even a Schellingian. What this means is that in Dussel's reconstruction, the fundamental method of Marx was not dialectics, but what he called analectics. Dussel thinks that the core philosophical and methodological insight in Marx's work is that the fountain of value, that which is appropriate as surplus value, and which gives the commodity its ability to generate value that is accumulated in capital, is living labor (*lebendige Arbeit*). The capitalist system does not produce value. Value is extracted and appropriated from the living corporeality of the laborer. A commodity, then, is a coagulation, a crystallization, of living labor. In Dussel's view, such an analysis of the processes of commodity production and the accumulation of surplus value into capital correspond more to a late Schellingian metaphysical perspective than to a Hegelian

dialectical perspective. For the late Schelling, specifically the Schelling of the *Philosophie der Offenbarung* (*Philosophy of Revelation*) of 1841/2, the ground of the world is the mystery of God's wholly otherness. What is, is revelation of the mystery of God. In terms of philosophy, Being is posterior to the non-Being of the wholly other. Or, to put it in the terms of German idealism, the identity of the identical and the non-identical is replaced in Schelling by the non-identity of the identical and the non-identical. There is always a surplus beyond the identical. The other is always the epiphany of an unsupersedeable alterity. In Dussel's view, this reverence and acknowledgment of the life of the other, as the living labor of the worker, is what makes Marx's method not Hegelian, but Schellingian, and one may add, Levinasian. The Marx Dussel discovered is what we would call today, of course anachronistically but entirely suggestively and appropriately, a Levinasian Marx.

Fourth, and consequently, Dussel's Marx is not one who is correctly read through the Althusserian distinction between the young and the late Marx; where the former is a humanist and dialectical Marx, while the latter is a scientific and materialist Marx. Nor is Marx correctly understood when we try to dissociate him from Engels's dialectical materialism, and appropriately associate him with historical materialism. Instead, and here Dussel enunciates a challenge for the twenty-first century Marxists, Marx is to be read metaphysically, humanistically, and as a critic of Hegelian, Aristotelian, and Platonist totalities. Dussel thus calls us to dispense with the distorting reading of Marx executed by Western Marxism, as well as *diamat* (Soviet-sanctioned, and dogmatically thought in the socialist bloc, dialectical materialism). In Dussel view, the really humanist Marx is he whom we encounter in *Capital*, where we are confronted not with a science of economics, but a critique of the political economy which produces the system for the expropriation of the life of the laborer. *Capital* is less a scientific treatise and more an ethics. A nice parallel would be to say that *Capital* is not like Hegel's *Logic*, but more like Levinas's *Totality and Infinity*, which at root is a fundamental ethics, a meta-ethics. The first philosophy, *prima philosophia*, of all philosophical speculation, in Levinas's view – and here Dussel concurs unequivocally – is ethics. In this sense, for Dussel, *Capital* is a *prima philosophia* which describes an ethics. In summary, Dussel discovers an ethical Marx who has been betrayed and eclipsed by decades of the ontologizing and Hegelinizing of his fundamental option for the creativity of the living corporeality of the worker.

The metaphysically criticized totalities of the first stage of Dussel's thought turned into the Marxistically unmasked systems of exploitation. History is not just a succession of ontological totalities; it is also a succession of systems of the exploitation, expropriation, and extraction of value from the living labor of workers. This exploitation and expropriation has taken place at regional, national, and continental levels. It is in this way that totality and transcendentality (the alterity of the other) are translated in Dussel's Schellingian Marx into the categories of center and periphery. Of course, such a reinscription takes place against the background of the concepts developed by dependency and underdevelopment theory (Frank 1970). In the 1970s and early 1980s the central question for Dussel became the *development of underdevelopment* on a global level. During this period Dussel's analysis of politics turns more economicist, in the sense that his books and essays are now suffused by careful studies of the flow of capital (i.e., accumulated value) from one continent to another (from Latin America to Europe, and from Latin America to the United States). From this perspective, then, the analysis of politics turns into the critique not just of political totalities, but most specifically into the critique of the political economies of imperial systems of the transfer of life coagulated into commodities from a sphere or region of production to a region or sphere of consumption. Here, Dussel's critique of the imperial political economy of world-systems converges with those critiques developed by Immanuel Wallerstein (1979) and Samir Amin (1974). During this second stage, Dussel adds to his analysis of anti-political politics the planetary and global perspective he assimilated from a Marxism read and discovered from a third-world perspective. In Dussel's view, whoever would like to speak of poverty and destitution, topics which are uncircumventable in the age of mass culture, world wars, and continental famines, must speak of global capitalism, imperialisms, and world accumulation of wealth for a minority and impoverishing expropriation of a majority. A nationalistic approach, an approach that only looks at most at regions within continents, and one which focuses only on the capitalist accumulation of certain "industrialized" Western nations, contributes only to the distortion of the global nature of the capitalist system of production and accumulation of wealth. In short, during his second stage the critique of Western philosophy as ontology has turned into a critique of the political and economic theories that misconstrued and contributed to the occlusion of the system of massive and global inequity.

The third stage of Dussel's philosophical development is traced by the trajectory from Marxism to discourse. Biographically, this stage overlaps, more or less, with the fall of the Berlin Wall, the voting out of office of the Sandinistas in 1991, and the splitting apart of the Soviet Union. This stage could be said to begin in 1989, when Enrique Dussel began a decade-long debate with Karl-Otto Apel, the founding father of discourse ethics.[7] Just as the first stage was summarized in his five-volume *Latin American Philosophical Ethics* (1973a, 1979a, 1980), and the second in his three-volume reconstruction and commentary on Marx's redactions of *Capital* (1985b, 1988, 1990a), this third stage is summarized in the monumental *Ética de la Liberación en la edad de globalización y de la exclusión* (*Ethics of Liberation in the Age of Globalization and Exclusion*) from 1998.[8] In this work Dussel sets out to reformulate the foundations of a planetary ethics of liberation of the oppressed and excluded, but now combining his particular brand of Levinasian and Ricoeurian phenomenology and hermeneutics with Apelian and Habermasian discourse ethics. Much of the preliminary work for the *Ethics of Liberation* has fortunately appeared in English under the title of *The Underside of Modernity* (Dussel 1996). In this collection of essays, as well as in the *Ethics* of 1998, Dussel confronts the challenges of the linguistic turn, and in particular the challenge of how to ground a universalist ethics in the face of the dismantling and critique of monological and logocentric philosophy of consciousness. While Dussel proceeds to offer a third way between abstract and universalist, but now dialogically reconstituted Kantianism, and particularist and historicist Hegelianism, with already dialogically constituted agents, in debate with Rorty, Taylor, Ricoeur, Vattimo, it is clear that the central dialogue partners are Apel and Habermas.

At the center of the debates, summarily put, are three questions: first, whether the community of communication (*kommunikationsgemeinschaft*), which acts as the *a priori* condition of possibility of all discourse (or that acts as a counterfactual idealization that is both precondition and telos of all communication, in Habermas's less strict formulation), is either prior or posterior to a community of life (*comunidad de vida*). In Dussel's terms, before discourse, there must be life (*bios*), in the sense that people must at the very least have secured the conditions for their survival and preservation. If these conditions are not met, then discourse, as conceived by both Apel and Habermas, becomes either an empty idealization, at best, or a way to conceal the factual lack of the conditions for true discourse (in which the only coercion is the non-coercion of the better argument, and in which the primary goal is agreement, and not deception or determination by fiat), at worst.

Second, whether we can dichotomize in practice what both Apel and Habermas had distinguished as discourses of justification (or grounding), and discourses of application. Discourses of justification attend to the theoretical dimension of ethical questions, namely whether we can offer rational and universal warrants that are not vitiated by their historical and local contexts of discovery. Discourses of application attend to the circumstantial, historicized, contextual, and very singular application of principles. Dussel thinks that this disjunction contributes to the misrepresentation of the very practical character of ethical questions; that is, that ethical questions emerge from very specific contexts and that universal principles are generalizations of concrete problems. More concretely, Dussel thinks the generalized principles of an ethics already anticipate their contexts of application; and vice versa, specific contexts of moral consideration become visible as such precisely because of a certain ethical outlook.

A third bone of contention is the degree to which any ethics should refer its affirmations to neurobiology or, philosophically articulated, to the fact that ethical entities are biological organisms with needs, desires, and neurological systems that filter the world and process it into ideas and perceptions. As Kantians, neither Apel nor Habermas are prepared to accept the empirical evidence or insights offered by neuro-biology in their moral philosophies, despite Habermas's call for a deflationary philoso-phy that works in close cooperation with the fallible sciences (Habermas 1984–7, 1987, 1990, 1992a,b). Dussel, instead, thinks that such extreme Kantianism leads to the erasure of the body or sentient corporeality. Most importantly, such intellectual rigorism and asceticism lead to the foreshortening of the ethical outlook. In other words, the exclusion of the body, as orienting being-in-the-world corporeality, leads to the misrepresentation of not just the source of ethics, but also its goals.

A brief discussion of the *Ethics of Liberation* of 1998 will make clear how Dussel has substantively replaced the philosophical infrastructure of his ethics, while retaining its fundamental concern and motivating telos: the oppression, exclusion, and genocide of the poor, destitute, suffering, vulnerable living corporeality of the victim.[9] After a lengthy introduction, which is a monograph on its own, that traces the history of world ethical systems, the book is divided into two major parts. The first deals with what Dussel calls foundational ethics. The second deals with critical ethics. Each part is divided into three chapters, each dealing with a major foundational aspect of ethics: the material moment, the formal moment, and the feasibility moment of ethics. The first chapter of the first part deals with the material or "content" moment of ethics. For Dussel, ethical questions have to do with our being in the world, not just in the Heideggerian sense of being interpreting entities whose world is always already inter-preted, but also in the sense that we are in the world by virtue of our needs and desires. All ethics deals with specific choices, and the principles that guide them, and these choices are "about" things and persons in the world. The second chapter of the first part deals with formal moralities, that is, with the question, or demand for, intersubjective validity. Validity remits us to the legitimation and application of the material principle. The next chapter deals with what Dussel calls the "good (*das Gute*)," or what he also calls *ethical feasibility*. From these considerations, three principles emerge: the practical principle of the preservation of life, the formal principle of the discursive legitimation of norms and principles, and the goodness, or feasibility, principle.

The second part of the *Ética de la liberación* develops the critical principles of his ethics of liberation in a negative vein; that is, if the foundational ethics, discussed in the first part, concerns the positive formulation of the principles that guide ethical action, critical ethics concerns the formulation of the critical principles that guide all ethical critique. Thus, chapter four, which is the first chapter of the second part, deals with the ethical critique of the ruling systems. This chapter concludes with the enunciation of the critical–material principle of ethics that commands that the affirmation of life calls for the critique of all systems in which the corporeality and dignity of the other is negated. All ethical critique emerges from the recognition of the suffering of the other. This suffering, however, is always material and bodily. The condition of possibility of all critique is the *recognition* of the dignity of the other subject, the co-subject, but from the perspective of their being seen and experienced above all as *human living beings*. The next chapter covers the anti-hegemonic validity of the community of victims. In this chapter Dussel deals with the problem that the ethical critique of the victims of any system always appears illegitimate from the standpoint of that system. To that extent, their critique turns into a delegitimizing critique of the legitimacy of the status quo. This chapter closes with the enunciation of the critical–discursive principle that commands that who *acts* ethically must participate in a community of victims, who having been excluded, recognized themselves as such, and thus issue a critique of the system. The closing chapter develops what Dussel has christened the "liberation principle." All ethics worth that name must culminate in the imperative to liberate all victims from the system that turns them into victims. Evidently, the question arises: how, under what conditions, and by what means is this liberation to be pursued and achieved? This chapter, in parallel with the preceding chapters, concludes with the elaboration of the "liberation principle," which commands that who *acts* critically–ethically *ought* to, or is compelled to pursue, a feasible and performable *transformation* of the present system that is the cause of the suffering of the victims, while also being compelled to pursue the *construction* of a new order in which the life of the victim will be made possible.

From this overview it becomes clear that Dussel has not simply fused his early ethics with the discourse ethics of Apel and Habermas. Instead, what we find is a very detailed, elaborate, comprehensive, and innovative discussion of ethics that synthesizes while superseding both teleological and deontological ethics. Most importantly, it is quite clear that for Dussel, politics is not extrinsic or foreign to ethics. Instead, politics becomes the horizon for the realization of the ethical. Dussel in fact has already announced (see Dussel 1997) that the ethics of liberation has as its logical and conceptual complement a politics of liberation, which like the ethics must proceed by way of the positive enunciation of certain principles, but also by way of the critique of political reason.

Critique of Political Reason

As we noted above, Enrique Dussel's philosophy is a philosophy of liberation that seeks to contribute to the actual liberation of victims and the oppressed by elucidating and unmasking the sources of that oppression. It is not because of hubris, or over-valorization of the philosophical disciplines, but precisely because every social science is informed by a series of acknowledged and unacknowledged preconceptions, which are at core philosophical ideas, that Dussel thinks that all projects of liberation must begin with a liberation of philosophy. In an unmistakable hermeneuticist attitude, social practices are seen as crystallizations of conceptual schemes, and vice versa. Social life is suffused by ideas, concepts, conceptual schemes, sometimes ossified into unchange-able verities and sacred truths. Liberation philosophy struggles against the tendency of both the social world and philosophy itself to conceal their interdependence (Dussel 1985a).[10] In this way, a liberation of philosophy must begin with a critique of most of its mystifications and divinification. A philosophy of liberation is a critique of philosophical fetishizations. And one of the areas Dussel has paid closest attention to is the fetishiza-tion of the inevitability and intractability of political systems of oppression (ibid).

In the 1970s one of the major targets of Dussel's anti-fetishistic critique, at the political level, was the myth of modernity and modernization.[11] Dussel demonstrated how the ideology of imposing on so-called third-world countries the expectation that they would overcome their poverty once they adopted the political and economic systems of the industrialized West, was in fact a way to mask the production of the underdevelopment of the underdeveloped. Dussel christened this ideology the devel-opmentalist fallacy (Dussel 1996), by which he meant to point out that it is a fallacy to suppose that underdeveloped countries are merely poor because they have failed to attain the stages of development of advanced northern countries. Instead, their condi-tion is dialectically related to the wealth and development of what is offered as the normative model. So, it is the case (and Dussel points this out) that we must both critique the myth of historical progress, if by this we mean the purported ascent through stages of development already traversed by the Western world, and critique the myth of the autonomy of nations. We cannot understand the success of the West by looking at internal and allegedly autochthonous factors, à la Hegel, Weber, and Habermas (Dussel 1992).

Another fundamental fallacy that Dussel has sought to unmask is what he calls (in the contribution to the present volume) the reductivist and formalist fallacy. By naming this fallacy, Dussel seeks to make explicit how most of the dominant political theory of the last five hundred years has been ruled by two overriding mystifications: first, that the political can only concern that which is not individual, material, or related to the corporeal survival of human beings; and second, that politics can only concern the arbitration of abstractly construed formal principles. If one aspect of the fallacy seeks to exclude the economic dimensions of human life from political deliberation, the other seeks to exclude questions of material and substantive values from the formulations of political principles. In Dussel's view, these ruling fallacies have turned politics not into the art of living in community, but into the science of control that reduces political agents to automatons, or mere numbers in a complex calculus of maximization or minimization of power accumulation. The scientization of politics, executed in tandem with the scientization of economics and sociology, has contributed to the denudation of all the social sciences of their practical and ethical aspects. All the social sciences, and in particular political science, have become disciplines of daily coercion, the regimentation of potentially subversive agents into docile and depoliticized consumers and agents of the state.[12] And this coercion and concomitant depoliticization becomes the more subtle and insidious the more the systems that enact it are baptized by the scientific social sciences as natural, logical, inevitable, or systematically autopoetic (à la Luhmann). It is for this reason that Dussel thinks that it is imperative that we abandon the already tired and sterile debate between communitarians and liberals. In the same vein, Dussel also admonishes us to relativize, or provincialize, the Western focus on rights and the state. Not because these are not fundamental to any viable political theory, but because the way they are debated in most of the contemporary political philosophy literature, broaches them from a series of unacceptable generalizations that are applicable to the West, and even within the West they are to be seen as wild generalizations.

Following the structure of his *Ethics of Liberation* (1998), Dussel has divided his contribution to this volume in two sections: fundamental and critical politics. The former deals positively with the principles that should guide all political reflection. The latter deals with the principles that motivate all political critique. However, and in contrast to his ethics, instead of deriving a series of principles, he proceeds by way of theses. The text is made up of six theses, and two corollaries. A note of clarification is in order. When Dussel refers to "fundamental politics" he has in mind both the Kantian sense of grounding, and the Aristotelian–Heideggerian sense of foundational, as in foundation and fountain (from whence something flows and grows out of). This means that Dussel is interested in grounding something in the rationalist sense of elucidating the principles without which political reason would be unthinkable and impossible, and the hermeneutical and metaphysical sense of providing an insight into the whence, the where-from, of our interest in the political. "Fundamental," therefore, should not be at all construed in the dogmatic or scholastic sense, in which we have a set of natural laws and principles which are unassailable and beyond criticism. It is imperative that this dual sense of Dussel's be kept in mind, lest we misinterpret him as another hubristic philosopher-king (in the tradition of Plato, Aquinas, Hobbes, Heidegger, and recently Rawls).[13]

The first thesis of Dussel's critique of political reason is that all political rationality is both practical and material. This means that politics is first and foremost a form of practical rationality, that is, a form of *prudentia* or *phronesis* that has to do with the reproduction of the life of individuals in contexts of community and mutual cooperation. Politics is uncircumventable for humans, for they are creatures of community (in the fashionable language of contemporary philosophy, humans are a dialogic species). Furthermore, their dialogicity, or linguistically constituted intersubjectivety, is practically oriented towards the production, reproduction, and development of human life. Political reason, *ratio politica*, is eminently practical, and precisely for that reason universal. But precisely because humans are dialogic creatures, their interactions must be discursively mediated. Hence the second thesis: political reason must proceed by way of discursive and legitimate procedures that neither mystify the rule of the majority nor sacrifice the autonomy of the political agent. Discursive legitimation, and democratically achieved validity, in which each political subject is both materially and formally a participant, do not exclude dissent, but rather incorporate it procedurally. But what kinds of projects are acceptable and feasible depends on the careful consideration of options, and a scrutiny of the means available for their realization. The third thesis, then, deals with the instrumental or strategic aspect of political rationality. It is this instrumental and even strategic rational aspect of political rationality that allows it to become a politics of the real and feasible, and not a politics of utopia, or atopia. In this way, a critique of political reason is also a critique of utopian reason, as Dussel already made explicit in his 1998 *Ethics* (partly inspired by Franz Hinkelammert 1990). A political reason that is too far beyond the horizon of the possible, and too close this side of the incipient, becomes either a politics of the unreal or a politics of the *modus vivendi*. The synthesis of the above three theses gives us the first corollary. Only those norms, laws, and institutions that have been guided in their execution by a political reason that is material and practical, although also universal; has been dialogically and democratically legitimated and validated; and has looked at the real possibilities of the actualization of these norms, laws, and institutions, can make a claim to political justice. If one of these conditions is exempted or excluded, we have a faulty politics, a politics of power, and coercion, of the powerful and the autocrats, a politics of utopia which quickly turns into a totalitarian politics. How is political reason mindful of its own faults? How does it monitor its own penchant to consecrate the present as the most perfect system of political organization? For politics to live closest to its own ideals it must turn into critical political reason. And it does so by turning critical from a particular perspective, guided by a particular series of concerns, advocating a specific agenda.

The second part of Dussel's critique of political reason develops the structure of a critical politics, what in the language of Dussel's earlier philosophical stage was called anti-politics. The fourth thesis, or first of critical politics, hypothesizes that when political reason takes charge of the negative effects of any norm, law, or system, then political reason turns into critical political reason. For this reason it now seeks not the legitimation of the existing system, but its de-legitimation, precisely because it is faulty and the cause of negative and adverse consequences. All systems have their victims, true. But this realization neither exempts any system, nor makes victimization acceptable. Instead, it renders political rationality realistic, in the sense that its realism makes it suspicious of the perfection of any norm, law, or system that claims such honor for itself. Consequently, thesis five: all systems have their own victims, and these victims owe their existence to heterogeneous factors. The interests of these diverse victims must be considered in the restructuring of the system. Critical political reason is discursively critical political reason, meaning, the claims of the excluded and victimized are brought to the fore and become the point of departure for future legislation or norm development. The guide is offered not by the best well off within a system, but rather by the worst off within that very system.[14]

All critical political reason has only one telos: *liberación* (liberation). Critical political reason, which is at core a critique of the establish political system, aims at a transformation of oppressive practices, be they institutional or existential (not that they can in practice be separated). But the transformation of the existing ruling and oppressive system, undertaken with the interest of the most disadvantaged of that system, must be guided by a politics of a realizable utopianism. Hence thesis six: mere critique is insufficient. This must be accompanied by the development of strategies and movements that aim at the heart of the oppressive present. In this way, critical political reason which is guided by the telos of liberation turns into a transformative politics, a politics of liberation. An anti-politics of the status quo, turns into the politics of liberation of the future system. But only, in Dussel's formulation, a politics which has been guided by the insights offered by the above six theses, as a synthesis of the positive and negative moments of political rationality, can claim to be a just critical political reason of liberation. Political justice, in other words, is the obverse side of political liberation. Both are unified in a politics of transformation which is always provisional and fallible. For every system produces its victims. In Dussel's view, however, political reason, and consequently political philosophy, must look at the world of the political not through the lens of the system, but of the victim. The more victims a system produces, and the more blind and deaf that system is to their suffering and interpellation, the more unjust, illegitimate that system becomes. Politics is the practical craft, a *phronesis*, of living together. If there are victims, politics has turned into a technology of genocide. This is why true politics must be always accompanied by a critical political philosophy that from the outset looks at the world through the eyes of the suffering and vulnerable materiality of the most dispossessed and exploited of the world. For this reason, Dussel thinks that the only viable politics for an age of unprecedented interdependence but simultaneous massive exclusion from the sharing of the most elemental goods necessary for a humane life (water, food, education) is a transformative politics that aims at liberation from the side of the least of the world.[15] In an age of globalization, our political solutions will not come from those who seek to include, but those who have been excluded. They understand best how our political systems have turned into machines of destitution and impoverishment. Despite all the changes and philosophical transformations, Dussel has remained obstinate in this principle: all truly liberating thinking must set out from the misery of the poor, the anguish of the destitute, the pain of the victim.

Notes

1   For biographical details see the autobiographical essay by Enrique Dussel (1998b), and the introduction to Alcoff and Mendieta (2000).
2   See in particular the essays gathered in Dussel (1974b). As Dussel notes repeatedly throughout his magisterial five-volume ethics (Dussel 1973a, 1979, 1980), the challenge was not only the inappropriateness of the methods, which not only neglected but contributed to the exclusion of Latin American, or for that matter all non-Western thought traditions, but also the lack of sources and materials. For this reason, Dussel's volumes on ethics contained lengthy reconstructions of what he calls Latin American pedagogics, erotics, politics, and archeology, each one dealing with a separate moment of the analectics. So, erotics deals with the analectical relation between men and women; pedagogic, with the analectical relationship between parent and child; politics with the analectical relationships brother to brother; and archeology with the analectical relationships between cultures and worlds of meaning that have met and clashed in the so-called New World.
3   For a discussion of the philosophy of liberation see Cerutti (1983) and Schelkshorn (1992). Liberation philosophy is a heterogeneous current with figures as different as Bondy and Zea, and Scannone and Cerutti himself.

4   For the following, see in particular volume 4 of Dussel's *Filosofía ética latinoamericana* (*Latin American Philosophical Ethics*) (1979), as well as Dussel (1979b, 1985a).

5   In the context of this introductory essay I will not address the unsubstantiated and misleading criticisms that impute to Dussel's thinking an uncritical and slovenly nationalism and populism. It would take too long to demonstrate that Dussel's references to the nation, pueblo, class, are overdetermined by contexts of relations *vis-à-vis* their hegemonic others. Thus, for instance, when Dussel refers to the symbolics of Latin American peoples (pueblos), which needs to be rescued and studied, he does so in light of the dominant national bourgeoisie's, whose orientation was towards Europe, and whose ethos was industrial and military modernization. At the same time, however, Dussel realizes that a pueblo is neither homogeneous nor historically stable. A people, as a people, also alterizes, others, its others: women, indigenous populations, other ethnicities, etc. It is truly unfortunate how the readings and commentaries of certain scholars can totally de-rail the reception of a thinker, and this has been the sorry case of Enrique Dussel's so-called populism and fideism. For a discussion of some of these criticisms, see Linda Martín Alcoff's wonderful essay on Dussel and Foucault in Alcoff and Mendieta (2000); see also Barber (1998).

6   For an analysis of Dussel's Marx, see Mendieta (1994), and Mario Sáenz in Alcoff and Mendieta (2000). For a summary of the main arguments in Dussel's own words see Dussel (1990b).

7   The earliest, and already fairly substantive, formulations of the principles and structure of discourse ethics can be found in Apel (1973) (partly translated in 1980) and (1988).

8   See Mendieta (1999) for an extended review of this work. A translation of this extremely important work is being prepared by Duke University Press.

9   For a summary of the *Ethics of Liberation*, see Dussel (1997).

10 For a fruitful and insightful comparison, see Bourdieu (2000), who among contemporary thinkers is the closest to Dussel's philosophical interests and inclinations.

11 See in particular Dussel (1994b).

12 As Dussel untiringly notes, what we call political science used to be called political philosophy, which in turn was another name for practical philosophy, or ethics. Politics, like economics, jurisprudence, aesthetics, and of course ethical philosophy, are the practical part of philosophy.

13 Compare also with Bourdieu (2000).

14 Notwithstanding Dussel's criticisms of Rawls in the present text, as well as in the *Ethics* of 1998, I think that Rawls Maximin principle is in accordance with this thesis. Freedom and participation in civil rights should be maximized as the adverse effects of all distributions of social goods are minimized for those most affected in the population. See Rawls (1971).

15 At the time of writing this essay, Dussel himself is writing what he has tentatively entitled *A Critique of Political Will and Reason*, which will be his Harvard Lectures for the years 2000–1. In fact, the essay included in this volume is a preliminary sketch of these lectures. The original text of the essay was twice its present size, but was edited for a book from which it was eventually excluded due to editorial pressures from the publisher.

References

Alcoff, Linda Martín and Mendieta, Eduardo, eds. 2000. *Thinking from the Underside of History: Enrique Dussel's Philosophy of Liberation*. Lanham, MD: Rowman & Littlefield.

Amin, Samir. 1974. *Accumulation on a World Scale: A Critique of the Theory of Underdevelopment*. New York: Monthly Review Press.

Amin, Samir. 1989. *Eurocentrism*. New York: Monthly Review Press.

Apel, Karl-Otto. 1963. *Die Idee der Sprache in der Tradition des Humanismus von Dante bis Vico.* Bonn: Bouvier.

Apel, Karl-Otto. 1973. *Transformation der Philosophie,* 2 vol. Frankfurt: Suhrkamp.

Apel, Karl-Otto. 1980. *Towards a Transformation of Philosophy,* trans. Glyn Adey and David Frisby. London: Routledge and Kegan Paul.

Apel, Karl-Otto. 1984. *Understanding and Explanation: A Transcendental–Pragmatic Perspective,* trans. Georgia Warnke. Cambridge, MA: MIT Press.

Apel, Karl-Otto. 1988. *Diskurs und Verantwortung. Das Problem des Übergangs zur postkonventionellen Moral.* Frankfurt: Suhrkamp.

Apel, Karl-Otto. 1994a. "Rationalitätskriterien und Rationalitätstheorien" in G. Meggle and A. Wüstehube, eds., *Pragmatische Rationalitätstheorien.* Berlin: de Gruyter.

Apel, Karl-Otto. 1994b. *Towards a Transcendental Semiotics: Selected Essays, Volume 1.* Atlantic Highlands, NJ: Humanities Press.

Apel, Karl-Otto. 1996. *Ethics and the Theory of Rationality: Selected Essays, Volume 2.* Atlantic Highlands, NJ: Humanities Press.

Apel, Karl-Otto, Adela Cortina, et. al., eds. 1991. *Ética comunicativa y Demócracia.* Barcelona: Editorial Critica.

Apel, Karl-Otto and Matthias Kettner, eds. 1992. *Zur Anwendung der Diskursethik in Politik, Recht und Wissenchaft.* Frankfurt: Suhrkamp.

Apel, Karl-Otto, Enrique Dussel, and Raúl Fornet-Betancourt, eds. 1992. *Fundamentación de la ética y filosofía de la liberación.* Mexico: Siglo XXI.

Barber, Michael D. 1998. *Ethical Hermeneutics: Rationalism in Enrique Dussel's Philosophy of Liberation.* New York: Fordham University Press.

Bondy, Augusto Salazar. 1968. *Existe una filosofía en nuestra América?* Mexico: Siglo XXI.

Bourdieu, Pierre. 2000. *Pascalian Meditations.* Stanford, NJ: Stanford University Press.

Cerutti, Horacio. 1983. *Filosofía de la liberación latinoamericana.* Mexico: FCE.

Dussel, Enrique. 1969. *El humanismo Semita.* Buenos Aires: EUDEBA.

Dussel, Enrique. 1972. *Para una de-strucción de la historia de la ética.* Mendoza: Ser y tiempo.

Dussel, Enrique. 1973a. *Para una ética de la liberación latinoamericana,* 5 vols. Buenos Aires: Siglos XXI.

Dussel, Enrique, ed. 1973b. *Hacia una Filosofía de la Liberación.* Buenos Aires: Bonum.

Dussel, Enrique. 1974a. *El dualismo de la antroplogía de la christiandad.* Buenos Aires: Guadalupe.

Dussel, Enrique. 1974b. *América latina, dependencia y liberación.* Buenos Aires: García Cambeiro.

Dussel, Enrique. 1975. *El humanismo helénico.* Buenos Aires: EUDEBA.

Dussel, Enrique. 1976. *Método para una Filosofía de la Liberación. Superación analéctica de la dialéctica hegeliana.* Sígueme: Salamanca.

Dussel, Enrique. 1977. *Filosofía ética latinoamericana,* vol. 3. México: Edicol.

Dussel, Enrique. 1979a. *Filosofía ética latinoamericana,* vol. 4. Bogotá: USTA.

Dussel, Enrique. 1979b. *Introducción a la filosofía de la liberación.* Bogotá: Editorial nueva américa.

Dussel, Enrique. 1980. *Filosofía ética latinoamericana,* vol. 5. Bogotá: USTA.

Dussel, Enrique. 1983a. *Praxis latinomaericana y filosofía de la Liberación.* Bogotá: Editorial nueva américa.

Dussel, Enrique. 1983b. *Filosofía de la producción.* Bogotá: Editorial nueva américa.

Dussel, Enrique. 1985a. *Philosophy of Liberation,* trans. Aquila Martinez and Christine Morkovsky. Maryknoll, NY: Orbis Books.

Dussel, Enrique. 1985b. *La producción teórica de Marx. Un comentario de los Grundrisse.* Mexico: Siglo XXI.

Dussel, Enrique. 1988. *Hacia un Marx desconcido. Un comentario a los Manuscritos del 61–63.* Mexico: Siglo XXI.

Dussel, Enrique. 1990a. *El último Marx (1863–1882) y la liberación latinoamericana*. Mexico: Siglo XXI.

Dussel, Enrique. 1990b. "Marx's Economic Manuscripts of 1861–63 and the 'Concept' of Dependency," *Latin American Perspectives*. 17, 2 (1990): 61–101.

Dussel, Enrique. 1992. *1492. El encubrimiento del otro. Hacia el origen del mito de la modernidad*. Madrid: Ed. nueva utopía.

Dussel, Enrique. 1993. *Las metáforas teológicas de Marx*. Navarra: Editorial Verbo Divino.

Dussel, Enrique. 1994a. *Historia de la Filosofía y Filosofía de la Liberación*. Bogotá: Editorial nueva américa.

Dussel, Enrique. 1994b. "The 'World-system': Europe as 'Center' and Its 'Periphery.' Beyond Eurocentrism." Lecture presented at the Seminar on Globalization, Duke University, November 1994. Edited version appeared in Fredric Jameson and Masao Miyoshi, eds., *Cultures of Globalization* (Durham, NC: Duke University Press, 1998), pp. 3–31.

Dussel, Enrique. 1996. *The Underside of Modernity: Apel, Ricoeur, Rorty, Taylor and the Philosophy of Liberation*. Atlantic Highlands, NJ: Humanities Press.

Dussel, Enrique. 1997. "Principles, Mediations and the 'Good' as Synthesis (From 'Discourse Ethics' to 'Ethics of Liberation')." *Philosophy Today*, vol. 41, supplement 1997: 55–66.

Dussel, Enrique. 1998a. *Ética de la Liberación en la edad de globalización y de la exclusión*. Madrid: Editorial Trotta.

Dussel, Enrique. 1998b. "Autopercepción intelectual de un proceso histórico," *Revista Anthropos*, no. 180 (Sept.–Oct.): 13–36.

Dussel, Enrique and Guillot, Dannel E. 1975. *Liberación y Emmanuel Levinas*. Buenos Aires: Editorial Bonum.

Fornert-Betancourt, Raúl, ed. 1990. *Ethik und Befreiung*. Aachen: Augustinus Buchhandlung.

Fornet-Betancourt, Raúl, ed. 1992. *Diskursethik oder Befreiungsthik?* Aachen: Augustinus Buchhandlung.

Frank, Ander Gunder. 1970. *Latin America: Underdevelopment or Revolution*. New York: Monthly Review Press.

Gadamer, Hans-Georg. 1993. *Truth and Method*, 2nd. rev. edn., trans. Joel Weinsheimer and Donald G. Marschall. New York: Continuum.

Goizueta, Roberto S. 1987. *Liberation, Method and Dialogue: Enrique Dussel and North American Theological Discourse*. Atlanta, GA: Scholars Press.

Habermas, Jürgen. 1984. *Vorstudien und Ergänzungen zur Theorie des kommunuitakiven Handelns*. Frankfurt: Suhrkamp.

Habermas, Jürgen. 1984–7. *The Theory of Communicative Action*, 2 vols., trans. Thomas McCarthy. Boston: Beacon Press.

Habermas, Jürgen. 1987. *The Philosophical Discourse of Modernity: Twelve Lectures*, trans. Frederick G. Lawrence. Cambridge, MA: MIT Press.

Habermas, Jürgen. 1990. *Moral Consciousness and Communicative Action*, trans. Christian Lenhardt and Shierry Weber Nicholsen. Cambridge, MA: MIT Press.

Habermas, Jürgen. 1992a. *Faktizität und Geltung*. Frankfurt: Suhrkamp.

Habermas, Jürgen. 1992b. *Postmetaphysical Thinking: Philosophical Essays*, trans. William Mark Hohengarten. Cambridge, MA: MIT Press.

Hinkelammert, Franz. 1990 [1984]. *Crítica de la razón utópica*. San José, Costa Rica: DEI.

Kogon, Eugene. 1960. *The Theory and Practice of Hell: The German Concentration Camps and the System Behind Them*. New York: Berkeley Publishing.

Levinas, Emmanuel. 1969. *Totality and Infinity: An Essay on Exteriority*, trans. Alphonso Lingis. Pittsburgh: Duquesne University Press.

Luhmann, Niklas. 1988. *Soziale Systeme*. Frankfurt: Suhrkamp.

Luhmann, Niklas. 1990. *Die Wissenchaft der Gesellschaft*. Frankfurt: Suhrkamp.

Marx, Karl. 1990 [1976]. *Capital*, vol. 1, trans. Ben Fowkes. New York: Penguin Books.

Marx, Karl. 1992 [1974]. *Early Writings*, trans. Rodney Livingstone and Gregor Benton. New York: Penguin Books.

Marx, Karl. 1993 [1973]. *Grundrisse*, trans. Martin Nicolaus. New York: Penguin Books.

Mendieta, Eduardo. 1994. "Marxism in a Post-Communist and Post-Colonial World: Four Thinkers of the boundary – Rosdolsky, Robinson, Dussel and West," *APA Newsletter on Philosophy and the Black Experience*, 93: 1, spring: 6–13.

Mendieta, Eduardo. 1995. "Discourse Ethics and Liberation Ethics: At the Boundaries of Moral Theory," *Philosophy and Social Criticism*, 21, 4: 111–26.

Mendieta, Eduardo. 1999. "Ethics for an Age of Globalization and Exclusion," *Philosophy and Social Criticism*, 25, 2: 115–21.

Rawls, John. 1971. *Theory of Justice*. Oxford: Clarendon Press.

Ricoeur, Paul. 1965. *History and Truth*, trans. Charles A. Kelbley. Evanston, IL: Northwestern University Press.

Ricoeur, Paul. 1967. *The Symbolism of Evil*, trans. Emerson, Buchanan. New York: Harper & Row.

Ricoeur, Paul. 1970. *Freud and Philosophy: An Essay on Interpretation*, trans. Denis Savage. New Haven, CT: Yale University Press.

Ricoeur, Paul. 1974. *The Conflict of Interpretations: Essays in Hermeneutics*, ed. Don Ihde. Evanston, IL: Northwestern University Press.

Ricoeur, Paul. 1991. *From Text to Action: Essays in Hermeneutics, II*, trans. Kathleen Blamey and John B. Thompson. Evanston, IL: Northwestern University Press.

Ricoeur, Paul. 1984–8. *Time and Narrative*, 3 vols, trans. Kathleen McLaughlin and David Pellauer. Chicago: University of Chicago Press.

Ricoeur, Paul. 1992. *Oneself as Another*, trans. Kathleen Blamey. Chicago: University of Chicago Press.

Rorty, Richard. 1979. *Philosophy and the Mirror of Nature*. Princeton, NJ: Princeton University Press.

Rorty, Richard. 1982. *Consequences of Pragmatism*. Minneapolis: Minnesota University Press.

Rorty, Richard. 1989. *Contingency, Irony and Solidarity*. New York: Cambridge University Press.

Schelskhorn, Hans. 1992. *Ethik der Befreiung. Eine Einführung in der Philosophie Enrique Dussels*. Freiburg: Herder.

Taylor, Charles. 1975. *Hegel*. Cambridge: Cambridge University Press.

Taylor, Charles. 1979. *Hegel and Modern Society*. Cambridge: Cambridge University Press.

Taylor, Charles. 1989. *Sources of the Self: The Making of the Modern Identity*. Cambridge, MA: Harvard University Press.

Taylor, Charles. 1992. *The Ethics of Authenticity*. Cambridge, MA: Harvard University Press.

Wallerstein, Emmanuel. 1974. *The Modern World System: Capitalist Agriculture and the Origins of the European World Economy in the Sixteenth Century*. New York: Academic Press.

Wallerstein, Emmanuel. 1979. *The Capitalist World-Economy*. Cambridge: Cambridge University Press.

Weber, Max. 1958. *The Protestant Ethic and the Spirit of Capitalism*. trans. Talcott Parsons. New York: Charles Scribner's Sons.

Zea, Leopoldo. 1992. *The Role of the Americas in History*, trans. Sonja Karsen. Lanham, MD: Rowman & Littlefield.

INDEX